Political Problems
and Personalities in
Contemporary Maryland

Lexington Studies in Political Communication

Series Editor: Robert E. Denton, Jr., Virginia Tech University

This series encourages focused work examining the role and function of communication in the realm of politics including campaigns and elections, media, and political institutions.

Recent Titles in This Series

Political Problems and Personalities in Contemporary Maryland
By Theodore F. Sheckels and Carl Hyden
Money in Politics: Campaign Fundraising in the 2020 Presidential Elections
By Marcus Cayce Myers
Democratic Disunity: Rhetorical Tribalism in 2020
By Colleen Elizabeth Kelley
Third Parties, Outsiders, and Renegades: Modern Challenges to the Two-Party System in Presidential Elections
By Melissa M. Smith
Studies of Communication in the 2020 Presidential Campaign
Edited by Robert E. Denton, Jr.
Horror Framing and the General Election: Ghosts and Ghouls in Twenty-First Century Presidential Campaign Advertisements
By Fielding Montgomery
Political Rhetoric, Social Media, and American Presidential Campaigns: Presidential Candidates' Use of New Media
By Janet Johnson
The Rhetoric of the American Political Party Conventions, 1948-2016
By Theodore F. Sheckels

Political Problems and Personalities in Contemporary Maryland

Theodore F. Sheckels and Carl T. Hyden

LEXINGTON BOOKS

Lanham • *Boulder* • *New York* • *London*

Published by Lexington Books
An imprint of The Rowman & Littlefield Publishing Group, Inc.
4501 Forbes Boulevard, Suite 200, Lanham, Maryland 20706
www.rowman.com

86-90 Paul Street, London EC2A 4NE, United Kingdom

British Library Cataloguing in Publication Information Available

Library of Congress Cataloging-in-Publication Data Available

ISBN 9781666928976 (cloth) | ISBN 9781666928983 (epub)

Contents

Preface   vii

1 Introduction: Studying State and Local Politics; Studying
Maryland   1

PART I: PEOPLE   **13**

2 Barbara Mikulski: Advocate and Mentor   15

3 Martin O'Malley's Failure to Communicate   29

4 Larry Hogan: A Look at His Record as Governor of Maryland   43

PART II: POLITICS   **67**

5 Baltimore in Search of Its Next Transformational Mayor   69

6 Why Haven't Maryland's African American Candidates
for Governor Been Elected?   95

7 Marylanders and Congress: Different Leaders for Different
Tasks   117

8 Why Has There Been No Marylander in the White House?
The Quests of Albert Ritchie, Spiro Agnew, Martin O'Malley,
and John Delaney   133

PART III: POLICIES   **151**

9 Race, Housing, and Segregation in Baltimore   153

10 Transportation Policy: Questions of Power, Questions of Identity 177

PART IV: PLACES **209**

11 Renewal, Revitalization, and Redevelopment across Baltimore from the Downtown Core to the Neighborhoods 211

12 Gerrymandering: Questions of Power, Questions of Identity 231

13 Has Change Come to Maryland's Eastern Shore? 245

14 Conclusions: The Communication Realities of State and Local Politics 263

Works Cited 273

Index 291

About the Authors 299

Preface

In a way, this book is a sequel to *Maryland Politics and Political Communication, 1950–2005* (2006), which one of the authors (Sheckels) wrote fifteen years ago. However, this book is rather different: it's not just an update. It's different because rhetorically based political communication research has evolved.

When the first book was written, political communication research tended to focus on elections. Occasionally, it would veer into what we might term the rhetoric of governance, looking at what the executive does or the legislature does or the courts do. But elections were front-and-center. But, even at that time, changes were brewing.

One change was the increasing recognition that places were worth studying rhetorically. These places were both memory sites and public locations such as parks and stadia and transportation centers. The architecture was relevant as were, of course, any inscriptions. So were the contexts these places were in—physical context and temporal context. So was how those who interact with these places respond.

Insofar as many of these places offered political messages, they were relevant to political communication research. What they "said" was relevant, but so was how they came about. Politics often led to a particular message. Politics even altered a message after the fact: consider the changes made to the Vietnam Veterans Memorial when its message was thought, by some, to be overly critical of the controversial war.

Memory sites cannot say all there is to say, so they often privilege one view—and one group—over others. This dynamic of empowering and disempowering was illuminated especially by the emergence of critical rhetoric. Influenced by the work of Foucault (and others) and crystallized as a method by McKerrow (and others), critical rhetoric insisted that questions of power and privilege be raised and that the material consequences of rhetorical acts be stressed.

Consider New York's Central Park. It is landscape architecture, and there are also structures—some with inscriptions—here and there. It exists in a New York City context, which has changed and changed again over time. And people most certainly respond to the place, with that response varying with both demographics and decades. So, there is much to read. But critical rhetoric would assume that the Park's creation was a rhetorical act and would ask who was privileged by it and who gained materially by its existence. And, when the Park was updated, how did the power dimensions and material dimensions change? Or did they? Critical rhetoric, then, supplements not supplants what a reading might reveal.

Critical rhetoric, however, is not just relevant to places. It's relevant to anything that might be conceived of as a rhetorical act. Traditionally, such acts were predominantly speeches; then, at least in campaign communication research, speeches and ads. But governing decisions are also rhetorical acts. Building a bridge is an act with effects critical rhetoric would discern; enacting a housing policy or pursuing a redevelopment scheme is such an act too. And so, of course, is the time-honored and increasing process of gerrymandering.

Along with critical rhetoric came constitutive rhetoric, influenced by Althusser (and others) and modeled by Charland (and others). Rhetorical acts, defined broadly, were connected with identity: they created identity; they challenged identity; they changed identity. Building a bridge that opened up a previously somewhat isolated area would likely change that area; so would downtown-based and neighborhood-based urban redevelopment. Gerrymandering, insofar as it created a new district, might also create a new political identity.

So, since 2005, the concerns of political communication researchers have grown, have broadened. Furthermore, the questions have moved beyond persuasion to include matters of power and issues of identity. The chapters in this book reflect this change. Yes, some chapters are traditional insofar as they look at elections and political players, but others move into territory that the 2005 book did not.

To make this move, additional expertise was needed. So, this new volume has two authors who have spent years looking at the many dimensions of the state and local politics of Maryland. A bit of biography is useful here.

Sheckels was born in Washington, D.C., but that's because the hospital was there. After a few days, he was a Marylander, living in the very close-in suburbs. He cut his political teeth there as a teenager working for the Democratic ticket in 1964, Carlton Sickles's gubernatorial campaign in 1966, and Senator Eugene McCarthy's presidential campaign in 1968. Then, he was off to college and Pennsylvania, where he worked for Humphrey/ Muskie in 1968 and future Pittsburgh Mayor Peter Flaherty's campaign in 1969. Graduate school was time consuming, but in the summer of 1976 he was back in Maryland working on future Senator Barbara Mikulski's initial (losing) campaign. After a two-year teaching stint in suburban Philadelphia, he moved to Virginia in 1980, but the work on Maryland continued with freelance speechwriting and campaign consulting in 2002 and 2008. He owns a second home in Garrett County, Maryland; so, although a Virginian, he is still Maryland-connected.

Hyden was born in Pennsylvania and educated there and in Ohio. He came to Maryland after receiving two master's degrees from Ohio University to work on communication-related projects for Baltimore Mayor William Donald Schaefer. When Schaefer moved on from Baltimore to Annapolis (as governor), so did Hyden. In total, Hyden worked for fifteen years on "real" political communication tasks. Then, after Schaefer's time in Annapolis was up, he turned to academe, becoming a professor and administrator at one of Maryland HBCU's. Working in Baltimore and living on its outskirts give him a Baltimore perspective on politics in Maryland, complementing Sheckels's, which is more that of suburban Washington, D.C.

Skimming this book's Table of Contents, one can readily see how important knowing the Baltimore scene is to discussing what has happened in the state. But the Washington, D.C. suburbs—in many ways, the Baltimore area's rival—are also crucial. Furthermore, one cannot ignore that Maryland has other regions—to its far West, its far South, and its far East. They may not have the numbers metro Baltimore and the DC suburbs have, but they play roles in the state's communication picture. And Sheckels and Hyden are quite conversant with the dynamics of these areas, even though their life experiences tie them more to the state's two big political regions.

We, the authors, play off the expertise we have accumulated quite a bit in this book. Sheckels, for example, knows the story of the beach towns dotted along the Chesapeake's western shore because he once went to them—as did his Washingtonian parents; Hyden knows what went on as Baltimore tried to revive its downtown because he was working in the Schaefer administration. We count on this expertise to give much of what we say credibility. We, therefore, do not clutter the chapters with note after note after note. There are notes, of course, but most are to news coverage or commentary, whether it be in-print or online. This dominance by non-scholarly sources is primarily because there are not very many scholarly sources. Some of the historical material referred to is indeed the product of scholarship on the state (or the city of Baltimore), but, once we move beyond what is considered history into more current matters, we are dependent on what we know and what the media present by way of information and opinion.

But we do offer references under certain circumstances—first, when something we talk about is either little known or extremely controversial; second, when we think a reference or two will take an interested reader to valuable supplementary material. We envision readers as falling into two categories, those interested in state and local political communication who will see this book as a case study and those interested in Maryland. It is the latter group that might find the supplementary material of interest.

Our approach is rhetorical in the broadest sense. We are interested in what persuaded people but also in what illustrated the operation of power and privilege and in what helped constitute (or undermine) political identity. We know we are perhaps stretching the domain of rhetoric a good bit, but we argue throughout the matters such as housing policy, urban redevelopment policy, and transportation policy are rhetorical. Actions by political players are not in a separate category from their messages. Far from it, for their actions are messages, often with very important material consequences.

As a rhetorical approach, we refer frequently to rhetorical theory, but we try not to bog down in discussing it. We see theory as a set of lenses that help illuminate what has happened, and we quite deliberately focus on what then becomes apparent, not how we theoretically got there. And we do not limit our lenses to just that of rhetoric. There is much in other areas of the communication discipline as well as in cognate fields such as social psychology and leadership studies that help illuminate the political scene. We turn to that work when relevant.

That this book is a sequel to one framed by 1950–2005 should suggest that we are dealing here with people, events, and policies from 2006 and later. Well, yes and no. The "no" is because, although stories may climax in or after 2006, they often have deeper roots. The urban redevelopment going on in the Baltimore area known as Port Covington is a current story, but one cannot fully understand it without also knowing what Baltimore tried before with both the Charles Center project and the Inner Harbor and its extensions to its East. The question of why Martin O'Malley and John Delaney got nowhere in seeking a presidential nomination cannot be fully understood without considering those Marylanders who got closer to the prize. We do not, however, explore history for the sake of doing so, but, rather, to contextualize what is currently in focus. The previous book was conceived of as focusing on several incidents or events in the state's political history. Some background was needed to understand each, but not to the extent as in this book. Why? Because just as rhetoric has broadened its focus, so has political communication.

The narrow view of political communication would have one saying that, of course, the topic in focus is the next gubernatorial election. Who will run? Will the Democrats regain the State House? Will Republican Governor Larry

Hogan's legacy be a Republican successor? We do not raise this topic for two reasons. The practical one is that the election story is only beginning to unfold: the election is eighteen months off as we write this. The philosophical one is that there are important political communication matters that are not about elections. In keeping with the shifts in political communication research and in rhetorical inquiry, we have chosen to give these non-election topics considerable space.

The result is that, unlike the first study, this is not an election book. Rather, it is a more comprehensive examination of all that state and local political communication is. We explore this matter in the book's concluding chapter, but, here, let us note one practical one—that being that some topics require more pages than others. Looking at a prominent Marylander's career does not require the lengthy discussion that the topics of race relations or transportation policy do. So, the reader will notice that the chapters are not of a uniform length. Rather than be confined by some "rule" that a chapter must have a specified number of words, we have allowed the topic to dictate the length.

We are both "fans" of Maryland politics, but we do not mean to suggest that they are any more important than politics elsewhere. There are, we know, fascinating topics that someone might explore involving neighboring Pennsylvania or Virginia, states we have some connection with. We imagine that there are equally compelling topics involving every state. In writing this study, we hope we inspire others to explore the political communication that is close to home and, thus, playing important roles in everyday lives. We also hope that, as an enlarging research community, we and others will contribute to an emerging understanding of state and local political communication.

Chapter 1

Introduction

Studying State and Local Politics; Studying Maryland

THE STATE AND LOCAL SCENE

The trend in studies of political communication continues to favor the national scene over the state and local—so much so the journals continue to push aside articles that discuss the state and local as exploring matters "not of national interest." This is a trend we would very much like to see reversed. The national scene is, of course, important, but so are the state and local.

One would hope that those studying political communication want to know *all* about it. Those who study anatomy are not interested just in the body's big organs. If there is indeed something more than just metaphor in the phrase "body politic," shouldn't researchers want to know about all of that body's parts? Put another way, do these researchers know their field if all they know is what's true nationally?

Researchers might respond that there are major topics and there are minor ones. True. But consider literary studies as a discipline. Do those who study any given period of any national literature only study the handful of major writers? They might be preferred, but there has long been a place in such scholarship for others. Consider political science. Do those who focus on comparative politics restrict their studies to just the major powers? Again, they might be preferred, but there has long been a place in such scholarship for studies of Uruguay or Kenya or Thailand.

The term "major" needs to be interrogated, for, although no one would label the state and localities "major" and the federal government "minor," there is a strong basis for rethinking the role the states and localities play in the national picture. As Gary Moncrief and Peverill Squire argue in the 2021 edition of *Why States Matter: An Introduction to State Politics*, major governmental responsibilities are likely to shift to the state-local level

1

because of financial constraints at the federal. They also note that, in most states and localities, the resources to undertake the additional work have significantly increased in recent decades. Furthermore, they note that, because state legislatures are now overwhelmingly dominated by one political party or the other, bills can actually be passed and proposals can actually become programs. Thus, the states—and, to a lesser extent, the local governments they create—can serve as the "laboratories" some have envisioned them as, trying out different approaches to matters such as healthcare, welfare, education, policing, and transportation. Given what is already emerging in terms of policy and program development at the state level, dismissing state and local government and the associate communication as minor is without a basis.

Another trend is noticeable in the political communication literature: it tends to be overwhelmingly focused not just on the national scene but one specific element in that scene: presidential elections. Occasionally, a noteworthy senatorial or gubernatorial race is thought to be "of national interest," but there are many, many state and local elections worth studying, especially if we are intrigued by how state and local campaigns may be similar to but different from the "big" ones. Also, political communication occurs during governance. Legislative bodies consider matters in committee and debate them on the assembly's floor. This communication is largely ignored by extant scholarship even when it is the U.S. Congress. State legislatures and city councils are almost totally ignored. And, political communication occurs in the appellate courts. Again, there is some discussion by scholars of the U.S. Supreme Court, but lower federal courts and state courts are ignored.

There is, in sum, far more than just what is national, and there is far more than just election campaigns. Political communication is a vast field, and one does not do it justice if the next presidential race is researchers' primary concern as soon as the current one concludes.

We certainly believe that, as our governments tend to be tripartite—executive, legislative, and judicial, that a three-part structure might have been a way to explore state and local political communication. We chose, however, another because the issues that we saw emerging in Maryland did not fit that structure. We saw people emerging as an important topic as well as the politics—that is, electoral politics—they engaged in; we also saw policies of various sorts emerging, not because of how they were enacted, but because of their rhetorical effects such as disempowering groups of people or altering how groups identify themselves. Finally, we saw places as important—how they may or may not change as constitutive spaces, including how partisan government might play a major role in the process. Proceeding through people, politics, policies, and places gives us not only a structure encompassing what has proven to be of consequence in Maryland but suggests how both political communication and rhetorical criticism now must extend beyond political campaigns and public addresses.

There is much more that could be explored on the state and local level. These major concerns for Maryland, as reflected in this book's next twelve chapters, may not be the major concerns for other states, although we suspect most are. But all concerns will play out differently in different states—and different cities. So, the number of chapters necessary to cover the nation's state and local political communication issues might well number into the several hundred! For example, we discuss Baltimore's mayors, tracing a period of weak leadership that, now, may be acquiring new and needed strength with Brandon Scott. Other books might discuss Pittsburgh's mayors or Detroit's mayors or Los Angeles' mayors. There would be common ground among the discussions, but there would also be differences due to different problems, different demographics, and different political traditions. So, many chapters would be necessary before this local political topic was explored and understood. Our goal is not to engage in comparative politics or comparative political communication but to sketch the picture in one state, with the hope that others will offer additional state case studies.

States are certainly not as different from each other as they were when the nation was founded; furthermore, in some ways, the federal-state-local distinction has blurred. When studying government, political scientists are quite attentive to differences. State governments do different things than the federal government, although it is sometimes challenging for the states to do much without some federal involvement. So, there is some blurring, but it seems even more pronounced when it comes to politics as opposed to government. As Daniel Hopkins has argued in *The Increasingly United States* (2008), the issues being raised in a state campaign may well be only slightly different from those being raised in a federal one—to the point where voters may be electing governors to do what only members of Congress can. What is changing then seems to be more the issues that resonate with voters as opposed to what happens day-to-day, month-to-month at the state level.

We see what we attempt in this book as moving political communication scholarship in the direction of fully exploring and understanding what occurs on the state and local level. This book is a sequel to one author's *Maryland Politics and Political Communication, 1950–2005* (2006). Looking back on that volume, we see it as fairly traditional in what it covered: most chapters dealt with—no surprise—elections. This volume is quite different, and the difference is because rhetorical criticism, changing back in 2006, has definitely changed in four crucial ways by 2021, fifteen years later.

THE BROADENING OF RHETORICAL CRITICISM

First, the subject matter has broadened. Once, of course, rhetorical criticism focused on oral texts such as speeches or largely visual texts such as advertisements. Much more is being explored today, most notably public places. Memory sites should, of course, be read, for they contain messages and are usually far from neutral, but other sites as well. In Baltimore, south of the tourist meccas of the Inner Harbor and Harbor East is the Fort McHenry historical site, where Francis Scott Key composed our national anthem during the War of 1812. But before one reaches Fort McHenry is Federal Hill, a neighborhood rich in meaning, and, beyond Fort McHenry are areas of the cities that are seeing urban redevelopment of different sorts. There is much to discuss—to read—in what is happening just in Baltimore's southern sectors.

Second, the reading of texts of all sorts is now frequently critical in the sense that the reader explicitly asks questions about power and privilege and is aware of the material consequences of power- and privilege-laden texts. Policies decisions, delivered via texts of various sorts, are rife with such issues. For example, the decision (by current Governor Larry Hogan) not to build the light rail "red line" in Baltimore materially affected the low-income residents who would have been the line's primary beneficiaries.

Third, the reading also frequently reflects an awareness of the constitutive effect of rhetoric. Traditionally, rhetoric concerns the means to persuasion. Now, it concerns that and the means to maintain (or challenge) power and privilege and the means whereby identity might be constituted or, if it already exists, reinforced or undermined. The ways rhetoric extends beyond persuasion are often not immediately apparent, but, when they are revealed, their importance is striking. Building the Chesapeake Bay Bridge back in the 1950s was a rhetorical act, and it played a role in changing both the Bay's eastern and western shores. The eastern became less insular and, perhaps, began a transition from a very southern identity to a different (still ill-defined) one. The western transitioned from a resort identity to a gambling one, from which it has further evolved based on housing prices and inter- and intra-state transportation patterns.

Fourth, rhetoricians seem willing to not only escape the more traditional theoretical frameworks but move into cognate communication areas when doing so enriches rhetorical understanding. There is, for example, social science work on persuasion that can help explain some of the dynamics of elections. There is also a large body of social science work on leadership that can explain such matters as who the voting public looks to as a presidential candidate and how those holding various political offices succeed—or fail. We refer to this work on leadership frequently in discussing Marylanders and the Presidency and Marylanders and the U.S. Congress. What might not be immediately clear is that the work is heavily empirical. The data undergirding one theory or another is fascinating to look at, but the ideas that emerge are very useful as rhetorical lenses to assess the behavior—heavily communicative behavior—of those aspiring to lead the nation in one branch or level of government or another.

We are pretty sure you will see how these four changes affect what we do in the twelve chapters that follow. Some are more traditional, some less. We are not abandoning traditional rhetorical practices in this case study of Maryland; rather, we are letting the newer directions enter in where relevant. They undoubtedly influenced the issues we have chosen to explore as well. Housing policy or transportation policy are not traditional rhetorical subjects, but we consider them as strongly rhetorical with important material consequences. Housing policy decisions affected race relations in Baltimore; those relations are crucial in the city's current politics. Transportation policy decisions affected what the Baltimore and Washington, D.C. areas are like, blending suburbs, creating a pronounced city-suburb divide, and almost destroying urban communities. The decisions, in part, altered the state's politics, with the suburban counties acquiring increasing power. This alteration affected what were thought to be spending priorities.

MARYLAND

We choose Maryland because, as explained in the preface, it is a state we know well. A public relations campaign decades ago declared Maryland to be "America in Miniature." And, yes, Maryland does have farmland and cities and suburbs, and it does have an oceanfront and mountains with valleys in between. There is some truth to the slogan. However, we are not claiming that what's true in Maryland is necessarily true in any of the other states. We suspect there are similarities, but what we are hoping is not that others will find those similarities and stop their investigations with a handful of generalizations, but, rather, explore their own places be they Michigan or Montana, West Virginia or Wyoming. The goal, then, would be to create the whole picture which, right now, we lack because so much of political communication work is devoted to limited aspects of the national scene.

To make this part—the Maryland part—clear to readers, we do need to offer some background information. So, we will now offer a tour of the state. We will be discussing physical and cultural geography, but will note political implications as we proceed, region-by-region, through the state. We'll conclude by talking more explicitly about a few political dimensions.

Southern Maryland

Although the first European settlement in Maryland may well be on an island hugging the eastern shore of the Chesapeake Bay, most point to a site on the western shore as the beginning. That is St. Mary's City, where the Ark and the Dove landed in 1634.

From there, the Maryland colony grew. The initial colonists were heavily Catholic, but, after the "Glorious Revolution" in England in 1688, there was a heavy influx of Presbyterians. With a sprinkling of Anglicans, the colony quickly became inter-denominational and strongly committed to religious freedom. There was, however, a tendency even early on for the different religious groups to take their own paths in populating southern Maryland, the area between the Bay on the East and the Potomac River on the West, southeast of present-day Washington, D.C.

Religious differences aside, the region became heavily agricultural, with the dominant crop being tobacco. Slaves worked the fields, as did indentured servants; and, although there were large farms one might term "plantations," the area was not like the large plantation-dominated areas in more southern states. Gradually, the entry point into Maryland will shift northward to Annapolis and Baltimore, and a steady flow of immigrants would come into the state. Some turned southward once arriving increasing both the population and ethnic diversity of southern Maryland. The mix resulted in the area never becoming as stridently conservative as the state's "Eastern Shore," which stayed isolated from the rest of the state for a long period. There was nonetheless a southern "feel" to the area, which until recently has given it a conservative political tinge. But do note that the region's representative in Congress has long been Democrat Steny Hoyer. So, that tinge has resulted in more a purple patch than either a red or blue one.

Baltimore

Baltimore quickly became the state's major city. It featured not only one of the nation's major harbors but a variety of industries. Immigration gave it ethnic diversity. It also acquired a sizeable free African American population with a lively culture and an excellent newspaper in the *Afro-American*. Although Maryland might be argued to be a southern state, Baltimore was not a southern city when it came to race relations. It might have had, at one point, some southern charm if compared to New York City or Philadelphia, but that is as far as the southerness went.

North of Baltimore

Northwest of Baltimore is Carroll County; arcing around Baltimore City is Baltimore County; northeast of Baltimore is Harford County. They are similar insofar as they all have had communities that one would characterize as suburban as well as more rural stretches. Baltimore County, however, was more suburban than the Carroll or Harford; Harford, along the Baltimore-to-New York route, a bit more developed than Carroll. If one were to compare Westminster (Carroll), Towson (Baltimore), and Aberdeen (Harford), one would be struck by the differences right away. Westminster strikes one as a country town; Aberdeen as a place touched by those passing-through and by nearby military installations. Towson would be a stereotypical suburb.

Eastern Shore

Cecil County sits at the top of the Chesapeake Bay. Today, commuter trains (MARC) from Baltimore cross the Susquehanna River from Harford and into Cecil and stop, signaling that Cecil is a different region. From Cecil, the "Eastern Shore" counties proceed downward on the eastern side of the Bay. Delaware is to their East except at the bottom of the map, where the "Eastern Shore" turns to the Atlantic under Delaware.

This region is more diverse than it initially seems to be. Its counties have different identities; its town different economic histories. Cambridge was once a cannery town; Salisbury, textiles and chickens. Still, as a whole, the "Eastern Shore" is the state's most southern-feeling region. Its relative isolation from the rest of the state until the mid-1950s resulted in minimal ethnic diversity; however, there was a sizeable African American presence. This was the result of plantation slavery, mixed with small farms, mixed with types of indenture.

Politically, the "Eastern Shore" is a distinct region, much more conservative than the populous core of the state. Like Western Maryland, the region has often expressed a measure of political alienation—as if it did not matter much in the affairs of the state. That feeling may hold the "Eastern Shore" together somewhat, but the communities that comprise the region are different. Salisbury, for example, has traditionally been more progressive than Cambridge, which was the site of violent civil rights demonstrations in the 1960s. Easton (in Talbot County) is different still, mixing residents with deep roots with others who have moved in from the Baltimore or Washington areas. And Ocean City, which boomed after the Chesapeake Bay Bridge opened in the early 1950s, is a stereotypical resort with thousands of visiting tourists, some vacation condo owners, and a small year-round population that seems far more conservative (and Republican) than most who visit.

Washington Suburbs

Montgomery and Prince George's Counties border the nation's capital. Both are largely suburban communities, but historically they have been quite different. Montgomery was more affluent and featured a strong public school system. Eventually, as housing stock aged, some areas in the county's southeastern corner became heavily Latino or Asian, with poverty and crime becoming problems. Prince George's was less affluent but predominantly white. Then, a migration of African Americans from DC into Prince George's developed, transforming the county into a majority minority one. The county features pockets of affluence and pockets of poverty, and race does not map onto the socioeconomic differences in a clear pattern: there are affluent black neighborhoods; there are poor white ones. There are also racially mixed areas as well as a large Latino one in the county's northwest corner.

Both counties have long voted Democrat more than Republican. But Montgomery traditionally exhibited a good deal of political independence, electing Republicans if they were perceived as good candidates. Prince George's, now very Democratic, was Democratic decades ago before it changed racially. But, back then, Democrats with a pronounced southern stripe sometimes had a fair amount of support. Thus, in the 1972 Democratic primary, Alabama's George Wallace chose to campaign in Prince George's but skipped Montgomery. And Republicans could win in Prince George's: Governor Larry Hogan's father (also Larry Hogan) represented the county in Congress back in the 1970s.

In Between the Big Cities

Baltimore and Washington are some 40 miles apart. Once, as late as the early 1960s, that was enough to create something of an empty zone between them consisting of Howard County and a part of Anne Arundel. Then, major highways were built: the Baltimore-Washington Parkway, I-95, and an expanded U.S. 29. One no longer had to creep along U.S. 1 which is often a congested long-distance route. Then, visionary developer James Rouse decided to build a planned city in this zone, and Columbia came into existence as an imaginatively designed bedroom community for both cities. Rural Howard County became progressively less rural. And, then, high-speed roads shot across Anne Arundel, spreading suburbia farther toward the South. The gap that once existed between Baltimore and Annapolis vanished as would the one between Washington and Annapolis.

The area, as a suburban one, has much in common with the Washington, D.C. suburban ones. Three elements make it a bit different. First, there is a Baltimore working-class element in the mix in northern Anne Arundel. Second, there is a distinctly southern element in the mix in the smaller towns, especially in southern Anne Arundel. Third, there is a different suburban attitude among the many residents of Columbia, for they fled the close-in suburbs not the cities. Arguably, they saw the close-in suburbs changing and sought out the larger homes, larger lawns, greater amenities, and heightened safety of the more distant model city. These elements result in the area being politically volatile. There is a Democratic base as in Montgomery and Prince George's but there are voters who can easily be swayed in a Republican or "blue dog" Democratic direction.

Western Maryland

German immigrants to Baltimore moved due west out of the city, giving the communities along the path a distinct German quality. Cumberland once brewed Old German Beer; Upper and Lower New Germany forests stand along the Allegany County-Garrett County line. The towns along the path—Frederick, Hagerstown, and Cumberland—featured light industry. Cumberland was also a railroading center. The path was not a fast one as it headed through this scenic region of mountains and valleys. That path scooted north into Pennsylvania, just skirting the northern edge of Garrett County, the county farthest west. When I-70 was built, the scooting occurred even sooner—in Washington County, leaving both Garrett and Allegany remote.

There was, however, a short period when Garrett boomed. Its county seat, Oakland, was another railroading center featuring more than twenty passenger trains per day, and Oakland and nearby Deer Park featured large resort hotels built by John Garrett's B & O. A sizeable Chautauqua resort community developed in Mountain Park, and a similar but "wet" one developed in neighboring Loch Lynn. These railroad-side communities faded in the early twentieth century, and Garrett County declined until the lake created by a Pennsylvania Electric Company dam (Deep Creek Lake) grew into a three-season vacation site.

The politics all along in this region were fairly conservative. Whatever would help small industry was popular. Also popular was what would promote the mining of the coal that the many freight trains hauled. Working-class enclaves in Frederick, Hagerstown, and Cumberland gave the region small "blue" pockets, but, for the most part, it was distinctly "red."

Political Patterns

If one were to color the state in blue or red following the descriptions we just offered, the surprise discovery would be that very little of the state is blue. To the west, it's red; to the east, it's red; and in between there are some purple spots mixed with a handful of deep blue ones. Fortunately for Democrats, those deep blue ones are the most populous. So, it is very possible for a

Democrat to win in Maryland while losing the vast majority of the state's jurisdictions (counties and one independent city). It has happened—frequently. So, calling Maryland a "blue state" is deceptive. It has a blue streak down the middle, but there is a lot of red. The divide is, to a large extent, an urban vs. rural one, a political reality true elsewhere in the nation. The need to point to it in the case of Maryland is because Maryland, as a geographically smaller state sandwiched in along an east coast corridor is often assumed to be almost uniformly blue by those living at a distance. No. Maryland has more counties that are red than blue.

Republican wins, then, are not shocking upsets—even if the media, especially the national media, present them that way. They usually occur if the Democrats either field a weak candidate or if the Democrat is too liberal. Marylanders of both parties tend to reject extreme candidates. Maryland Democrats are more moderate than the national party has become; Maryland Republicans are more moderate than the national party has become. The members of the Maryland parties are, of course, not of one mind. That fact and all of the vagaries of campaigns have led to a few exceptions. Liberal Barbara Mikulski won repeatedly because of her strong Baltimore roots: people voted for "Aunt Barb" while disagreeing with her; conservative J. Glenn Beall, Jr. (from Cumberland) won a U.S. Senate seat because the National Rifle Association dumped money in the state to defeat a liberal-leaning incumbent. These exceptions aside, Marylanders have tended to be politically moderate.

Traditionally, Maryland politics was dominated by the city of Baltimore. That dominance reflected both the city's population and its prominence in the economy. That dominance had to be "watered-down" with nods to other areas. So, candidates from other parts of the state would be included on statewide tickets. Doing so also helped overcome Baltimore's reputation for political corruption as well. But once elections were done and legislators in Annapolis began their work, Baltimore regained much of its strength.

Other parts of the state, of course, resented this dominance. Those on the Eastern Shore, in Southern Maryland, and in Western Maryland muttered many a curse word directed at those from the City. Those in the Washington suburbs, because they were numerous and growing, did more. They challenged Baltimore's dominance, creating a tension throughout the middle of the twentieth century. Those from the DC suburbs did not want to vote for a Baltimorean; those from Baltimore, fearing economic revenge, would not vote for someone from Montgomery or Prince George's. This rivalry between the two numerically dominant regions surfaces during the governorships of William Donald Schaefer, Parris Glendenning, and even Martin O'Malley. It now seems to be fading, but it is nonetheless a Maryland political reality. Baltimore City and the DC suburbs eye each other suspiciously. Meanwhile, the rest of the state envies both.

Perhaps one reason the tension is fading is that the two areas have blurred together somewhat. Suburbs grew outward; Columbia developed out of farmland. The time to drive from Washington to Baltimore shrank. Some in the Washington suburbs began to think of "Baltimore-Washington International Airport" as—maybe—not just Baltimore's airport with a somewhat misleading name. And, after the second rendition of the Washington senators left for Texas, many D.C. area baseball fans embraced the Orioles. And, after the 1968 urban rioting, both areas shared common problems.

CONCLUSION

Maryland is like other states, but not like other states. This is true whether the focus be geography, economy, or politics. It may indeed have features that link it with what's true nationally—it may be "America in Miniature," but quite a few other states can make that claim too. New Jersey, for example, has mountains, farmlands, cities, suburbs, and a seacoast, although some might scratch their heads at "mountains" until consulting a map. So, the goal of a study such as this is not to establish what is true of state and local political communication nationwide. But it is also not to posit ideas that are just relevant to a single state.

Knowing how political communication functions, state by state, is a noble goal indeed, but probably not an easily reached one. Political communication scholars will ideally know the dynamics of a few states well and a few others a bit. That's the academic reality. But what scholars should know are the commonalities, for there are some. So, this study, immersed in many Maryland particulars, tries ultimately to reach for those commonalities, which are offered in the book's final chapter.

When considering those commonalities, one should be struck by the fact that, to apply them to a particular state, one needs to know a fair amount about the state. Matters such as its geography and its economy can be readily gleaned from any number of research sources. In rather short order, we could tell you about the geography of Colorado or the economy of Kentucky. What requires research and, perhaps, insights gained from living in the state is the state's politics, particularly because that subject is a dynamic one, different in 2020 than in 1990 or in 1960. The information we have offered in this chapter blends geography, economy, and politics. All three are important, but it is the political information that one so often needs to make sense of this version of state and local politics and fit this version into a larger picture.

Part I

PEOPLE

Chapter 2

Barbara Mikulski

Advocate and Mentor

Careers in the U.S. Senate are often assessed based on if and how quickly one makes it into the leadership. By that standard, Maryland senator Barbara Mikulski's career was, at best, slowly successful. But is that the standard she would have used to assess her career, and, if not, what was the measure she would have used and how did she fare based on her chosen measure? This question is a useful one to pose because it is not true that all who arrive in the U. S. Senate aspire to be party leader or whip or even chair of a particularly powerful committee. There are probably many different goals and paths in view. Tracing Mikulski's, then, should alert one studying legislators to the possibility of others. Recognizing the multiple ways to be an effective U.S. senator should prompt one to study the different members in their terms, not what is presumed to be a universally accepted standard.

Mikulski did play a major role in the post-1968 Democratic Party reform efforts, chairing an important committee in the early 1970s while serving on the Baltimore City Council. This role might suggest that she would indeed try to climb the party ladder, but other interests became dominant. Except for a curiosity about and commitment to space exploration, all of these interests are rooted in her life story.

So, we begin with that story before focusing on her four major concerns as first a member of the U.S. House of Representatives (1977–1987) and then a member of the U.S. Senate.

FROM HIGHLANDTOWN TO WASHINGTON

Mikulski grew up in a somewhat ethnic (Polish) area of east Baltimore.[1] It was, at the time, a working-class area. She attended a private Catholic

Figure 2.1 Maryland Senator Barbara Mikulski. *Source*: Public domain.

high school (two years ahead of Nancy D'Alessandro Pelosi) and a private Catholic college in Baltimore, where she studied sociology. That education and a follow-up master's degree propelled her into social work in the city, most of it focused on the welfare of children. Some point to a 1970 address she delivered at a national Catholic conference, a speech that saluted ethnic, working-class neighborhoods, as the beginning of her political career, but a more likely starting point was her activism against an interstate highway project (I-95) that would have torn apart her Fells Point neighborhood and the adjoining Canton one. That activism allied her with African American groups in west Baltimore who were rallying against a related project (the I-170 spur off I-70N or I-70).[2] (Some may recall the somewhat iconic picture of Mikulski speaking to a rally standing atop a picnic table, but some of these don't realize that she stood there, not to lead the charge against the highway, but because at 4'10," she would otherwise not have been seen speaking.) And with a reputation for both her activism and her community organizing, she won election to the City Council shortly after stopping the expressway project.

Well-known in the city and its immediate surroundings, she was the "sacrificial lamb" in the 1974 U.S. Senate race against the very popular Republican incumbent Charles Mathias. Democrat Paul Sarbanes's decision to run for the Senate in 1976 left his 3rd District House seat open. She ran for it and won. Then, upon Mathias' retirement, she ran again for the Senate in 1986, retiring from that body at the end of 2016. Her margins winning election and reelection were never close, although Republican challengers, citing her ultra-liberal record, fared better in later ones than initially. Her toughest race might well have been her first, not based on the margin of victory (which was sizeable) but how viciously her challenger attacked her.[3] Her margin of victory in Baltimore City in all races was impressive, giving her a lead that Republicans, even if they won most of the state's counties, could not overcome. As the vote in Baltimore suggests, Mikulski was very much "Baltimore's gal."[4]

SERVING HER STATE AND HER CITY

A legislator's committee service is often an indicator of how she or he plans to represent voters. Mikulski long served on the Committee on Appropriations (eventually becoming its chair) and the Committee on Health, Education, Labor, and Pensions. She was interested in getting federal money to her state—especially her city, and she was interested in addressing the issues that affected the working class and the children in working-class areas. Not a prolific law-writer, she was the sponsor of a 2013 measure reforming how childcare was federally funded and administered in working-class communities. This law reflects both her Highlandtown-Fells Point-Canton area upbringing and her social work career. More broadly, she worked on urban development issues and harbor issues. If Mikulski can be faulted, she can be for focusing more on Baltimore's concerns than those of the rest of the state. In doing so, however, she was not alone: many Baltimoreans who make it to either the State House or to the Congress have fallen into the trap of being too city-focused. (Democrat Martin O'Malley was sometimes labeled "Governor of Baltimore," as was Republican Theodore McKeldin.)

Mikulski might also be faulted somewhat for never making the House-to-Senate transition as fully as some in the Senate might have desired. Historically, the House has been a good bit more raucous than the Senate with members having the chance to speak up sooner and more loudly. The Senate, supposedly, was a more restrained, more polite body, the supposed saucer to cool off the hot tea cup. This different atmosphere meant that men and women who transitioned across Capitol Hill often had to adjust their behavior. Mikulski was not alone in not adjusting as quickly or as fully as the established members of the Senate expected—and to some extent demanded. She could be very outspoken in the House; she would initially try to be just as outspoken in the Senate. She gradually altered her communication behavior a bit, counseled to do so by senior colleagues such as Texas senator Lloyd Bentsen, but one should note that the Senate was changing too, becoming a less polite debating society. Also, one should note that her not adjusting was probably not tied to gender: Pennsylvania Congressman turned senator Rick Santorum, for example, ran into the exact same difficulty. In Mikulski's case, her tendency to not always observe the Senate's traditional decorum might be responsible for a relatively slow movement through the Senate ranks. She had to wait longer for her important chairpersonship than others who played the "Senate game" better. So, an outspoken style that was not necessarily gender-based may have posed problems for Mikulski. However, there were other ways in which gender did, if for no other reason than, when Mikulski joined the Senate, she was one of only two female members. In ways the men in the Senate didn't even realize, it was a very male-defined space.

ADDRESSING GENDER INJUSTICES

Most U.S. senators pass through a period of seeming inactivity upon election. Partially, they are learning the proverbial ropes, but they are also stuck in a structure that values—perhaps overvalues—seniority. In Mikulski's case, there was the other obstacle to progress: her gender. The U.S. Senate was not only defined by its deference to seniority but its overwhelming white maleness. Perhaps also holding Mikulski back was her reputation. Some in her office thought her mean, not just as demanding of them as she was of herself.[5] Some of her colleagues thought her "volcanic" (her term) in her anger, even though they had never witnessed an instance of it.

So, Mikulski was slow in gaining prominence in the "Senate Club." But, she was quite prominent in a 1993 debate over the retirement rank of Admiral Frank Kelso.[6] Admirals (and generals) routinely retire with two stars. Anything higher requires a presidential recommendation, a Senate Armed Services Committee recommendation, and a full Senate vote. The latter two are usually pro forma, but the case of Kelso was different in the eyes of the women of the Senate—now seven following the 1992 "Year of the Woman" election. The case was different because Kelso had been in charge when the notorious "Tailhook '91" naval aviators' "conference" was held in Las Vegas. The annual "conference" had long featured excessive alcohol consumption, pornography, and strippers, but the out-of-control behavior there was kept quiet. In 1991, however, several female officers went public, claiming they were assaulted by the rowdy "boys." Kelso not only must have known what the "conference" was like but did nothing to crack down on it and, arguably, did a poor job investigating it after the women went public.

So, the women of the Senate—led by Mikulski—requested six hours of that august body's time to debate the four-star recommendation by Armed Services. Much of the commentary offered by the female senators, primarily Diane Feinstein and Barbara Boxer of California, Carol Moseley-Braun of Illinois, Patty Murray of Washington, and Mikulski, dealt with the specifics of either the event or the follow-up investigations. Feinstein, for example, cited specific rules of conduct that had been violated while Boxer told the stories of the women who had reported assault. Occasionally, however, the commentary would glance at matters other than "Tailhook '91." At the debate's end, Mikulski is quite explicit in saying that the women were not concerned only about the naval aviators' gathering. She said:

> We hope we win this, But whether we win the vote or not, we feel we have won a victory here today because we have raised this issue to show from now on when we look at what is going to happen in promotions and in retirements and in rewards, the issues will be raised, and they will be raised not only about the United States military, they will be raised about the FBI, they will be raised about the Bureau of Alcohol and Firearms, they will be raised about Social Security, they will be raised about gender discrimination going on at the National Institutes of Health. They will be raised.[7]

Interestingly, she did not mention the U.S. Senate itself as a site of sexist behavior, for that would have been a breach of Senate decorum; however, her listing makes it very clear that she believed the problem of sexism to be systemic throughout government. Although Mikulski did not explicitly voice her view that the "Club" was not friendly toward women, it did reveal itself in the "revolt" she and Moseley-Braun staged by wearing pants on the Senate floor.[8] Doing so had been prohibited, but they defied the rule and thereby prompted a rule change. Not a major matter, but an indication of Mikulski's awareness of institutional sexism. Here, the institution was the U.S. Senate. In 2014, the institution was business, characterized by gender differences in pay. She authored and pushed through the *Paycheck Fairness Act*, which attempts to make it more possible for women to challenge wage inequities and win. On the issue, Mikulski said, "I get angry, I get outraged and I get volcanic."[9]

SPACE

One fully understands why Mikulski might be interested in America's harbors. Baltimore was a major one, and her native neighborhood was on that harbor. Mikulski's interest in space is a bit difficult to explain. She promoted the Space Telescope Science Institute in Baltimore, securing it NASA funding. An astronomy database there is named in her honor, as is an exploding star NASA discovered in 2012. It is "Supernova Mikulski." Perhaps its naming was a glance at her personality, which could be explosive. But too much can be made of that. There were undoubtedly moments when issues made her "volcanic" or staff failures made her explode. However, some of her most noteworthy work was much quieter, much less dramatic, such as that benefiting Baltimore harbor or space exploration.

A space telescope will be, at best, a story for well into a newspaper's "A" section. It might even be saved for a once-a-week science section that many discard unread. Harbors, although important in international commerce and in certain states, also do not rate the front page. Mikulski will get headlines when she raises questions about gender equity and about sexual harassment, and her work on these matters, increasingly in concert with other women in Congress, should not be underrated. However, while noting this important crusading that gained media attention, one should also point to the work she did on issues (the Baltimore harbor) that mattered to her city and her state (the Chesapeake Bay) as well as work she did just because it intrigued her (space exploration).

PROMOTING WOMEN IN POLITICS

Opposing Kelso for a four-star retirement put Mikulski front-and-center on a number of issues important to women; gender-based wage discrepancies made her "volcanic." These and other matters that arose during her near-thirty years in the U.S. Senate constituted her legislative side, but there was another that might actually be more important.

Throughout the Kelso debate, Mikulski emphasized that there were seven women in the U.S. Senate. Years later, a growing group wrote and edited *Nine and Counting*.[10] Barbara Boxer of California gets credit as "lead author," but the work was a collaborative project. When they began writing, there were nine women in the U.S. Senate; by the time they published, there were thirteen. This—and further growth to twenty-four as we write—happened for a number of reasons. Some deal with election politics; others deal with whether or not the institution would allow them to truly serve, for one's reelection might depend on one's success, and success for a woman might be a challenge.

Achieving the requisite success was, as Mikulski knew, a genuine issue, for there were recognized and unrecognized barriers to gender equity in the austere body. The House of Representatives, although arguably more open to women, also featured barriers as Mikulski knew from her nine years of service there representing Maryland's 3rd District. Mikulski would probably say that all legislatures featured barriers; French thinker Michel Foucault would go farther and posit that all institutions set-up to support the prevailing "discourse" had not only barriers but visible and invisible ways to discipline those who did not observe the barriers.[11] In Mikulski's view, one might not want to challenge too overtly, but, nonetheless, one, facing the barriers and the disciplining, should challenge. If one did not, one could not truly serve and thereby gain the recognition necessary for reelection. Wearing pants on the Senate floor would not be challenge enough.

So, how were the women elected to the Senate to learn how to proceed? They would need skillful mentoring, and Mikulski devoted much of her time and energy on Capitol Hill to providing this mentoring. Some of it grew out of the regular dinners the group would have—at Washington, D.C. restaurants and in private homes. Over the years, it took various forms and was sometimes formal and sometimes informal. The mentoring was also bipartisan: Mikulski— and those who joined her—helped along Republican women as well as Democrat, although Democrats numerically dominated the group.[12]

Men, who join the House of Representatives or the Senate, are undoubtedly mentored, although there does not seem to be a systematic procedure. Typically, a new member latches on to an established one and learns "the ropes" rather informally. The system seems to work; however, it is rather hegemonic, for the mentoring typically stresses both the structures that be and the powers that be. This type of mentoring was in theory available for women entering the legislature, but it often did not occur. "Why" is a matter for speculation. Was sexism so inherent in the two governmental bodies that newly elected men were embraced in the system and newly elected women ignored? Did too much of the mentoring involve activities—the gym, the bar after hours—that were male-defined and male-only? Whatever the reason, women needed assistance and were not getting it. Mikulski made it her mission to fill in the gap.

And the mentoring involved different topics. The men did not have to be told, in some detail, how to locate the few restrooms available to them near the legislative floor. The men did not have to be told how to adjust—not change—their rhetorical inclinations for (still) male-defined communication activities such as debating on the floor or questioning witnesses in a hearing. Mikulski had a distinct style, and she would not change it, but adjusting and changing are not the same thing.

As Mikulski closed-in on retirement from the Senate, more and more colleagues pointed to this mentoring work as her major achievement. One might not think much of it: it resulted in no legislation; it did not influence policy discussions or decisions. But, if one considers how the number of women has grown in both the House and Senate since Mikulski arrived, one might change one's mind about her work. Mikulski joined the House in January 1977. There were a handful of women in that body then; now, there are many. Mikulski joined the Senate in January 1987. There were only two women in that body then; now, twenty-four. Mikulski, of course, did not mentor all, but she played a major role in introducing many to legislative life and work, and she establish a mentoring precedent for other Senate women to follow.

One might think of the Senate pre-Mikulski. What accomplishments by women can be noted? What women emerged from the group of senators as leaders? The only person one might point to is Maine senator Margaret

Chase Smith. She spoke up against Joseph McCarthy long before others; she was mentioned as a Republican candidate for the presidency or vice presidency. But Smith, who got to the Senate upon her husband's death, stands alone. Now, think of the Senate today. Washington's Patty Murray and Maine's Susan Collins have strong records as legislators; California's Diane Feinstein has become an authority on national security matters; Alaska's Lisa Murkowski and West Virginia's Shelly Moore Capito have emerged as bipartisan coalition-builders. And, in 2020, three female members of the Senate, Minnesota's Amy Klobuchar, New York's Kirsten Gillibrand, and California's Kamala Harris sought the Democratic presidential nomination. One cannot point to Mikulski's mentoring work as causing this dramatic change. However, based on what many of these women said upon Mikulski's retirement, that on-going mentoring effort was indeed a major factor.

IMPLICATIONS FOR COMMUNICATION

Upon her retirement, many paid tribute to Mikulski. Her many years in the Congress justified that, even if there were no grand titles or genuinely landmark pieces of legislation to associate her with. Her leadership—and, thus, her communication—focused mainly on issues of gender. When these issues became prominent, she was in the lead, as with Admiral Frank Kelso's retirement rank in 1993. There, she led the way; on other matters of gender she was part of a group that equally led. So, when one looks for major speeches on the floor of the Senate that Mikulski delivered, one finds few. Before 1992, she was a lone spokesperson for gender equity, and, in 1993, she had to be the leading one because all but one (Republican Nancy Kassebaum of Kansas) of her female colleagues were new to the body. But, after 1993, she proceeded more as part of a collective than as the spokesperson. Doing so is, of course, in line with what theorists during Second Wave Feminism pointed to as the "female style."[13] Yes, this term essentializes those gendered female, but it also pointed to an approach to politics that was indeed the preferred one for women in the legislature. One is tempted to say "at that time." Recently, for example, New York senator Kirsten Gillibrand has been upfront on the issue of sexual harassment and assault in the military. She has been very much the "point person," with former Missouri senator Claire McCaskill also playing a major role until her reelection defeat. So, now, perhaps, we see women not working communally quite as much as in previous decades, but working communally was seemingly Mikulski's preference and is still common among the much larger number of women in the Senate.

This preference is very much evident in the work she did to orient women to Congress. Having been there longer, she initially took the lead, but quickly the various activities became more of a shared project. People will still point to Mikulski as the leader because she was the force behind the efforts, but she was not always the one at the helm. That very fact perhaps played a role in these activities being somewhat non-partisan. Mikulski was, after all, widely recognized as a liberal Democrat, and, therefore, newly elected Republican women might have shied away from a Mikulski-orchestrated orientation. That the women of the Congress provided the introduction perhaps gave it less of a liberal tinge. The correct term for Mikulski's role is difficult to find: "inspired" suggests that she receded from the effort, which is not true; "orchestrated" suggests that she coordinated to a degree, she didn't. So, without the accurate verb, the best we can say is that Mikulski made sure the efforts to welcome women into the Congress occurred. And all involved recognized Mikulski as being the guiding force. The absence of the precise term should not be totally surprising. A basic tenet of Second Wave Feminism was that many experiences known to those gendered female had not made it fully into the language. Thus, we may not have the term with which to label Mikulski's role, but, as many noted, it was significant.

The communication being described is largely interpersonal or group, not oratorical. As such, it is difficult to study. There are no records of it. All we have are scattered comments by women about it—always appreciative. There are, however, enough of these scattered comments to offer some informed guesses. As already noted, there were few if any speeches—maybe a brief welcome; there was, at best, a very loose agenda. Rather than anything remotely resembling a seminar or a meeting, the gatherings were social ones, focused on a shared meal and much conversation. The conversational pattern sometimes had a group talking, but often was one-on-one. Three generalizations might well be offered about these sessions. First, they did not resemble what someone in an organization—a corporate one or an educational one or a governmental one—would expect for an orientation. They were far more casual. Second, they were very much in line with what those who theorized gendered communication would predict— no hierarchy, many stories, much turn-taking. Yes, this conception of a "feminine" communication style does run the risk of essentializing the gender; nonetheless, there seemed to be a match between the conception and the reality at these gatherings Third, they reflected Mikulski's communication skills, even though she was not "running" them in the manner that a sit-down in a committee or caucus room might be "run." Mikulski was evidently talented in one-on-one as well as in setting-up and participating in appropriate ways in groups. In fact, these communication skills are noted in comments offered about the senator by the men she worked with. They found her cooperative but also sometimes determined in interpersonal interactions; and they would characterize her group work to be productive. They did not point to any dramatic moments on the floor of the Senate, but they did assess her senatorial work—and the associated communication—as both results-focused and cordial. There is a great deal of consonance between this assessment of Mikulski's work and what we imagine she did as convener of these informal orientation gatherings. In the official work, there would often be an edginess, for Mikulski could be a battler. Subtract that edginess, add in the camaraderie she wished to develop among the women in Congress, and you would have a good sense of what her interpersonal and group communication skills were. Mikulski could deliver a rip-roaring speech, with her pronounced Baltimore accent and, maybe, a few lapses in grammar, but it is not her oratorical accomplishments one would point to in assessing her work in the Congress. Rather, it is her interpersonal, group communication, especially as it displayed itself in her mentoring efforts, as well as those time she stood up for those—usually women—who were disadvantaged in the workplace or other venues.

This assessment, focusing on what might be termed "cordiality"—might surprise some, for Mikulski had a Capitol Hill reputation as being very difficult to work with—as being "mean."[14] This was the view of some who joined her staff but rather dramatically not the view of others there over lengthy periods. The conclusion one arrives at is that she was as demanding of staff as she was of herself and, when workers fell short of the mark, she told them as much, perhaps strongly. One should keep in mind that a member of Congress acquires staffers through various means: some a congressperson or senator chooses, others may get in for political reasons. So, it is quite possible that some on Mikulski's staff were there because her senior Democratic colleague in the Senate recommended them or her state's Democratic governor recommended them. They may not have been in sync with the demands that she would make of those hired to support her work. Those clearly in sync were the ones who stayed with the senator and the ones who described their working relationship in positive terms.

It is also worth noting that, whereas many senators might be on the "meaner" side of a "nice"-to-"mean" continuum, the only time it seems to become an issue is when the senator is female. Thus, during the 2020 presidential campaign, *Vanity Fair* ran an article indicting Minnesota's Amy Klobuchar for her supposedly overly tough treatment of staffers.[15] Do women need to be perceived as tougher than men? Or do the media choose to cover the tough women while treating the tough men as normal? *Politico* in 2018 listed the ten U.S. senators with the worst records keeping staff members. Presumably, these were the ten who were the worst to work for. Curiously, seven of the ten were women. Does that statistic—70 percent—say something about the women or about the contexts in which women senators and their staffers work? And why isn't there media coverage of the "meanness" of West Virginia's Joe Manchin or Colorado's Michael Bennet (who was a

2020 presidential aspirant)? Both were on the list. The *Vanity Fair* prompted defenses of Klobuchar. Back in time, there were comparable defenses of Mikulski.

If one reads the praise Mikulski received upon her retirement, one is very reluctant to conclude that it and its reflections on her communication were pro forma. She was certainly not described as a push-over: many noted her strong commitment on certain issues as well as her determination to respond to those issues in certain ways. But the picture is not of one who is hostile—or "mean," but, rather, one who is a strong advocate whose legislative flexibility is often apparent but sometimes not. And such a description might well be the way many successful legislators, female or male, would be described—and would want to be described. Mikulski, then, may not have been the easiest senator to work for or with, but the "mean" label must be seen in a context where the women in the legislature are disproportionately so characterized.

Her communication as a legislator, although not grand Senate oratory, was then effective. Although it left no public record, it did leave a record with her colleagues, especially her female colleagues. Group communication in a legislative body sometimes is recorded: for example, one can read or watch committee hearings and assess how individual members of the body—or the committee as a group—handle the structured communication of a committee. Because of its structure, the communication does not conform to what one might find in a group communication textbook, but it is nonetheless group communication. Furthermore, its nuances as political communication are fascinating, as Lisa Gring-Pemble has ably noted, nuances introduced because of a structure that gives the committee chair power to highlight testimony and interrogation and suppress testimony and interrogation.[16] Other examples of legislative group communication are unfortunately off-the-record. Imagine how fascinating it would be to study the communication in a conference committee set-up to reconcile very different versions of a bill passed by the House and the Senate. Interpersonal communication in the legislature is even rarer. In the course of Senate debates, two members will stage a "colloquy," but it is a staged dialogue not genuine interpersonal communication. The same can be said for a joint press conference. Two members are involved but it is scarcely the same thing as a one-on-one conversation over lunch or the cloakroom (still called that) at the rear of the Senate chamber.

So, much of what Mikulski accomplished through both group gatherings and one-on-one mentoring sessions is not recorded and cannot be studied. We have testimony as to its effectiveness. And we can also speak to its importance. All one really needs to do is look at the composition of the U.S. Senate when Mikulski arrived there. Many have noted that when Anita Hill appeared before the Senate Judiciary Committee in 1991, she faced an array of white males, all wearing the "required" dark suits. That was the case because it was very rare to find any Senate committee that would not match that description back then. Consider again the Senate today. It is not as diverse as one might like, but there is much more diversity when it comes to gender and some diversity on other counts. The Senate is, then, a different place today than in 1987 when Mikulski arrived or 1991 when Hill testified. Many events, including the treatment of Hill, pushed the legislature toward greater diversity. But electing diversity and orienting diversity—so that those new to the body could succeed—are two different matters. Without the second, one can envision electoral wins as voters wonder why there is so little diversity followed by electoral losses as voters assess new members as not effectively serving. The work Mikulski did through communication not on any official record was intended to prevent this scenario: that work would help new members who represented gender diversity serve and succeed.

NOTES

1. Theodore F. Sheckels, Nichola D. Gutgold, and Diana B. Carlin, *Gender and the American Presidency: Nine Presidential Women and the Barriers They Faced* (Lanham, MD: Lexington Books, 2012), pp. 53–68.

2. Dan Rodricks, "Mikulski's Legacy Starts with 'The Battle of the Road," *Baltimore Sun*, https://www.baltimoresun.com/Maryland/bs-md-rodricks-0303 -20150302-column.html. At one point in time, I-70 split into I-70S (to Washington) and I-70N (to Baltimore) in Frederick. MD. Then, I-70S was renamed I-270, and I70N became simply I-70. The continuation of I-70 beyond I-695 and into the center of Baltimore was termed I-70 in some reports but I-170 in others.

3. Theodore F. Sheckels, "Mikulski vs. Chavez for the Senate from Maryland in 1986 and the 'Rules' for Attack Politics," *Communication Quarterly* 42.1 (1994): 311–26.

4. One of us recalls a conversation with a *Baltimore Sun* employee while doing research in its archives of the 1986 Senate race. The employee said she disagreed with Mikulski on most issues but still voted for her because she was "Baltimore's gal."

5. "The Best and Worst of Congress 2014," *Washingtonian.* http://www.washintonian.com/article/people/the-bestworst-of-Congress-2014

6. Theodore F. Sheckels, "The Rhetorical Use of Double-Voiced Discourse and Feminine Style: The U. S. Senate Debate over the Impact of Tailhook '91 on Admiral Frank B. Kelso II's Retirement Rank," *Southern Communication Journal* 63.1 (1997): 56–68.

7. *Congressional Record*, April 19, 1994. p. S4453.

8. Luke Wenger, Erin Broadwater, and Yvonne Cox, "Mikulski Remembered a Plain-speaking Trailblazer for Women in Politics," *Baltimore Sun*, https://www.baltimoresun.com/politics/bs-md-mikulski-career-20150302-story-html

9. Ramsey Cox and Alexander Bolton, "Senate GOP Blocks Paycheck Fairness Bill," *The Hill*, April 9, 2014, http://thehill.com/blogs/floor-action/Senate/203064-senate-gop-blocks-paycheck-fairness-bill/2199/all-archives/

10. *Nine and Counting: The Women of the Senate* (New York: Harper Collins, 2000). The book's cover lists all nine women as co-authors, with Catherine Whitney working with them. Listings for the book put Barbara Boxer as author.

11. Michel Foucault, *Discipline and Punish: The Birth of the Prison,* trans. Alan Sheridan (New York: Pantheon Books, 1978).

12. Dana Bash, "Mikulski Makes History While Creating Zone of Civility for Senate Women," *CNN,* http://www.cnn.com/2012/03116/politics/mikulski-history /index.html?hpt=hp_t3; Marc Fisher, "Mikulski, a Role Model for Generations of Women in Politics, to Retire in 2016," *Washington Post.* March 2, 2015. https:// www.washingtonpost.com/local/dc-politics/mikulski-a-role-model-for-generatio ns-of-women-to--retire-in-2016/2015/03/02/c6770396c0e4-9ec2-b418f57a4a99-st ory.html

13. Jane Blankenship and Debrah C. Robson, "A 'Feminine Style' in Women's Political Discourse: An Exploratory Essay," *Communication Quarterly* 43.3 (1995): 353–66.

14. "The Best and Worst of Congress 2014."

15. Tina Nguyen, "Terrified Aides Say Amy Klobuchar is Just Like Trump," *Vanity Fair,* February 8, 2019.

16. Lisa Gring Pemble, "'Are We Going to Govern by Anecdote?' Rhetorical Constructions of Welfare Recipients in Congressional Hearings, Debates, and Legislation, 1992-1996," *Quarterly Journal of Speech* 87.3 (2001): 341–65.

Chapter 3

Martin O'Malley's Failure to Communicate

In 2020, Maryland governor Parris Glendening was concluding his second term, and most presumed that his lieutenant, Kathleen Kennedy Townsend, would run to succeed him. She did, but, before she could secure the Democrats' nomination, she and her campaign had to deal with rumors that another was eyeing the office. That other was Baltimore mayor Martin O'Malley.[1]Charismatic, O'Malley had an appeal that Townsend lacked. He deferred; she lost, but, in 2006, it was his turn. That year, he used that charisma or charm to make the incumbent Republican Robert Ehrlich a one-term governor. In retrospect, this moment may well be the high point of O'Malley's political career. Marty O'Malley had won statewide office, but messaging problems, ones already apparent during his time as mayor, would weaken him politically from 2006 onward.

This chapter considers two matters: first, how O'Malley rose to this high point; second, how did his political appeal erode during his eight years as governor. Both stories involve communication. Both stories involve communication that O'Malley was not adequately controlling. The problems were not entirely communication ones: there were inconsistences in O'Malley's record—positions that were quite strikingly progressive and others arguably not, but these inconsistencies could have been explained. A political progressive, for example, has to also keep his (or her) eyes peeled on the economy, for a faltering one would weaken reelection or advancement chances. "Keeping Maryland strong while promoting social justice" could have been O'Malley's mantra; but, instead, he allowed the inconsistencies to remain unreconciled. Not clearly defining himself, he allowed opponents to define him—a fatal communication error in politics.

O'Malley was a surprising success early in his political career. He was arguably an underdog when elected to the Baltimore City Council, and he was arguably an underdog when he won the Democratic primary and became the party's nominee for mayor. (Winning the nomination was tantamount to winning the office in the Democrat-dominated city.) Then, his career moved forward based on a combination of image and policy. One reason he was something of a surprise winner was his race. Baltimore, a heavily African American city, had seen more and more African Americans in leadership positions. In fact, O'Malley's primary opponents were African American. O'Malley was, however, able to muster considerable support among black civic leaders and voters. Presumably, they saw in O'Malley the potential for progressive leadership.

CHARISMA TOO

O'Malley was young and handsome. He also seemed "with it" insofar as he was able to bring modern, computerized accounting into city finances (a program called CitiStat), created in imitation of a similar one pioneered in New York City. He also seemed the proverbial "breath of fresh air" because, through this system, he brought a measure of transparency to city affairs. City affairs had arguably escaped the control of "bosses" during

Figure 3.1 Martin O'Malley Fronting His Celtic Rock Band, "O'Malley's March." *Source*: Photo by Edward Kimmel of Takoma Park, MD. Reprinted with permission under the Creative Commons Attribution-Share Alike 2.0 Generic license: https://creativecommons.org/licenses/by-sa/2.0/legalcode

William Donald Schaefer's terms, but there was both lingering murkiness and a remembered history of past corruption. O'Malley used high-tech to surmount both.

He was also a rock star, albeit for a limited audience. He was front man—guitar and vocals—for a Celtic rock group called "O'Malley's March," who performed frequently in the city.[2] Some still recall the promotional pictures used for the band, ones showing O'Malley in a sleeveless shirt that displayed rather buff biceps. So, in some eyes, "with it" meant "cool." And, in conjunction with this image was his role as husband in a very photogenic family. One might also argue that the fact that his spouse's father was attorney general and very influential politico Joseph Curran also sped O'Malley along his political path. The average voters might be more likely to know about the rock band, but the political insiders whom O'Malley needed to have in his corner knew about the Curran connection. He was something of the "golden boy," both cool and well-connected.

These matters of image undoubtedly helped O'Malley as he attempted to advance his career whereas his record raised some questions. The record raised eyebrows, although his charisma as well as a generally progressive philosophy kept concerns at bay.

RECORD AS MAYOR

When O'Malley sought election as mayor, Baltimore was suffering from typical urban problems—and then some. The story is one shared by most major American cities. As suburbs grew, cities declined in population and acquired a different racial and economic demographic. Parallel was a major economic shift as industry relocated to areas with lower labor costs. Abandoned factories and warehouses joined blighted blocks of housing, with the tax base continually shrinking. American cities, especially in the North, had to devise redevelopment projects and, in some cases, reinvent themselves in response. Meanwhile, with impoverishment came crime, and O'Malley chose to make fighting crime a centerpiece of his campaign. In the primary, he was the sole white person running against six African Americans. Nonetheless, he secured the endorsement of several prominent African American civic and church leaders, as well as that of former mayor and governor William Donald Schaefer. His firm stance on crime played a role in gaining him this support. O'Malley won the primary; then, he won the general election with 90 percent of the vote. There was then an expectation that O'Malley would take action to combat the city's crime problem.

The tracking system called "CitiStat" that O'Malley initiated won considerable applause. It kept track of many city matters, including incidents of reported crime. Knowing its level and its details was one thing but zero-tolerance policing was another. O'Malley enacted that, leading to the alleged targeting of black communities and a loss of some African American support.[3] O'Malley claimed the tough strategy worked, and he cited declines in city crime when running for governor in 2006. Those claims, however, were questioned by his opponent in that race. The *Washington Post*, reporting on the campaign, rejected his opponent's (Republican incumbent Robert Ehrlich) claim that O'Malley was playing with statistics in order to look good, but the newspaper also noted that definitive data were lacking and that O'Malley's claim of a 36 percent reduction in violent crime was therefore impossible to either prove or disprove.[4] One then finds it difficult to assess O'Malley's crime-fighting record. The best conclusion to offer is, first, that it was effective (although we do not know how effective) and, second, that it did raise concern among the city's African American residents and leaders. "Concern," however, does not necessarily mean lack of support. African Americans were negatively affected by crime in the city: they wanted to see it reduced. So, O'Malley was to be applauded, but the policing methods he advocated were concerning because of the racist edge they seemed to have.

So, O'Malley's record on crime may have helped him with some voters but hurt him with others. What certainly helped him was the fiscal responsibility he showed as mayor. So, with a liberal reputation but some credentials that more conservative voters might find appealing, he defeated Ehrlich 53 percent to 46 percent and made the move from Baltimore City to Annapolis. That winning margin is good for a Democrat, but not as good as achieved by other Democrats in a state where Democrats do hold a sizeable voting registration edge. One might draw two conclusions: first, there were elements in O'Malley's record that bothered both liberals and conservatives; second, he was not doing the job he needed to do in presenting a consistent political identity. In 2002, he was named "The Best Young Mayor in the Country." His relative youth and the charisma gained him acclaim and some support, but many voters wanted a more substantive picture. Who precisely was Marty O'Malley? Yes, he was the "front man" for a Celtic rock group, but what exactly did he stand for?

A note on Maryland politics is useful here. Most assume that Maryland is a very blue state, one of the bluest in the nation. While that may be so if one is looking only at the political party preference expressed at voter registration, Democrats do not always win big. There are large blocs of Republican voters in the western and eastern reaches of the state. They are usually outnumbered by the Democrats living along the state's "metropolitan" core, but, should the Republicans nominate a candidate who is both reasonably moderate and reasonably competent, he or she can make inroads among those "metropolitan" voters. Historically, one could cite U.S. senator Charles Matthias, Governor

Theodore McKeldin, and any number of Congressional representatives. If the Democratic candidate is not strong—for example, George Mahoney in 1966, Kathleen Townsend in 2002, and Ben Jealous in 2018—then Republicans can win statewide. Thus, in those example cases, Republicans Spiro Agnew, Robert Ehrlich, and Larry Hogan became governor. O'Malley's six-point win over incumbent Ehrlich, then, should be seen as a win but not an overpowering one, especially given the poor relations Ehrlich had had with the state legislature during his tenure. O'Malley should have been perceived as a bit less the "golden boy" and more a promising Democrat who perhaps needed to shore-up his image.

As he moved from Baltimore City Hall to the governor's mansion in Annapolis, three matters chased him. Not scandals, although there were a few rumored ones, but, first, his ambition; second, inconsistencies that blurred the picture of who he was; and, third, his lack of message control.

AMBITION

As noted at the outset of this chapter, he was rumored to be interested in running for governor as early as 2002, and that rumor held many back from supporting Lieutenant Governor Kathleen Kennedy Townsend to succeed Parris Glendenning. He had the charisma, which she arguably lacked. But he had not served long as mayor then, and some thought charisma was all he had at that point. But the fact that he seriously considered running marked him as one who was always looking at the next office he would seek. As mayor, he was running for governor, and, as governor, he was running for president. This apparent ambition did not appeal to those citizens who wanted him to focus on the job at hand, not the next one.

INCONSISTENCIES

The envisioned presidential run would require that O'Malley position himself as a liberal. Primary voters tend to support "edge" candidates (liberal Democrats, conservative Republicans), so positioning himself as a liberal conformed to time-honored election reality. Also, in 2016, Hillary Clinton was hugging the moderate-liberal divide, and, looking toward 2016, she seemed the more formidable opponent than very liberal Vermont senator Bernie Sanders, who many perceived as inspiring but not especially presidential. So, during his two terms as governor, he pursued what one might label a progressive agenda. He advocated penal system reform, made "dreamers" eligible for in-state tuition at Maryland's colleges and universities, abolished capital punishment, campaigned for strict gun control measures, and supported the legalization of same-sex marriage. His pursuit of this liberal agenda evoked opposition: the legislation he supported on "dreamers" and same-sex marriage were sent, by petition, to referenda where "dreamers" won 58 percent of the vote and same-sex marriage won 52.4. On the latter, O'Malley's stance also evoked opposition from Baltimore's Roman Catholic Archbishop Edwin O'Brien, who lobbied O'Malley as a devout Catholic, to reverse his position. Needing to be a good liberal more so than a good Catholic, O'Malley chose to disagree with the Archbishop.[5]

On the environment, O'Malley did support a ban on the practice of shark finning, but that was probably an issue that involved few votes to either gain or lose. (How many voters even knew what shark finning was?) On other environmental issues, where more votes were at stake, he did not pursue an especially liberal course. On Maryland's Eastern Shore, there are many chicken farms, small ones as well as big ones such as the collection owned by Salisbury's Frank Perdue. Allegedly, these farms were polluting the Chesapeake Bay. Chicken waste is high in phosphorus, and large quantities of phosphorus were running off Eastern Shore farmland into the lower Bay. The twin results were pollution and damage to the state's shellfishing industry. The University of Maryland's Environmental Law Clinic sued Perdue Farms; O'Malley opposed the lawsuit. The State Assembly considered measures imposing clean-up taxes on Perdue Farms and others; O'Malley said he would veto any such legislation.[6] O'Malley was probably not trying to gain "Eastern Shore" support; rather, as governor, he was probably focused on preserving the state's strong economy. The "Eastern Shore" needed chickens to be prosperous.

In Western Maryland, the issue was not chickens; rather, it was fracking. In areas where coal was once mined, it was becoming popular to use hydraulic fracturing to get at the natural gas that was otherwise difficult to extract. Using the fracking techniques, mines could extend their lifespan. That, of course, would benefit state commerce. O'Malley was cautious on this issue: rather than join liberal environmental voices in denouncing the process, he commissioned a study and waited years for it to be completed. Then, he approved fracking, although he did insist on tight regulation.[7] Arguably, O'Malley was trying to appeal to both business interests and environmentalists, but environmentalists were not pleased. They wondered about O'Malley's supposed progressive posture. Yes, O'Malley did in late 2014 issue an executive order committing the state to a "zero-waste" future (an order current governor Larry Hogan has revoked), but some saw it as liberal window-dressing that did not correspond with O'Malley's refusal to crack down on chicken farm waste and fracking. O'Malley certainly could have taken a more progressive stance; however, he, as governor, had his eyes on the state's economy. He could have explained his need to balance environmental protection and economic stability in terms most Democrats would have understood. Instead, he let the seeming inconsistency between his support for the liberal agenda and his reluctance to be extremely "green" stand.

MESSAGE CONTROL

If Hillary Clinton had won the presidency in 2016, O'Malley might have been in her Cabinet as Secretary of Homeland Security.[8] That position might seem odd to some who followed O'Malley's career as mayor and governor, but security had indeed been a matter O'Malley had focused on as mayor and governor, just not one that attracted headlines. His particular concern was port security, a matter he felt President George W. Bush's administration was particularly weak on. In general, O'Malley had a very negative view of Bush policies. He thought they were so-so on urban security and, more generally, anti-urban. At the National Press Club in 2005, O'Malley compared Bush's urban affairs budget to the terrorists' 9/11 attacks on New York City and Washington, D.C. sites. All were attacks, he argued. His analogy was not received well by both Republicans and Democrats. O'Malley was guilty of hyperbole that grated with people who recalled Bush's nobility in the wake of the 9/11 attacks.[9]

O'Malley also allegedly went after David Simon, creator of the television show *The Wire*. O'Malley thought the Baltimore mayor in the show was an unflattering fictitious version of himself. He threatened to prevent the show's continued filming in the city if Simon did not alter the way the mayor was depicted.[10] That incident occurred before O'Malley was governor. Years later, after he was governor, O'Malley went after Trump's Homeland Security Acting Deputy Secretary, Virginia's Ken Cuccinelli. O'Malley encountered Cuccinelli at Hawk and Dove, a well-known Capitol Hill bar, and loudly berated Cuccinelli for Trump's immigration policies.[11] In both these instances, O'Malley lost control. Those who agreed with him and those who disagreed felt he damaged his image by not controlling his messaging.

Controlling one's message, of course, means two things. In these three incidents, O'Malley did not control his communicating: he attacked when he probably should not have, he seemed petty when nobility would have been preferable, and he made the news by making a scene. The control in these cases is control of what one says and does. O'Malley sometimes lacked that control. The other type of control is larger: control of the overall message one sends about one's politics. O'Malley lacked that control too.

SPENDING AND TAXES

O'Malley's tendency to be hyperbolic or unduly aggressive might have lost him votes if he had been able to seek a third term as governor, but what really cost him was how he lost control of what should have been a positive fiscal message. In Baltimore, when mayor, O'Malley wanted to run a "tight ship" and used computer technology to do so. So, as governor, he imitated "CitiStat" on a statewide basis to provide fiscal transparency. In Baltimore, there had been a long history of corruption. Long-serving Mayor William Donald Schaefer combated it, but people still fretted over whether city affairs were on the up-and-up. The same was arguably true at the state level. One recalls Vice President Spiro Agnew's defense in 1973 when he was charged with accepting bribes as governor: everybody did it, it was normal. So, O'Malley's focus on transparency was as necessary in Annapolis as it had been in Baltimore. Also necessary at the state level was providing a high level of services while eliminating debt. So, in Annapolis, O'Malley pushed through the State Assembly a plan that would eliminate a projected $1.7 billion state budget deficit. Fiscal responsibility was certainly a message O'Malley could have sent with transparency and a sound budget as hallmarks; instead, he let his opponents dominate messaging with attacks on how O'Malley's plan would raise taxes.

Gradually, as the years in Annapolis progressed, the "raising taxes" message would drown out many of the good things that might have been said about O'Malley's government. The anti-O'Malley message suggested that he would tax anything he could. The message was so strong that a proposal to raise revenue using traffic speed cameras experienced difficulty getting through an overwhelmingly Democratic Assembly.[12] The message reached its climax in Republican-sponsored messages that claimed O'Malley was going to tax "the rain."

O'Malley certainly did raise taxes and fees. Wanting a balanced state budget but also wanting to pursue an agenda requiring considerable spending on vital programs, he had no choice but to do so. And, as taxes went up, O'Malley's popularity went down. But did he really want to tax "the rain"? No. O'Malley was sometimes concerned about the health of Maryland's treasured Chesapeake Bay. Although he did not favor punitive taxes on the chicken farmers on the Eastern Shore, he did look for other sources of pollution that he thought he might target without a pronounced negative impact. One he noticed was parking lots—acres and acres of them from which there was polluting runoff when it rained. Parking lots were not typically viewed as structures the way buildings were; thus, they escaped taxation imposed on commercial real estate. The land might be taxed, but there were no structures or "improvements" on the land. Or were acres of non-porous asphalt an "improvement"? If so, then a tax could be imposed and revenue collected to offset the costs of combating the dirty run-off from the lots, run-off when it rained. Opponents chose not to term the levy "the parking lot tax," for constituents might have concluded that such a levy made sense. (Most Marylanders are united in wanting to protect the Chesapeake.) Rather, opponents termed it "the rain tax."[13]

The term did not cost O'Malley reelection in 2010, but the saying, "He'll even tax the rain" haunted him because he had acquired a stereotypically liberal tax-and-spend reputation. Looking back on O'Malley's campaign in 2010, one has to wonder how much voters understood about "the rain tax." One would hope that they found the very notion absurd and dismissed the idea that O'Malley was in support of such a thing. (Same for the less talked-about "flush tax.") Truth be told, some voters, without the time to interrogate the charge, probably did believe O'Malley, somehow, wanted to tax the rain. The idea was consonant with his image, so there were probably some swayed by the charge, not understanding that the governor was attempting to raise revenue (yes) but also help improve the declining condition of the northern section of the Chesapeake, which was affected by the run-off heavy in leaked motor oil into the bay's watershed.

What it also reveals is O'Malley's inability to control the messaging about him. In this case, he was not able to remove from public discourse an absurd notion. In others, he was not able to communicate a clear image of himself and his politics to the public. He was guilty of inconsistencies, and he was guilty of not restraining himself when the restraint one might want in a statesman was expected. Much in O'Malley's two terms deserves praise, but his communication—before, during, and after—was a problem. He was a much weaker political figure in 2012 than in 2006. This weakness hurt the campaign of his lieutenant governor, Anthony Brown, who was attempting to succeed O'Malley. This weakness also did not provide a strong foundation for a 2016 presidential campaign.

In another chapter, we talk about O'Malley's campaign for the presidency, but a few matters related to it should be noted here.

First, he seemed to be running while he should have been focusing on the state he was governing. In doing so, he was repeating his earlier pattern of seeming to run for governor early—arguably too early—in his tenure as Baltimore mayor. O'Malley, thus, marked himself as overly ambitious, and this probably turned some people off and away from his presidential campaign. Voters in Iowa probably did not know how ambitious O'Malley had seemed to be, but political insiders, especially those he might have involved in his campaign did. They might have asked if ambition defined O'Malley more than what he had accomplished and stood for as a public servant.

Second, like others who have served as governor after serving as Baltimore mayor (e.g., Theodore McKeldin, William Donald Schaefer), he seemed to many to be too Baltimore-oriented. As such, he had lukewarm support for a future office from parts of the state other than Baltimore and, perhaps, its immediate environs. This accusation may well not be objectively true (just as it may not be true for McKeldin or Schaefer), but perception rooted in a long-standing rivalry among the state's regions may have trumped truth. (Elsewhere, we talk about the rivalry between the Baltimore area and the Washington, D.C. area when it comes to state spending.) A presidential aspirant needs a strong core of support. For a governor, one expects it to come from the candidate's state. In O'Malley's case, there may well have been large swaths of the state that were more indifferent than supportive. And, pundits might ask, if Marylanders don't strongly support him, why should voters in Iowa or New Hampshire or South Carolina?

Third, although there was much that was positive in his political record, the inconsistencies were worrisome. They prevented a totally coherent image of O'Malley from emerging. Was he closer to Bernie Sanders or Hillary Clinton on the political spectrum? Or in between? A brief examination of his record might push him in the Sanders direction, but, then, there would be the inconsistencies that made some wonder if he was truly a progressive. And he had been a Clinton supporter back in 2008, not an Obama one. Lacking a clear image, he lacked a clearly identifiable group of supporters. His problems controlling the messaging about him exacerbated the problem. In the eyes of too many Marylanders, he was a governor who raised taxes and fees. In the eyes of others, he was a governor with few noteworthy achievements they could cite because the achievements—genuine ones—were not being highlighted. People were not talking about his demonstrated commitment to social justice, for example; they were instead talking about how he wanted to tax the rain.

CONCLUSION

Those who study political communication, more often than not, examine what a candidate or an office-holder says. They then assess whether the communication was effective or ineffective. But there is more to being ineffective than delivering a faulty message. O'Malley was guilty of three types of miscommunication that might escape one focused on examining texts such as speeches or advertisements or debates.

First, he communicated through his words, actions, and even his bearing that he was ambitious. He did not squelch talk of running for mayor when he was a city councilman, governor when he was mayor, and president when he was governor. O'Malley, despite many actions that helped Baltimore and Maryland, was perceived as being not especially focused on the job he had. He, instead, desired the next one.

Second, O'Malley did not communicate a totally consistent sense of what he stood for politically. Most identified him as politically liberal, but some of his actions—on crime, on the environment—did not quite fit that picture. He never tried to clarify the picture either, making some wonder whether he was more interested in attaining an office than governing along predictable, consistent lines.

Third, O'Malley did not control communication about him. Increasing taxes made him politically vulnerable, but his position was one he could have explained by noting how Marylanders wanted—expected—a very high level of certain services and revenue was needed to provide them. Rather than explain why he raised taxes and fees, O'Malley let his opponents stereotype him as a tax-raising Democrat and, then, suggest that O'Malley was so tax-crazy that he'd even tax the rain. One can imagine a number of responses he might have offered to the "rain tax" notion—for example, a picture of a parking lot with clearly polluting water running off of it into a nearby creek. But there was no such response. Much as Michael Dukakis lost control of his image during the 1988 presidential campaign, letting the Bush campaign define him in a number of negative ways, O'Malley lost control of his image. He became the governor "who'd even tax the rain."

The Dukakis analogy is an apt one. Dukakis's record as Massachusetts governor was, on balance, a progressive. Although not the most progressive candidate seeking the Democratic presidential nomination in 1988, he was more the progressive than the moderate. After the Democratic National Convention, Dukakis had a sizeable lead in the polls over the incumbent Vice President George H. W. Bush. Moreover, he had a clear identity: he was a governor who had done miraculous things in Massachusetts that he would now pursue nationwide; he would blend competence and vison. Both this image and the lead were lost when internal problems in the Dukakis campaign allowed attack ads by the Bush forces to go unanswered. These ads either redefined Dukakis as foolish and dangerous or so blurred his image that voters no longer knew who he was. Dukakis, of course, never recovered from the Bush attack. His image was lost because, during a period when communication was essential, his campaigned remained largely silent. O'Malley's image problem was not because an opponent had run highly effective ads against him. Rather, it was because, during his years in public service, he did not pay sufficient attention to creating and sustaining an image. But, much as in the case of Dukakis, voters, as a consequence of poor communication, did not know who Marty O'Malley really was.

In 2016, he stood on the debate stage with Hillary Clinton and Bernie Sanders—and also with Rhode Island's Lincoln Chafee and Virginia's Jim Webb, until they faded. But most who viewed those debates probably would have had a difficult time assessing O'Malley. Part of the problem was, of course, that the media focused on Clinton and Sanders, but another part was that O'Malley, despite many successes as mayor and governor that he could have trumpeted, was undefined.

NOTES

1. Daniel LeDuc. "Coy O'Malley Scrutinized—Challenge to Townsend," *Washington Post,* December 25, 2001; Matthew Mosk, "Baltimore Mayor's Profile Is Rising," *Washington Post*, October 15, 2001; Daniel LeDuc, "O'Malley Raises Funds, Raises Roof," *Washington Post*, March 25, 2002.

2. "O'Malley's March," *Washington Post*, March 17, 2000, http://www.omalleysmarch.com/acclaimwp.htm; "Rock and Roll Governor: The Wild Side of Maryland's Martin O'Malley," https://news.yahoo.com/blogs/power-playersabc -news/rock-n-roll-governor-the-wild-side-of-marylands-Martin-O'Malley-1102 44497.html

3. Paul Schwartzman and John Wagner, "As Baltimore's Mayor, Critics Say, O'Malley's Policing Tactics Sewed Distrust," *Washington Post*, April 25, 2015, https://www.washingtonpost.com/local/dc-politics/as-mayor-of-baltimore-omall eys-policing-strategy-sewed-mistrust/2015/24/25/af81178a-ea9l-11e4-9767-627 6fc9bOadastory.html

4. John Wagner, "O'Malley Finds Issue Can Cut Both Ways," *Washington Post*, https://www.washingtonpost.com/wp-dyn/content/article/2016/c3/02/AR200608 0201812.html

5. John Wagner, "O'Malley, Archbishop at Odds over Same-Sex Marriage, Letters Show," *Washington Post*, August 8, 2011. https://www.washingtonpost.com /local/dc-politics/omalley-archbishop-at-odds-over-same-sex-marriageletters-show /2011/08/08/g/QAL/vR02L_story.html

6. Jennifer Shutt, "Governor O'Malley Says He'll Veto Chicken Tax Bill," https://web.archive.org/web/20151117065247; http://archive.delmarvanow.com/ article/20140207/NEWS/302070009/Governor-Martin-O-Malley-says-he-ll-veto-ch icken-tax-bill-poultry-S-cent

7. Timothy Wheeler, "O'Malley Administration Sets Out Path to Fracking in Maryland," *Baltimore Sun*, http://www.baltimoresun.com/feature/green/blog/bs-md-f racking-regulation-20141125-story.html

8. https://www.politico.com/story/2016/08/insiders-game-out-clintons-cabinet -226599

9. Lori Montgomery, "O'Malley Likens Bush's Proposed Cuts to Sept 11 Attack," *Washington Post*, February 9, 2005, https://www.washingtonpost.com/wp/ hyn/articles/A9117-2005Feb8.2005.html

10. Ben Jacobs, "Martin O'Malley, Tommy Carcetti, and 2016," http://www.the-dailybeast.com/articles/203/05/09/martin-o-malley-tommy-carcetti-and-2016.html

11. "Ken Cuccinelli Walked into a Bar and Martin O'Malley Lit Into Him," *Washington Post*, November 28, 2019, https://washingtonpost.com/local/ken-cucc

inelli-walked-into-a-bar-and-martin-omalley-lit-intohim/2019/11/28/d27742lc1191-llea-bOfc-b2cc38411ebb-story.html

12. "O'Malley's Budget Cuts Kick Off Long Process," *Ocean City Maryland News*, July 12, 2007, http://www.mdcoastdispatch.com/articles/2012/11/09/Top-Stor ies/OMalleys-Budget-Cuts-Kick-Off-Long-Process

13. Travis Brown, "When It Rains, It Pours Tax Dollars in Maryland," *Forbes*, https://www.forbes.com/sites/travisbrown/2013/01/03/when-it-rains-it-pours-tax-do llars-in-Maryland/?sh=360b223f7c69

Chapter 4

Larry Hogan

A Look at His Record as Governor of Maryland

On November 6, 2018, Maryland's Republican governor, Larry Hogan, Jr., did the almost unimaginable. He won reelection to a second term. To put that in perspective, the first Republican governor in Maryland came into office in 1862. Since then, there have been only nine Republican governors. And only one of them, Theodore McKeldin, had succeeded in being reelected—and that had been more than sixty-five years earlier.

That Larry Hogan won as a Republican in Maryland is unusual. Maryland is a deeply blue state. Registered Democrats outnumber Republicans by more than two to one. Even when you include independents and those registered in other parties, Democrats still enjoy a 10 percentage point advantage. For Republicans to win a statewide elective office, they must pull a substantial majority of Republican votes and a good number of votes from the independents. But in addition to those, they must convince some Democrats to vote for them.

For a man who in 2014 and 2018 ran gubernatorial campaigns claiming that he was just an ordinary Marylander and not a politician, Hogan has a fascinating political résumé. His father, Larry Hogan, Sr., served as the Congressman from Maryland's 5th Congressional District from 1969 until 1975. He was the first Republican member of the House Judiciary Committee to call for Richard Nixon's impeachment.

Larry, Jr. worked in the Florida State Legislature while he was in college at Florida State University majoring in government and political science. After graduation, he went to work on Capitol Hill. He also helped his father run a successful 1978 campaign for Prince George's County Executive. During the 1970s and 1980s, Hogan, Jr. was a delegate to the Republican National Conventions.

Hogan ran two unsuccessful campaigns for his father's old seat in the U.S. House of Representatives. The first defeat came in the 1981 special election to fill the 5th District seat which became vacant when the incumbent suffered a heart attack and was in a coma. The second was in 1992. In the latter, he won the Republican nomination but lost the general election to Steny Hoyer, who still holds that seat. Between 2003 and 2007, Hogan served as Secretary of Appointments in the administration of Republican governor Robert Ehrlich.

While he had not held elective office when he ran for governor, he was by no means a political novice. He was "plugged in" to Maryland politics generally and to Maryland Republican politics particularly.

During his two campaigns for governor, Hogan also claimed to be just a small businessman concerned about the state's economy and business climate. But while he may have been a businessman, the business was not a small operation. He had founded the Hogan Companies in 1985. The company's website says it handles land, commercial, and residential brokerage as well as consulting, investment, and development. It has done more than $2 billion in real estate transactions in Maryland and beyond.

In 2011, Hogan formed Change Maryland, an advocacy group for "people who believe we ought to have more common sense in Annapolis, and who want to lower spending and lower taxes." When he sat down with Len Lazarick of the marylandreporter.com a month after forming Change Maryland, Hogan also said, "It's not a fight about the right and the left; it's more about the distance between right and wrong."[1] This is all standard Larry Hogan stuff.

But the standard Hogan rhetoric wasn't what was interesting about the interview. Robert Ehrlich, in whose Cabinet Hogan had served, ran unsuccessfully for reelection in 2006, beaten by Martin O'Malley, then Baltimore's mayor. The interesting part was that Ehrlich wanted a rematch with O'Malley in 2010 (which also turned out to be unsuccessful). Hogan said he'd have run in 2010 if Ehrlich hadn't. Since the 2010 run didn't happen, Hogan formed Change Maryland instead.

Lazarick wrote that, at the time of the interview, Change Maryland had 2,000 Facebook followers and that certainly was a way to keep his name out there. About those followers, Hogan did admit that having them "certainly wouldn't hurt if I run."[2]

The previously mentioned reasons for forming Change Maryland, lower spending, and lower taxes, would become important themes when Hogan did decide to run in 2014. Change also said Maryland's economic future was at stake. It said it wanted to be a voice for people who didn't seem to have one.[3] These, too, would become important campaign themes in 2014.

As I wrote in chapter 6, the establishment of Change Maryland essentially marks the beginning of Hogan's 2014 campaign for governor. In his second term by this point, Governor Martin O'Malley could not run for another term as governor. It was assumed (accurately) that his lieutenant governor, Anthony Brown, would run for his own term. Seemingly confident of his potential to capture the Republican nomination three years hence, Hogan began using Change Maryland as an "anti-O'Malley clearinghouse" as Kevin Robillard wrote in a *Politico* post-2014 election analysis after Hogan had won.[4]

Change Maryland issued reports and press releases on every conceivable topic, and many of them criticized the O'Malley administration. Another post-2014 election analysis article, this one in the *Baltimore Sun*, said that Hogan had used Change Maryland to gather the information that he would use to defeat Brown.[5]

And extremely important to the Hogan's 2014 campaign was the attention Change Maryland paid to Republican and independent voters. The critical piece, though, was its focus on conservative Democrats who were upset with state government and who might be persuaded to vote Republican. If Change had had 2,000 Facebook followers in 2011 just a month or so after it had formed, by the time of the 2014 election, it had 120,000 followers.

THE 2014 CAMPAIGN

The first real test for Larry Hogan's Change Maryland strategy was his 2014 run for governor. An important early decision was to hire Maryland-based Russell Schriefer as his lead campaign strategist and media consultant. A major Republican political strategist, Schriefer has worked on six of the last seven presidential campaigns and also on campaigns with many Republican governors, senators, and congressmen, including Robert Ehrlich.

In the 2014 campaign against Lt. Governor Anthony Brown, the message would be critical. The Hogan campaign, through its Change Maryland research, knew that the things that most concerned voters in 2014 were the economy, jobs, taxes, and education. The Hogan message lumped the first three as "economy" and focused his messaging almost exclusively on that single issue.[6] That narrow focus helped keep the campaign on message.

Hogan's main campaign promise was that he would be a good financial manager for the state. His pro-business message also won votes.[7] More than anything, though, Hogan relentlessly promised to roll back the O'Malley tax increases, which, without providing evidence, he said came to about 40. He emphasized his private sector negotiating skills and pledged to work with the veto-proof Democratic majority in the General Assembly—something the previous Republican governor had seemed unable to do.[8]

The taxes messages seemed to especially resonate with the voters. Voters interviewed on Election Day mentioned taxes over and over as a reason that they voted for Hogan.

Campaign advertising tended to be very negative. In late September, Michael Dresser writing for the *Baltimore Sun* said that both the Brown and Hogan campaigns were "flooding the airwaves with apocalyptic messages about the dire consequences of choosing the other guy."[9] None of the reporting I found for that election cycle differentiated between ads run by the campaigns themselves and ads run on their behalf by PACs or the parties' governors associations.

The anti-Hogan ads called him dangerous. They said he wanted to give corporations big tax cuts. And they said he wanted to deny pre-K to children to pay for those cuts. He would block women's access to abortion and birth control, they said.

The anti-Brown ads claimed he wasn't ready to be governor. They blamed him for an alleged (and unsubstantiated) mass exodus from Maryland of businesses and individuals leaving to escape regulations and high taxes. Ads called Brown the most incompetent man in Maryland and blamed him for the disastrous rollout of Maryland's health exchange designed to operationalize "Obamacare."[10]

Barry Rascover in an October 5, 2014, piece in his blog "Maryland Reporter" wrote that Larry Hogan came across as likeable and engaging. He had a simple message, "let's get a handle on excess government spending and then let's see if we can lower taxes."[11]

Election turnout that year was low. There was a fair amount of ambivalence for both Hogan and Brown among voters, who were saying that neither candidate had provided much insight about what they would do if elected. One voter said she wasn't a fan of either one.[12] Hogan's campaign did get a boost by the national political climate that seemed to be rejecting Democrats. Longtime political commentator Blair Lee IV said after the election that a lot of angry Democrats voted for Hogan and a lot of traditional Democrats stayed home.[13]

While many Democrats appeared to have deserted the party's candidate for governor that didn't go for the down ballot races. All seven of the Democratic candidates for Congress won their elections—most handily. Democrats running for county executive in both Montgomery and Prince George's Counties also won their races. And Democrats kept their veto-proof lock on the General Assembly. Maryland Democrats weren't rejecting their party, only its candidate for governor.

Figure 4.1   Maryland Governor Larry Hogan. *Source*: Photo provided by Maryland GovPics and reprinted with permission under the Creative Commons Attribution 2.0 Generic license: https://creativecommons.org/licenses/by/2.0/legalcode

THE 2018 CAMPAIGN

With the success of the 2014 campaign media strategies, Hogan brought Russell Schiefer back to run his 2018 campaign against Democrat Ben Jealous. As it did in 2014, the Hogan campaign placed a heavy emphasis on TV advertising despite the presence of so much social media during the 2016 presidential campaign. Although Hogan had no competition for the primary election, the campaign spent a great deal to air an ad called "Maryland Strong," which defined Hogan as almost heroic in the way he dealt with his 2015 diagnosis of non-Hodgkin lymphoma. Using the cancer diagnosis, while perhaps risky as *Baltimore Sun* media critic David Zurawik noted, actually served to humanize Hogan in ways that connected him with so many Marylanders. Nearly everyone is touched in some way by cancer.

Schriefer justified the almost saturation media buy during the uncontested primary on two reasons. One he called a practical one based on the cost of airtime during the primary season. Purchasing airtime is less expensive during the primaries. He called the second reason political. The Democrats had a very crowded field. Nine candidates were trying to get their messages heard. Schriefer wanted to be sure that the Hogan message got heard despite the "noise" from so many Democratic primary candidates.[14]

Though Hogan used a lot of TV advertising in 2018, that didn't mean the campaign had ignored or rejected social media. As mentioned in chapter 6, the Hogan campaign was on Facebook on the night of the primary election with an ad it called, "Introducing Ben Jealous" which cast Jealous as "too extreme" and "too risky" for Maryland. To some extent Hogan's campaign was using Facebook not just for its inherent value in reaching followers, but also as a testing ground for possible TV ads. The "too extreme" and "too risky" ads later ran on Maryland TV stations.

Not only was the Hogan campaign using social media, they were very good at it. By the time of Jealous's primary election victory, it was already almost too late to make up any ground. Hogan's crack social media team was already blending the earlier TV ad buys with effective use of social media. And they weren't just good at it; they were very fast in responding to any mistakes the Jealous campaign made.

And the Jealous campaign made a number of mistakes to the point that he almost became one of Hogan's most effective campaigners. One of the most serious is described in chapter 6. One of the more interesting ones, though, happened when Jealous said that Hogan had responsibly managed the state for four years, but had no real vision for the next four. The first part of that was ammunition for Hogan. It was not a sensible admission for a candidate trying to toss an incumbent out of office.[15]

Chapter 6 also describes the Jealous campaign's lack of money. By the time Jealous ran his first ads in September, he had already been defined by the Hogan campaign. Jealous never really recovered from that first "too extreme" and "too risky" ad.

If Larry Hogan successfully defined Ben Jealous, he was at least as successful in defining himself. He was bipartisan. He worked effectively with the majority Democrats. He was a business-friendly leader. He was turning the state around. To illustrate this last point, a Hogan ad painted a dismal pre-Hogan picture of 8,000 business and 100,000 jobs lost. The ad provided no documentation for this claim. For many Marylanders, though, the assertion was enough.[16]

Other claims made by the Hogan campaign included $1.2 billion in tax, toll and fee relief, no tax increases, record funding for schools, the healthiest Chesapeake Bay in a generation, repairs to the infrastructure, and rising employment and wages. Again the campaign provided no documentation. It failed to mention that some of his accomplishments were due to an improved national economy. It also failed to mention that much of what he was touting had to have been enacted by the Democrat-dominated General Assembly. Like other aspects of his campaign messaging, mere assertion seemed enough to get the support of many Marylanders.[17]

Analysis of several Hogan campaign ads by Erin Cox and Michael Dresser of the *Sun* found some of the claims to be inflated. Others were misleading. Others used cherry-picked information to enhance the preferred narrative.[18]

One ad focused on Hogan himself was particularly interesting. It evoked the 2015 Baltimore riots after the death of Freddie Gray. The narrator says, "When we needed a leader, Larry Hogan was there." The ad then shifted to footage of Hogan receiving chemotherapy treatment for his cancer. The ad says, "When Larry Hogan needed us, we returned the favor." It ends with Hogan running a race and the audience hears, "Together we're stronger. Maryland strong. Larry Hogan. Governor."[19]

Perhaps the smartest thing Hogan and his campaign did was to maintain distance from President Trump. The Jealous campaign and groups supporting him tried unsuccessfully several times to tie Hogan to Trump. As an example, the Democratic Governors Association ran TV ads criticizing Hogan's educational policies and attempting to equate him with Betsy DeVos, Trump's controversial and unpopular Secretary of Education. The ad came very late in the campaign and by then Hogan's image had been firmly established in voters' minds.

In an Op-Ed opinion piece written for the *Baltimore Sun* the day after the election, Mileah Kromer, an associate professor of political science at Goucher College that conducts the widely respected Goucher Political Poll, wrote that attempts to question his image as a moderate, "worked only to bolster his centrist credentials." The attempts to compare Hogan to Trump allowed Hogan to "deftly highlight the differences in style and substance." In addition, Kromer wrote, "complaints that Mr. Hogan had co-opted the Democrats' policy agenda only provided him with evidence of a willingness to work across the partisan aisle."[20]

As was the case in 2014, Republican Larry Hogan's electoral success didn't translate to Republican successes down ballot. Todd Eberly, a political scientist at St. Mary's College, quoted in Donovan's and Dresser's post-election article in the *Baltimore Sun* said, "Voters viewed Larry Hogan as Larry Hogan, and they were willing to vote for him, but that does not mean that they were willing to vote for other Republicans as well."[21]

As was also the case in 2014, Democrats didn't desert their party; they deserted its candidate for governor. All the Democratic Congressional Democrats won reelection. So did Democratic candidates for county executive in counties already held by Democrats. And in 2018, Democratic candidates defeated incumbent Republican county executives in Anne Arundel and Howard Counties. Democrats also added seven seats to their already large majority in the House of Delegates.

WORKING WITH A DEMOCRATIC
GENERAL ASSEMBLY

After both the 2014 and 2018 elections, reporters wrote of Hogan's need to work cooperatively with the Democrats in the General Assembly if he wanted to achieve any of his goals. Hogan was urged to focus on governing, to compromise with Democrats, and to work to pass as much bipartisan legislation as possible. Hogan did make some effort. Though the relationship with the General Assembly has been rocky, he's had more success than the previous governor Republican Robert Ehrlich did when he was in office.

There is really very little specific information about how Hogan has worked with the General Assembly. In the October 2018 issue of *Baltimore* magazine, writer Ron Cassie's article, "Likable Larry," referred to "Hogan's remarkable skill in navigating a General Assembly with veto-proof majorities in the state House and Senate." Cassie also mentioned Hogan's rapport with the late senate president Thomas V. "Mike" Miller. Cassie doesn't document these and other evidence is hard to find.[22]

Some of what we have about his working relationship with the General Assembly is found in Hogan's 2020 memoir, *Still Standing: Surviving Cancer, Riots, a Global Pandemic and the Toxic Politics That Divide America.* There's actually very little in the memoir focused on governing and even what's there is sketchy and doesn't say much. Articles published at the time the memoir was released were critical of the way he described it. There are only two specific examples.

Because it played such a big role in his election campaign against Anthony Brown, he made sure he mentioned his success in repealing what he and his campaign had named "the rain tax." His description of that was less about negotiation than it was about gloating about its repeal.[23]

He mentions negotiations with the General Assembly over the *2016 Justice Reinvestment Act*, a criminal justice reform bill. Though it was a good piece of legislation and must surely have required negotiation, Hogan's memoir gives no indication of what those negotiations were or with whom he had been negotiating.[24]

The problem with sorting out his legislative accomplishments is complicated by the fact that Hogan has sometimes claimed as legislative victories things for which he had little or no role. As an example, an ad during the 2018 campaign claimed credit for some tax relief measures pressed by Democrats and for tax credits given to already existing programs such as the film industry and cybersecurity. In addition, he would sometimes hijack as his own legislation to which he had earlier been opposed. The fracking ban and the education lockbox amendment to the constitution are examples. He even referred to the latter as the "Hogan Lockbox" in a 2018 campaign ad.[25]

This hijacking of legislation and claiming credit for its passage was a point made several times in media coverage in the run up to the 2018 election. In an Op-Ed piece in the *Baltimore Sun*, Mileah Kromer of the Goucher Poll wrote that the General Assembly could view Hogan's "penchant for adopting parts of their agenda as an opportunity rather than an irritant."[26]

THE PANDEMIC

Almost from the beginning of his first term, Larry Hogan has enjoyed astoundingly high approval ratings in both major polls that focus on Maryland, its politics, and its issues. That support extended to his handling of the COVID-19 pandemic. In October 2020, the Goucher Poll found that 70 percent of Marylanders approved of the job Hogan was doing. In addition, 82 percent approved of how he was handling the pandemic.[27] The Gonzales Poll of the same month found 73.3 percent job approval and 77 percent approval of how he was handling the pandemic.[28]

I was unable to find the March 2021 Gonzales Poll, but the March 2021 Goucher Poll found that 65 percent approved of the job Hogan was doing and about 75 percent approved of his handling of the pandemic. Though still high, they do represent a decline, which might be attributed in part to the poll's finding that 66 percent of those polled thought the state was doing only a fair or poor job distributing vaccines.[29]

It is interesting to note that the March 2021 Goucher Poll was conducted at exactly the time that the governor was under fire for saying that Baltimore had received far more vaccine doses "than they really were entitled to."[30]

From the beginning of the pandemic, Hogan received high marks for his handling. Columnist Dan Rodricks wrote that from the start Hogan was at the center of the state's response. He praised Hogan for seeking out and accepting the best scientific evidence available, for preparing for a coming crisis and for declaring a state of emergency in early March 2020. He closed schools, senior centers, bars, and restaurants.[31] State employees who could do their jobs remotely were required to do so. Those who could not were tested frequently.

Hogan held daily news briefings to keep Marylanders abreast of what was happening and how the state was responding. He turned some of the day-to-day operations of state government over to his Lt. Governor Boyd Rutherford so he could devote full attention to the crisis. During the early days of the pandemic, Hogan emerged as a national figure. He not only advocated for aid to Maryland but he advocated for all the states in his role as chair of the National Governors Association.

By listening to the medical experts and constantly repeating the message of wearing masks, social distancing and handwashing, Hogan was able to persuade most Marylanders to accept those messages. The October 2020 Goucher Poll found that 89 percent of Marylanders agreed that these kinds of individual actions made a difference. Mileah Kromer commented that, unlike some Republicans, Hogan had not turned these actions into a wedge issue.[32]

It helped his credibility that Hogan did all he could to model appropriate behavior. He reduced official travel, limited the staff around him, required screening procedures at the State House, and required social distancing protocols. He also sharply limited the numbers of journalists at his news briefings, required that they sit apart from one another, and submit to screenings that involved temperature checks and answering questions about symptoms and possible exposure.

Hogan regularly wore a mask in public. He and the First Lady Yumi Hogan were tested regularly. The governor's staff were also screened every day and those who shared offices worked on a teleworking rotation.[33]

Marylanders liked Hogan's forthrightness. At the outset, his air of competence and patience, his willingness to defer to the experts, and his refusal to play partisan politics impressed people. As Dan Rodricks wrote, first impressions last. He took seriously the threats posed by the pandemic. People particularly liked his "Just wear the damn masks" comment as he urged people back in November 2020 not to be complacent. That even became the tagline in a public service advertisement the state ran on Maryland TV stations.

Hogan's handling of the pandemic began to come in for criticism as the pandemic went on longer and longer. Though there were multiple examples of such criticism, I will mention only three: the vaccine rollout, early loosening of restrictions and school reopening.

There was a certain degree of irony to his handling of the vaccine rollout. In his campaign for governor in 2014, he sharply criticized his opponent, Lt. Governor Anthony Brown, for the disastrous rollout of Maryland's "Obamacare" health exchange. He called Brown the most incompetent man in Maryland. The state's rollout of COVID-19 vaccines was confusing and frustrating to average Marylanders. They encountered a variety of problems trying to register to get a vaccine. There seemed to be competing agencies, hospitals, pharmacies, among others, responsible for those registrations. Even if you were qualified to receive the vaccine, finding doses was nearly impossible.

The Hogan administration's "Maryland Strong: Roadmap to Recovery" was released on April 24, 2020. Shortly after that, Hogan began to loosen some of the restrictions put in place during the state of emergency. This came as Maryland had just experienced record numbers of hospitalizations. On May 14, the Editorial Board at the *Baltimore Sun* criticized the action, which was set to take effect in only a few days. His announcement had been made without consulting (or even warning) city and county leaders who were caught off guard, especially by his statement that they could determine for themselves if their jurisdictions would participate in the announced Stage 1 reopening or keep stricter restrictions in place. The Editorial Board said this felt as if he were washing his hands of decision making. The Board was also concerned by what it called compliance confusion; in other words, people not knowing what restrictions were in place where.[34] They were right to have been concerned. Compliance confusion was a problem well into 2021 as well. It is interesting to note that by July, Hogan had to expand mask-wearing mandates.

School reopening became a huge problem in practically every school district in the state. Nearly everyone involved wanted to reopen schools, but there were disagreements about how and when that should happen. Most districts had been in the planning stages about how to safely reopen their school systems.

Hogan created a firestorm in a January 20, 2021, news conference in which he called on all Maryland's school systems to *immediately* make every effort to get back to some form of in-person learning by March 1. If he had left it at that, it probably wouldn't have been that newsworthy and this portion of this chapter would not have been necessary. But then he issued threats. After saying (not quite accurately) that there was no public health reason to keep schools closed, he threatened legal action against any school board that didn't comply.[35]

The threat didn't end there, though. At the same news conference, Hogan and State School Superintendent Karen Salmon revealed that they had sent a letter to the head of the state's teachers union telling her, "roadblocks to resuming in-person instruction must cease."

Cheryl Bost, President of the Maryland State Teachers Association, said that state leaders had not worked collaboratively with the teachers union or sought their opinion since August 2020, some five months before. In addition, she said this letter was Hogan's first correspondence with the union.[36]

From the start, teachers had wanted to be assured that there would be in place clear plans, availability of personal protective equipment, cleaning protocols for school buildings, and, most of all, vaccines before returning to in-person instruction. At the time of the press conference, all teachers were eligible to receive vaccines, but vaccines were still in extremely short supply so fewer teachers had actually been vaccinated.

Hogan's acting deputy secretary for public health, Dr. Jinlene Chan, didn't help the situation. She said, "I would emphasize that school reopening decisions should not be based on the availability of vaccinations or the level of vaccination among staff."[37]

In their editorial on Hogan's news conference, the *Baltimore Sun*'s Editorial Board wrote, "All we're asking for is a return of the Larry Hogan of months ago with his empathy, non-partisanship and 'we're all in this together' outlook regarding the pandemic. And, particularly given the states' own shortcomings in vaccine distribution, one would expect just a little bit of humility, too."[38]

BALTIMORE—RIOTS AFTER THE DEATH OF FREDDIE GRAY

If Governor Hogan's methods of handling the pandemic devolved from empathy, non-partisanship, and "we're all in this together" to argumentative, demanding, and threatening, his disdain and callousness toward the City of Baltimore were both notable and disturbing, and was in evidence almost from the day he took office.

In April 2015, barely three months after he took office, Baltimore erupted into violence in reaction to the death of Freddie Gray, a young African American man. He sustained spinal cord injuries that killed him while he was in police custody.

In his memoir, Hogan devotes several chapters to the riot and his handling of it. His recounting of some events has been criticized for not being backed up with evidence or for not correlating with what is publicly known about events.

Freddie Gray was no angel. He had a lengthy court record, mostly involving charges for selling or possessing drugs. Hogan referred to him as being connected with the Crips gang and called him a street-level drug dealer. Pamela Wood and Justin Fenton in their *Baltimore Sun* article about Hogan's memoir point out that there is no publicly known connection between Gray and the Crips.[39]

As to the matter of Gray's injuries, Hogan wrote that the cause of those injuries was disputed. Hogan puts forward a tragic accident or murder, but nothing in between. The medical examiner gave the cause of death as homicide as a result of the officers' failure to follow safety procedures.[40]

The memoir attacked Baltimore Mayor Stephanie Rawlings-Blake, criticizing her for not cracking down on demonstrators immediately. He wrote that he couldn't trust her leadership. He characterized her as paralyzed with fear and indecision and accused her of making poor decisions and being missing in action. Hogan claimed he saved the city.[41]

Hogan was also critical of Baltimore City State's Attorney Marilyn Mosby who had charged the six police officers in Gray's death. All the officers were either acquitted or had the charges against them dropped. Hogan called that a complete defeat and said Mosby was 0 for 6.[42]

The governor was even critical of President Barack Obama. Obama had called Hogan to urge restraint and caution in his response. About the call, Hogan wrote that Obama had attempted to guide "me, the rookie white Republican governor who had recently defeated his candidate for governor of Maryland in this overwhelmingly Democratic state and whose majority-black largest city was now in flames. A lot of landmines there."[43]

None of the three commented on Hogan's recollection of events.

Among the missing pieces in Hogan's recall was any important mention of the late U.S. Representative Elijah Cummings. During the riots, Cummings had often been in the streets with a bullhorn urging people to go home as the nightly curfew was approaching. The only mention Cummings gets in the entire memoir is as one of those who attended Gray's funeral, a serious omission considering the role Cummings played in attempting to calm the situation.

Hogan's heavy-handed approach to the riots caused a lot of anger in the city. Though his memoir claimed he told Obama that he would, there are many in Baltimore who would argue that he exercised neither restraint nor caution. Kwame Rose, a Baltimore activist quoted by Pamela Wood in her article about the memoir, said that bringing the National Guard to Baltimore made things worse. "It's given young people trauma. We don't need over-policing. The policing was the problem in the first place."[44]

BALTIMORE—THE RED LINE GETS CANCELED

A major blow to Baltimore came just two months after the riots when Hogan canceled the construction of the Red Line light rail project and returned $900 million in federal money that would have helped fund the $2.9 billion project. The Red Line would have been a 14-mile-long east-west light rail line that would have provided reliable public transportation to parts of economically disadvantaged and largely Black West Baltimore. It would have connected them to jobs in Baltimore County and other parts of the city. Glen Smith of the Baltimore Equity Transit Coalition called the move punitive and mean-spirited.

But it got worse. The state funding that had already been allocated for the Red Line project was then redirected to highway projects in other parts of the state—parts with higher concentrations of white Marylanders. This resulted in a civil rights complaint filed by the NAACP's Legal Defense Fund and the ACLU. The Trump administration quietly dismissed the complaint without comment.

And then it got even worse when Hogan approved the Purple Line light rail project that would connect parts of Prince George's and Montgomery Counties, both DC suburbs. It was pointed out that many (but not all) of those who would use the Purple Line would be better off white people.

To give the Purple Line its due, though, it will include several stations that will connect to existing DC Metro lines thus creating further integration of what is admittedly an excellent system. One terminus for the Purple Line will be New Carrollton, MD, which will connect people with the DC Metro as well as with AMTRAK and the MARC commuter rail.

For Baltimore, Hogan proposed a much less expensive project he called CityLink that he promised would be a transformational public transit system Baltimore needed. At a cost of some $135 million, the effort has not brought the promised transformation. On-time records have not improved and access to jobs actually decreased.[45]

There has been no substantive progress in fixing the public transportation system in Baltimore. The Hogan administration has said there are no plans to address the problems. The lack of reliable, on-time public transportation makes life extremely difficult for many Baltimoreans who must rely on it to get to their jobs. Bus commute times of more than an hour are not unusual—and that's if the bus shows up.

While Hogan has not supported public transportation in Baltimore, he has signaled his support for a Baltimore-to-Washington maglev project, which would cut the trip down to roughly fifteen minutes. A one-way ticket is projected to cost $60. The project, which would cost about $10 billion, is more than three times what it would have cost to build the Red Line. Baltimore City is opposing the maglev's construction over concerns about equity and the effects it would have on the environment. Of special concern were the potential effects on the communities surrounding the two places that have been proposed as the Baltimore terminus for the line, one of which is Cherry Hill, a community whose people are largely low-income and Black.[46]

The cost and scope of the maglev project has caused agitation outside government as well. In 2018, Baltimore historian and Johns Hopkins University professor emeritus Matthew Crenson commented, "The big problem for Baltimoreans is not getting to Washington but getting across the city. Moving east-west has been a problem since the 19th century."[47]

BALTIMORE—THE STATE CENTER
REDEVELOPMENT PROJECT GETS CANCELED

As far as Baltimore was concerned its experiences with the Hogan administration would not be any better in 2016 that they had been in 2015. In December, the state's Board of Public Works, which consisted of the governor, the Comptroller Peter Franchot, and then-State Treasurer Nancy Kopp who must approve all large expenditures of state funds, voted unanimously to void the lease agreements the state had made with the private developers selected to undertake the State Center project. In voiding the leases the governor said that he was still committed to redevelopment of State Center. It is a claim he has made repeatedly to increasingly skeptical audiences.

State Center is a 28-acre site at Eutaw and Preston streets near Martin Luther King Boulevard. It is occupied by the Fifth Regiment Armory and by several large state government office buildings of 1960s vintage. The office buildings are outdated, expensive to maintain, and badly in need of replacement. The site is also at the edge of West Baltimore about which much is written in this book. West Baltimore itself is badly in need of attention and the State Center project would have been of enormous benefit to the area. As Pamela Wood wrote in the *Baltimore Sun*, "The area along Martin Luther King, Jr. Boulevard has long been eyed for redevelopment, potentially opening a path for the affluence of downtown Baltimore to spread into impoverished neighborhoods in West Baltimore."[48]

The plan to redevelop State Center originated under former Governor Robert Ehrlich and continued under Governor Martin O'Malley. State Center was to be a $1.5 billion effort and would have included demolishing the existing state office buildings. Redevelopment included new state office buildings, other office buildings, housing (some classified as affordable), and retail (including a very badly needed grocery store in what has been termed a food desert). Located at a light rail stop, a subway station, and stops for multiple bus lines, the area would have been well-served by public transit. In addition, the project would have created construction jobs as well as other permanent jobs once the project had been completed.

The scope and character of the proposed redevelopment was determined over about a decade with extensive conversations with those who would be directly impacted. The State Center Neighborhood Alliance was a multiracial group of nine neighborhood groups that had united behind the project's potential. They pushed developers for economic inclusion, community benefit agreements and local hiring.

Though the community was behind it, the State Center project faced opposition. In 2010, a group of Baltimore businesses filed a lawsuit to stop the project. They maintained that the city had high vacancy rates in buildings downtown. The suit was eventually thrown out of court, but some four years had passed with no progress on redevelopment.[49]

Once the Board of Public Works voided the leases, the governor asked that the Maryland Stadium Authority conduct a land-use study about options for the State Center site. A separate study was requested to evaluate the viability of building a new arena on the site as was proposed by Comptroller Peter Franchot.

Less than a month later, some ninety-nine state employees were moved out of State Center to a building in Anne Arundel County. Some in West Baltimore feared that that would be only the first of many such moves until the Center was gutted. Maryland Senator Bill Ferguson (who is now senate president) said he had not been notified. Ferguson said, "I want to believe that the administration had the best intentions. Unfortunately, when we've consistently seen this administration forcefully withdraw planned public investments in Baltimore City, it is hard to believe there isn't some broader strategy at play."[50]

There were suits and countersuits involving the state and the developer and things were not resolved. For the extremely frustrated residents of the adjoining communities, the State Center project was on hold yet again. According to *Baltimore Sun* reporter Natalie Sherman, some of the nearby residents saw institutional racism in the decision to void the leases and pointed to investments bypassing West Baltimore while they go elsewhere. Janet Allen, a resident asked, "Why is it that nothing in our community is viable? I feel like it's redlining. It's redlining all over again in a new form." James Hamlin, a business owner, didn't want to get into the role of politics and race in the decision but did say that it's a fact that West Baltimore and Pennsylvania Avenue had been neglected for more than forty years.[51]

Near the end of the 2017 session of the General Assembly, members of the Baltimore delegation were pressing the governor to drop the lawsuit against the developer and get the project back on track. John Kyle, who headed the State Center Neighborhood Alliance, said that the group's repeated requests for a meeting with Hogan had been ignored. Del. Robbyn Lewis, who represented the area in which State Center is located, connected the governor's State Center decision with his decision to cancel the Red Line. She worried that the 3,300 state employees at the Center would be moved with nothing to replace them. The result, she said, would be a deserted site.[52]

The Maryland Stadium Authority study was released in January 2018. It found that high probability uses included "retail sites for development, various types of restaurant concepts, a freestanding grocery store, convenience/office space, all categories of medical uses, parkland/recreation space, varying university influences and public/private school uses." Ranking as moderate to low probability of potential uses were large office sites and high-rise office spaces. What the study did not include was any discussion of options for state government office space. It also recommended that there be further studies.[53] More delay. By June 2018, Hogan was calling for developers interested in taking over the project and was expecting to have the process completed by September. With an audience of state workers, Hogan said he hoped to deliver open-space, high-tech office spaces. He said that the new proposals would connect State Center with the surrounding neighborhoods and provide jobs and a grocery store. But significantly and perhaps missed by some in his audience, he also said that more high-rise state office buildings wouldn't benefit the community.

Baltimore leaders called the announcement election season grandstanding. John Kyle said he suspected the announcement was timed to coincide with the first day of early voting for the primary election. Kathleen Matthews, chair of the Maryland Democratic Party said, "In less than four years, Larry Hogan blocked both State Center and the Red Line, and he's hoping that today's announcement will make Baltimoreans forget. It won't."[54]

Not quite a year-and-a-half later, Hogan announced that the state would begin seeking bidders for the redevelopment State Center. He called it bold and said it would have a transformative effect on the surrounding communities. He also announced that the state would begin the process of relocating the 3,300 state employees to office spaces downtown and pledged to keep all those employees in Baltimore. There were no real details provided but Hogan said it was possible that one or two agencies might return to State Center in the future.

Adrienne Jones, Speaker of the House of Delegates, said that Hogan had not spoken with legislative leaders before making the announcement. She asked why the community had not been involved and added that West Baltimore needed a solid anchor.

State Center Neighborhood Alliance chair John Kyle said Hogan had not involved the community groups and professed his disappointment. He said, "It's wasteful of the 15 years the community has put into coming up with good ideas until this administration and the developer had a falling out. We in the neighborhoods are the victims of all this."[55]

Hogan said there would be a lengthy process to select a new developer. Still more delays.

BALTIMORE—SHORTCHANGED BY STATE BUDGETS

Governor Hogan's budgets have not been Baltimore-friendly at all. In 2018, when Hogan opened his campaign office for his reelection bid, State Delegate Brooke Lierman and Baltimore City Councilman Zeke Cohen organized a counter news conference across the street. As described in Cassie's *Baltimore* magazine 2018 article, Lierman said in an interview with Real News Network, "There is a record here, and it is not a good record for Baltimore. I'm on the Appropriations Committee. Every year it is a battle to make sure we are funding the priorities in Baltimore. Whether that's the Baltimore Regional Neighborhoods Initiative, whether that's funding for the Enoch Pratt [Free Library], every year he cuts those initiatives out of his budget, and the General Assembly has to put that money back in and find money." Cohen, a former teacher, said that Hogan had underfunded city schools by between $290 million and $360 million per year depending on which study one was reading. He also called out the governor for referring to unionized teachers as "thugs."[56]

In further budgetary slights to the city, Hogan vetoed the legislation connected with the findings of the Kirwan Commission, which had been created to come up with a plan to improve K-12 education. The legislation would have brought substantial funding to Baltimore City schools. He claimed Maryland couldn't afford it. He vetoed the legislation that would have funded the settlement the state had reached with its four historically Black universities (two of which are located in Baltimore) after discrimination litigation that had lasted some fourteen years. He said Maryland couldn't afford that, either (though he did finally sign it in the next session when the General Assembly passed it again, essentially daring him to veto it again). He also withheld a bridge grant to the Baltimore Symphony Orchestra, the state's premier performing arts organization. The grant was meant to give the BSO some breathing space while it reworked its finances. That was something else Hogan said the state couldn't afford. Money, of course, talks, and so does its absence. Repeated refusals to fund what was important to Baltimore were as much a rhetorical act as a fiscal one.

CONCLUSION

How do you assess Larry Hogan, a governor whose time as governor hasn't ended? You can't give a complete picture. And it isn't safe to speculate about what his future might hold for him except to say that he and the First Lady will move out of Government House and into the mansion they recently purchased.

He spent the better part of two campaigns for governor working hard to convince Marylanders that he was a moderate Republican, a regular Marylander, and just a small businessman. He wasn't a politician, he said. He was bipartisan, he said. He said he'd work cooperatively with the Democratic majority in the General Assembly. And people believed him and voted for him.

Cassie in his *Baltimore Magazine* article said, "his ability to defuse problematic issues and appear pragmatic and reasonable have become hallmark." The same article referred to his "flair for branding" and his "political agility." He's an "astute political animal." He's a "happy warrior on the campaign trail . . . and disciplined off it." He's "fun to be around." It also quoted Hogan's ex-boss, former governor Robert Ehrlich, who called him "charismatic," a "people person and he loves to talk." Ehrlich also called him outgoing.[57]

In a post-2018 election commentary in the *Baltimore Sun*, Mileah Kromer of the Goucher Poll wrote that Hogan had "weaponized his gregarious personality and advanced retail politics skills." She continued, "The only voters [at fairs and community events] who didn't get gubernatorial selfies were the ones who didn't ask."[58]

There were columnists and reporters who in the early days of the COVID-19 pandemic praised Hogan for his decisive action. They liked his advocacy for federal aid for state governments reeling from the pandemic. They commented favorably on his modeling of the behaviors appropriate to helping stem the pandemic.

But there's another side to Larry Hogan; one that isn't so nice. It's the Larry Hogan that is revealed in his memoir. It's a Larry Hogan who went around the General Assembly and used Executive Orders to get his way. He claimed he worked with the General Assembly but provided only two examples. He claimed credit for legislation in which he had no part. It is also a Larry Hogan who would allow a wide variety of legislation become law without his signature so he didn't have to face the embarrassment of having his vetoes overridden. This is the Larry Hogan who had nothing positive to say about any Democrats. His memoir shows particular enmity to former Baltimore Mayor Stephanie Rawlings-Blake. It was clear he had no respect for Baltimore City State's Attorney Marilyn Mosby. And as he shown time and time again during his term, he has a special hatred for former governor Martin O'Malley.

There was the Larry Hogan who told Baltimore that it had got more doses of COVID vaccine than it was entitled to have. This was the same Larry Hogan who threatened legal actions against teachers who voiced concerns about going back to the classroom without proper precautions in place and ordered the teachers union to stop setting up roadblocks to getting kids back in school (it wasn't).

We see a Larry Hogan who canceled the Red Line light rail project that would have been had major benefits to the lower-income, mostly African Americans living in West Baltimore and redirected hundreds of millions of dollars to road projects that mostly benefited white suburbanites.

This is the same Larry Hogan that engineered the voiding of leases that effectively pulled the state out of a major project that would have redeveloped State Center. This project, too, would have been of enormous benefit to those same West Baltimoreans who were impacted by cancellation of the Red Line. The proposed replacement hasn't been found yet, but the land-use study Hogan commissioned is a much watered-down project that moves more than 3,000 state workers downtown with almost no likelihood that they'll ever return to a redeveloped State Center.

Finally, it's a Larry Hogan who, in budget after budget, has shown that he has little concern about the needs of Baltimore or the people who live there and the immense challenges they face. I won't argue the point that there are certainly areas of the state that have benefited from Hogan's time as governor. There have been. But Baltimore certainly wasn't one of them.

Is this evaluation harsh? Possibly. But then Hogan the campaigner and Hogan the governor turned out to be very different indeed. What Maryland elected to two terms was not what they got as governor. The image didn't match the reality.

In what I perceive as a rebuke to Hogan's governorship, the *Baltimore Sun* Editorial Board wrote on July 12, 2021, about the shifts in political influence from Baltimore City toward Montgomery and Prince George's Counties and discussed from where all the twelve candidates currently declared candidates for governor come. Only two are from Baltimore. The Board wrote that all the candidates need to be questioned about their plans for Baltimore because, "The health of Baltimore's surrounding counties and the state as a whole are tied to the health of the city." The editorial was headlined, "Maryland's next governor doesn't have to come from Baltimore but must care about it."[59] This is something Larry Hogan apparently forgot and he certainly didn't care.

NOTES

1. Len Lazarick, "'Change Maryland' Looks for Middle Ground," *Maryland Reporter*, June 13, 2011. https://marylandreporter.com/2011/06/13/change-maryland%E2%80%99-looksfor-middle-ground/

2. Ibid.

3. Ibid.

4. Kevin Robillard, "How Larry Hogan Won in Maryland," *Politico*, November 7, 2014. https://www.politico.com/story/2014/11/larry-hogan-maryland-governor-112681

5. Erin Cox and Michael Dresser, "Hogan Defeats Brown," *Baltimore Sun*, November 5, 2014. https://www.baltimoresun.com/maryland/anne-arundel/bs-md-governor-20141105story.html

6. Lejla Sarcevic and Max Bennett, "How Larry Hogan Won In a Blue State," *Capital News Service*, November 6, 2014. https://cnsmaryland.org/2014/11/06/how-republican-larryhogan-won-in-blue-maryland/

7. Ibid.

8. John Wagner and Jenna Johnson, "Republican Larry Hogan Wins MD Governor's Race in Stunning Upset," *Washington Post*, November 5, 2014. https://www.washingtonpost.com/local/md-politics/republican-larry-hogan-wins-md-governorsrace-in-stunning-upset/2014/11/05

9. Michael Dresser, "Ads in Governor's Race Are Narrow, Negative," *Baltimore Sun*, September 25, 2014. https://www.baltimoresun.com/maryland/bs-md-governor-ads-20140924story.html

10. Ibid.

11. Barry Rascovar, "Rascovar: Why Brown Could Lose Race for Governor," *Maryland Reporter*, October 5, 2015. https://marylandreporter.com/2014/10/05/rascovar-why-browncould-lose-race-for-maryland-governor/

12. Barry Rascovar, "Rascovar: Why Brown Could Lose Race for Governor," *Maryland Reporter*, October 5, 2015. https://marylandreporter.com/2014/10/05/rascovar-why-browncould-lose-race-for-maryland-governor/

13. Lejla Sarcevic and Max Bennett, "How Larry Hogan Won In a Blue State," *Capital News Service*, November 6, 2014. https://cnsmaryland.org/2014/11/06/how-republican-larryhogan-won-in-blue-maryland/

14. David Zurawik, "Five Unconventional Takeaways on Media Campaigns from Hogan's Big Win," *Baltimore Sun*, November 6, 2018. https://www.baltimoresun.com/opinion/columnists/zurawik/bs-fe-zontv-larry-hogan-mediacampaign-20181106-story.html

15. Martin Austermuhle, "Ben Jealous Has Big Ideas for Maryland. But, First He Needs People to Know He's Running for Governor," *WAMU*, November 1, 2018. https://wamu.org/story/18/11/01/ben-jealous-has-big-ideas-for-maryland-but-first-he-needspeople-to-know-hes-running-for-governor/

16. Erin Cox, "Ad Watch: Maryland Gov. Larry Hogan Inflates Tax Relief Claims in Campaign Commercial," *Baltimore Sun*, May 30, 2018. https://www.baltimoresun.com/politics/bs-md-hogan-ad-watch-20180529-story.html

17. Michael Dresser, "Gov. Larry Hogan Blankets Maryland with Positive TV Ads as Ben Jealous Watches," *Baltimore Sun*, August 27, 2018. https://www.baltimoresun.com/politics/bs-md-hogan-ad-campaign-20180824-story.html

18. Erin Cox, "Ad Watch: Maryland Gov. Larry Hogan Inflates Tax Relief Claims in Campaign Commercial," *Baltimore Sun*, May 30, 2018. https://www.baltimoresun.com/politics/bs-md-hogan-ad-watch-20180529-story.html

19. Ibid.

20. Mileah Kromer, "Jealous Didn't So Much Lose MD Gubernatorial Race as Hogan Won It," *Baltimore Sun*, November 7, 2018. https://www.baltimoresun.com/opinion/op-ed/bs-ed-op-1108-h, ogan-wins-20181106-story.html

21. Doug Donovan and Michael Dresser, "No Coattails: Maryland Voters Backed Republican Gov. Hogan, But Also Showed Their Disdain for Trump," *Baltimore Sun*, November 7, 2018. https://www.baltimoresun.com/politics/bs-md-hogan-coattails-20181107story.html

22. Ron Cassie, "Likable Larry," *Baltimore Magazine*. October 2018. https://www.baltimoremagazine.com/section/historypolitics/how-did-larry-hogan-becomesecond-most-popular-governor-in-the-country/

23. Hogan, Larry and Ellis Henican, *Still Standing: Surviving Cancer, Riots, A Global Pandemic and the Toxic Politics That Divide America*. Dallas: BenBella Books, Inc., 2020, pp. 103–4.

24. Hogan, pp. 203–4.

25. Ron Cassie, "Likable Larry," *Baltimore Magazine*. October 2018. https://www.baltimoremagazine.com/section/historypolitics/how-did-larry-hogan-becomesecond-most-popular-governor-in-the-country/

26. Mileah Kromer, "Jealous Didn't So Much Lose MD Gubernatorial Race as Hogan Won It," *Baltimore Sun*, November 7, 2018. https://www.baltimoresun.com/opinion/op-ed/bs-ed-op-1108-h, ogan-wins-20181106-story.html

27. Goucher College Poll, *Goucher College Poll: October 2020*. Sarah T. Hughes Field Politics Center, October 2020.

28. Gonzalez Research & Media Services, *Gonzalez Maryland Poll: October 2020*. Gonzalez Polls, Inc., October 2020.

29. Goucher College Poll, *Goucher College Poll: March 2021*. Sarah T. Hughes Field Politics Center, March 2021.

30. Alex Mann, "Hogan Says Baltimore Has Gotten More COVID Vaccines Than It's 'Entitled to,' Drawing Outrage from City Leaders," *Baltimore Sun*, February 26, 2021. https://www.baltimoresun.com/coronavirus/bs-md-hogan-remarks-2021022 6wdph6hrsarh23jscsgjo2csfi4-story.html

31. Dan Rodericks, "In Facing Pandemic, Hogan Has Been Sensible, Trump Reckless. Will That Matter in 2024?/Commentary," *Baltimore Sun*, November 6, 2020. https://www.baltimoresun.com/opinion/columnists/dan-rodricks/bs-md -rodricks-1108-20201106-szoqixa4djg3bhj4xsh3qqaeti-story.html

32. Talia Richman, "Poll: Majority of Marylanders Surveyed Approve of Hogan's Response to the Coronavirus Pandemic," *Baltimore Sun*, October 13, 2020. https:// www.baltimoresun.com/politics/bs-md-pol-poll-approval-20201013mbo4gunw2bc k7kqglh6ftox6nu-story.html

33. Pamela Wood, "Maryland Gov. Hogan's Coronavirus Precautions: Tests, Masks, Fewer Staff," *Baltimore Sun*, October 20, 2020. https://www.baltimoresun .com/coronavirus/bs-mdtrump-hogan-coronavirus-20201002-kvtn6ua5efdg5js4kks 52ib5hi-story.html

34. Editorial Board, "Gov. Hogan Washes His Hands of Coronavirus Decision-Making/Commentary," *Baltimore Sun*, May 14, 2020. https://www.baltimoresun .com/opinion/editorial/bs-ed-0517-stage-one-hogan-20200514nob6y6ffrnbh3pdcgor hm66x54-story.html

35. Editorial Board, "On School Reopening, Hogan Does Not Work Well With Others/Commentary," *Baltimore Sun*, January 22, 2021. https://www.baltimoresun .com/opinion/editorial/bs-ed-0125-hogan-schools-reopening-20210122-3jy2a63uaza f3fp26y6gnvxvty-story.html

36. Pamela Wood, Bryn Stole and Liz Bowie, "Maryland Gov. Hogan Calls on Schools to Bring Students Back to Classrooms by March Under Hybrid Learning Plan," *Baltimore Sun*, January 21, 2021. https://www.baltimoresun.com/coronavirus/bs-md -hogan-salmon-covidschools-update-20210121-5r74ewa7nnfg7bq4hjsdrwcfju-story.html

37. Ibid.

38. Editorial Board, "On School Reopening, Hogan Does Not Work Well With Others/Commentary," *Baltimore Sun*, January 22, 2021. https://www.baltimoresun .com/opinion/editorial/bs-ed-0125-hogan-schools-reopening-20210122-3jy2a63uaza f3fp26y6gnvxvty-story.html

39. Pamela Wood and Justin Fenton, "We've Examined 5 Chapters of Maryland Gov. Larry Hogan's Book. We Have Questions," *Baltimore Sun*, July 16, 2020. https://www.baltimoresun.com/politics/bs-md-pol-hogan-chapters-2020071671lfg2s5 3wrb55npxjpli7wndry-story.html

40. Hogan, pp. 106–8.

41. Pamela Wood, "In Upcoming Political Memoir, Maryland Gov. Hogan Calls 2015 Baltimore Unrest His 'Baptism of Fire,'" *Baltimore Sun*, July 14, 2020. https:// www.baltimoresun.com/politics/bs-pr-pol-hogan-book-20200714yepqs2x5xfhdhkg hn6zu4zfowa-story.html

42. Hogan, p. 144.

43. Hogan, pp. 121–3.

44. Pamela Wood, "In Upcoming Political Memoir, Maryland Gov. Hogan Calls 2015 Baltimore Unrest His 'Baptism of Fire,'" *Baltimore Sun*, July 14, 2020. https://www.baltimoresun.com/politics/bs-pr-pol-hogan-book-20200714yepqs2x5xfhdhkg hn6zu4zfowa-story.html

45. Ron Cassie, "Likable Larry," *Baltimore Magazine*. October 2018. https://www .baltimoremagazine.com/section/historypolitics/how-did-larry-hogan-becomesecond -most-popular-governor-in-the-country/

46. Colin Campbell, "Baltimore City Recommends Against Building Proposed $10 Billion High-Speech Maglev Train to Washington," *Baltimore Sun*, June 23, 2021. https://www.baltimoresun.com/politics/bs-md-ci-baltimore-says-no-maglev -20210623itzlcpa7tnbi3d7ty6p2vpfx4a-story.html

47. Ron Cassie, "Likable Larry," *Baltimore Magazine*. October 2018. https://www .baltimoremagazine.com/section/historypolitics/how-did-larry-hogan-becomesecond -most-popular-governor-in-the-country/

48. Pamela Wood, "Study Recommends Offices, Retail, Park for State Center in Baltimore, But Not an Arena," *Baltimore Sun*, January 23, 2018. https://www.chica-gotribune.com/bs-mdstate-center-study-20180123-story.html

49. Natalie Sherman, "What Now for State Center Site? Anxious Neighbors Wait for Answers," *Baltimore Sun*, March 31, 2017. https://www.baltimoresun.com/busi-ness/bs-bzstate-center-next-20170331-story.html

50. Natalie Sherman and Pamela Wood, "99 Workers Moved from Baltimore's State Center," *Baltimore Sun*, January 26, 2017. https://www.baltimoresun.com/maryland/baltimorecity/bs-md-state-center-jobs-20170126-story.html

51. Natalie Sherman, "What Now for State Center Site? Anxious Neighbors Wait for Answers," *Baltimore Sun*, March 31, 2017. https://www.baltimoresun.com/busi-ness/bs-bzstate-center-next-20170331-story.html

52. Michael Dresser, "Baltimore Lawmakers Press Hogan to Get State Center Project on Track," *Baltimore Sun*, April 7, 2017. https://www.baltimoresun.com/maryland/baltimorecity/bs-md-state-center-delegation-20170407-story.html

53. Maryland Stadium Authority, *Baltimore State Center Alternative Land Use Study*. January 2018. pp. 94–100. https://mdstad.com/sites/default/files/State_Center _Site_Final_Report_January_2018.pdf

54. Maryland Stadium Authority, *Baltimore State Center Alternative Land Use Study*. January 2018. pp. 94–100. https://mdstad.com/sites/default/files/State_Center _Site_Final_Report_January_2018.pdf

55. Luke Broadwater, "Despite Lawsuit, Hogan Says He's Relocating Workers, Moving Forward with State Center Project in Baltimore," *Baltimore Sun*, November 26, 2019. https://www.baltimoresun.com/politics/bs-md-pol-hogan-state-center -20191126-7ucinlgbcjf77pl47xylm6utmu-story.html

56. Ron Cassie, "Likable Larry," *Baltimore Magazine*. October 2018. https://www .baltimoremagazine.com/section/historypolitics/how-did-larry-hogan-becomesecond -most-popular-governor-in-the-country/

57. Ibid.

58. Mileah Kromer, "Jealous Didn't So Much Lose MD Gubernatorial Race as Hogan Won It," *Baltimore Sun*, November 7, 2018. https://www.baltimoresun.com/opinion/op-ed/bs-ed-op-1108-h, ogan-wins-20181106-story.html

59. Editorial Board, "Maryland's Next Governor Doesn't Have to Be From Baltimore, But Must Care About It," *Baltimore Sun*, July 12, 2021. https://www.baltimoresun.com/opinion/editorial/bs-ed-0707-maryland-governor-race-20210709yst qvarmtrf7vkqpbbb7yhg2ui-story.html

Part II

POLITICS

Chapter 5

Baltimore in Search of Its Next Transformational Mayor

There have been fifty-two mayors in Baltimore, though because of the multiple but not sequential terms of six of them, the office has changed hands sixty-two times. Baltimore's first mayor was James Calhoun, first elected in 1794. He served until 1804. As was the case in too many places, to be elected to public office at that time required that a person be a man who owned taxable property of a certain amount—a requirement that effectively prevented African Americans and people of color from running for office. In Baltimore, to be mayor required a man to own at least $2,000 worth of assessed property which was a significant amount at that time. Calhoun owned $12,600 in real estate and eleven slaves.[1]

Under the original City Charter of 1797, Baltimore's mayors were elected to two-year terms. Following an amendment to the current City Charter, mayors serve four-year terms with no limit on how many terms they may serve. The first mayor to serve a four-year term was Thomas G. Hayes who served a single term from 1899 until 1903.

For many years, the elections for the mayor and city council were held in the year before the presidential election. This meant that Baltimore held elections in three of every four years. In 2012, city elections were moved to coincide with presidential elections. This changed the next city's elections from 2015 until 2016 and gave those elected in 2011 a five-year term before having to run for reelection.

To attempt to cover all fifty-two people who have served as mayor, one would need at least one book of its own; maybe two. In fact, one recent mayor is the subject of a comprehensive biography. Instead, the focus will be on the eleven people who have served during the past almost sixty years. Of these, two resigned after having been elected governor. Two were forced to resign during corruption scandals. Two served partial terms but did not win their party's nomination for a full term. And four chose not to run for reelection (two after serving a single term and two who served more than one term). The incumbent took office in December 2020. I will not cover all these mayors in depth since not all of them are significant.

THEODORE MCKELDIN

(1943–1947 and 1963–1967)

Theodore Roosevelt McKeldin was a Republican. He served two non-sequential terms as Baltimore's mayor. The first was from 1943 to 1947. The second was from 1963 to 1967. In addition, he served as governor of Maryland from 1951 to 1959. Until Larry Hogan won reelection in 2018, McKeldin had been the only Republican in Maryland history to be elected to a second term as governor.

One can't discuss McKeldin without recognizing his first term. When he was elected in 1943, the United States was at war. That first term was concerned with wartime priorities such as industrial mobilization and shortages of consumer goods.[2] Despite those challenges, however, in that first term he also completed Friendship Municipal Airport (now called Baltimore/Washington International Thurgood Marshall) and constructed a new civic center. He appointed the first African American to the Baltimore School Board.[3] He laid the groundwork for an expressway system and for renewal of downtown Baltimore.[4]

It is also impossible to appreciate McKeldin without knowing what he did as governor. His two terms as governor coincided with a period of enormous post-war prosperity.[5] The Maryland that he inherited was one undergoing fundamental economic and social changes. Increasing suburbanization created enormous demand for public spending. His administration created a twelve-year plan for state highway construction which included both the Baltimore Beltway and the Maryland portion of the Washington Beltway. Also among his accomplishments as governor was the opening of the Baltimore Harbor Tunnel, the first car tunnel under the Patapsco River.[6]

In addition to highways, the budget increases made possible by the general prosperity also allowed McKeldin to provide aid for higher education and hospitals and to create parks and recreational facilities. His Commission on Administrative Organization of the State made sweeping reforms in state government.

McKeldin returned to City Hall as mayor in 1963. By that point, urban renewal efforts were underway and Charles Center was becoming a reality. But McKeldin envisioned more. In his inaugural address, he laid out a vision of a redeveloped Inner Harbor and began the groundwork for it. His second term also saw the construction of a new municipal building.

Urban renewal projects were reviving the downtown core, but the Baltimore of McKeldin's second term was increasingly non-white and poorer. There was crime, racial tension, and economic stagnation. McKeldin pushed for civil rights legislation in public accommodations and open housing, legislation introduced into city council by then city council president Thomas "Young Tommy" D'Alesandro III. McKeldin also called for non-discrimination in employment.[7]

When the Congress on Racial Equality (CORE) announced at its 1966 convention in Baltimore that the city would be its target city for the next year, McKeldin addressed the convention. He embraced its goals and promised his full cooperation.[8]

Renowned for his strong advocacy of civil rights, during his second term there was negative impact on communities of color as a result of the urban renewal efforts to eliminate slums. Urban renewal programs resulted in displacement of 800 households and about 3,000 residents of predominantly African American neighborhoods. Hundreds of homes were demolished. Businesses were also displaced with some 500 jobs lost.[9]

The physical legacy McKeldin left behind in his terms as mayor and governor is important, but the most important and impactful legacy is found in civil rights. Publicly and behind the scenes, McKeldin worked to end segregation in Baltimore theaters, stores, and lunch counters. As governor he ordered the integration of state ferries and beaches, abolished racially based lists for state jobs, and played a crucial role in ending school and hotel segregation.

McKeldin was a forceful advocate. He appointed African Americans to posts long before other Maryland politicians did, not only as clerks, but as executive aides and magistrates and to school boards and commissions.[10] He also appointed Jews and women to offices they had not previously occupied.[11]

McKeldin was a firm opponent of capital punishment on moral grounds. He cited reasons such as race, economic hardships, and mental impairment among the reasons for his opposition.

His civil rights advocacy resulted in death threats. On one occasion someone burned a cross on the grounds of the governor's mansion in Annapolis. His advocacy extended to supporting various Jewish causes, including support for the State of Israel.[12]

In addition to his many accomplishments, many people remembered Theodore McKeldin as a highly skilled speaker. William Thompson writing about McKeldin in *The Washington Post* said, "But it was McKeldin the campaigner and speechmaker who shone brightest." He was comfortable in any situation speaking as easily to crowds as to individuals one-on-one.[13] His skill as a speaker was certainly a factor in his being asked to give a speech nominating Dwight D. Eisenhower at the 1952 Republican National Convention.[14]

Thompson also wrote that as a speaker McKeldin had few peers. He was able to switch styles to meet the audiences in front of him. As Thompson puts it, "using lofty rhetoric at one event, homey language at the next." He especially enjoyed speaking to religious groups and would often spend weekends speaking at churches and synagogues.[15] McKeldin's papers are held in the special collections archive at the University of Maryland Libraries. Among the contents are boxes of speeches, including some on audio tape. [16] Not available there but maybe in the University's undergraduate library named after him would be a copy of *The Art of Eloquence: A Governor and a Scientist Look at Public Speaking*, a 1952 textbook he coauthored with pharmacology professor John C. Krantz, Jr., which was published by the Williams and Wilkins Company of Baltimore. After more than a 100 pages of instruction, the book anthologized more than a dozen McKeldin speeches.

When his second term as mayor ended, he chose not to run for reelection. After retiring from public office, he served as one member of a panel of observers charged with supervising the 1967 elections in South Vietnam. The following year, he testified against capital punishment before Congress. He also remained an active supporter of Israel.[17]

Theodore Roosevelt McKeldin died on August 10, 1974. He was seventy-three.

THOMAS "YOUNG TOMMY" D'ALESANDRO III

(1967–1971)

Thomas "Young Tommy" D'Alesandro III was the son of Thomas "Big Tommy" D'Alesandro, Jr. and Annuciata (Nancy) Lombardi D'Alesandro. "Big Tommy" served in Congress beginning in 1939. He ran successfully for mayor and served three consecutive terms.[18]

"Young Tommy" was mayor as well, though he served only one term. His career as a politician was relatively short; just sixteen years. It began in 1956 with a seat on the Board of Election Supervisors. In 1962, he won a seat on city council. A year later, he was elected city council president. He replaced Phillip H. Goodman who became mayor when Mayor J. Harold Grady resigned to accept a judgeship.

During his time as council president, D'Alesandro worked closely with Republican mayor Theodore McKeldin. Most notably, he introduced in Council McKeldin's proposed civil rights legislation for which D'Alesandro was also a strong advocate.[19]

In 1967, D'Alesandro ran successfully for mayor. To get there he ran in the primary against Peter Angelos, a former city councilman who would eventually be majority owner of the Baltimore Orioles baseball team. Running on the D'Alesandro ticket for the office of city council president was William Donald Schaefer, the man who would be D'Alesandro's successor as mayor.[20]

In an interesting twist of history, after each of his terms as mayor ended Theodore McKeldin was succeeded by a D'Alesandro. "Big Tommy" succeeded him in 1947. "Young Tommy" succeeded him twenty years later in 1967.

In his inaugural address, D'Alesandro said he would root out discrimination. As one of his first appointments, D'Alesandro named George Russell to be city solicitor and to a seat on the Board of Estimates. Russell had been the first African American judge of the Superior Court and was the first to be city solicitor and sit on the Board of Estimates. He would go on to appoint Roland Patterson as the first African American superintendent of the Baltimore City Public Schools and the Rev. Marion Bascomb as the first African American on the city's Board of Fire Commissioners.[21]

D'Alesandro's first months in office were momentous. He proposed new ordinances to ban discrimination in housing and public accommodations. They had not been successful in the McKeldin administration. He created mayor's stations in city neighborhoods where citizens could bring complaints and find out about city services. He created neighborhood development corporations and centers at which public and private agencies could provide a range of services.

D'Alesandro came into office at a time of enormous racial tension. There had recently been riots in Harlem, Watts, Chicago, Cleveland, Detroit, and Newark. He knew tensions were high in Baltimore, but so far nothing had happened. He also knew some kind of action was necessary if Baltimore was to escape what was happening in other cities.

The first mayor's station opened two months into his term. He compromised with Black leaders wanting control of the Model Cities program. He asked public and private leaders to plan for summer programs for city youth. Bills went to Annapolis to eliminate all exceptions from open-housing and public accommodations laws. He urged the Greater Baltimore Committee to create jobs for the unemployed.[22]

Other efforts to prevent riots from erupting included the Baltimore Police Department's expansion of its community relations department and creating police service centers staffed by officers. These, combined with the mayor's stations and other programs, were meant to intercept citizen complaints and grievances and to deal with them before they became serious issues causing public protests.

In early 1968, D'Alesandro revived the defunct Baltimore Office of Civil Defense. Created to respond to the aftermath of a nuclear attack, D'Alesandro gave it new purpose. It was to lead city agencies in creating workable plans for responding to nearly every kind of crisis from fires to rioting to looting. Plans would also be put in place for things like distribution of food and medical supplies.[23]

Unfortunately, the crisis for which the Office of Civil Defense was making plans occurred in April 1968 after the assassination of Martin Luther King—and just four months into D'Alesandro's term. Unlike in some cities which erupted almost immediately, Baltimore endured two very tense days before violence broke out, though there had been a few isolated fire bombings.

The first large-scale disorders began on Saturday, April 6. A firebomb was tossed into a vacant house and a growing crowd moved up the street. Two furniture stores were set on fire. The uprising spread and there was extensive looting in some areas. The next day it spread along what would eventually become the "Highway to Nowhere," about which more has been written in other chapters.[24]

Police were outmatched, and Governor Spiro Agnew declared a state of emergency. D'Alesandro asked Agnew to impose a curfew and dispatch the National Guard. Agnew asked for federal troops which arrived on Sunday, April 7. Though the next days were difficult, disorders gradually subsided and were over by April 10.[25] These actions by Agnew may have helped, but as discussed in chapter 8, Agnew's decision to deliver a stern lecture to the city's black leaders did not.

Calm came at a heavy price. There had been 1,032 fires. Six people died and 700 were injured. There were 4,500 arrests (mostly for curfew violations) as well as 1,075 lootings and hundreds of businesses burned out. Many would never reopen.[26]

That it took two days before rioting began has been ascribed by some to the progressive policies put in place by McKeldin and D'Alesandro. And that Baltimore made it past the riots can be partly credited to D'Alesandro's leadership and to the open lines of communication between his office and the African American community. His handling of the riots and the many complex challenges the city faced led Rev. Bascom to call D'Alesandro the greatest mayor in Baltimore's modern history.[27]

The aftermath of the riots brought many challenges. The city's anti-poverty agency unraveled when its three top administrators resigned. About half the Community Action Commission resigned. Disputes within the Model Cities program delayed the launch of programs and services. There were garbage, transit, and symphony orchestra strikes. And always looming was the east/west expressway project more fully described in chapters 9 and 10.[28]

Despite the challenges, there were some significant accomplishments during his term. He got the civil rights bill passed. He got Baltimoreans to approve an $80 million bond issue to build schools. He created summer recreation programs for city youth. And he laid the legislative groundwork that would make the redevelopment of the Inner Harbor possible.

D'Alesandro is also credited with bringing many bright, young people into city government. Some of them are still active and playing important roles in Baltimore.[29]

When he announced that he would not seek a second term, many people assumed that it was the riot that disillusioned him; that wore him out. He never really said until a 1998 interview with Richard O'Mara of the *Baltimore Sun* on the thirtieth anniversary of Dr. King's death. When O'Mara asked him why he left, D'Alesandro said, "I had no money." He continued, "I was clearing $695 every two weeks. I had five children. I couldn't make ends meet."[30] It really wasn't that simple. Things never are. But it's the only real answer D'Alesandro ever gave. After City Hall, D'Alesandro practiced worker's compensation and personal injury law. He was an informal advisor to Kurt Schmoke and Martin O'Malley when they were mayor. Thomas, "Young Tommy" D'Alesandro died in October 2019 at age ninety. None of D'Alesandro's five children are in politics. But his baby sister, Nancy D'Alessandro Pelosi, is Speaker of the House of Representatives.

WILLIAM DONALD SCHAEFER

(1971–1987)

Of all the mayors in this chapter, perhaps the most interesting (and quirkiest) is William Donald Schaefer. He served four terms as mayor; from 1971 until 1987 when he resigned to assume the office of governor. He was Baltimore's longest-serving mayor.

An entire book has been written about Schaefer. Titled *William Donald Schaefer: A Political Biography*, it was written by C. Fraser Smith. Smith was a longtime journalist who worked at both the *Baltimore Sun* and the *Daily Record*, among others. Smith covered Schaefer for the *Baltimore Sun* when Schaefer was both mayor and governor. Schaefer also has a significant presence in Matthew Crenson's book, *Baltimore: A Political History*. Crenson is professor emeritus of political science at Johns Hopkins University.

This chapter cannot be as thorough as these two books. Though I will draw parts of this chapter from Smith's book and from other sources, I will also draw significantly upon my own experiences working in his administrations for the sixteen years between 1979 when he was mayor and 1995 when he left office as governor (focusing on those years as mayor).

William Donald Schaefer's first successful election came after two unsuccessful runs for the Maryland House of Delegates in 1950 and 1954. His first successful campaign was for a city council seat representing District 5. He was successful partly because of his interest in city planning and housing issues and partly because of Irv Kovens, one of the last of Baltimore's old-time political bosses.

Schaefer then ran successfully for president of the city council in 1967. Four years later, in 1971, he would run for mayor when the incumbent, Thomas D'Alesandro III chose not to run for reelection.

Throughout his terms as both mayor and governor, Schaefer's mantra was, "Do it now!" The origin of that may be found in his devotion and attention to Baltimore's many neighborhoods. He wanted them to look good; to be good. When he was being driven to appointments or appearances, he would take notes on the locations of potholes, piles of trash, burned-out streetlights, signs in bad condition, among others. Sometimes he would spend parts of his weekends traveling around the city looking for such things. The next day, or on Monday, the notes would go out to the appropriate agencies. Scrawled on the note would be, "Do it now!" These even became known as the Do It Now Memos. This was so much a part of things that after he went to Annapolis as governor, one of the staff of his appointments office had a sign over his desk that said, "I did it yesterday."

Because he seemed so "blue collar" (though he really wasn't), something people sometimes found unusual about Schaefer was his strong support for the arts. He viewed them as crucial to the life of the city and to attracting new businesses to the city. Among the things he did was get a percent for art ordinance passed that required a percentage of the construction costs of city-building projects be set aside for including artworks. The program didn't last long after he left office, but it's rumored that the new mayor, Brandon Scott, may revive it.

His support for the arts extended to the creation of the Mayor's Advisory Committee on Art and Culture (MACAC), a quasi-city agency that coordinated a variety of arts projects and programs. It was the agency for which I worked.

MACAC oversaw the Beautiful Walls for Baltimore mural program, coordinated the Mayor's Ball for the Benefit of the Arts and managed the City Arts Grant program that gave modest grants to community-based arts projects. MACAC also created Artscape, which is still the largest free arts festival in the county. It helped lobby the General Assembly for funding for the city's major cultural institutions and tracked arts-related legislation at all levels of government. There was a great deal that was in MACAC's portfolio.

When Schaefer became governor a slimmed-down version of this was created and reported directly to his office. Schaefer's reputation as an outspoken supporter of the arts was such that he was invited to give the keynote address for the American Association of Museums.

Schaefer did not like to make remarks from manuscripts. In fact, when he was required to do that, the speech had no life to it. He preferred to deliver speeches extemporaneously. We would prepare a set of talking points accompanied by a detailed briefing book with all the information about the event. He'd absorb the contents of the book and, using the talking points, deliver an animated and effective speech.

When Schaefer came into office as mayor, a number of the major urban renewal projects were already completed or underway. They included a federal office building (1963), the Sun Life Building (1963), the Baltimore Gas and Electric Building (1964), the Morris Mechanic Theatre (1964), the Maryland Science Center (1965), and the opening of an office tower at 2 Charles Center (1969). City Council had also approved the development of the Inner Harbor. Though Schaefer's name seems permanently attached to the Inner Harbor, he always credited mayors McKeldin and D'Alesandro for getting that project started.[31] But Schaefer knew all that building needed to continue.

And the momentum did continue. The Baltimore Convention Center, Harborplace, the National Aquarium, and the World Trade Center all came in relatively short order. It would be the aquarium that would arguably give Schaefer national attention. At a meeting with reporters in January 1981, an unscripted Schafer declared that if the aquarium didn't open on time, he jump in the seal pool. C. Fraser Smith described the run up to the swim. Would the aquarium open on time? If it didn't, would the mayor keep his word? There were press inquiries from around the country; what was going to happen? Scheduled to open on July 1, 1981, the opening was pushed back until August. Free publicity.[32]

On July 15, Schaefer took his swim in the aquarium's seal pool. He came out from the aquarium in a bathrobe and a boater hat. He had an inflatable plastic duck in his hand and rubber ducks in the bathrobe. He tossed those into the pool. When he slipped off the robe, it revealed a red and gold striped Victorian bathing costume. He went in the pool, submerged, and took his swim. He then sat on a rock next to a young woman in a mermaid costume. She gave him a kiss on the cheek. And at that point the seals were let into the pool. I was actually there that day and remember it well.

Because this was 1981, it took a while for it to go around the country. Today it would have gone "viral." Many people played up the swim and focused on how ridiculous it seemed. Even though he said it at the time, they were forgetting that Schaefer had promised he would. Smith reminded readers in his biography of Schaefer that at the event Schaefer had said, "I'm a man of my word. It would have been beneath my dignity to make a promise and not keep it." He was playing it broadly, but the truth was there.[33]

An important aspect of Schaefer's tenure as mayor was that he, like McKeldin and D'Alesandro before him, appointed African Americans to important city posts. The most notable of these was the appointment in 1984 of Bishop L. Robinson as Baltimore's first African American Police Commissioner.

For Schaefer, I'm sure the low point of his tenure as mayor was the loss of the Baltimore Colts. The threats to take the team out of Baltimore began about 1976 shortly after owner Robert Irsay had purchased the team. The story got long and complicated. But the short version is that Irsay was shopping the team around while negotiating with the city about keeping it in Baltimore. Whether Irsay was negotiating in good faith or not is unclear, but when he heard that the Maryland State Senate had on, March 27, 1984, passed a bill that would allow the city to seize the team under eminent domain he gave the order to pack up and leave. Mayflower moving vans went to the Colts training facility in the middle of the night, packed up, and left town for Indianapolis in a snowstorm. Football wouldn't return to Baltimore until Art Modell moved the Cleveland Browns to the city in 1996 shortly after Schaefer left office as governor.

As one of the major projects that occupied Schaefer's attention in the last years of his terms as mayor and for the first part of his terms as governor was getting stadiums built for the Baltimore Orioles and the Baltimore Ravens. Oriole Park at Camden Yards opened in 1992. The Ravens' stadium, now called M&T Bank Stadium, opened in 1999.

William Donald Schaefer was not an easy man for whom to work. He was impatient. He wanted Baltimore to be world class and he wanted it done now. To do that, he created mechanisms that allowed funds to flow into the projects that would make Baltimore into what he envisioned. They were mechanisms that probably could have used greater oversight. But the one thing I never heard, though, was anyone questioning his integrity.

Schaefer served two terms as governor. He ran for Comptroller of Maryland in a special election held after the incumbent, Louis Goldstein, died in office. Schaefer was reelected for two full terms. He died in 2011 at the age of eighty-nine.

There is so much more that could be written here, but it would largely repeat what Matthew Crenson and C. Fraser Smith wrote in their books and what so many journalists wrote in their reporting. The years I worked in his administrations as mayor and governor were both the start of my career and among the best years of my career. If I had to sum up William Donald Schaefer as mayor (and as governor), it would be to say that he loved

Baltimore and its people and that serving them was more important than probably anything else. And that was a very good thing.

CLARENCE H. "DU" BURNS

(1987–1987)

Clarence H. "Du" Burns didn't accomplish much as mayor. He really didn't have time. He served for only eleven months. As President of the City Council, he became mayor when William Donald Schafer resigned to become governor. When Burns ran for a full term in 1987, he was defeated. Many of his significant contributions came during his years on city council.

Burns came up through old-style Baltimore politics. Though he wasn't even legally old enough to vote, at age nineteen he became the first African American member of the 7thWard's powerful Bohemian Club. He started by corralling votes for members while at the same time building a political base that would eventually become the Eastside Democratic Organization. In the 1940s he delivered votes for Mayor Thomas "Big Tommy" D'Alesandro, Jr. through that connection he landed a job as a locker room attendant at Dunbar High School. During the twenty-two years he spent there, he was also learning very practical politics. He started as a precinct worker and rose to ward boss. From the Eastside Democratic Organization, he launched a campaign for city council from the 2nd District, winning that election in 1971.[34]

For more than ten years, he chaired the city council Urban Affairs Committee which handled matters such as urban renewal. He would hold hearings in the evenings to engage the neighborhoods in the process. He was Council vice president from 1977 to 1982 when he rose to president upon the resignation of then president Walter Orlinsky who was caught up in a bribery scandal. When he assumed that post he became the first African American to be President of the City Council.

In 1987, Mayor Schaefer resigned to become governor and, as city council president, Burns became mayor. He was the city's first African American mayor; a job he said he loved. While he was mayor, he created the first city program to help the homeless, started several housing initiatives, found money to keep five library branches open, and increased school funding. He did all that without raising taxes, laying off workers, or cutting services.[35]

When he ran for a full term as mayor in 1987, Burns took some of the credit for some major projects of the Schaefer administration, including new low-income housing for East Baltimore, Dunbar High School, East Baltimore Medical Center, the Hyatt Hotel, and Harborplace. Some activists said he played only minor roles in those. Schaefer said, however, that Burns's role in those projects had been very significant.[36] He was a longtime Schaefer ally and the city council floor leader on many of those projects.[37] He had been the link between City Hall and the neighborhoods that were affected.[38] Burns was defeated by Kurt Schmoke in that primary election. He would try again in 1991 but would be defeated again.

KURT SCHMOKE

(1987–1999)

Though he was not the first African American to hold the office of mayor, Kurt Schmoke was the first African American to be elected to that office.

Schmoke may be the brightest person to have ever held the office of mayor. He attended Baltimore City College, a prestigious public high school. He went on to attend Yale University. He studied at Oxford University as a Rhodes Scholar. After that, he went to Harvard Law School to earn his law degree.

In 1983 in his first try for elective office, he challenged William Swisher, the incumbent Baltimore City State's Attorney. He won by a very large margin. He served only one term, though. In 1987, rather than run for reelection, he chose to challenge the incumbent mayor, "Du" Burns, who was running for a full term.

As mayor, Schmoke was never one to shy away from controversy. Arguably, his most controversial stance was his opposition to the so-called "war on drugs." He famously called for decriminalizing drugs, though that term is actually an over-simplification of his stance. For many that meant legalizing drugs, which is not at all what Schmoke meant. His stance was that drug *use* ought to be decriminalized; that people should not go to prison because they were addicted to drugs. One of the programs put forward by Schmoke's administration was a needle exchange program for addicts.

Schmoke did not abandon economic development as an engine for Baltimore going forward. He did shift priorities around and focused a lot of attention on the schools. Matthew Crenson wrote that Schmoke's focus on the school system was risky because, "No one had developed a formula for enhancing the educational performance of poor black children in a big city with thousands of single-parent households."[39]

Schmoke's more hands-on approach to the school system did indeed prove risky. His choice for president of the Board of School Commissioners proved a very bad choice. So was his choice for a new school superintendent who proved so controversial that he was not renewed when his contract expired.[40]

Although Schmoke had been City State's Attorney, crime didn't seem to be high on his mayoral agenda. This was despite a surging homicide rate. He was forced to cut police budgets because of a reduction in state aid; morale was low and officers were leaving the department for other departments with better pay. Yet Schmoke seemed disengaged. In his political history of Baltimore, Crenson quoted a police commander. "In the past, when we got near 200 felonies a day in the city, you'd have Schaefer demanding that something be done. Now we're routinely over 300 a day and no one bats and eye."[41]

Schmoke's three terms were not without accomplishments. He was able to improve the environments of the city's low-income housing projects and he kept the tax rates stable. His needle exchange program was working. And, very important for many Baltimoreans of all kinds, he was key to attracting the Cleveland Browns football team to Baltimore. They, of course, became the Baltimore Ravens who filled the hole created when the city's beloved Colts left town for Indianapolis in the middle of the night in a snowstorm.

Kurt Schmoke chose not to run for a fourth term and left office in 1999.

MARTIN O'MALLEY

(1999–2007)

Martin O'Malley was elected mayor in 1999. He decided to run when incumbent Kurt Schmoke announced that he would not seek a fourth term. It was not his first political office, however. He served on city council from 1991 until 1999 representing District 3.

At first, his run for mayor sparked controversy. He was a white candidate running for mayor of a majority Black city that had seen two successive African American mayors. There were two Black politicians who were already seen as candidates. They were city council president Lawrence Bell and Carl Stokes, a member of the school board and a former councilman.

According to Matthew Crenson, a number of influential Black leaders were unsatisfied with both these candidates. Howard "Pete" Rawlings, a member of the Maryland House of Delegates, widely regarded as the most powerful Black politician in Baltimore, tried to recruit then NAACP president Kweisi Mfume to run. He eventually declined.

When O'Malley declared his candidacy, he was attacked by some Black leaders as a political opportunist who was cynically taking advantage of a split in the Black community. Crenson wrote, however, that O'Malley had, in fact, been one of those who had been actively trying to persuade Mfume to run. He decided to run only after Mfume declined to do so. Attacks on O'Malley faded when Rawlings and other Black leaders endorsed him.[42]

O'Malley based his campaign on reducing crime in a city with a high homicide rate. After winning the election, his administration adopted a statistics-based tool called CitiStat which was based on a similar program used in New York City. CitiStat logged every call for service into a database that could then be analyzed. It has been reported that CitiStat saved the city some $350 million and helped generate the city's first budget surplus in years.[43]

Perhaps the most controversial aspect of his drive to reduce crime was his adoption of a zero-tolerance strategy. This was based on the idea that when there is a lot of low-level crime, it creates an atmosphere that encourages more serious crime.[44]

Baltimore's Black leaders were concerned that this kind of policing would end up targeting Black communities with racial profiling and aggressive, abusive police conduct. This would, in turn, aggravate already existing animosities between the police and the communities they were supposed to serve, which could then lead to civil unrest as would be seen in 2015 after the death of Freddie Gray.[45] These concerns may explain, at least in part, why O'Malley's successor, Sheila Dixon, shifted the emphasis to community policing.

O'Malley ran for reelection as mayor in 2004 and served a partial term. In 2006, he ran successfully for governor, resigning as mayor to assume that office.

While there is a good deal of information readily available for O'Malley's two terms as governor (and less for his terms as mayor), those terms as governor are not the subject of this chapter. They are discussed, in the context of his aspirations for the presidency, in another chapter.

There have been a number of observers of Maryland politics, including myself, who are critical of what appears to be O'Malley's focus on what comes next. As a councilman, he was looking to be mayor. As mayor, he was looking to be governor. As governor, he was looking to be president (and he eventually did declare his candidacy for that office). As was observed elsewhere in this book, O'Malley was criticized for spending too much time in 2014 laying the groundwork for that run for president and not enough time helping his lieutenant governor win election as governor.

SHEILA DIXON

(2007–2010)

Sheila Dixon was the president of the city council when she was elevated to the mayor's office in 2007 upon the resignation of Martin O'Malley when he became governor. She was the first African American woman to be council president, the first woman to be mayor, and the third African American mayor.

Dixon was first elected to city council in 1987 to represent District 4. She served on the Council until 1999 when she was elected city council president. She was re-elected in 2003, serving as president until becoming mayor. Later that year she successfully ran for a full term.

In the 2007 mayoral election, crime was a major issue. Homicides were on pace to exceed 300. After she became mayor, Dixon made tackling crime a major focus of her administration. While she was mayor homicides dropped for the first time in decades. By the end of 2008, there had been a 17 percent reduction. Her crime plan, supported by her Police Commissioner, Fred Bealefeld, emphasized community policing and using police resources to target the most violent offenders.

Her crime-fighting strategy did have its critics. The record shows, though, that she had increased police patrols, cracked down on illegal gun possession, and secured federal and state funding for crime-fighting programs.

Though begun under other mayors, several major projects were finished while she was mayor. They included Harbor East, the Legg Mason Tower, and the Baltimore Hilton Hotel.

In the end, Sheila Dixon was undone by gift cards. Of course, it wasn't really that simple. The Office of the State Prosecutor executed search warrants on her home and subpoenaed several aides. They were looking into gifts (including fur coats) as well as into her spending habits. Two associates pleaded guilty to tax charges and cooperated with prosecutors.

As reported in the *Baltimore Sun* on January 9, 2009, she was indicted on four counts of perjury, two counts of misconduct, three counts of felony theft, and three counts of fraudulent misappropriation. She went to trial in November 2009 on the felony theft and fraudulent misappropriation charges (one each of which was dropped) as well as one count of misconduct. She was found guilty on only one charge of fraudulent misappropriation for her use of $600 worth of gift cards intended for distribution to those in need.

She resigned as mayor on February 2, 2010, as part of a plea deal to avoid prosecution on the remaining charges. In return for her resignation, she got to keep her $83,000 per year pension. She had threatened to stay in office while she appealed her conviction if she weren't allowed to keep the pension.[46]

Dixon wasn't finished though. She attempted a comeback in 2016 but was defeated in the primary by Catherine Pugh (more on her later). She tried again in 2020 but was narrowly beaten in the primary by current mayor, Brandon Scott.

During that 2020 campaign, Joan Jacobson, writing for the *Baltimore Brew* described Dixon's long history of corruption going back to her years as city council president. Included among her transgressions were accepting lavish gifts from her developer boyfriend and then voting in favor of tax breaks for his project in Harbor East. She also lied on required ethics forms.

Dixon was never really genuinely sorry. As reported in *Baltimore Brew*, she apologized for what she called mistakes. When asked how she would characterize them, she said only that she had failed to disclose a personal relationship.[47]

STEPHANIE RAWLINGS-BLAKE

(2010–2016)

Stephanie Rawlings-Blake became mayor on February 4, 2010, upon the resignation of Sheila Dixon.

Rawlings-Blake's entry into politics should not be regarded as a surprise. Her father was Howard Peters "Pete" Rawlings who, from 1979 until his death in 2003, was a member of the Maryland House of Delegates representing the 40th District. He chaired the powerful House Appropriations Committee.

Rawlings-Blake didn't enter politics through elective office but rather as a member of the Baltimore City Democratic State Central Committee. In 1995, she became the youngest person to win election to the city council. She represented District 5 until district lines were redrawn after which she represented District 6. In her second term she was chosen vice president of the Council.

In 2007, she became President of the city council when then president Sheila Dixon became mayor following Martin O'Malley's resignation to become governor. She ran for a full term in 2007 on a platform focused on education and crime reduction. She won handily. Before that term was over, Rawlings-Blake ascended to the mayor's office when Dixon resigned.

Stephanie Rawlings-Blake did not have an easy time of it as mayor. She had barely taken office when Baltimore was hit by a series of snowstorms that buried the city under feet rather than inches of snow. To say that those storms taxed the city's ability to respond might be an understatement. Nevertheless, despite the difficulties, she was generally regarded as having handled that crisis very well.

Among her successes was a program called the Vacant to Value Initiative to reduce the blight caused by the thousands of vacant buildings. The initiative streamlined code enforcement and disposition of city-owned vacant property. Included among the strategies was offering incentives to people who would buy and renovate vacant homes. It included redevelopment in distressed areas as well as targeted demolition of vacant properties to enhance the value of those which remained. The initiative won an Urban Land Institute award along with a number of other awards.

What damaged her term as mayor and what may have been an impetus in her decision to not seek a second full term was the rioting that occurred after the death of Freddie Gray while in police custody. What began as peaceful protests erupted into violence on April 25, 2015. Within hours, she requested assistance from the Maryland National Guard. Two days later she asked Governor Hogan to declare a state of emergency. A day after that she asked for additional help from the National Guard.

Rawlings-Blake received criticism for her handling of the disturbances. She was accused of acting too slowly to respond and especially (by some) of waiting too long to ask the state for help.

In an especially unfortunate moment in a press conference, Rawlings-Blake said that while trying to make sure people were protected, the city also gave space to those who wanted to destroy property. This was pounced on by conservative media and by Governor Hogan to attack a Democratic mayor's handling of the crisis.[48] There were, however, some conservative media who said that some of what the mayor said had been taken out of context and that anyone who read the whole statement knew that she had meant something completely different, though she could have said it more clearly.

Rawlings-Blake came under particularly vicious criticism in Larry Hogan's political memoir *Still Standing*. He characterized her as paralyzed with fear. He accused her of indecision and of being missing in action. He criticized her for not cracking down on demonstrators. He said he couldn't trust her. Hogan portrayed himself as the superhero who saved Baltimore from destruction.[49]

In September 2015, Stephanie Rawlings-Blake announced that she would not seek reelection. Had she run again, it may have been more difficult than in her first campaign for mayor, but she likely would have won. I don't know if others share this opinion, but I think the riots took all the energy out of her and she believed she needed to step aside and refocus. Her term ended in December 2020.

CATHERINE PUGH

2016–2019

Catherine Pugh's political career began in 1999 when she was first elected to Baltimore City Council to represent District 4. In 2004, she was elected to the Maryland House of Delegates from the 40th District. In the next election cycle, she ran successfully for the Maryland Senate where she served until 2016. During 2015 and 2016 she was the Senate's Majority Leader.

Pugh ran for mayor in 2016 and won. She succeeded Stephanie Rawlings-Blake who had chosen not to run for reelection. Pugh was mayor for about two-and-a-half years when she resigned in the midst of a corruption scandal.

When Pugh became mayor, she had a serious set of issues facing her, issues left over from the previous administration. Chief among them was the Justice Department's investigation into the Baltimore Police Department after the death of Freddie Gray in police custody. This became a priority and within a few months of taking office, she was able to sign the consent decree on behalf of the city.

That wasn't the only issue, though. Crime was rapidly increasing, especially homicides. There were thousands of vacant homes. Governor Hogan canceled the Red Line light rail line. He also launched the BaltimoreLink, a revised transit system that proved to be problematic at best. Revitalization and redevelopment were on the table, too, including the Port Covington project's request for $660 million in tax increment financing.

As a state senator, Pugh had been an advocate of a minimum living wage. She went further. She promised during her campaign for mayor that she would sign such an ordinance if it passed. When it came to her desk, though, she vetoed it earning criticism from many quarters. She suffered a legislative defeat when Council watered down a bill which would have instituted a one-year minimum sentence for illegal possession of a gun.

The challenges of being mayor would be dwarfed by the legal problems that would soon surface. An FBI investigation was opened in January 2017 after state prosecutors had been unable to trace the sources of the money with which Pugh's aide Gary Brown made contributions to her campaign for mayor; contributions that exceeded campaign limits.

The FBI investigation lasted for some time before anyone caught wind of it. In February 2019, they were preparing search warrants. On March 13, the *Baltimore Sun* broke what would be only the first of a months-long series of stories.

The case was a complicated one and would take too long to recount in detail here. It involved various entities paying large sums of money for copies of Pugh's self-published *Healthy Holly* books. They include $500,000 from the University of Maryland Medical System (UMMS) for 100,000 copies of the books to be donated to the schools (Pugh was a UMMS trustee). Payments for these books dated back to the time when Pugh was a senator and chaired a committee dealing with health matters and lasted through her time as mayor. Pugh neither disclosed those payments nor recused herself from voting on matters involving UMMS.

The *Baltimore Sun* reported that Kaiser Permanente had paid more than $100,000 for copies and Associated Black Charities more than $80,000. Both did business with Baltimore City. Though the numbers of copies supposedly purchased weren't revealed, the publisher said that only 60,000 had actually been printed. Remember that UMMS thought that it had purchased 100,000 copies. No one from these groups was indicted since it could not be shown that they were aware that the money paid was not going for books to be donated.[50]

On April 8, 2019, all the members of the city council signed a memorandum calling for Pugh to resign as mayor. She took a leave of absence instead saying that she needed time to rest and recover from pneumonia. In the middle of that leave, on April 25, the FBI raided two homes Pugh owned, her City Hall office, and other locations. She resigned on May 2.

Catherine Pugh was indicted by a grand jury on November 20, 2019, on eleven counts including fraud, tax evasion, and conspiracy. They next day she signed a plea deal pleading guilty to four counts of tax evasion and conspiracy. On February 2, 2020, she was sentenced to three years in prison followed by three years of probation.

BERNARD C. "JACK" YOUNG

2019–2020

Bernard C. "Jack" Young, like "Du" Burns, served only briefly as mayor before being defeated in the primary election in which he was seeking a full term. Young entered political office in 1996 when he was elected to city council from the District 2, which he represented until 2003 when councilmanic district lines were redrawn. Following the redistricting, he represented District 12.

In 2010 he was elected city council president after then council president Stephanie Rawlings-Blake had become mayor when Sheila Dixon resigned. He remained council president until April 2019 when he became acting mayor. As already recounted, Mayor Catherine Pugh had taken an indefinite leave of absence, ostensibly to recover from pneumonia. Her leave coincided with a developing scandal over a book sales arrangement. She resigned in May and Young became mayor.

Young had been in office for only a very short time when Baltimore City government was hit with a ransomware attack. The attack crippled the city's computer network, severely impacting many city services. Young refused to pay the ransom. It cost the city more than $18 million to resolve the problem.

In an interview with John Rydell of *Maryland Matters*, Young reflected on his time as mayor. His term was not without accomplishments. He found funding to open city recreation centers on Saturdays, something which hadn't happened in many years. He also created the Mayor's Office of Children and Success to help families in need. In the interview, Young defended his handling of the COVID-19 pandemic saying that he was able to set aside some of the stimulus money to help businesses impacted by the pandemic.[51]

Arguably his most significant achievement was resetting the city's relationship with the Stronach Group, owners of Pimlico and Laurel racecourses. Pimlico, in Baltimore, is the home of the Preakness Stakes. The relationship had become strained when Pugh and the city sued Stronach to keep the Preakness in Baltimore.

Young got the city to drop the lawsuit and to revive negotiations with Stronach. The General Assembly approved a multimillion-dollar public financing deal that resulted in keeping the Preakness where it is and which will overhaul Pimlico. The adjacent Park Heights community will benefit from the project as well.[52]

Jack Young ran for election to a full term as mayor in a crowded Democratic primary. He finished fifth in the primary.

BRANDON SCOTT

(2020–Incumbent)

Baltimore's 52nd mayor is Brandon Scott. Elected in 2020, Scott is a relative newcomer to politics as compared with some of his predecessors in the office. And at age thirty-six when he assumed office, he is also among the youngest to have been elected mayor.

Scott was born and raised in the Park Heights neighborhood, one of the areas of the city now undergoing a community-led revitalization; something that is described in another chapter of this book. A 2006 political science graduate of St. Mary's College, Scott made his first bid for elective office the following year when he tried unsuccessfully to gain the city council seat being vacated by Stephanie Rawlings-Blake. As mentioned before, Rawlings-Blake had just been selected as city council president during a political shuffle following Mayor Martin O'Malley's resignation when he became governor. When Scott wasn't elected, Rawlings-Blake offered him a job in the council president's office.

His first elective office was representing District 2 on city council, which he won in 2011. He was elected for a second term in 2016. In 2018, he was a candidate for lieutenant governor on the unsuccessful ticket headed by Jim Smith. In 2019, he was elected council president when that office was vacated when its incumbent, Jack Young, became mayor in the wake of Mayor

Figure 5.1   Baltimore Mayor Brandon Scott. *Source*: Photo provided by user Praxidicae and reprinted with permission under the Creative Commons Attribution-Share Alike 4.0 International license: https://creativecommons.org/licenses/by-sa/4.0/legalcode

Catherine Pugh's resignation following a corruption scandal. Scott ran for Mayor in 2020 and was elected.

While he has been in public office, he has pushed for new, more creative ways of thinking in City Hall. With younger, more left-leaning newer members of city council replacing many of the "old guard," Scott pushed through charter amendments that change how the city is administered, gave Council greater power over the budget, and changed the legislative process. These changes upended in many ways the "strong mayor" governance available to previous administrations. They would have been inconceivable to many previous mayors who were often able to get things done with little oversight.[53]

In 2018, while still on city council, Scott successfully sponsored a racial equality bill that requires city agencies to determine whether policies have differing outcomes with regard to race, gender, and income, and if they do, to develop policies to address them. He proposed a $15 million annual fund to address institutional racism. He also sponsored legislation that makes city data more easily available to the public.[54] This has included something called "Open Checkbook," which makes city expenditure and employee salary data available on the mayor's office website.

In a carefully focused inaugural address, Scott specifically addressed the public health challenges facing the city with COVID-19. But he also called gun violence a public health emergency and made it clear that he regards gun violence as matter not just for the police but one on which all city agencies must focus.[55]

Brandon Scott has said more than once that he is ready to reimagine Baltimore. He would also say that large-scale ongoing projects such as Park Heights and Port Covington, and a proposed one in Westport, are good for Baltimore only if they benefit everyone; especially the communities in which they are located. He made that clear with Baltimore's objection to the mag-lev project's Cherry Hill/Westport neighborhoods as the Baltimore terminus because of concerns over equity and the environment.[56]

CONCLUSION

People are always impacted by the action or inaction of the mayors who run the cities in which they live. But who is impacted and how becomes the question. The first three in this chapter were certainly transformational. All three presided over a city undergoing major physical changes. Redevelopment of significant parts of the downtown core transformed Baltimore into a genuine world-class destination. Downtown came alive. These changes tended to most benefit those in power; those with money.

Much more important to ordinary Baltimoreans was that these three also transformed the governmental power structure so that it became more inclusive. They appointed African Americans to important positions in government and paved the way for Baltimore to have its first Black mayor. Major civil rights legislation was passed under the first two of these mayors.

As we have seen, none of the next seven mayors was outstanding in ways the first three mayors in this chapter were. Two really weren't mayor long enough to have made much of a difference. Two were caught up in corruption scandals that overshadowed any accomplishments made during their administrations. One seemed disengaged. Another always seemed to be eyeing up the next higher office. And one was overwhelmed by events out of her control.

That leaves Baltimore's current mayor, Brandon Scott. As this chapter is written, Scott has not been in office even a year. Predictions involving politics are always dangerous. Things can change very quickly and what may have been a sure thing today may fall apart tomorrow. Scott will be under a great deal of scrutiny. He has made a good start, though, and it will be a good thing for Baltimore if he can continue that.

POSTSCRIPT

After this chapter was completed, Mayor Brandon Scott released a five-year plan to tackle crime in Baltimore; especially violent crime. Writing for the *Baltimore Sun* on July 23, Rose Wagner reported that in broad terms the plan seeks to reduce violence by treating crime as a public health issue (something

Scott discussed in his inaugural address). This framing is a rhetorical choice that could well extend beyond wording into policing policies. The plan also calls for better coordination of the efforts of law enforcement, community groups, and the business ·community. Most important, perhaps, will be the creation of systems to measure progress.

Wagner also wrote, "One of the most striking aspects is its goal: a reduction of gun violence by 15 percent every year for the next five years." If Scott's plan can pull this off, Scott *will* be Baltimore's next transformational mayor.[57]

NOTES

1. Matthew A. Crenson, *Baltimore: A Political History* (Baltimore: Johns Hopkins University Press, 2017), p. 59.

2. William J. Thompson, "So What Did He Do," *Washington Post*, August 22, 1999. https://www.washingtonpost.com/archive/opinions/1999/08/22/so-what-did-he -do/762dac88-646c-463b-9ba6-72b2a05fc93a/

3. Social Network and Archival Cooperative, "McKeldin, Theodore R." https:// snaccooperative.org/ark:/99166/w63v3ctt

4. William J. Thompson, "So What Did He Do," *Washington Post*, August 22, 1999. https://www.washingtonpost.com/archive/opinions/1999/08/22/so-what-did-he -do/762dac88646c-463b-9ba6-72b2a05fc93a/

5. Ibid.

6. Editorial Board, "Theodore R. McKeldin Modernized Maryland; Governor and Mayor; Baltimorean Envisioned Today's Airport and Inner Harbor; Practice Racial Equality; Marylanders of the Century," *Baltimore Sun* August 31, 1999. https://www.baltimoresun.com/news/bs-xpm-1999-08-31-9909010432-story.html

7. William J. Thompson, "So What Did He Do," *Washington Post*, August 22, 1999. https://www.washingtonpost.com/archive/opinions/1999/08/22/so-what-did-he -do/762dac88-646c-463b-9ba6-72b2a05fc93a/

8. Editorial Board, "Theodore R. McKeldin Modernized Maryland; Governor and Mayor; Baltimorean Envisioned Today's Airport and Inner Harbor; Practice Racial Equality; Marylanders of the Century," *Baltimore Sun*, August 31, 1999. https://www.baltimoresun.com/news/bs-xpm-1999-08-31-9909010432-story.html

9. University of Maryland Libraries, "Theodore Roosevelt McKeldin Biography." https://archives.lib.umd.edu/repositories/2/resources/1051#, November 26, 2019.

10. William J. Thompson, "So What Did He Do," *Washington Post*, August 22, 1999. https://www.washingtonpost.com/archive/opinions/1999/08/22/so-what-did-he -do/762dac88-646c-463b-9ba6-72b2a05fc93a/

11. Editorial Board, "Theodore R. McKeldin Modernized Maryland; Governor and Mayor; Baltimorean Envisioned Today's Airport and Inner Harbor; Practice Racial Equality; Marylanders of the Century," *Baltimore Sun*, August 31, 1999. https://www.baltimoresun.com/news/bs-xpm-1999-08-31-9909010432-story.html

12. William J. Thompson, "So What Did He Do," *Washington Post*, August 22, 1999. https://www.washingtonpost.com/archive/opinions/1999/08/22/so-what-did-he-do/762dac88646c-463b-9ba6-72b2a05fc93a/

13. Ibid.

14. Editorial Board, "Theodore R. McKeldin Modernized Maryland; Governor and Mayor; Baltimorean Envisioned Today's Airport and Inner Harbor; Practice Racial Equality; Marylanders of the Century," *Baltimore Sun*, August 31, 1999. https://www.baltimoresun.com/news/bs-xpm-1999-08-31-9909010432-story.html

15. William J. Thompson, "So What Did He Do," *Washington Post*, August 22, 1999. https://www.washingtonpost.com/archive/opinions/1999/08/22/so-what-did-he-do/762dac88-646c-463b-9ba6-72b2a05fc93a/

16. University of Maryland Libraries, "Theodore Roosevelt McKeldin Biography,"https://archives.lib.umd.edu/repositories/2/resources/1051#, November 26, 2019.

17. Ibid.

18. Richard O'Mara, "At Peace in Quiet: For 30 Years, People Have Wondered How Tommy D'Alesandro III, a Born Winner, Could Walk Away from Politics. It Wasn't the '68 Riot, He Insists," *Baltimore Sun*, April 4, 1998. https://www.baltimoresun.com/news/bs-xpm-1998-04-04-1998094106-story.html

19. Jean Marbella and Luke Broadwater, "Former Baltimore Mayor Thomas 'Young Tommy' D'Alesandro III, Brother of Nancy Pelosi, Dies at 90," *Baltimore Sun*, October 20, 2019. https://www.baltimoresun.com/obituaries/bs-md-ob-tommy-dalesandro-20191020dzzetsbbi5cehdiqupcp5slwca-story.html

20. Matthew A. Crenson, *Baltimore: A Political History* (Baltimore: Johns Hopkins University Press, 2017), p. 454.

21. Ron Cassie, "Former Baltimore Mayor Thomas D'Alesandro III, Brother of Nancy Pelosi, Dies at 90," *Baltimore Magazine*, October 21, 2019. https://www.baltimoremagazine.com/section/community/former-baltimore-mayor-thomasdalesandro-iii-nancy-pelosi-brother-dies/

22. Crenson, p. 455.

23. Ibid., p. 463.

24. Ibid., p. 462.

25. Ibid., p. 464.

26. Richard, O'Mara, "At Peace in Quiet: For 30 Years, People Have Wondered How Tommy D'Alesandro III, a Born Winner, Could Walk Away from Politics. It Wasn't the '68 Riot, He Insists," *Baltimore Sun*, April 4, 1998. https://www.baltimoresun.com/news/bs-xpm-1998-04-04-1998094106-story.html

27. Jean Marbella and Luke Broadwater, "Former Baltimore Mayor Thomas 'Young Tommy D'Alesandro III, Brother of Nancy Pelosi, Dies at 90," *Baltimore Sun*, October 20, 2019. https://www.baltimoresun.com/obituaries/bs-md-ob-tommy-dalesandro-20191020dzzetsbbi5cehdiqupcp5slwca-story.html

28. Crenson, pp. 466–7.

29. Richard, O'Mara, "At Peace in Quiet: For 30 Years, People Have Wondered How Tommy D'Alesandro III, a Born Winner, Could Walk Away from Politics. It

Wasn't the '68 Riot, He Insists," *Baltimore Sun*, April 4, 1998. https://www.baltimoresun.com/news/bs-xpm1998-04-04-1998094106-story.html

30. Ibid.

31. C. Fraser Smith, *William Donald Schaefer: A Political Biography* (Baltimore: Johns Hopkins University Press, 1999), p. 113.

32. Smith, p. 206.

33. Ibid., p. 207.

34. Jonathan E. Briggs and Laura Vozzella, "Clarence H. Du Burns, First Black Mayor of Baltimore," *Baltimore Sun*, February 21, 2007 (originally published January 13, 2003). https://www.baltimoresun.com/features/bal-blackhistory-burns-story.html

35. Ibid.

36. Ibid.

37. Richard Pearson, "Clarence 'Du' Burns, 84, Dies," *Washington Post*, January 14, 2003. https://www.washingtonpost.com/archive/local/2003/01/14/clarence-du-burns-84dies/b90638a5-fd6c-4e34-9b00-77f4b1d098e6/

38. Jonathan E. Briggs and Laura Vozzella, "Clarence H. Du Burns, First Black Mayor of Baltimore," *Baltimore Sun*, February 21, 2007 (originally published January 13, 2003). https://www.baltimoresun.com/features/bal-blackhistory-burns-story.html

39. Crenson, p. 509.

40. Ibid., pp. 509–10.

41. Ibid., p. 510.

42. Ibid., p. 511.

43. Paul Schwartzman and John Wagner, "As Baltimore's Mayor, Critics Say, O'Malley's Policing Tactics Sewed Distrust," *Washington Post.* April 25, 2015. https://washingtonpost.com/local/dc-politics/as-mayor-of-baltimore-omalleys-policing-strategysewed-mistrust/2015/24/25/af81178a-ea91-11e4-0767-6276fc9b0ada-story.html

44. Crenson, p. 512.

45. Ibid.

46. Joan Jacobson, "The Sheila Dixon Story: It Wasn't Just About the Gift Cards," *Baltimore Sun*, May 18, 2020. https://baltimorebrew.com/2020/05/18/the-sheila-dixon-story-it-wasnt-justabout-the-gift-cards/

47. Ibid.

48. Pamela Wood, "In Upcoming Political Memoir, Maryland Gov. Hogan Calls 2015 Baltimore Unrest His 'Baptism of Fire,'" *Baltimore Sun*, July 14, 2020. https://www.baltimoresun.com/politics/bs-pr-pol-hogan-book-20200714yepqs2x5xfhdhkghn6zu4zfowa-story.html

49. Ibid.

50. Justin Fenton, "How the Feds Investigated 'Healthy Holly': Prosecutors Share New Details of Case Against Former Baltimore Mayor Pugh," *Baltimore Sun*, March 18, 2021. https://www.baltimoresun.com/news/crime/bs-pr-md-ci-cr-healthy-holly-investigationbackstory-20210318-rwd5w3xsuzczrhnkj27uw4lce4-story.html

51. John Rydell, "As Scott Delivers His First State of the City Speech, Jack Young Speaks," *Maryland Matters*, March 19, 2021. https://www.marylandmatters.org/2021/03/19/as-scottdelivers-his-first-state-of-the-city-speech-jack-young-speaks/

52. Jean Marbella, Childs Walker and Daniel Oyefusi, "As Preakness Approaches, the Real Winner Could Be Pimlico and the Surrounding Neighborhoods. Here's Why," *Baltimore Sun*, May 6, 2021. https://www.baltimoresun.com/maryland/bs-prem-md-pimlico-redevelopmentpreakness-20210506-vpt7v57sjbcbfcwrcbm rx3iqcq-story.html

53. Emily Opiolo and Ben Leonard, "Brandon Scott Sworn in as Baltimore Mayor, Addresses 'Public Health Emergencies' of COVID-19 and Gun Violence," *Baltimore Sun*, December 8, 2020. https://www.baltimoresun.com/politics/bs-md-pol-brandon-scottinauguration-20201208-e6plg5omprh33lecpchscxf6g4-story.html

54. Ibid.

55. Ibid.

56. Colin Campbell, "Baltimore City Recommends Against Building Proposed $10 Billion High-Speech Maglev Train to Washington," *Baltimore Sun*, June 23, 2021. https://www.baltimoresun.com/politics/bs-md-ci-baltimore-says-no-maglev-20210623itzlcpa7tnbi3d7ty6p2vpfx4a-story.html

57. Rose Wagner, "Five Takeaways from Baltimore Mayor Brandon Scott's New Crime Plan," *Baltimore Sun*, July 23, 2021. https://www.baltimoresun.com/politics/bs-prem-md-cimayor-scott-crime-plan-takeaways-20210723-z3uquzlzwng4dmltrgb jxiq75e-story.html

Chapter 6

Why Haven't Maryland's African American Candidates for Governor Been Elected?

In Maryland, only four state government offices are elected in statewide elections. Two of them are comptroller and attorney general. Each is elected separately. The other two, governor and lieutenant governor are elected as a team. This chapter will focus on the office of governor.

In the history of Maryland, no African America has been nominated by a major party to run in the general election for either comptroller or attorney general. Only twice has one been nominated to run for governor—Anthony Brown in 2014 and Ben Jealous in 2018. Both are Democrats.

There have, however, been three African American lieutenant governors. Republican Michael Steele was running mate with Robert Ehrlich in his successful bid in 2002. Anthony Brown served with Governor Martin O'Malley from 2007 until 2015. As this chapter is written, Boyd Rutherford is the current lieutenant governor under Governor Larry Hogan and serving since 2015.

When Ehrlich ran for reelection in 2006, Steele opted out and instead attempted a run for the U.S. Senate. He was soundly defeated by Democrat Ben Cardin for the seat made vacant by the retirement of Paul Sarbanes. With a gubernatorial election looming in 2022, Steele had not decided whether he would run for governor, though he did tell the *Baltimore Sun* that he was "taking a hard, serious look at an opportunity to serve Marylanders again."[1] At the time this chapter was written, Rutherford had already announced his decision *not* to run to succeed Larry Hogan who is term-limited out.

Of the three African American lieutenant governors, that leaves only Anthony Brown. He did have the advantage of running for governor from the position of having served two terms as lieutenant governor under a generally popular governor. He was unable to translate that into success at the polls, though, and he lost to Larry Hogan in 2014. The only other African American to had so far run for governor in a general election was former NAACP President Benjamin Jealous—a Democrat in a very blue state. But he, too, lost to Hogan when he ran in 2018.

So why has no African American candidate been elected to a statewide office? Like so much of Maryland history, the answers are complicated. It certainly isn't for lack of a deep talent pool. African Americans have been elected to Congress (including the aforementioned Anthony Brown in 2016). African Americans have served or are serving as County Executives in several Maryland counties, including two who currently hold office. And African Americans have been elected to all the top posts in Baltimore City.

What are the reasons then? It's easy to say that systemic racism prevents African Americans from winning statewide office (though admittedly, racism may have some role). But that on its own would not explain why two African American Democrats running in an overwhelmingly Democratic state would be unsuccessful in their attempts to be governor. The answer, as I said, is complicated. To understand why, it is important to understand Maryland politics and, to a certain extent, Maryland itself.

In Maryland, registered Democrats outnumber registered Republicans by more than two to one. Even if you include those who are registered in all other parties as well as those who are registered as unaffiliated, Democrats still enjoy an advantage of 10 percentage points.

Democrats outnumber Republicans in only ten of Maryland's twenty-four jurisdictions. The key, however, is that in seven of those ten jurisdictions, the differences are substantial. In addition, six of those jurisdictions are the Baltimore/Washington metropolitan area with quite substantial populations. Though the Republican majority jurisdictions outnumber the Democratic majority jurisdictions, many are the counties in Western Maryland and on the Eastern Shore which have much smaller populations.[2]

To successfully win a statewide race, Democrats need only win solid majorities in Baltimore City, Montgomery County, and Prince George's County as long as they win solid vote totals in the other counties that comprise the Baltimore metro counties. With those behind them, the remainder of Maryland's counties, though largely Republican, have populations small enough that Republicans can't outvote Democrats statewide.

And therein lies a challenge for Republicans. A Republican candidate for statewide office must capture a substantial majority of Republican voters. The greater challenge, though, is that they must also have a strong showing among Independents and siphon off a significant number of Democrats willing to vote Republican. In Maryland, it's a really big deal when a Republican wins statewide office.

Party considerations aside, however, Marylanders tend to like their politicians on the more moderate side. They're often uncomfortable with politicians who are either too liberal or too conservative. While this may or may not be as much a problem for Democrats with their large voter registration advantage, it can cause Republicans headaches. Generally speaking, for Republicans to take the State House, they have to be (or at least be perceived to be) more centrist while still appealing to conservative Republicans. And Republicans must be able to work with a veto-proof Democratic majority in both houses of the General Assembly if they want to get anything accomplished.

Another thing to understand about Maryland and how Marylanders will often perceive things is to know that in the minds of many Marylanders, in order to be a real, true Marylander, one has to have been born in Maryland. This is admittedly anecdotal but I've seen it play out for me. Though I have lived in Maryland for more than forty years, I still run into people who don't consider me a real, true Marylander. And I've seen that play out with other non-natives I know. There will be more on this idea as I look at the two African Americans who have run for governor.

The two largest racial groups in Maryland are non-Hispanic whites and African Americans. In 1970, those groups represented 80.4 percent and 17.8 percent, respectively. In the fifty years since then there has been a seismic shift in the numbers. These groups now represent 49.9 percent and 29.6 percent, respectively. African Americans are in the majority in two of Maryland's most populous jurisdictions, Baltimore City and Prince George's County where they comprise 63 percent and 63.5 percent of the populations, respectively. In addition, African Americans represent significant segments of the populations of Charles County (42.6 percent) and Somerset County (41.8 percent). They are also 28.0 percent of the population in Dorchester County and 27.5 percent of the population of Baltimore County.[3]

Given both the voter registration numbers and the demographic composition of Maryland's population, how is it that neither African American Democratic candidate for governor was able to assemble enough "blue votes" to win the election? Yes, race probably did play a role, but it is interesting to note that both unsuccessful African American candidates lost to the same Republican, Larry Hogan.

We can probably trace Larry Hogan's formula for victory back to 2011 when he founded Change Maryland after deciding not to run for governor in 2010. As Kevin Robillard wrote in *Politico* just after Hogan won the 2014 election, Hogan used the group as an "anti-O'Malley clearinghouse." Change Maryland issued press releases on every conceivable topic criticizing the O'Malley administration in which Anthony Brown was Lt. Governor.[4] A Baltimore *Sun* article that appeared the day after the election said that Hogan used Change Maryland to gather the research he would use as ammunition in a race for Governor.[5] Hogan's goal was to organize the Republicans and Independents, both critical to a Republican statewide win. But Change

Maryland also focused a great deal of attention on disgruntled conservative Democrats who might be frustrated with the state government. Change Maryland had 120,000 Facebook members at the time of the 2014 election.[6]

THE 2014 ANTHONY BROWN CAMPAIGN

In 2014, the primary election for governor was wide open. Martin O'Malley was term-limited out, so the Democratic field was wide open. And since the Republicans were out of office, their field was, too.

On the Republican side, Larry Hogan had an advantage in name recognition over his three opponents. Despite this (and the advantage of the Change Maryland organization and its Facebook members), the Hogan ticket garnered only 43 percent of the vote—a plurality yes, but not a majority even in his own party.

On the Democratic side, Anthony Brown had an advantage as the sitting lieutenant governor. He also had high name recognition, but so did Maryland Attorney General Doug Gansler who was one of Brown's opponents. Brown won the primary with slightly more than 51 percent of the vote.[7]

Though there had been an office of lieutenant governor under the Constitution of 1864, it was abolished under the current constitution adopted in 1867. The office was reestablished by a constitutional amendment in 1970. Anthony Brown was Maryland's eighth lieutenant governor. Since the office was reestablished, no incumbent lieutenant governor has been elected governor, so in some ways history was against Brown from the start. But Brown's almost incomprehensible 2014 defeat by Republican Larry Hogan in a very blue state cannot be ascribed simply to that. It, like most things in Maryland, was more complicated. Before getting into how and why that defeat came about, we need some background on Anthony Brown.

At the time he was elected lieutenant governor in 2006, Anthony Brown had an almost perfect political biography. He is the biracial son of immigrant parents. His father was a physician who was born in Cuba, grew up in Jamaica, and earned his medical degree in Switzerland. Brown's mother was Swiss.

Brown was the first African American student council president at his high school in Huntington, New York, and was often the only one in his Advanced Placement classes. He studied government at Harvard from which he graduated *cum laude*. Because Harvard didn't have an ROTC program, he had enrolled in one at nearby MIT. After five years active duty, Brown entered the U.S. Army Reserve and earned a law degree from Harvard.

He came to Maryland for his law clerkship and stayed. He volunteered with the PTA. He served on the board of Prince George's Community College. He became part of the community. His career in politics began in 1999 with the first of his two terms in the Maryland House of Delegates where he was mentored by longtime House Speaker Michael Busch. Still in the Reserve, Brown was deployed to Iraq for ten months during his second term in the House. He continued his military service as a Judge Advocate General in the Reserve until 2014 when he reached mandatory retirement age. He had risen to the rank of Colonel.

In 2006, he was chosen by Baltimore Mayor Martin O'Malley to be his running mate in his bid to be governor. O'Malley served two terms, the second of which ended in 2015. As the incumbent lieutenant governor, Brown announced his candidacy to be governor and won the primary. Some of what happened during his two terms as lieutenant governor would haunt him in his quest.[8]

In the 2014 election, Brown carried Baltimore City and Montgomery and Prince George's Counties all by substantial margins over Hogan. In addition, he carried Charles County, though the margin there was much less in a county that has double the number of Democrats than Republicans. To win, though, he didn't necessarily have to carry Anne Arundel, Baltimore, and Howard Counties, but he did have to do reasonably well in them. He lost those counties by a combined total of 165,656 votes. Because turnout was low, there was little room for error by either campaign. Hogan won the election by only 3.8 percentage points.[9] As a candidate for governor, Anthony Brown should have been near perfect. He was the incumbent lieutenant governor with a governor who had been popular through much of his time in the State House. Brown was attractive. He was a military veteran who had served in a war zone. In Ken Ulman, he had a popular term-limited county executive from Howard County as his running mate. The Brown/Ulman ticket had a clear, coherent, potentially popular campaign platform that was articulately written. (I may be one of only a very small handful of people who actually read its 157 pages.) He had so much going for him. So why didn't he win?

While perhaps an oversimplification, the reasons can be boiled down to two things. Anthony Brown ran an inept, lackluster campaign that was often misdirected. And Larry Hogan ran a skilled, strong campaign that was kept tightly focused.

To begin, Brown was not a dynamic campaigner and that was sometimes reflected in the media coverage of his campaign. Whether intended or not, an Erin Cox profile in the *Baltimore Sun* created a negative impression of Brown's personality. Though Cox quoted Brown, who said that he was just a deliberate person, that comment came after Cox had already called Brown, stiff, stuffy, and stilted. She commented that critics had said that Brown had been too cautious to lay out his plan for Maryland. She even quoted Brown's twin brother, Andrew, who characterized Brown's deployment to Baghdad as politically motivated. The article appeared about two weeks before Election Day and did nothing to help Brown in a race that was already tightening.[10]

Negative characterizations of the campaign were reported in post-election analysis. In a *New Republic* article the day after the election, Alec MacGillis wrote that Brown had run one of the worst campaigns he'd ever observed up close. He called the campaign defensive and unimaginative. As reported in *Politico*, Senator Chris Van Hollen told MSNBC that Democrats didn't have a lot of excitement or energy for the election. *Politico* also called Brown an uninspiring candidate whose campaign had alienated Democrats who otherwise would have been allies.[11] In counting votes in his district, Baltimore City Councilman Robert Curran said some 10 percent of the voters in his district skipped voting on the governor's race but voted for the down ballot Democrats.[12]

Though the O'Malley camp denied it, the governor was accused of not doing enough by way of campaigning for his own lieutenant governor. And Brown really didn't get the help he should have had from Governor O'Malley who was spending a good deal of his time outside Maryland traveling the country trying to lay the groundwork for his own campaign to be president. The day after the election political commentator Blair Lee IV told Capital News Service that O'Malley's aspirations to be president cost Brown votes. He called O'Malley's presidential campaign "an affront to Maryland voters." Lee also remarked that angry Democrats came out to vote for Hogan while many traditional Democrats stayed home.

Post-election analysis showed that the Democratic Party did not have an effective ground game in two key counties. Capital News Service reported Montgomery County Delegate, Democrat Ana Sol Gutierrez as saying that Montgomery County did not live up to its turnout standards. In the same article, Delegate Aisha Braveboy, a Democrat from Prince George's County, cited a lack of grassroots organization and efforts supporting Brown at the precinct level as having had a negative effect on voter turnout in her county.[13]

The fault for the lack of an effective ground game doesn't lie solely with the party. The Brown campaign does bear at least some responsibility. Though I am not aware of anyone who may have actually reported on this, I did hear it whispered that Brown, because he is African American, may have taken the African American vote as a done deal. If that is the case, that may have been another factor in the smaller than usual voter turnout in Baltimore City and Prince George's County.

Even if that were not the case, it is accurate to say that in a state in which Democrats outnumber Republicans by more than two to one, too many Democrats did take the 2014 election for granted. That complacency may have been based on polling which showed Brown with a substantial lead. The models used by FiveThirtyEight had Brown defeating Hogan by nearly 10 percentage points. Their models rely on the accumulation of the polls they collect and analyze. Unfortunately, the most reliable pollsters had stopped polling the Brown/Hogan race a month before the election.

FiveThirtyEight tends not to use party-sponsored polls or those sponsored by the campaigns themselves because they're often biased. This time they might have wanted to do that. A poll by Wilson Perkins Allen Opinion Research (WPF) taken for the Hogan campaign a week before the election showed Hogan with a lead of 5 percentage points—very nearly the percentage by which he won the election.[14]

Not all political observers were convinced by the polling showing Brown with a significant point lead. Barry Rascovar, in his "Maryland Reporter" blog a month before the election, said that Brown was about to "blow a sure thing." He called the Brown campaign "badly off track."

According to Rascovar, among the campaign's problems was that Brown had hired national campaign specialists rather than Maryland ones. In reading the text of that October 5 blog posting, it's clear Rascovar thought it was from that decision that other campaign problems flowed.

The campaign staff isolated Brown from the media and from the public. He was even largely MIA in many of the campaign ads. Staff picked the wrong issues on which to run. Focusing the campaign on abortion and gun control missed the mark. Rascovar referred to those issues as "settled matters" and that even "Larry Hogan, Jr. agrees on that." Rascovar knew as well as Hogan did that "pocketbook issues will decide this election."

Rascovar characterized Brown's campaign ads as "Harsh. Negative. Hostile. Incendiary. The sky is falling if you vote for Hogan." He contrasted this with Hogan's main message of too much government spending and high taxes. Hogan presented himself as likeable and gregarious. Rascovar's concluded that if Brown "continues to come across as arrogant, aloof and unwilling to speak directly to ordinary voters and to the media," then "he might end up handing the governor's mansion to Hogan."[15]

Whatever the cause, Democratic voter complacency or a bad campaign or some other reason or reasons, the resulting turnout was low—especially in critical jurisdictions. And that ultimately sank Brown's campaign and his ambition to be governor.

Larry Hogan, on the other hand, ran a tightly focused campaign in 2014. He knew that Maryland voters were most worried about the economy, jobs, taxes, and education. He took the first three of those worries, combined them, and made the campaign into a single-issue campaign focusing on the economy.[16]

Hampered by a bad economy caused by a recession that began barely two years into their first term, the O'Malley/Brown administration was faced with extraordinarily difficult fiscal problems. A series of tax increases that were passed became a yoke on Brown's neck during the 2014 campaign for governor. Given Maryland's dependence upon and love for the Chesapeake Bay, two minor taxes should not have faced particularly strong opposition, but the administration allowed Republicans to attach to them the names "flush tax," the proceeds of which would go to upgrade sewage treatment plants, and "rain tax," the proceeds of which would go toward keeping stormwater runoff from polluting the Bay. There were also tax increases on alcohol, cigarettes, and gasoline. The Hogan campaign took full advantage and effectively tied Brown to Governor O'Malley's record.[17]

Without citing sources, Hogan created an image of a Maryland in economic crisis. Hogan claimed that businesses and individuals were leaving Maryland because of high taxes and too many regulations. Among his campaign promises was one to roll back O'Malley's "40 consecutive tax increases" though he didn't give any details of just how he would accomplish that.

Though this message certainly resonated with voters, so did one that Hogan would cut taxes without reducing services. He would do this, he said, by eliminating the oft-used waste, fraud, and abuse. Critics of this promise pointed out that his $1.75 billion plan was full of errors and almost certainly could not be accomplished.[18]

During the campaign, Hogan tried to capitalize on his perceived status as a relative unknown and that appeared to benefit him. Hogan worked very hard to portray himself as just a small businessman who was concerned about the state's economy and the effects of the O'Malley tax increases. He wasn't a politician, he said.[19] Because voters weren't as familiar with him as they were with Brown, many voters saw him as a breath of fresh air.[20]

While both these self-characterizations are superficially true, he left out a few key details. First, he left out that he was owner and president of The Hogan Companies that had handled more than $2 billion in property transactions and had made him a millionaire several times over. Second, he left out that he'd been involved in politics since his father, Larry Hogan, Sr., ran for Congress. He also left out that he'd been a Cabinet secretary in the administration of former governor Robert Ehrlich.[21]

Like Brown's ads did, Hogan's ads went negative. His first ad ran the day after the primary election. It called Brown "the most incompetent man in Maryland," a not-so-veiled reference to Brown's role in the disastrous roll out of Maryland's Affordable Care Act online health insurance marketplace.[22] The Hogan campaign ads generally hammered home the message that Maryland was in bad shape, that Brown had a role in that and that he (Hogan) would use his experience as a businessman to fix the state.

One positive ad did draw a lot of attention. The Brown campaign had run ads saying that Hogan would roll back Maryland's abortion laws and accused him of being anti-women. That accusation was countered by an ad featuring Hogan's daughter, Jaymi Sterling, defending her father's record as a supporter of women's rights.

Hogan's campaign also ran a round of ads featuring regular Marylanders talking directly to the camera. The ads were intended to give Democrats, independents, and women "permission" to vote for a Republican for governor.

Some of Brown's negative ads apparently did hit a little too close to home. Hogan was forced to explicitly say that he would not repeal O'Malley's social policies. He swore he would not touch the state's abortion laws or attempt to roll back gun control laws.[23]

The 2014 gubernatorial campaign was interesting in a number of respects. It was the first time an African American had been a candidate for governor. Though Anthony Brown should have won the election rather handily, he didn't. The Hogan campaign effectively tied him to high taxes and a bad economy. Combining that with Brown's lackluster campaign and his inability to articulate a clear direction in which he would steer Maryland essentially doomed his campaign.

Probably, the biggest reason for Brown's defeat was the low voter turnout overall, but especially in some key areas. Had a "normal" level of Democratic voter turnout happened, there is every likelihood that Brown would have won the election. Brown's career as an elected official didn't end with the 2014 election, though. In 2016, he was elected to represent Maryland's Fourth Congressional District in Washington, D.C., an office to which he was easily reelected in 2018 and 2020. As this chapter was being written, Brown is said to be considering another run for governor though no announcement has been made.

THE 2018 BEN JEALOUS ELECTION CAMPAIGN

For most Democrats, the 2018 gubernatorial election would not have any happier conclusion than the 2014 election had. For the incumbent, Governor Larry Hogan, the primary was a cakewalk. As an incumbent with incredibly strong approval numbers, he ran unopposed and, of course, received 100 percent of the vote. There weren't even any write-ins. It should be noted, however, that only roughly 20 percent of registered Republicans turned up at the polls for the primary.

The eventual Democratic opponent to Hogan, Ben Jealous, had a far more difficult time. The Democratic primary field had nine tickets which included the popular African American County Executive of Prince George's County Rushern Baker and the popular County Executive of Baltimore County Kevin Kamenetz.

The primary was thrown into some turmoil by Kamenetz's sudden death just six weeks before the primary election. Had he lived, it was expected that

Figure 6.1 2018 Democratic Gubernatorial Nominee Ben Jealous Campaigning.
Source: Photo by Edward Kimmel of Takoma Park, MD. Reprinted with permission under the Creative Commons Attribution-Share Alike 2.0 Generic license: https://creativecommons.org/licenses/by-sa/2.0/legalcode.

he would have done very well. At first, his running mate said she would not run, but changed her mind at the last minute and ran as a candidate for governor with her own running mate.

Despite the drama, Jealous received nearly 40 percent of the vote in the June 26 primary to Baker's just over 29 percent. The other seven candidates each received vote totals in the single digits.[24] With just over four months until the November 6 general election, Jealous now faced a significant problem. The Jealous campaign had had to spend a good deal of its money to win the primary election. There wasn't time to replenish his campaign treasury to effectively compete in the general election.

Hogan on the other hand already had substantial funds in the bank before the primary campaign. Running unopposed, he didn't have to spend much to win the Republican nomination. With a fat bank account, Hogan was able to spend money to go after Jealous before Jealous would have been able to respond in any substantive way.

Before taking on the election results and the reasons for Ben Jealous's loss, it is important to know a little bit about him.

Ben Jealous has a very interesting background just as Anthony Brown did. Like Brown, he is mixed race. Jealous's mother was biracial and his father was white. Both parents were active in the Civil Rights Movement. They met in Baltimore in 1966 but had to date surreptitiously. They had to be married in Washington, D.C., because at that time interracial marriages were still illegal in Maryland. They moved to California in 1970 where Jealous was born.

Jealous earned a BA in political science from Columbia University and was a Rhodes Scholar. He later earned an MS in comparative social research from St. Anthony's College, Oxford.

Jealous had been an activist and a journalist. He served as Executive Director of the National Newspaper Publishers Association. In 2008, he was elected President and CEO of the National Association for the Advancement of Colored People (NAACP). He left that position in 2013. In 2014, he became a senior partner at Kapor Capital. He also became a senior fellow at the Center for American Progress.

Both Brown and Jealous carried the same four jurisdictions; Baltimore City and Charles, Montgomery and Prince George's Counties. Even though Jealous had higher vote totals in those counties, Brown won them by larger margins. In looking at the vote totals in the three other Baltimore metro counties, Jealous lost Anne Arundel and Baltimore Counties by substantially larger margins that Brown did in 2014. Brown, however, lost Howard County by a far larger margin than Jealous did four years later. While the turnout for the 2018 election was nearly double that of 2014, Jealous lost to Larry Hogan by 11.9 percentage points as compared with Brown's 3.8 percentage point loss.

There are so many reasons for Ben Jealous's loss to Larry Hogan that it's hard to know where to begin. There may have been nearly a dozen reasons and though racism may have played a very minor role, it's not one of those six I would highlight.

Though he received some 40 percent of the vote in the June Democratic primary, Jealous began the general election campaign with a severe "name recognition deficit." In July, the Jealous campaign's own internal polling showed that at least a third of Maryland's voters didn't know who he was. Perhaps more ominous for him was that the same internal polling also showed that one quarter of Democratic voters didn't know who he was.[25]

Name recognition was a problem as late as one week before the election. A Martin Austermuhle report posted on the WAMU website recounted the example of a Jealous campaign stop at a Giant supermarket in Prince George's County. There he was criticized by a store employee about the campaign's lack of visibility. Jealous seemed almost puzzled by that criticism.[26]

When name recognition is low at the start of the general election campaign, a candidate already has problems. If it's still low as the election gets nearer, the campaign is in serious trouble. By contrast, if a lot of people didn't know who Ben Jealous was, everybody knew who Larry Hogan was. After all, he'd been governor for four years. The Hogan campaign had an enormous name recognition advantage.

Adding to the name recognition problem was a lack of political experience and a voting record to go with it. Lacking that record made it even more difficult to get to know Jealous and how he might govern if elected. In some ways that also made it easier for the Hogan campaign to label Jealous in just about any way it might choose.

While Hogan had faced a similar lack of a voting record in his 2014 race against Anthony Brown, he at least had experience working at the Cabinet level in state government. In addition, there were people who remembered his father, Larry Hogan, Sr., when he served in Congress. Finally, his activities with his Change Maryland organization gave voters a fairly clear picture about how he might govern.

Often cited in post-election analysis as *the* reason Jealous lost was the enormous money differential between his campaign and Hogan's. Fundraising was a problem for Jealous from the start. With eight opponents in the primary, he had to spend a good deal of money just to get past the noise. At the end of August, Jealous had only $385,000 in the bank and for the last two weeks before the general election, he had a mere $275,000. Jealous thought he could change the dynamics after Labor Day. He was wrong. By then it was far too late. By then people didn't want to donate to what was already seen as a losing effort, something that compounded his already difficult financial situation.

Hogan on the other hand, had no real financial worries. He began with several million dollars in the bank. At the end of August, he had $9.4 million. He still had $3.3 million for the campaign's last two weeks.[27]

Some media outlets said that Jealous lost because of lukewarm support from the Democratic establishment. To an extent they were right. Much of Maryland's Democratic leadership had backed Rushern Baker in the primary. Ryan Miner in his blog, aminerdertail.com, cited as one of the reasons Jealous lost was his failure to woo Maryland's Democratic elected officials. Miner didn't suggest that Jealous should have sucked up to those officials, but rather that he should have sat down with them and listened and learned how to work their districts.[28]

He did end up getting endorsements from many of the state's Democratic elected officials, but as Rachel Cohen of *The Intercept* puts it, "some were much slower to voice their support, and many remained muted in their enthusiasm."[29]

Hogan had the Republican Party firmly behind him. They'd seen him in operation during his first term. Watching the Jealous campaign, they could smell blood. They could already envision a second Hogan term.

The Jealous platform had problems, too. But they weren't the problems one might think would be the case with a very progressive platform in a relatively moderate state. The platform included single payer healthcare which had support from 54 percent of Marylanders. Seventy-one percent supported a $15 per hour minimum wage and 62 percent favored legalization of recreational marijuana.[30] Other popular platform planks included free in-state tuition, ending mass incarceration, ending the student debt crisis, and protecting the environment. What the campaign didn't put forward was any realistic idea of how to pay for all these. And the voters knew that. One voter interviewed on Election Day said he didn't think that some of the things Jealous had promised were economically doable.

The Hogan campaign didn't put forward much beyond saying it would continue the administration's effort to improve the economy for ordinary Marylanders, lower taxes, and improve the business climate. For many voters, that was enough. Comments such as "Mr. Hogan's been getting things done" and "He's been a great leader" were not unusual reactions, even from Democrats.[31]

Jealous sometimes proved to be his own worst enemy. There were times he didn't think before answering reporters' questions. During the campaign, Hogan called Jealous a "far left socialist." When asked by *Washington Post* reporter Erin Cox (previously of the *Baltimore Sun*) if he identified as a socialist, Jealous responded, "Are you fucking kidding me." Dropping the F-bomb was unwise at best and may actually have cost him at least some votes. Though it should probably be taken with a healthy dose of skepticism, the results of a focus group of 110 women assembled by the Hogan campaign claimed that one word influenced their perceptions of Jealous.[32] A self-described liberal Baltimore Democrat who voted for Hogan said she didn't know anything about Jealous but didn't like that he cursed at a reporter for asking a question.[33]

The rest of that exchange with Cox came back to bite Jealous big time. He went on to say, "Go ahead, call me a socialist. It doesn't change the fact that I'm a venture capitalist." The Republican Governors Association ran an ad featuring Jealous using only the first of those two sentences.[34] That ad did some serious damage in a state whose voters usually like their politicians on the moderate side.

The Jealous campaign demanded that TV stations pull the ad for being false and misleading.[35] Unfortunately, there is no requirement that a political ad be truthful much less that it avoids misleading the public. Even if the ad had been pulled, it was too late. The damage had already been done.

Jealous was not helped by the fact that his campaign staff consisted mostly of Maryland outsiders with little understanding of what it takes to get elected to statewide office in Maryland. As a result, the campaign made some really awful decisions. High on the list of bad decisions was skipping the conference of the Maryland Association of Counties held every year in Ocean

City. Jealous justified this by saying that the conference was nothing more than partying with lobbyists. And while there's some truth to that, it's the last day of the conference that would have been Jealous's big opportunity to talk with hundreds of Maryland's elected county officials. The final agenda item for the conference was a gubernatorial forum. What did he do instead? He attended a poorly organized Democratic Party event in Frederick County which attracted about seventy-five people.[36]

The Jealous campaign itself made generating and maintaining support difficult. Supporters noted that the campaign's website had no place from which to order lawn signs, bumper stickers, and other things that made people's support visible. Supporters had to ask around only to find out that they had to go to a campaign office to get such items. Even that piece of information wasn't on the website. The Hogan campaign website on the other hand made very clear how supporters could purchase campaign materials.

Social media also seemed to be a problem area for Jealous. While candidates across the country were increasingly using a variety of social media platforms in creative and effective ways, the Jealous campaign relied on clunky, less popular platforms like Facebook Live.[37]

Hogan on the other hand had a crack social media team that was really quick to take advantage of every Jealous gaffe and to push out messages on issues of concern to voters. It also seemed that the Hogan team was using Facebook as an inexpensive way to "test market" messages that often later made their ways into more traditional TV advertising.[38]

With all the difficulties it was facing, the Jealous campaign knew it had to invest in the ground game. Complacency over the ground game had helped sink Anthony Brown's campaign in 2014 and Jealous wanted to avoid that. The campaign nearly quadrupled the number of organizers used by the Brown campaign four years earlier.[39] In crafting the ground game Jealous employed some of the same tactics used by the NAACP during voter registration drives and other efforts during the Civil Rights Movement. It may be that Jealous just didn't quite grasp how bad things really were when he was thinking things would turn around after Labor Day. The previously mentioned Austermuhle article on the WAMU website the week before the election ended by quoting Jealous. "It feels like it's all coming together at the right moment," he said, "This is how we won the primary. The establishment had written us off, but we had built a bigger ground army than anyone else, and we put out a clearer, more positive vision than anybody else, and we won. And that's been our plan for the general, and it feels like it's coming together exactly at the right time."[40]

Although there was no primary opponent for the 2018 campaign, the Hogan campaign hit the airwaves during the primary season. Running an ad called, "Maryland Strong," had two purposes. First it touted Hogan's leadership and accomplishments as Governor—no tax increases, record funding for schools, a healthier Chesapeake Bay, infrastructure repairs, more jobs, and higher wages, to name some. What the ad didn't mention was that the statistics used in it were seriously cherry picked.[41]

The ad's second purpose was to humanize Hogan by using how he dealt with his 2015 cancer diagnosis; something that *Sun* media critic David Zurawik called risky. Risky or not, the ad worked. Voters were left with very positive feelings about Hogan.

As it did against Brown in 2014, the Hogan camp hit Jealous hard and early; on the night of the primary in fact. Titled, "Introducing Ben Jealous," the ad, which ran on Facebook, called him, "Too Extreme. Too Risky." Using dark images of Jealous overlaid with those words against a red background, the ad's message was that Jealous as governor would be bad for Maryland. Being able to hit Jealous even before his campaign could possibly start was highly effective. And the words extreme and risky stuck.[42]

In general, the Hogan campaign kept its ads positive, focusing many of them on his successes in improving the Maryland economy, though the claims made in some of the ads were inflated. He left it to the Republican Governors Association to do the really negative attack ads that among other things labeled Jealous as free-spending socialist. At least one of the ads used images of Jealous that made him look like an angry and aggressive Black man.

In addition to an effective media campaign, Hogan was helped by astoundingly high approval ratings that were typically in the high 60s. One national survey even ranked Hogan as the second most popular governor in the United States.

Handicapped by a nearly empty treasury, little success in raising money, and lackluster support from Maryland's Democratic leaders, the Jealous campaign didn't run its first ads until mid-September. He did get some help from ads run by PACs, including some $3 million from Maryland Together We Rise. Most of the PAC ads didn't appear until the last weeks of the campaign, though.[43] By then it was far too late to counter a negative narrative that had been solidified in voters' minds long before Labor Day.

Leading a large not-for-profit organization like the NAACP is certainly a complex and difficult task. But it is very different from leading a government when you need the General Assembly to enact the legislation that makes your platform possible. As I watched the Jealous campaign during the summer and early fall of 2018, it was very clear that Jealous did not have a good understanding of how state government really operated and what level of government was responsible for what. As only one example, he promised in his campaign that he would raise teacher salaries. Teacher salaries are a function of county government and not state government. It was also clear that even if he had been elected, he would not have had the trust or confidence of the Democrats in the General Assembly any more than Larry Hogan did.

As stated earlier, there are so many reasons to which Ben Jealous's 2018 loss to Larry Hogan can be traced. They included lack of name recognition, lack of political experience and a voting record, lack of funds, lukewarm support from the Democratic establishment, the price tag of his platform, being his own worst enemy, a campaign staff of mostly Maryland outsiders who made some very poor choices, a poor web presence, lack of social media savviness, an overdependence on the ground game, and an obvious lack of knowledge about how state government operated. The combination of these factors stalled the campaign's primary election momentum and made it seem like a losing proposition.

Anthony Brown and Ben Jealous, two African American Democrats in a very heavily Democratic state, managed to lose gubernatorial elections to their Republican opponent Larry Hogan. Were there any common threads?

It wasn't really money. In 2014 Hogan was the financial underdog and was significantly outspent by the Brown campaign. Conventional wisdom is that the candidate with the most money will win the election, so it was a surprise when Brown lost. In 2018, Jealous was the financial underdog and was substantially outspent by Hogan. Not surprisingly, Hogan swamped Jealous.

It wasn't really their platforms. Both Brown and Jealous had solid ideas that were generally popular with Marylanders. Brown's platform was more pragmatic and much of it could have been enacted. He didn't communicate it well, however. The Jealous platform would have been very expensive to enact, and Marylanders knew that. They were reluctant to support a candidate whose platform, if enacted, would almost certainly have raised their taxes and polling in 2018 showed that some 56 percent of Marylanders believed their taxes were too high.[44]

It wasn't really name recognition. Brown was well known to Marylanders from his two terms in the House of Delegates and his eight years as Lt. Governor, yet he still lost. Jealous was an unknown. Even in the last week before the general election, large numbers of Marylanders didn't know anything about him. They wanted to stick with someone familiar in 2018.

It wasn't really the ground game. In 2014, there wasn't much of a get-out-the-vote effort. A number of Maryland politicians recognized that and included that among the reasons that Brown lost. In 2018, though, the ground game was a major piece of the Jealous strategy and he still lost.

It really wasn't that Brown and Jealous weren't born in Maryland. Brown managed to transcend that. He arrived in Maryland in the early 1990s when he came to do his law clerkship. He became involved in the community. He was elected to the House of Delegates in 1998 and served two terms. In 2006, he was the lieutenant governor half of the O'Malley/Brown ticket and served two terms as lieutenant governor.

Though he had family in Maryland, Ben Jealous didn't move to the state until 2008 when he became President of the NAACP. That job didn't really give him any real chance to become entrenched into the community in ways that would benefit political candidates running for public office. Seth Grimes in a post-election blog posting on theseventhstate.com wrote that Jealous's Maryland association was too weak. He came "across as a movement guy more than as someone you'd look to craft a state budget." Grimes also wrote that to voters Jealous didn't seem like a candidate who was in it for the long haul for Maryland.[45] Post-election analysis showed that there were a good number of voters who just didn't like Ben Jealous. They voted for Anthony Brown, but they couldn't bring themselves to vote for Jealous.

If it isn't any of these, what is the common thread to these candidate's losses? Why did Republican Larry Hogan win two terms as governor in a state as overwhelmingly Democratic as Maryland? The simple reason is that Hogan ran far better, tighter, savvier, and more disciplined campaigns than either of his opponents did. He outmaneuvered the Brown and Jealous campaigns at just about every turn. Everything else flows from that.

Anthony Brown and Ben Jealous got bad campaign advice from out of state strategists who did not have any real understanding of Maryland, its politics, and its voters. Larry Hogan's strategist for both those campaigns was highly skilled and had worked many successful national-level Republican campaigns. He was also based in Maryland and knew Maryland voters.

Neither Brown nor Jealous campaigned on the right issues. In Brown's case, abortion and gun control were settled issues in Maryland, but he based most of his attack ads on them. Jealous's progressive agenda had popular pieces but would have been very expensive to implement. Hogan knew that the economy was the most important thing on voters' minds and he ran on that.

Brown and Jealous both lost control of the perceptions people had of them almost from the moment each had won his primary. Brown was, "the most incompetent man in Maryland." Jealous was "too extreme" and "too risky" for Maryland. Hogan kept tight control over his own image as a likeable, regular person; a moderate Republican willing to work across the aisle to get things done for Maryland.

Brown's strategists largely kept him away from the media making it difficult for them to interview him or ask questions at public appearances. Jealous, while more accessible to the media, made no friends there when he, as mentioned before, cursed at a reporter for doing her job. Hogan was always available and gregarious, especially at campaign events.

Brown's campaign ads were largely negative and tried to craft a negative image of Hogan. Jealous's campaign, when it ran ads, ran negative ads. Hogan's ads were generally positive and extremely tightly focused on the economy. During the 2014 campaign the economic message was that Maryland was a mess and it was Brown's fault. During the 2018 campaign, the economic message was one of a Maryland that was much better off under his four years as governor. He let the Republican Governors Association do the dirty work.

It seemed that neither Anthony Brown nor Ben Jealous really knew their Republican opponent, Larry Hogan. Larry Hogan certainly knew them, though. He knew where they were vulnerable and exploited that. Neither Brown nor Jealous were able to find a chink in Hogan's armor and were never able to develop a workable attack strategy. Hogan had a genuinely savvy media team who knew how and when to use what particular medium from standard "old-fashioned" television ads to the newest social media. Neither Brown nor Jealous were able use the media as effectively as Hogan. When Brown did run ads that emphasized his personal story, he made much better headway than when Jealous tried the same thing. Even at that, Hogan did it better.

The 2014 and 2018 Maryland gubernatorial elections were interesting. In both elections, Democrats were not rejecting their party, but rather its candidates for governor. While many Democrats voted for Hogan (or for no one) as governor, they were still supporting other Democrats. In 2014 and 2018, all of Maryland's congressional Democratic candidates easily won reelection. In 2018 the Democrats added seven seats to their already veto-proof majority in the House of Delegates. And voters in Anne Arundel and Howard Counties flipped their county executives from red to blue (and the Howard County victor was African American).

This chapter began by wondering why two African American Democrats failed to win governors races in an overwhelmingly Democratic state. While it would be easy to chalk it all up to racism, I don't think that was anything more than a very minor factor. Both Anthony Brown and Ben Jealous lost to the same Republican. Larry Hogan really knew Maryland voters and what was important to them. He crafted incredibly smart campaigns around those ideas and beat the odds.

At the time this chapter was written, there were already nine people who had declared their candidacy for the Democratic nomination for governor in the 2022 election. Of those seven, four are candidates of color. Three are African Americans and the fourth is the son of immigrants from India. There is no reason why any of those four should be unsuccessful if nominated—as long as they pay attention to the lessons provided by the unsuccessful 2014 and 2018 campaigns.

NOTES

1. Jeff Barker, "Maverick Michael Steele Says He's Seriously Considering a Run for Maryland Governor and Won't Leave the Republican Party: 'It's My House, Too.'" *Baltimore Sun*, April 22, 2021. https://www.baltimoresun.com/politics/bs-md -pol-michael-steele-20210422-h7ruh6cevrbexcubebwav4zm44-story.html

2. Maryland State Board of Elections, "Elections," https://elections.maryland .gov/elections/2022/index.html

3. United States Census Bureau. https://census.gov

4. Kevin Robillard, "How Larry Hogan Won in Maryland," *Politico*, November 7, 2014. https://www.politico.com/story/2014/11/larry-hogan-maryland-governor-112681

5. Erin Cox and Michael Dresser, "Hogan Defeats Brown," *Baltimore Sun*, November 5, 2014. https://www.baltimoresun.com/maryland/anne-arundel/bs-md -governor-20141105story.html

6. Kevin Robillard, "How Larry Hogan Won in Maryland," *Politico*, November 7, 2014. https://www.politico.com/story/2014/11/larry-hogan-maryland-governor -112681

7. Maryland State Board of Elections, "Elections," https://elections.maryland .gov/elections/2022/index.html

8. Erin Cox, "Brown on a Deliberate March Toward Goal Years in the Making," *Baltimore Sun*, October 18, 2014. https://www.baltimoresun.com/politics/bs-md -brown-profile-20141018story.html

9. Maryland State Board of Elections, "Elections," https://elections.maryland .gov/elections/2022/index.html

10. Erin Cox, "Brown on a Deliberate March Toward Goal Years in the Making," *Baltimore Sun*, October 18, 2014. https://www.baltimoresun.com/politics/bs-md -brown-profile-20141018story.html

11. Kevin Robillard, "How Larry Hogan Won in Maryland," *Politico*, November 7, 2014. https://www.politico.com/story/2014/11/larry-hogan-maryland-governor -112681

12. Erin Cox and Michael Dresser, "Hogan Defeats Brown," *Baltimore Sun*, November 5, 2014. https://www.baltimoresun.com/maryland/anne-arundel/bs-md -governor-20141105story.html

13. Lejla Sarcevic and Max Bennett, "How Larry Hogan Won In a Blue State," *Capital News Service*, November 6, 2014. https://cnsmaryland.org/2014/11/06/how -republican-larryhogan-won-in-blue-maryland/

14. Harry Enten, "Flying Blind Toward Hogan's Upset Win in Maryland," *Five Thirty Eight*, November 7, 2014. https://fivethirtyeight.com/features/governor-mary-land-surprisebrown-hogan/

15. Barry Rascovar, "Rascovar: Why Brown Could Lose Race for Governor," *Maryland Reporter*, October 5, 2015. https://marylandreporter.com/2014/10/05/ rascovar-why-browncould-lose-race-for-maryland-governor/

16. Lejla Sarcevic and Max Bennett, "How Larry Hogan Won In a Blue State," *Capital News Service*, November 6, 2014. https://cnsmaryland.org/2014/11/06/how -republican-larryhogan-won-in-blue-maryland/

17. Alec MacGillis, "Democrats Didn't Lose Governor's Races Because of a GOP Wave. They Lost Because of Bad Candidates," *New Republic,* November 5, 2014. https://newrepublic.com/article/120152/anthony-brown-didnt-lose-maryland-because -republicanwave

18. Erin Cox and Michael Dresser, "Hogan Defeats Brown," *Baltimore Sun,* November 5, 2014. https://www.baltimoresun.com/maryland/anne-arundel/bs-md -governor-20141105story.html

19. Lejla Sarcevic and Max Bennett, "How Larry Hogan Won In a Blue State," *Capital News Service,* November 6, 2014. https://cnsmaryland.org/2014/11/06/how -republican-larryhogan-won-in-blue-maryland/

20. Carissa DiMargo, "Maryland Governor: Larry Hogan Defeats Anthony Brown," *NBC Washington,* November 5, 2014. https://www.nbcwashington.com /news/local/marylandgovernor-republican-larry-hogan-democrat-anthony-brown /67640/

21. Lejla Sarcevic and Max Bennett, "How Larry Hogan Won In a Blue State," *Capital News Service,* November 6, 2014. https://cnsmaryland.org/2014/11/06/how -republican-larryhogan-won-in-blue-maryland/

22. Michael Dresser, "Ads in Governor's Race Are Narrow, Negative," *Baltimore Sun,* September 25, 2014. https://www.baltimoresun.com/maryland/bs-md-governor -ads-20140924story.html

23. Kevin Robillard, "How Larry Hogan Won in Maryland," *Politico,* November 7, 2014.https://www.politico.com/story/2014/11/larry-hogan-maryland-governor -112681

24. Maryland State Board of Elections, "Elections," https://elections.maryland .gov/elections/2022/index.html

25. Rachel Cohen, "Why Ben Jealous Lost the Maryland Governor's Race," *The Seventh State,* November 7, 2018. https://theintercept.com/2018/11/07/maryland -governor-election-benjealous-larry-hogan/

26. Martin Austermuhle, "Ben Jealous Has Big Ideas for Maryland. But, First He Needs People to Know He's Running for Governor," *WAMU,* November 1, 2018. https://wamu.org/story/18/11/01/ben-jealous-has-big-ideas-for-maryland-but-first -he- needspeople-to-know-hes-running-for-governor/

27. Rachel Cohen, "Why Ben Jealous Lost the Maryland Governor's Race," *The Seventh State,* November 7, 2018. https://theintercept.com/2018/11/07/maryland -governor-election-benjealous-larry-hogan/

28. Ryan Miner, "Ben Jealous Still Wants to Be Governor – But Can He Clean Up His 2018 Mess?" *A Miner Detail,* September 8, 2019. https://aminerdetail.com/ben -jealous-still-wants-tobe-governor-but-can-he-clean-up-his-2018-mess/

29. Rachel Cohen, "Why Ben Jealous Lost the Maryland Governor's Race," *The Seventh State,* November 7, 2018. https://theintercept.com/2018/11/07/maryland -governor-election-benjealous-larry-hogan/

30. Ibid.

31. Doug Donovan and Michael Dresser, "No Coattails: Maryland Voters Backed Republican Gov. Hogan, But Also Showed Their Disdain for Trump," *Baltimore Sun,*

November 7, 2018. https://www.baltimoresun.com/politics/bs-md-hogan-coattails-20181107-story.html

32. Ryan Miner, "Ben Jealous Still Wants to Be Governor – But Can He Clean Up His 2018 Mess?" *A Miner Detail*, September 8, 2019. https://aminerdetail.com/ben-jealous-still-wants-tobe-governor-but-can-he-clean-up-his-2018-mess/

33. Doug Donovan and Michael Dresser, "No Coattails: Maryland Voters Backed Republican Gov. Hogan, But Also Showed Their Disdain for Trump," *Baltimore Sun*, November 7, 2018. https://www.baltimoresun.com/politics/bs-md-hogan-coattails-20181107story.html

34. Rachel Cohen, "Why Ben Jealous Lost the Maryland Governor's Race," *The Seventh State*, November 7, 2018. https://theintercept.com/2018/11/07/maryland-governor-election-benjealous-larry-hogan/

35. Ibid.

36. Ryan Miner, "Ben Jealous Still Wants to Be Governor – But Can He Clean Up His 2018 Mess?" *A Miner Detail*, September 8, 2019. https://aminerdetail.com/ben-jealous-still-wants-tobe-governor-but-can-he-clean-up-his-2018-mess/

37. Rachel Cohen, "Why Ben Jealous Lost the Maryland Governor's Race," *The Seventh State*, November 7, 2018. https://theintercept.com/2018/11/07/maryland-governor-election-benjealous-larry-hogan/

38. David Zurawik, "Five Unconventional Takeaways on Media Campaigns from Hogan's Big Win," *Baltimore Sun*, November 6, 2018. https://www.baltimoresun.com/opinion/columnists/zurawik/bs-fe-zontv-larry-hogan-mediacampaign-20181106-story.html

39. Rachel Cohen, "Why Ben Jealous Lost the Maryland Governor's Race," *The Seventh State*, November 7, 2018. https://theintercept.com/2018/11/07/maryland-governor-election-benjealous-larry-hogan/

40. Martin Austermuhle, "Ben Jealous Has Big Ideas for Maryland. But, First He Needs People to Know He's Running for Governor," *WAMU*, November 1, 2018. https://wamu.org/story/18/11/01/ben-jealous-has-big-ideas-for-maryland-but-first-he-needspeople-to-know-hes-running-for-governor/

41. Erin Cox, "Ad Watch: Maryland Gov. Larry Hogan Inflates Tax Relief Claims in Campaign Commercial," *Baltimore Sun*, May 30, 2018. https://www.baltimoresun.com/politics/bs-md-hogan-ad-watch-20180529-story.html

42. David Zurawik, "Five Unconventional Takeaways on Media Campaigns from Hogan's Big Win," *Baltimore Sun*, November 6, 2018. https://www.baltimoresun.com/opinion/columnists/zurawik/bs-fe-zontv-larry-hogan-mediacampaign-20181106-story.html

43. Ibid.

44. Rachel Cohen, "Why Ben Jealous Lost the Maryland Governor's Race," *The Seventh State*, November 7, 2018. https://theintercept.com/2018/11/07/maryland-governor-election-benjealous-larry-hogan/

45. Seth Grimes, "Nancy Floreen Split the Republican Vote, Not the Democratic!, And Three Other 2018 Lessons Learned," *The Seventh State*, November 7, 2018. http://www.theseventhstate.com/?paged=50&ref=xranks

Chapter 7

Marylanders and Congress

Different Leaders for Different Tasks

In another chapter, we talk about leadership in the context of assessing who might—or might not—be considered for a presidential nomination. There, we note that the multidisciplinary studies of leadership have developed a long list of theories or approaches. Finding ones that fit the question of who might be president was relatively easy.[1] One quickly rejects early theories as being too based on rather simplistic work on personality and often quite sexist and turns to those that presume that a leader's most important role is transforming those led. How a leader does so depends on characteristics that are simultaneously focused on the leader and the process the leader initiates. For example, motivating followers to embrace high expectations entails both the communication the leader engages in and what the audience feels and does in response to it. The transformative approach to studying leadership communication is, then, to a large extent, future-focused. We select presidential nominees based on what we imagine will happen under their leadership.

Leadership in Congress is more complex, for not only is there not really the kind of transformative leader we expect a president to be but there are several types of leaders with different profiles. The most obvious leader would be the one with the title, "Majority Leader" or "Minority Leader" with "Speaker of the House" fitting into that category in recent decades. Party "whips" fit into this category too. The focus for this group is split between party and legislation. Once, all of these offices were not especially powerful or prestigious. In the 1950s, for example, being Majority or Minority Whip in either house was an inconsequential job no one wanted, and being Leader was not that much better. These roles would change with time, and, if we had time to trace the roles, we could point to the men who changed them. Sam Rayburn, for example, significantly altered the role of Speaker of the House, transforming it from ceremonial and neutral to quite partisan; another Texan, Lyndon Johnson, significantly altered the role of Majority Leader, giving it its present-day power to regulate legislation going to the floor for debate and a vote.[2] So, when we speak here of these offices, we are speaking about the present-day versions occupied by the likes of Harry Reid and Mitch McConnell in the Senate, and Paul Ryan and Nancy Pelosi in the House. Post-Johnson and post-Rayburn, the roles were enacted in various ways with some leaders not as controlling as LBJ and "Mr. Sam," but the roles were not what they were earlier in the twentieth century.[3]

Then, there are more purely political leaders—for example, those who direct fundraising efforts or orchestrate reelection efforts. The leaders mentioned before are indeed involved in these matters, but there have been, of late, in both houses, members with these specific party-focused responsibilities. It almost seems as if they are told to put legislative duties aside and focus on what's necessary to increase the party's power in the legislature. This role is a relatively new one, perhaps embraced first by California Congressman Tony Coelho, although, back in Johnson's days in the Senate, the role was played by aide Bobby Baker. Whatever its origin, it exists now in both House and Senate. Furthermore, although originally weak and originally controlled by the party leader, the person now in this purely party position wields power—because he or she wields money—and has a measure of independence in determining who gets it.[4]

Congress is, of course, more about legislation than elections, although some doubt that in recent times during which important legislation has frequently stalled. And there are leaders who craft legislation, a task often involving collaboration with others with somewhat different views on the matter at hand. These leaders are frequently behind the scenes, known to fellow legislators but not the general public. Then, more visible are the interrogators whose leadership (of a different sort) is evident during high-profile as well as low-profile hearings. They make the news, asking the difficult question or making the compelling statement.

These four categories—party leaders, pure party leaders, legislative leaders, and investigative leaders—are not necessarily distinct: a given member of Congress could fit into more than one. However, they are worth considering separately for they require different leadership skills. For example, a party leader must have the ability to both muster votes and rally members behind a cause. The first may require strong interpersonal communication skills; the latter, more public performance ones. A pure party leader must have the ability to persuade, often one-on-one, coupled with strong organizational skills. A legislative leader must have the ability to assess staff research and carefully craft legislation as well as the conflict communication skills that foster compromise or collaboration. And an investigative leader needs to know how to frame and sequence queries—and what to make out of answers in offering her or his remarks.

Whereas a prospective president is best assessed as a transformational leader who will, based on who he/she is, communicate about and inspire what's done in the future, these Congressional leaders, regardless of type, are more focused on present action—amassing votes now, getting money now, crafting a bill that will pass now, revealing the truth now. This action focus shifts one's attention from leadership skills dealing with transforming to those that get things done in the here-and-now. Those skills will vary from type to type.

A number of leadership theories illuminate these action-focused roles. Some fit one role more than another, but one need not necessarily choose among them. They are lenses that help one see the leadership. The different lenses let one see different things just as different lenses change what's highlighted when one looks through a microscope or a telescope. We'll consider three here as especially relevant to the different actions a member of the Congress takes.

Probably the most traditional approach to leadership is the trait one. Beginning in 1948 with the work of Stogdill, this approach derives from case studies and then lists the traits associated with those who are proven leaders.[5] This approach is dismissed by many because the traits were ill-defined and because the traits often seemed to have a masculinist bias, but the approach did not cease developing. Zaccaro, Kemp, and Bader in 2004 offered an empirically derived list that seems applicable to much of the work in Congress—and without the limitations of earlier ones. According to their work, a leader possesses a good measure of eleven qualities: (1) cognitive ability, (2) extraversion, (3) conscientiousness, (4) emotional stability, (5) openness, (6) agreeableness, (7) motivation, (8) social intelligence, (9) self-monitoring, (10) emotional intelligence, and (11) problem-solving ability.[6] Many of these traits made earlier lists. What was strikingly new in the Zaccaro, Kemp, and Bader formulation were social intelligence and emotional intelligence. They are, basically, the ability to understand how emotions function (emotional intelligence) and how they function in a group (social intelligence). Yes, a leader should be smart, outgoing, pleasant, motivated, conscientious, and self-aware, but these are traits defining the leader. Social intelligence and emotional intelligence go beyond the leader and consider how he or she understands what is happening in a group being led. A political leader, we would suggest, would not get far without this understanding.

Closely related to trait theory is skills theory. Mumford, Zaccaro, Harding, Jacobs, and Fleischman (and, also, Connelly and Marks) developed the fullest skills theory in 2000.[7] It lists individual attributes (general cognitive ability, crystallized—i.e., learned through experience-cognitive ability, motivation, personality) and competencies (problem-solving skills, social judgment skills). The difference between the trait approach and the skills approach is that the latter would be more likely observed if one were studying leadership in process. We might then step back from a long observation of a leader such as South Africa's Nelson Mandela and tick off the traits he has, but, if we were to study how another leader, let's say Canada's Pierre Elliot Trudeau, and how he dealt with Quebec separatism, we would want to study the full dynamics of the discussions he conducted and note his attributes and his competencies. We would want to note skills, not traits. The trait approach offers a photograph; the skills approach, a videograph. But many of the same "things" will get noted in either.

Another approach, later to develop, is George's authentic leadership.[8] In George's model, the authentic leader possesses passion, compassion, consistency due to self-discipline, connectedness rooted in good relationships, and behaviors rooted in values. Another authentic leadership model from the same year, 2003, was developed by Luthans and Avolio. In George's model, there are five "secrets" (that's the term he uses); in Luthans and Avolio's there's a developmental movement.[9] Based on positive psychological capacities and sound moral reasoning, a leader lives his or her life becoming self-aware, acquiring an internalized moral perspective, exhibiting balanced processing of information, and being transparent when it comes to relationships. Put these four together and, voila, an authentic leader.

We will consider seven Marylanders who might be consider party leaders, pure party leaders, legislators, and investigators with these different leadership theory perspectives in view. The value of these perspectives is that they root an analysis of political behavior in not a pundit's view of the men and women but in what a sustained program of interdisciplinary research tells us about what leaders do. Three of the Marylanders take us back in time: former senator Paul Sarbanes, former Congresswoman Constance (or "Connie") Morella, and former Congressman Elijah Cummings. Three are in the Congress now: Senator Chris Van Hollen, Congressman Jamie Raskin, and Congressman Steny Hoyer. The seventh will strike some as unusual: Maryland-born, Maryland-bred Congresswoman Nancy Pelosi.

PAUL SARBANES, LEGISLATOR

Sarbanes rose to the U.S. Senate after serving six years as representative for Maryland's 4th and 3rd Congressional Districts.[10] His office had a reputation for excellent constituent service; he had a reputation for intelligence. He intended to put that intelligence to work, not so much on partisan matters as on problems besetting the nation. He was especially interested in the financial dimension of governmental affairs, and they are neither the easiest to understand nor the most likely to attract newspaper headlines. So, Sarbanes led important efforts that few outside of government were conversant with. These dealt with both banking and military appropriations. Sarbanes's name is often heard as coauthor of the important but obscure *Sarbanes-Oxley Act of 2002.*[11] It regulates financial record-keeping broadly, reflecting the senator's interest in financial matters whether they involve the Congress or the banks or businesses.

He was known for a quiet, deliberative style.[12] This allowed him to legislate but did not win him either party positions nor committee chairmanships. Long-serving and well-respected, he did the work of a U.S. senator but rarely won the glory.[13]

Much of what Sarbanes did, he did behind closed doors, so we cannot look at his leadership as a process and point to skills he had, although it was clear he had many. But we can step back from his career and note how he possessed almost all of the leadership traits Zaccaro, Kemp, and Bader note. What seems a tad lacking in Sarbanes is extraversion, and that lack perhaps partially explains why he was a quiet legislative success but never a chair of an important committee. He did not adequately stand out.

CONSTANCE MORELLA, LEGISLATOR

Connie Morella represented Maryland 8th District for sixteen years. She was a Republican, but her district was strongly Democratic. She was not alone in being a long-serving Republican representing the 8th: Gilbert Gude had done the same between 1967 and 1977, and, long before, with the district drawn differently, Charles Matthias (later U.S. senator) had done so. The 8th, although "blue," had no trouble electing a Republican if the Republican was moderate, was interested in compromising on legislation for the good of the district or state, and was excellent when it came to constituency service. Mathias, Gude, and Morella all fit this description. In Morella's case, she fit the description so fully that the Republican Party tried repeatedly to "primary" her out of office. She was not, in the judgment of some, a "true" Republican. She was a RINO ("Republican in Name Only") before the term was coined. At a time when Reagan's conservatism ruled the party, Morella would often vote against Reagan-Bush proposals because either they were opposed by too many of her constituents or they were, in her judgment, not good for the district or state. She voted against Clinton proposals as well, but did not support his impeachment.

Willing to work with the other party, Morella played a role in crafting legislation that Republicans and Democrats might agree on. The legislation usually did not draw national headlines, but it did draw attention in the 8th. Many in her district were federal government workers: the 8th was a fairly affluent bedroom suburb of Washington, D.C.; and federal workers had needs. Her voting record also coincided with the liberal attitude on many social matters that her constituents possessed. She was, for example, supportive of women's reproductive rights, gay rights, the legalization of medical marijuana, and environmental protection. Thus, she was not at all aligned with the conservative drift of her party.

Like Sarbanes, she was primarily a legislator, although she was also a forceful advocate on a range of what were then identified as women's issues.[14] But unlike Sarbanes, she was not always quiet. She, for example, was quite "loud" (i.e., noticed) when she refused to vote for Republican colleague Newt Gingrich as Speaker of the House or for renaming Washington National Airport after Reagan.[15] She did, throughout her rather non-partisan stint, seem to have strong psychological and moral capacities that she had used to become very self-aware, very moral in her judgments, very balanced when processing ideas, and very transparent when it came to relationships. She knew who she was, people knew where they stood with her, and her reasoning was careful and principled. She would then be an authentic leader.

Unfortunately, she was not appreciated as such by her own party. Democrats perhaps appreciated Morella more than Republicans, but they could not afford to appreciate her too much, for they wanted her district to be (in later day terms) blue, not red.

Arguably, she was gerrymandered out of office.[16] Not disliking her but disliking the fact that she added to the Republican count in the House, moderate voters were moved out of the 8th and liberal voters were moved in. The shift allowed Chris Van Hollen to defeat her in 2002.

ELIJAH CUMMINGS, INTERROGATOR

Elijah Cummings joined the House when Kweisi Mfume decided to head-up the NAACP and gave up his 7th District seat. Quickly, Cummings rose within the House Black Caucus. In speaking out for African Americans, he was also speaking up for his constituents. The 7th District, largely comprising Baltimore City, was heavily African American and, in many parts, impoverished.

In the House, Cummings quickly rose to the position of leader of the Black Caucus. He thus frequently represented the interests of an African American constituency that extended beyond the city of Baltimore. Cummings, however, was not just an advocate for African American causes. He positioned himself as a champion of the truth and had little tolerance for any posturing that got in the way of the truth. Thus, as minority leader of the Oversight and Government Reform Committee investigating steroid use in sports, he did not let baseball slugger Mark McGwire off the hook when he tried to dodge questions about his use of performance-enhancing drugs.[17] And, as minority leader on a committee than endlessly investigated Benghazi, he did not let Republicans use hearings to discredit either Barack Obama or Hillary Clinton by distorting the facts of the case. His assertiveness and skill as an interrogator, in fact, earned him the Democrats' leadership role on the House Oversight and Government Reform Committee. There, Democrats expected Darrell Issa to stir up partisan-inspired trouble; they pushed aside other Democrats arguably more in line for the committee leadership position to set Cummings's assertiveness and skill against Issa's.[18]

Cummings was given these positions because he had the "stuff" necessary to get the job done.[19] If one were to look again at Zaccaro, Kemp, and Bader's list of leadership traits, Cummings possessed them. In particular, he had the motivation and extraversion to take on witnesses—and colleagues, but he also had the emotional and social intelligence to pull it off plus self-monitoring preventing him from pushing too hard and an agreeableness that soften others' anger.

CHRIS VAN HOLLEN, PURE PARTY LEADER

Like Connie Morella, Chris Van Hollen represented Maryland's 8th District. In Morella's days, the 8th was pretty much synonymous with Montgomery County, but, by Van Hollen's time, a small piece of Prince George's—quite liberal-leaning—had been added in while some more moderate areas in Montgomery were sent elsewhere. The shifts were just enough to change the district from heavily Democratic but willing to vote for a moderate Republican such as Morella to more heavily Democratic and unwilling to vote for any Republican.[20]

Van Hollen served his liberal district well, but he also quickly became vocal on issues one would term more national and international. This involvement attracted the attention of the party leadership in the House, and, according to many, he was soon fast-tracking his way to a leadership post. In fact, with no post to elect him to, Nancy Pelosi created a new one, Assistant to the Speaker, just for Van Hollen to occupy.[21]

But then he decided to abandon the House of Representatives, where, one day, he might have been Speaker, to run for the U.S. Senate upon Barbara Mikulski's retirement. He was easily elected. And, so, a rising star in the House became a rising star in the Senate. That he was such had more to do with political work than legislative work, however. In the House, he was chair of Democratic Congressional Campaign Committee, and, in the Senate, he was chair (very quickly) of the Democratic Senatorial Campaign Committee. DCCC to DSCC. He was not just "in charge" of getting Democrats elected; he pushed forward legislation to help federal employees and promote clean energy, and he spoke often on Afghanistan, Iraq, and Pakistan, where he had been born. But it is with his political party work that Van Hollen, at least for the moment, is most associated.

The partisan role he has assumed is odd given his background before running for the House. He began his political career as a defense and foreign policy aide to U.S. senator Charles Mathias, a moderate Republican. From Mathias's office, he moved to Maryland Governor William Donald Schaefer's, where he served as advisor on federal government relations; from there, to the Maryland House of Delegates and the State Senate.[22] Along the way, his advocacy broadened: he authored legislation on taxes, oil drilling in the Bay, and gun safety; he tilted more and more to the left while still winning praise from Republicans and from the media for his ability to get things done. He brought that "get things done" attitude to his work leading the DCCC and DSCC. One should therefore conclude that, although we think of Van Hollen in 2021 in political party terms, he has talents that could easily fit roles more involving crafting or pushing forward legislation.

Van Hollen is a skilled leader. He is bright with global experiences that made him seem even more so. He was motivated to help Democrats win elections, and he possessed, by all counts, a personality that oozed encouragement. He could solve problems; he could read a room; and he knew—rather quickly for he was a very quick study—what he needed to know to get the party's business done.

JAMIE RASKIN, LEGISLATOR

Van Hollen was succeeded in the Maryland 8th by Jamie Raskin, a law professor at American University and decade-long Maryland State senator. Raskin ran for the Democratic nomination in a crowded field in which he was arguably the most liberal.[23] Born in Washington, D.C., to a journalist mother and White House staff member father, Raskin attended Harvard for both his undergraduate education and his legal education, becoming a Constitutional law scholar under the tutelage of Lawrence Tribe. A liberal bent was obvious in his advocacy for the legalization of same-sex marriage and marijuana. He strongly denounced discrimination based on religion (including atheism), and he strongly called for election reform (including replacing the electoral college with a national popular vote).

Raskin sees himself as offering a moral perspective, not just a legal one.[24]Perhaps that is why his House Democratic colleagues chose him to write and present to the Senate the second set of impeachment articles against President Donald Trump. Raskin was a moral voice, not a purely partisan one.

Easily reelected in 2018 (68.2 percent) and 2020 (also 86.2 percent), Raskin is on track as a multifaceted leader. He is an expert on the Constitution; he is a self-proclaimed advocate of moral government, and he is a legislator members of both parties respect. Like Van Hollen, Raskin has skills that qualify him for a number of different roles that might come his way.

One, then, might look at Raskin from a skills perspective, but the better lens is that of authentic leadership. One sees in his behavior passion and compassion, self-discipline and connectedness, and behavior rooted in strongly held moral values. Not long before Raskin served as the House's chief prosecutor in Trump's second impeachment trial, his son Tom committed suicide. When, on January 6, 2021, a mob stormed the U.S. Capitol, Raskin was hosting his young daughter at work. One cannot read Raskin's comments on his son's death or hear Raskin's comments on his daughter's fear without detecting how deeply compassionate the man is.[25] The other traits of the authentic leader as sketched by George are present too, especially the strong moral values that undergird his conduct as a member of Congress. He may be a Constitutional law scholar, but his reasoning is as much moral as legal.

STENY HOYER, PARTY LEADER

We have mentioned several Marylanders who made their way through the House of Representatives over the years. Throughout most of the story, representing Maryland's 5th was Steny Hoyer. A New Yorker, Hoyer moved to Maryland (a fairly rural spot in Prince George's) where he attended the state university and, then, its law school. After law school, he became a legislative aide to Maryland senator Daniel Brewster. He served on Capitol Hill for a brief period, and, then, after a fourteen-year stint as legislator in Annapolis, he ran for Congress in 1981 in one of Maryland's most interesting districts insofar as it mixes suburban and rural, Washington, D.C. exurbs and Maryland forests, farms, and fisheries, Democrats and Republicans. And many of the Democrats were "southern Democrats," who voted for George Wallace in the 1964 and 1972 Democratic presidential primaries. The district was not the easiest one for a Democrat with decent liberal credentials to win or to hold.

That difficulty might explain why, as soon as people refer to him as a liberal, they back off the claim. He is, yes, but a cautious liberal, perhaps better labeled a moderate. Being such, he became the perfect person to use political acumen and one-on-one communication to hold the House Democratic caucus together. He could work with "Blue Dogs"; he could work with the much more liberal New York delegation. His positioning was sufficient to win Hoyer reelection fourteen times, the closest race being in 1992 when he beat a young Republican named Larry Hogan, Jr., with 53 percent of the district vote.

Hoyer has been consistently pro-choice and anti-gun; he has supported affirmative action and LGBTQ rights. And on February 2021, he strongly denounced Republican Congresswoman Marjorie Taylor Greene on the House floor.[26] A strikingly liberal record, but his independence is evident when he chose to disagree with Obama on tax cuts and agree with Trump on recognizing Jerusalem as Israel's capital.[27] One can point to Hoyer votes and Hoyer speeches but not much legislation, for his work has been heavily party work. Here, he butt heads with Nancy Pelosi, for they both wanted the top job among House Democrats. The rivalry came to a head when Pelosi, the Speaker, lost that position in 2010 when Democrats lost control of the House. She wanted then to be Leader, the position Hoyer held when she was Speaker and for which she had not even supported Hoyer (preferring Pennsylvania's John Murtha).[28] They worked things out, creating a Democratic leadership team with similar skill sets, although, perhaps, different styles.[29] Both could raise a prodigious sum of money for the party; both could steer favored legislation through the House; both could keep Democrats in-line while granting them a measure of independence when deemed appropriate.[30]

Hoyer is a skilled leader. He has the basic smarts, and he has certainly crystallized them through years of political experience. He is strongly motivated, and those who know him well attest to how cordial he is. He can work through problems well, he can understand what's happening emotionally well, and he knows what he needs to know about legislation as well as about specific legislators.

NANCY PELOSI, PARTY LEADER
AND PURE PARTY LEADER

Some may not know Nancy Pelosi's biography. She is a Baltimore girl. More than that, she is the youngest child—and only daughter—of Baltimore's legendary mayor Thomas J. D'Alessandro (known as "Big Tommy"). She learned politics by observing—and occasionally helping out—her father. But her mother wanted Nancy to get out of Baltimore's "Little Italy" and acquire some polish. So, she was sent to a private Catholic girls school in Baltimore—just a few years behind Barbara Mikulski—and then to a small private Catholic girls college in Washington, D.C. Trinity was a good school, but it was a "finishing school" as well as an academic one.[31]

After graduation, she stayed in Washington. She got a job working—largely as a receptionist—in Maryland senator Daniel Brewster's office. And, yes, she and Steny Hoyer were there at the same time. Pelosi married, moved to California, and raised a family. She increasingly did fundraising work for the Democratic Party (taking advantage of her wealthy husband Paul's connections) but did not enter politics herself until her youngest daughter was sixteen. With that daughter's permission, she ran for a vacated seat and has held it ever since. A very liberal-leaning district in the heart of San Francisco, it proved to offer the epitome of a "safe seat" to Pelosi.

Pelosi has been written about more than Hoyer, but, in many ways, what one might say of the one could be said of the other when it comes to leadership skills. She is more predictably liberal on issues, but Hoyer is not as much the moderate as many claim. He has done an excellent job packaging himself in Maryland's 5th District so as to seem not that liberal, something increasingly less necessary as the 5th's demographics change. But, looking at voting records, one does not see much of an ideological gap between the Baltimore "girl" and the southern Maryland "boy." They both are accomplished fund-raisers; they both work well with party colleagues, being tough when needed and being easy-going (Hoyer) or charming (Pelosi) when needed.

Pelosi's profile is much the same as Hoyer's. Different styles. Hoyer will slap on the back; Pelosi will offer chocolates. But both are pleasant, although sometimes pleasantly firm. Given their similar leadership profiles, one might wonder why Pelosi is so loathed and Hoyer goes largely unattacked by Republicans. Is the difference that she's a bit more liberal. We doubt that. We suspect it has to do with motivation, a leadership skill according to Mumford, et al. Both were motivated by the same goal—to sit in the Speaker's chair. Such motivation was understandable for a man, but unseemly for a woman. So, the gender bias against Pelosi is not because she is in the Congress or even prominent in the Congress; rather, it is because she sought the leadership position her skills well-qualified her for.

Pelosi has, of course, become the "poster child" in many anti-Democratic campaigns. Democratic candidates all over the country have been depicted with her or, worse, morphed into her. The result is a great deal of Pelosi-loathing, but, when Republicans in the House are asked candidly about her, they express admiration. Some even say they like her. These Republicans may use anti-Pelosi rhetoric back home when seeking reelection, but, in Washington, they seem to recognize the leadership skills sets she and Hoyer share.

CONCLUSION

A fundamental point made repeatedly in this chapter is that there are different types of leaders in the Congress. When one examines leadership communication textbooks, one gets the impression that there is a single correct theory and that researchers and theorists have been working toward it for decades. Thus, some of the earlier approaches such as trait theory and skills theory are treated as outdated with the stress being on theories that put group over individual and social justice as, of course, the goal. Dugan's *Leadership Theory* (2017), for example, explicitly uses critical social theory to evaluate a succession of approaches.[32] That emphasis on critical social theory, often associated with Loyola University in Chicago, has pushed many in communication who talk about leadership to treat the earlier chapters in a typical textbook as background, as inaccurate approaches that emerged before there was the needed critical "turn."

What the communication realities of the Congress show, however, is that the different types of leaders exhibit different modes of leadership. And some of the earlier approaches better fit these realities than the newer ones. Once one grasps that trait theory and skills theory (early in any textbook) are just as useful as authentic leadership theory (about two-thirds into the book), one then notices that the earlier theories really have not disappeared. As noted earlier in this chapter, major trait theories appeared from Stogdill in 1948 to Zaccaro, Kemp, and Bader in 2004.[33] There is in the communication literature often a less than subtle attempt to associate the earlier theories that linger with academic areas, such as management studies, that are stereotyped as conservative and more than a tad masculinist, but Stephen Zaccaro is a widely published, highly regarded professor of psychology, not a management "guy." What the communication realities of Congress show us then is that we need to use the different approaches as lenses, applying the ones that make sense in the different communication and leadership situations. Elijah Cummings's leadership as committee chair or committee minority leader is exhibited very differently from Steny Hoyer's leadership in fundraising or Chris Van Hollen's in maximizing Democratic chances to gain House or Senate seats.

Maryland has produced its fair share of Congressional leaders, and it has also produced women and men who had the leadership communication skills but did not get to use them fully (Morella) or who have the skills and are not yet centerstage (Raskin). The same might be said for most states. So, the argument in this chapter is not that Maryland has been productive or unproductive. Rather, the argument has to do with what we conceive of as leadership and leadership communication. We can, then, point to the political figures highlighted in this chapter—or others—as exemplifying leadership. In doing so, we recognize that leadership is not one thing, but different qualities, aptitudes, and skills arrayed in different configurations for the very different tasks facing those elected to the U. S. Congress.

NOTES

1. John P. Dugan, *Leadership Theory: Cultivating Critical Perspectives* (San Francisco: Jossey-Bass, 2017); Peter Northouse, *Leadership: Theory and Practice,* 7th ed. (Los Angeles: Sage, 2016).

2. Robert A. Caro, *The Years of Lyndon Johnson: Master of the Senate* (New York: Vintage Books, 2002).

3. Adam Jentleson, *Kill Switch: The Rise of the Modern Senate and the Crippling of American Democracy* (New York: Liveright Publishing, 2021).

4. Jettleson, pp. 170–2.

5. R. M. Stogdill, "Personal Factors Associated with Leadership: A Survey of the Literature," *Journal of Psychology* 25.1 (1948): 35–71; R. R. Stogdill, *Handbook of Leadership: A Survey of Theory and Research* (New York: Free Press, 1974).

6. S. J. Zaccaro, "Organizational Leadership and Social Intelligence," in *Multiple Intelligence and Leadership,* edited by R. Riggio, 29–54 (Mahwah, NJ: Lawrence Erlbaum, 2002); S. J. Zaccaro, "Trait-based Perspectives of Leadership," *American Psychologist* 62.1 (2007): 6–16; S. J. Zaccaro, C. Kemp, and P. Bader, "Leader Traits and Attributes," in *The Nature of Leadership,* edited by J. Antonakis, A. T. Cianciolo, and R. J. Sternberg (Thousand Oaks, CA: Sage, 2004).

7. M. D. Mumford, S. J. Zaccaro, M. S. Connelly, and M. A. Marks, "Leadership Skills: Conclusions and Future Directions," *Leadership Quarterly* 11.1 (2000): 155–70; M. D. Mumford, S. J. Zaccaro, F. D. Harding, T. O. Jacobs, and E. A. Fleischman, "Leadership Skills for a Changing World: Solving Complex Social Problems," *Leadership Quarterly* 11.1 (2000): 11–35.

8. B. George, *Authentic Leadership: Rediscovering the Secrets to Creating Lasting Value* (San Francisco: Jossey-Bass, 2003); B. George and P. Sims, *True North: Discover Your Authentic Leadership* (San Francisco: Jossey-Bass, 2007).

9. F. Luthans and B. J. Avolio, "Authentic Leadership Development," in *Positive Organizational Scholarship,* edited by K. S. Cameron, J. E. Dutton, and R. E. Quinn (San Francisco: Berrett-Koehler, 2003).

10. Sarbanes did not move; rather, district boundaries changed.

11. Greg Farrell, "The Men Behind the Sarbanes-Oxley Act," *U.S.A Today,* July 30, 2007, http://usatoday30.usatoday.com/manuf/companies/regulation/2007-07-30 -sarbanes-oxley-men_N.htm

12. Charles Babbington, "Cerebral Sarbanes Aloof into Limelight," *Washington Post,* March 12, 2005.

13. David Kirkpatrick, "Senator Sarbanes, Maryland Democrat, Will Retire in '06," *New York Times,* March 12, 2005, https://www.nytimes.com/2005/03/12/poli-tics/12sarbanes.html

14. Morella was inducted into the Maryland Women's Hall of Fame in 2007. The program for the ceremony cites the many ways she advocated for women while in Congress.

15. Mike Householder, "Morella Votes Present on Speaker Matter, Avoids Taking Position," *CNS Maryland,* https://cnsmaryland.org/1997/01/07/morella-votes-pre sent-on-speaker-matter-avoids-taking-position/; Richard Tapscott, "Congress Votes

to Put Reagan's Name on Airport," *Washington Post*, February 5, 1995, https://www.washingtonpost.com/archive/politics/1998/02/05/congress-votes-to-pur-reagans-name-onairport/096c/dd6-7084-48f8-aee2a-71f575afbb0/

16. Thomas Schaller, *Whistling Past Dixie* (New York: Simon and Schuster, 2008). See p. 292.

17. Clemens Pressed by Congress, Denies Accusations," https://www.starnewsonline.com/article/NC/200802131/News/605128348/WM/. "Pelosi Power Play Doomed Towns on Oversight Committee," https://tpmdc.talkingpoints-memo.com/2010/12/pelosi-power-doomed-towns-on-oversight-committee.php

18. Brian Boutler, "Pelosi Power Play Doomed Towns on Oversight Committee," https://tpmdc.talkingpointsmemo.com/2010/12/pelosi-power-doomed-towns-on-oversight-committee.php

19. David Zurawik, "Maryland Congressman Cummings Redeems Cohen Hearing with His Passionate, Poetic Closing Remarks," *Capital Gazette* (Annapolis, MD), February 27, 2019.

20. David LeDuc, "Maryland Democrats Redistrict Morella's District," *Washington Post.* January 15, 2002; Jo Becker, "Van Hollen Ousts Morella," *Washington Post*, November 6, 2002.

21. Pelosi Names Conferees to FY 2014 Budget Conference," https://web.archive.org/web/20146704622207/http://www.democraticleader.gov/Pelosi-_Statement_on_Conference_to_FY_2014_Budget_Conference

22. "Christopher Van Hollen, Jr. Biography," http://msa.maryland.gov/megafile/msa/speccol/sc3500/sc3520/0/2100/012178/html/12178bo.html

23. Bill Turque, "Jamie Raskin: The Most Liberal Congressional Candidate in a Crowded Field," *Washington Post.* April 5, 2016.

24. "Maryland Representative Jamie Raskin Named Lead Impeachment Manager for Trial against President Donald Trump," *Baltimore Sun,* January 13, 2021, https://www.baltimoresun.com/politics/bs-md-pol-raskin-impeachment-manager-20210113-ftx5yje5ljaadmm3hkxutt4wbu-story.html; David Smith, "'The Moral Centre': How Jamie Raskin Dominated the Stage at Trump's Trial," February 13, 2021, https://www.theguardian.com/us-news/2021/feb/13/jamie-raskin-trump-impeachment-trial

25. Will Weissert, "Representative Jamie Raskin Links Impeachment with Personal Tragedy," https://apnews.com/articles/donald-trump-capitol-siege-politics-impeachments-trumpimpeachment.878fc4csdba85111cecS2f1e8ebd2002772/10/21

26. Tom Bachelor, "Steny Hoyer Viral Speech Denouncing Marjorie Taylor Greene Viewed Two Million Times," *Newsweek*, February 5, 2021, http://www.newsweek.com/steny-hoyer-speech-marjorie-taylor-greene-1567062

27. Matt Laslo, "Hoyer Seeks to Change Obama's Tax Compromise," https://wamu.org/story/10/12/13/hoyer_seeks_to_change_obamas_tax_compromise/

28. "Christopher Van Hollen, Jr. Biography," http://msa.maryland.gov/megafile/msa/speccol/sc3500/sc3520/0/2100/012178/html/12178bo.html

29. https://www.politico.com/story/2011/08/hoyerlet-israel-build-in-e-jerusalem-061145

30. News coverage was extensive. See Catalina Comia, "Democrats Hoyer, Clyburn Fight for Leadership Post," *U.S.A. Today*, November 8, 2010; Patrick O'Connor, "Hoyer, Clyburn: An Impromptu Leadership Fight," *Wall Street Journal*, November 8, 2010; "High Profile Democrats Back Hoyer in Whip Race," http://tpmdc.talkingpointsmemo.com/2010/11/high-profile-democrats-back-hoyer-in-whip-race.php; Paul Kane, "In Race for Whip, Hoyer Gets Liberal Support," *Washington Post*, November 10, 2010; James Rawley, "Pelosi Heads Off Democratic Leadership Fight, Backs Hoyer for No 2 Post," https://www.bloomberg.com/news/2010-11-13/pelosi-holds-off-democratic-leadership-fight-backs-hoyer-for-no-2-post.html

31. See David Sandalow, *Madam Speaker Nancy Pelosi: Life, Times, and Rise* (New York: Modern Times, 2008); Jeff Bzdek, *Woman of the House: The Rise of Nancy Pelosi* (New York: St. Martin's, 2009); and Molly Ball, *Pelosi* (New York: Henry Holt, 2020). A briefer biography is in Theodore F. Sheckels, Nichola D. Guttgold, and Diana B. Carlin, *Gender and the American Presidency: Nine Presidential Women and the Barriers They Faced* (Lanham, MD: Lexington Books, 2012).

32. News coverage was extensive. See Catalina Comia, "Democrats Hoyer, Clyburn Fight for Leadership Post," *U.S.A. Today*, November 8, 2010; Patrick O'Connor, "Hoyer, Clyburn: An Impromptu Leadership Fight," *Wall Street Journal*, November 8, 2010; "High Profile Democrats Back Hoyer in Whip Race," http://tpmdc.talkingpointsmemo.com/2010/11/high-profile-democrats-back-hoyer-in-whip-race.php; Paul Kane, "In Race for Whip, Hoyer Gets Liberal Support," *Washington Post*, November 10, 2010; James Rawley, "Pelosi Heads Off Democratic Leadership Fight, Backs Hoyer for No 2 Post," *Bloomberg*, https://www.bloomberg.com/news/2010-11-13/pelosi-holds-off-democratic-leadership-fight-backs-hoyer-for-no-2-post.html

33. John P. Dugan, *Leadership Theory: Cultivating Critical Perspectives* (San Francisco: Jossey-Bass, 2017).

Chapter 8

Why Has There Been No Marylander in the White House?

The Quests of Albert Ritchie, Spiro Agnew, Martin O'Malley, and John Delaney

Data tell us that U.S. presidents have hailed from some states more than others. We can point to the edge Virginia had in the nation's beginning to explain its numbers; we can point to Ohio's size and centrality to explain its. But what of the nearly thirty states at the other end of the list, the ones that have never produced a president? Is there something that makes political figures from these states less appealing?

One is tempted to list these states and look for patterns. And there are some: the South doesn't fare well; neither do the Southwest and the Northwest and what one might label the prairie or the plains. Size seems to matter too. Yes, Joe Biden lived most of his life in Delaware and is therefore more associated with that state than with his native Pennsylvania, but, even if we give Biden to Delaware, only four presidents hail from the ten smallest states while twenty-three hail from the ten largest.

Some might think that this admittedly amateurish data analysis explains why Maryland has not produced a president, but those people are making a telling mistake: assuming that Maryland is small when it is not. Out of fifty states, it ranks nineteenth—in the top half—in population. But it is presumed to be small. One who has governed there has presumably governed "small"; one who has gone to Congress from there has not worn a big state cloak with its accompanying power. These assumptions are highly questionable: governing Rhode Island may well be more qualifying than governing Texas; representing Montana may be as prestigious as representing Florida. But the Maryland problem is not that it's small but that it's thought to be so.

Arguably the closest Marylander to the presidency was Spiro T. Agnew, Nixon's vice president. Facing federal indictment for tax fraud, Agnew resigned the office, but let's assume he didn't and let's assume Nixon served out his full second term. Would Agnew have been a strong candidate for the 1976 Republican nomination? No. Neither Martin O'Malley in 2016 nor John Delaney in 2020 received much support when seeking the Democratic nomination. Delaney's record was indeed quite limited, but O'Malley had been six years a big city mayor and eight years a governor, but he evoked minimal interest from voters. There were certainly many reasons, but one might well have been that these voters did not consider Maryland "the cradle of presidents." Virginia just next door, yes, but not Maryland.

Another variable that seems to affect the voters' choice is the governing position the possible president served in. Vice Presidents do not fare as well as one might think. Some become president because the sitting president dies in office (e.g., Theodore Roosevelt, Calvin Coolidge, Harry Truman, Lyndon Johnson) or resigns (Gerald Ford). In the twentieth and twenty-first centuries, George H. W. Bush was able to go from vice president to president immediately, but Richard Nixon and Joe Biden had to wait years, and Walter Mondale and Al Gore never made the leap. Governors seem to fare better than Senators, and Senators fare much better than "lowly" members of Congress, who are presumed to be too focused on their districts' issues, not national ones.

This variable should have helped O'Malley a great deal and Agnew a bit. Delaney, on other hand, as a "lowly" Congressman was not able to repeat the feat accomplished by only James Garfield. This variable should also have helped along a fourth Marylander, Albert Ritchie, who served as the state's governor for many, many years.

So, the perception of being small may be a problem for Marylanders aspiring to the presidency, but it may also not be the only one: previous service may be an issue as well. This chapter will consider the political figures who, one way or another, found themselves in the presidential spotlight and try to discern what held them back. The assumption is that the state's perceived size and the men's previous service may have been issues, but there is another, which will necessitate a detour: perceived leadership qualities.

Here and in the chapter on Marylanders and Congress, the multidisciplinary theory and research on leadership must be examined, albeit briefly. John Dugan in *Leadership Theory* (2017) discusses seven categories of leadership. In roughly chronological order, they are (1) person-centered theories, (2) theories of production and effectiveness, (3) group-centered theories, (4) theories of transformation, (5) relationship-centered theories, (6) vanguard theories, and (7) an emerging justice-based model.[1] That these are roughly chronological is important, for earlier theories have, to a large extent, fallen out of vogue and been replaced with newer ones. Peter Northouse in the seventh edition of *Leadership: Theory and Practice* (2016) discusses eleven approaches—again, in roughly chronological order: (1) trait, (2) skills,

(3) behavioral, (4) situational, (5) path-goal, (6) leader-member exchange, (7) transformational, (8) authentic, (9) servant, (10) adaptive, and (11) psychodynamic.[2]

People clearly expect a president of the United States to be a leader, but of what sort? What theory or theories apply? One might make a case for a number, but we will here—and in the chapter on Congress—make a distinction between the role of the president and the many roles played in the Congress. In the Congress, there are party leaders who whip members into line, there are legislative leaders who take bills forward to ultimate approval, there are investigative leaders who ask the tough, important questions, and there are those who seem to be auditioning for a higher leadership position—that is, president or vice president. Whipping, working, interrogating, auditioning— these different activities will map onto different theories or approaches. The auditioning one is most relevant here, for it maps onto the theory/approach that seems to account for what voters want prospective presidents to be. That theory/approach is the one Dugan and Northouse list as transformational.

Several have developed this theory. Bass, in 1985, offered, in *Leadership and Performance Beyond Expectations*, a schema depicting how a transformative leader appeared and how this leader performed.[3] The latter is largely irrelevant in this case, for the public is focused on appearance, not the nuts and bolts of managing or governing. So, a better articulation of the transformational approach might be House's earlier (1976) in a chapter in Hunt and Larson's *Leadership: The Cutting Edge*.[4] There, House points to five traits that leaders he termed "charismatic" possess: they (1) are a strong role model, (2) demonstrate competence, (3) articulate ideological goals, (4) communicate high expectations, and (5) arouse important, high motives. Not all presidents and not all presidential candidates possess all five traits. Furthermore, members of the public may well not agree on whether a person does. Did Donald Trump demonstrate competence? Some would say yes; some would say no. But, our premise here is that these are the five qualities people look for in a president.

So, the state might matter; so might the office/s the prospective president has held. These five leadership qualities, however, might be more decisive. Within a framework provided by these criteria, we will consider four Marylanders who have been mentioned in presidential conversations: Spiro T. Agnew, John Delaney, Martin O'Malley, and Albert Ritchie. The first was the proverbial heartbeat away; the other three sought the office.

One other variable should be mentioned: how the prospect positions himself in the race— or is positioned by media coverage. The trick in understanding this variable is to recognize that the desired position is far from a constant; rather, it depends on the particular political moment. Consider the Republican Party in 1952 and in 1968. In the former year, although there were some opposed to the New Deal policies of Franklin Roosevelt and there were some wanting to retreat from an international role for the nation, most had embraced much of the New Deal and the continuation of American global leadership. Thus, Eisenhower's positioning was far better than the more conservative Taft's. In the latter year, there was growing opposition to both LBJ's spending on social programs and his advocacy of civil rights legislation. Thus, Nixon, who had been a conservative in 1952 and 1956 but more of a moderate in 1960 drifted back toward conservatism. There was also concern about urban rioting and anti-war demonstrations. Thus, he positioned himself as the "law-and-order" candidate. What the GOP was seeking in these two years was quite different. A prospect either has to match-up with the desired positioning or package himself so that he seems to.

SPIRO T. AGNEW

There are a few indications that Spiro T. Agnew thought of himself as Richard Nixon's possible successor. Others did, although their musing had more to do with Agnew's popularity with certain audiences than the man's ability.[5] Yes, in January 1973, Agnew was looking at the second term as vice president with no indication that either he or his boss would have to resign before the term was over. From that perspective, the thought of moving from Number 2 to Number 1 certainly dawned on Agnew, but there are many indications that, if he was thinking in these terms with a gleam in his eye, others were doing so with reservations, for there seemed to be a widespread assumption that Agnew was not presidential material. Someone else would get the GOP nod in 1976, probably a Californian named Reagan who had been lurking in the background since an inspiring 1964 television address on behalf of conservative Barry Goldwater. Agnew, with his own rhetoric and that provided by speechwriters Patrick Buchanan (primarily) and William Safire (a bit), had developed a following.

That Agnew might be mentioned as potential president, of course, raises the question of how Agnew got a "heartbeat away" from being president. His story features a great deal of what must be termed "dumb luck."[6]

The consensus is that Agnew was competent but far from brilliant. He was the Republican Party's candidate for Baltimore County Executive in 1962 with the expectation that he would, of course, lose in a heavily Democratic jurisdiction. A split in the Democrats' ranks gained him the office where he would have to work with a majority Democratic County Council. He did so, following a common sense pragmatism that would characterize his early political career. He attempted to moderate positions he thought too extreme, especially on issues that would affect business, but he also sought compromise positions on highly divisive issues, such as civil rights ones. He was, for example, instrumental in forging a compromise on the matter of Gwynn Oak Amusement Park's swimming pool. He did far better in Baltimore County than leaders in the arguably more enlightened Montgomery County, who could not bring disputing groups together over the Glen Echo Amusement Park's pool. Glen Echo shut down; Gwynn Oak remained open.

This common sense pragmatism made him an attractive party nominee for governor in 1966. It was, again, a race the Republicans thought they would lose, but Agnew's moderate persona gave them a chance, although they would probably need the Democrats to once again open the door. And the Democrats did.

There were three candidates in the Democratic primary. Outgoing Governor J. Millard Tawes favored his attorney general, Thomas Finan, from Hagerstown. Finan would continue in the moderately progressive footsteps of Tawes. On Finan's left was Maryland's Congressman at-large, Carlton Sickles from Prince George's County. He was a liberal with the backing of liberal senator Joseph Tydings. On Finan's right was perennial candidate George P. Mahoney, a Baltimore contractor, who, borrowing energy from Alabama governor George Wallace's success in Maryland in 1964, was basing his campaign on opposition to federal equal-housing legislation. Each man won approximately one-third of the primary vote, with Mahoney's third slightly larger than Sickles's (which was slightly larger than Finan's).[7]

"Democrats for Agnew" offices opened all over the state, as liberal and moderate Democrats abandoned Mahoney. And, for Democrats squeamish about voting for a Republican, there was independent candidate Hyman Pressman, Baltimore City's Comptroller. Mahoney lost; Agnew won. Once in office in Annapolis, Agnew proceeded to govern in much the same manner as he had in Baltimore County. One might argue that, given the Democrats' control of the State Assembly, he had little choice. However, Agnew's common sense pragmatism seemed less a political choice than a reflection of what he thought government was. Neither brilliant nor inspiring, Agnew, businessman-like, wanted to get done what might get done.

As a governor, he became associated with other governors, especially with northeastern Republican ones. Thus, in 1968, he was a leader of the movement to draft New York governor Nelson Rockefeller to be the party's nominee for president. Rockefeller wavered, and, at a crucial moment, decided not to run but failed to alert Agnew. Agnew found himself in the embarrassing position of hosting a pro-Rockefeller gathering during which Rockefeller demurred. Agnew then turned to Richard Nixon.

Nixon, still somewhat identified with the party's conservative wing, might have wanted a moderate running mate to balance the ticket. But Nixon, executing his very controversial "southern strategy," also needed someone who could attract white voters in the South. In fact, Nixon had given South Carolina's Strom Thurmond (now a Republican) virtual veto power over the vice presidential choice in exchange for Thurmond's support.[8] Agnew, even though from a "border state," might not be conservative enough to please the South Carolinian.

Here, several factors seem to converge: Nixon's fears, Nixon's ego, and Agnew's drift in an increasingly conservative direction. Nixon knew he had enemies, some of whom, he feared, might try to assassinate him if he were ever elected. What better way to discourage that than to install as Number 2 someone the enemies would never want in the White House. Nixon also had a fragile ego and did not want to be upstaged during either the campaign or in office. What better way than to choose a man for the ticket who most found rather dull.

Agnew's drift toward conservatism is premised on the assumption that, as Baltimore County Executive and as Governor, he did not have a strong political philosophy. His pragmatism was based on a desire to get something done, not ideology. But, then, in 1967, the small Eastern Shore town of Cambridge erupted (again) into racial conflict. There had been sit-ins in 1962 and 1963, skirmishes in 1963 that led Tawes to send in the National Guard, and more skirmishes in 1964 evoked by a George Wallace campaign rally. Since 1964, tensions had diminished for a number of reasons: Attorney General Bobby Kennedy's intervention in 1963, CPAC leader Gloria Richardson's departure to New York City, and some progress on issues in the town. But, in 1967, SNCC leader H. Rap Brown delivered an incendiary speech on a vacant lot along the Race Street border separating the black ward from the rest of the town. He referred to a previous fire at Pine Street Elementary School in Ward 2, saying that the town's African American population should have let the school burn down, given how inferior it was to the others in Cambridge. Hours after Brown left, a fire broke out at the school. Because white firemen would not cross Race Street to fight the blaze, it destroyed not only the school but many other buildings before the Attorney General (a volunteer fireman in Baltimore County) commandeered the Cambridge trucks and put the fire out. Agnew, then vacationing in Ocean City, was enraged—at the outside agitation by H. Rap Brown and SNCC. Agnew's rhetoric was strongly anti-black activism and strongly pro-law and order.[9]

Then came April 1968 and the assassination of Dr. Martin Luther King, Jr., in Memphis. Initially, Baltimore did not experience the urban riots that followed the shooting, but on the Saturday after King's murder rioting did break out and on the Sunday it spread to other parts of the city. Mayor Thomas J. D'Alessandro III (Nancy Pelosi's older brother, not father) tried to address the violence by working through community leaders; Governor Agnew's response was different: he ordered in troops, and, then, he summoned black leaders to a meeting at the federal building in the city. Some who went expected that they would be praised by Agnew for their work keeping the rioting from spreading; some feared what Agnew would say and stayed away. The latter group was right to be fearful, for Agnew was not there to praise black leaders but to criticize them for allowing outside agitators to walk their communities and rile up residents. By the time Agnew had finished, 80 percent of his audience had walked out in protest. With the black audience, his speech was a disaster; but, according to the governor's office, the address was so successful with the white audience that Agnew replayed it on Maryland public television. Phone calls and telegrams were supposedly overwhelmingly supportive of this speech that Agnew himself had written—and was quite proud of.[10] Arguably, he had found a voice—against the radical element in the civil rights movement and for law and order. Cambridge had inched him toward it; the rioting in April 1968 took him the rest of the way.

So, Agnew, not likely to encourage an attack on Nixon and not likely to threaten Nixon's ego, became a vice presidential candidate whom Strom Thurmond could endorse. Furthermore, Agnew's embrace of a law-and-order message coincided with one of the major thrusts the Nixon 1968 campaign was going to make against whomever the Democrats nominated.

Nixon did not ask himself a crucial question in picking a running mate: Is he ready to serve as president? From the moment of the pick, many were asking that question. That question did not go away after Nixon won and began to serve. If Agnew had been given key assignments that gave him visibility as a leader, the question might have faded. Some presidents do indeed give their vice presidents major responsibilities, but Nixon was more like John F. Kennedy than Jimmy Carter. Kennedy largely froze Lyndon Johnson out of White House matters, turning to the Texan only occasionally when his expertise dealing with the Congress was felt to be necessary.

Nixon treated Agnew in much the same manner, turning to him not from Congressional expertise (because he had none) but to give speeches that Nixon wanted to but couldn't without drawing fire from moderates. Agnew dutifully read words written by others and approved by Nixon and thereby became a prominent extreme conservative spokesperson.

There was talk in 1972 of dumping Agnew from the Republican ticket in favor of someone who might be groomed as a successor, but Nixon stuck with the Marylander. So, at that point, the possibility of an Agnew presidential run in 1976 must have been raised. He was from a state perceived as small, but had overcome that by serving on the national stage. He had been a governor. So, the quick negative reaction to the notion of him as president must have involved how he was perceived as a leader. He had gradually become one who espoused ideological goals, and those who agreed with these goals might well have found his rhetoric—provided by others— motivating. But that rhetoric did not evoke high expectations. It focused on what was wrong with America but not the better path that he would lead the nation along. As Nixon's "attack dog," he surrounded himself with a negativity that inspired anger not the high expectations people seek in a charismatic, transformational leader.

Agnew was weaker on two other counts—being a role model and demonstrating competence. He was perceived as a weak vice president, not doing much and certainly not inspiring imitation. No one would have wanted to be like Spiro T. Agnew. Those who did not like him saw him as Nixon's stooge; those who perhaps liked him a bit saw him as Nixon's "Yes-man." Because vice presidents necessarily serve in a subordinate role, many have problems with the role model and the competence dimensions of leadership. George H. W. Bush turned to Reagan speechwriter Peggy Noonan to pen for him a convention address that would address these weaknesses; Al Gore, in planning the 2000 Democratic National Convention, worked diligently to define himself in positive terms (and escape Bill Clinton's shadow). It is very doubtful that Agnew could have achieved what Bush (who won the White House) and Gore (who won the popular vote) both did. Agnew, of course, never had the opportunity, for he was forced to resign the vice presidency when indicted on federal charges for income tax evasion.[11]

The years leading up to the 1976 presidential contest were tumultuous ones for the Republicans. When Nixon was inaugurated the second time in 1973, commentators undoubtedly interpreted the nation's overwhelming rejection of South Dakota senator George McGovern as an embrace of core conservative principles such as law and order. Thus, in 1973, despite his many personal liabilities, Agnew might have been positioned well for a 1976 run. If he had not been compelled to resign the vice presidency, he might have found himself in a good position only if he re-packaged himself with freedom from corruption replacing the insistence on law and order. After "Watergate," a position as far away as possible from corruption—and Nixon, became the one most likely to succeed. Agnew, thought to be saying what Nixon wanted to say, might have had difficulty asserting the necessary distance, although he was clearly not a Nixon administration insider. However, Agnew could have plausibly distanced himself from all-things-"Watergate," for no one was even hinting that he had any knowledge whatsoever of what the Nixon people were doing. So, Agnew might have been able to position himself in an advantageous manner, but his own ethical problems of course removed him from the picture before "Watergate" exploded and brought down the Nixon presidency.

JOHN DELANEY

Many who heard John Delaney speak on the issues in 2020 without knowing who was speaking were impressed by his command of the facts and the clarity with which he presented policies. Delaney undoubtedly had a grasp of what was facing the nation. Unfortunately, that grasp was not enough to overcome his fundamental liabilities. Despite being elected three times to the U.S. House of Representatives, he was still just a member of a body that had only sent James Garfield to the presidency.

In the House, he had a strong bipartisan record. Despite progressive stands on a few issues, Delaney was consistently labeled a moderate, a label he himself accepted, declaring himself "a solutions-oriented moderate who wants to get things done."[12] This philosophy may reflect the fact that Delaney came into politics from the business world. He had co-founded Health Care Financial Partners in 1993 and CapitalSource in 2000. Ironically, one of the areas Delaney proposed legislation in was partisan gerrymandering. He proposed the creation of independent redistricting commissions. The irony is based on the fact that Delaney won his Maryland 6th District seat only because the Democrats had moved voters around so that Democrats from parts of Montgomery County (who had been part of the 8th) outnumbered Republicans from the western counties.[13] Thus, Delaney defeated aging incumbent Republican Roscoe Bartlett with 59 percent of the vote and Republican challengers the next two times with 54 percent and 56 percent, respectively.

His record in the House was strong enough that many Democrats wanted him to challenge Larry Hogan for the governorship in 2018. He elected to run for president in 2020 instead, announcing first and considerably ahead of other prospects. Perhaps he thought the early announcement would gain him media attention before others were in the race. It really did not: his candidacy was noted and largely dismissed, as the media were waiting for the "big names" to jump in.

His moderation and his bipartisanship might have hurt him in the race as well. In the primaries, the extreme elements of the two parties vote more and, thus, moderate candidates do not fare as well as they might in the general election. Delaney, based on his political stance, had little appeal for party activists. He also had a matter-of-fact style that might have made him a fine legislator but not a strongly compelling candidate. He did win his House seat three times, but, in the first election, he faced a rather elderly Bartlett and, in the third, he faced an extreme conservative in Amie Hoeber. The second race against a Republican neither elderly nor extreme was surprisingly close, suggesting that Delaney was not especially compelling on the stump. So, although quite knowledgeable on an array of issues, Delaney simply could not gain any traction.

It is generally true that, during the primary season, prospective candidates move to the extremes—in recent times, liberal for Democrats, conservative for Republicans. In 2020, many Democrats sought the nomination. Most were left-leaning with the crucial question being how close to avowed socialist

Bernie Sanders they were. A few, including Joe Biden, were labeled more moderate, but even those in this grouping were positioning themselves as more pragmatic than moderate. Delaney was almost alone in associating himself with the "moderate" label. Positioned in such a way, he fit neither the liberal inclination nor the pragmatic modification of that inclination. His positioning as well as his less than lustrous record and his seeming lack of the desired leadership qualities made him a weak candidate from the offing, despite the knowledge of the issues that interviews with him revealed.

MARTIN O'MALLEY

As the front man for the Irish rock band "O'Malley's March," Martin O'Malley had a lot of appeal that might be termed charisma. He also had a record—as mayor of Baltimore and as governor of Maryland. He struck many as wanting to be mayor when he was on the city council, as wanting to be governor when he was mayor, and as wanting to be president when he was governor. He seemed to be always running for the next office, exhibiting ambition that was not only his but, arguably, also his politically influential father in-law's. Many in Maryland held this ambition against O'Malley and were, thus, ready to fault him when he did not take care of immediate business or did not take care of that immediate business well. As discussed in another chapter, O'Malley's record was both positive and progressive but with a few lapses that might have caused some to wonder if he was genuinely progressive. So, in 2016 debates against Hillary Clinton and Bernie Sanders, he came across as offering liberal slogans without the passion of Bernie and surprisingly not talking about his record. All knew how much O'Malley opposed the National Rifle Association, but what he had accomplished as governor and what he would do as president on guns or other issues remained vague.

Perhaps O'Malley did not want to raise his Maryland record for fear people would dismiss it as a "small state" one. Or, perhaps, there was simply a failure to communicate well. The definition of leadership we are using here as a lens points to qualities that depend on communication. A voter might know a candidate's record by reading a newspaper or visiting a website, but the candidate needed to be the source of the requisite high expectations and strong motivation. Furthermore, the candidate needed to enact the role of role model through campaign conduct. Reading about grand accomplishments would not be enough.

As discussed in another chapter, O'Malley exhibited a lack of control over messaging throughout his political career. That lack revealed itself in his inability to deal quickly with what seemed to be inconsistencies in his record. This inability finally undermined his standing as he was set to leave

Maryland behind and turn the State House over to his lieutenant governor Anthony Brown. So, he did not suffer electoral defeat (Brown did) but he did suffer a major dent in his image. The matter of the so-called "rain tax" might seem a small one: Republicans were able to label a justifiable tax on parking lot owners tied to these lots' polluting run-off into not only a joke but a glaring example of how O'Malley (and Democrats) would tax anything. Having raised taxes and fees as governor—in order to pay for the services residents did indeed desire but with a balanced budget—O'Malley was quite vulnerable. His taxation record certainly hurt O'Malley with the voters, but his inability to respond to the comic idea that he would even tax the rain was devastating. If O'Malley had been able to seek a third term, he probably would have lost.

He was, therefore, not well-positioned to be a presidential aspirant. He was not the overwhelmingly popular governor, but he might have been able to rise from this weak position if he had handled campaign communication better. He was, on paper, a serious alternative to Clinton and Sanders. He was a something of a rock star with a solid resume (despite a few inconsistencies). Clinton had what some saw as negative marks on her record (Benghazi); Sanders was thought to be too extreme. There was an opening, but O'Malley could not communicate a clear ideology, could not communicate his high expectations for government, and could not communicate in a manner that motivated people to take the path he charted.

One must ask whether the fault was O'Malley's or his staff's or the media's. The answer is probably all three. That communication problems were evident before the presidential campaign points the finger at O'Malley and/or his staff, but the media in 2016 certainly did him few favors by framing the Democratic race in Clinton vs. Sanders terms.[14] There were two other announced candidates. The media gave one, Rhode Islander Lincoln Chafee, virtually no coverage, and he very quickly faded, as Virginian Jim Webb— also ignored by the media—earlier had. The media gave O'Malley just a bit more but not much, and he faded. Could O'Malley have overcome this media framing? Perhaps if he had been a stronger communicator, offering a message the media would have to cover. But O'Malley was not that communicator. Unable to overcome the way the Republicans framed his revenue gathering as imposing "rain tax," O'Malley was unable to push the media away from its Hillary or Bernie story.

MORE ON THE MEDIA

It is appropriate at this point to take a detour and discuss two important dimensions of media coverage, for they affected Delaney and O'Malley.

The media cannot effectively cover 20-plus candidates. So, in the "surfacing" phase of a presidential campaign, candidates try to make it into the four or so the media can indeed cover.[15] Knowing this, Delaney may have entered the race early, but the media was not really ready to process the candidates until later, when there were 20-plus. Unknown, with just service in the House, and nothing exceptional in either his substance or style, Delaney did not have much of a chance of making it into the group the media would focus on.

In O'Malley's case, the story is different, for the number seeking the nomination was much smaller—just three or four or five if one counts Rhode Island's Lincoln Chafee and Virginia's Jim Webb. O'Malley was the victim of media framing, which presented the race as mainstreamer Hillary Clinton vs. left-winger Bernie Sanders, as establishment vs. anti-establishment. O'Malley was on stage with Clinton and Sanders throughout, but he might as well not have been since the lead-up to debates and the follow-up after debates had this dominant frame.

So, in both the cases of Delaney and O'Malley, although there were flaws in their candidacies, they were also "victims" of the realities of media coverage. Delaney could not "surface" in a large field; O'Malley could not break the prevailing media frame.

ALBERT RITCHIE

Delaney sought the Democratic nomination in 2020; O'Malley in 2008. They are fairly recent aspirants. Agnew's political star was high in the sky not that long ago. Albert Ritchie takes us back to the earlier part of the twentieth century. Most reading this chapter have probably never even heard of Ritchie. (Many who daily travel on Ritchie Highway probably have no idea whom the road was named after.)

Ritchie first came to statewide attention as Attorney General. Competent and attractive, the Democrats in Maryland chose him as their gubernatorial candidate in 1920. It was traditional but not legislated that governors in the state serve only a single term. Ritchie defied that traditional, serving four terms and running for a fifth. Thus, for a lengthy period, 1921–1934, Ritchie and Maryland were synonymous. Thus, not surprisingly, his name is found throughout the state: Fort Ritchie in Washington County; Ritchie Coliseum on the University of Maryland's College Park campus; and Ritchie Highway running south out of Baltimore to Annapolis. His politics and his accomplishments will be addressed shortly, but his longevity in office alone provided him with the basis for seeking a grander position.

And he actively sought that position. Although reportedly reserved, he spoke often throughout the state and nation, attempting to solidify his Maryland base and to attract support from elsewhere. He received considerable support, as attested to by pro-Ritchie demonstrations in convention cities and at the party's convention itself in 1924, 1928, and even 1932.[16] However, these demonstrations did not translate to large delegate pools. In 1924, he lost the nomination to James Cox; in 1928, he acceded to New York's Al Smith; and in 1932, he reluctantly gave way to the affable New York governor, Franklin D. Roosevelt.

The 1920s were arguably not good for Democrats. The nation was prosperous and happy with the pro-business, limited federal government philosophy espoused by Harding, Coolidge, and Hoover. That the Republican core constituency was shrinking a bit gave the Democrats an opening, but the true opening did not occur until prosperity came crashing down, taking the nation unto the "Great Depression." In 1932, any Democrat could have won the White House against the very unpopular Hoover. Ritchie was especially well-positioned to do so, for he could have easily assembled a winning coalition.

On some issues, Ritchie was slow to come around—on women's suffrage and civil rights, for example. On the latter, he withheld judgment until the KKK rose in prominence. Then, as an ardent opponent of the Klan, he won a measure of African American support.[17] On the former, he deflected, insisting that the matter of who voted was a state one and opposing federal action on the basis of states' rights. And he was a very ardent supporter of states' right, a stance that should have had considerable appeal among those in the southern wing of the national Democratic Party. His key states' rights issue, however, had nothing to do with race relations; rather, it was liquor and other forms of alcoholic beverage. Ritchie was a "wet," supported in that position by the urban portions of Maryland and opposed vehemently by the rural. As a "wet" governor who believed in states' rights, he refused to enforce federal prohibition and argued publicly that the "dry" position was foolish government meddling in personal behavior.

By 1932, Ritchie's "wetness" would be forgotten, but not his insistence on states' rights. Alcohol was not, however, Ritchie's only concern. He, as governor, embraced issues appealing to both progressives and business concerns. He debuted the "executive budget," which gave the governor a great deal of power to direct state spending. Assisted by federal largesse, which Ritchie said Maryland, states' rights notwithstanding, would be foolish not to take, he spent on hospitals, public employees' salaries, environmental protection, and—especially—education. He also did what was necessary with state funds to make Baltimore the third largest port in the nation, the Baltimore area a center for the developing aviation industry, and the state a prominent and diversified farming region (fast-burning tobacco in southern Maryland, "truck farming," and a mix of poultry and seafood on the Eastern Shore). Reorganizing the state government permitted allowed Ritchie to accomplish all of this while reducing taxes.

Ritchie mirrored state sentiment in resisting organized labor's call for a "closed shop," so he was not labor's man in 1932. But his record was strongly progressive, although he was a tad late on suffrage and civil rights. Still, he was a candidate progressives could support, as well as states' rights southerners who rarely found common ground with progressives. And to this emerging coalition, Ritchie could add those, perhaps many of them nominal Republicans, who were impressed with all that the governor was doing for the states' business interests while keeping government size and taxes down.

The problem for Ritchie was that there was another, arguably with less of a record, who was also building a strong coalition. That was, of course, New York governor Franklin D. Roosevelt. We could debate who had the better coalition, but that was probably beside the point, for Democrats turned to Roosevelt over Ritchie because of their perceived leadership traits.

Ritchie's record was arguably stronger: serving longer, he had done more. So, Ritchie probably was seen as more competent than Roosevelt. On the other counts, however, Roosevelt probably had Ritchie beat, for the Ritchie's rhetoric was constrained by his twin beliefs in state action and carefully limited government action. The people wanted—needed—something bigger. Roosevelt offered it. Furthermore, Roosevelt, because of his outgoing personality and his uplifting rhetoric, was simply more inspiring.

Ritchie, despite the many political speeches he might deliver, seemed to many aloof. He did not hail from money as FDR did, but FDR had the ability to connect with the average person whereas Ritchie seemed to be stuck in an older oratorical tradition. Ritchie gave speeches; FDR had conversations. Or so it seemed. Ritchie was also much more reserved. He could become passionate when denouncing prohibition or defending states' rights against other federal intrusions, but more people admired and wanted to be like the very affable New Yorker. Ritchie had competence galore, but not the charm that would inspire both high expectations and noble motives. Ritchie also may have had the wrong ideology for the 1932 moment. In normal times, Ritchie's record would have proved compelling, but, in 1932, it seemed restrained compared to Roosevelt's big promises. Ritchie seemed timid.

Roosevelt thought highly enough of Ritchie to offer him the vice presidency in 1932. Ritchie declined, saying he preferred being Governor of Maryland to being FDR's Number 2. As Ritchie's popularity in Maryland began to fade during his unprecedented fourth term as governor, he is said to have regretted the decision.[18] He was urged in 1934 to run for a U.S. Senate seat, not a fifth term. He refused and, then, almost lost in the primary to a political unknown who taunted him as "Prince Albert the Fourth." The near-loss caused him to abandon his somewhat cautious persona and become an ardent "New Dealer," but it was too late. With lukewarm support from Labor and African Americans, he narrowly lost to Republican Harry Nice.

Ritchie came closer to the presidency than Agnew, Delaney, and O'Malley. He had achieved sufficient national prominence to overcome the "small state" label, and he was a governor—again and again. His record provided him with the ability to assemble a strong coalition, but his ideological goals seemed slightly off the mark for 1932 and he was not as inspiring as his New York rival. But what about 1924 and 1928? One might conjecture that 1924 was too early: Ritchie had not yet established much visibility beyond Maryland, which was perceived as small. In 1928, with more visibility, he had another New York rival in Al Smith. One might conjecture that, sensing that a Democrat could not win that year, Ritchie gave his support to Smith on the assumption that Smith would return the favor four years hence. Smith did not, however, prefer fellow New Yorker FDR to the Marylander. New York politics, then, had much to do with Ritchie's failure to win a presidential nod and, presumably in 1932, the presidency. But more important were his record that seemed opposed to the federal action the nation so desperately needed and his somewhat shy, somewhat timid streak. He wasn't offering a "New Deal," and he didn't possess Franklin Roosevelt's charisma.

Ritchie, arguably, was not as well-positioned for 1932 as Roosevelt. Ritchie's failure was not just because FDR out-charmed him. Suffering from the economic hardships of the Great Depression, voters wanted action. An examination of Ritchie's record as governor revealed plenty of action, but also a measure of caution. He responded to causes and needs, but a tad slowly. The only issue that seemed to propel Ritchie forward quickly was prohibition, which, as an ardent "wet," he opposed, but that was not a relevant issue in 1932. Without Roosevelt in the race, Ritchie might have been perceived as active enough. He might then have been able to position himself to win both the nomination and the general election. FDR, however, was in the race and fit the needs of the time—as interpreted by the Democrats—better than the more cautious Marylander.

CONCLUSION

The process of selecting a presidential nominee is not straightforward: there are many variables involved, and the process has changed over time. Furthermore, odd things can occur such as the nomination of newspaperman Wendell Wilkie in 1940 and business man and reality TV star Donald Trump in 2016. But, based on almost 250 years of history, one can say that the state a prospect hails from matters and what office or offices a prospect has held matter(s). They are not determinative, but they play a role in how the public perceives a nominee. Small states—or states perceived to be small—are then

Figure 8.1   Crowd Greets Maryland Governor and 1932 Presidential Aspirant Albert Ritchie upon His Arrival at Congress Hotel in Chicago for the Upcoming Convention. *Source*: Photo originally via ACME Newspictures, now public domain.

at a disadvantage, as are political figures who have only served as mayors or members of the House.

Those who select the nominees, be they political insiders or voters, however, look for more than just the right residence and the right current or previous job. They look for leadership. There are many ways to define what leadership is. Some, as noted in another chapter deal with how a person enacts the role. But when selecting a presidential nominee, the emphasis is less on the enactment and more on the qualities the prospect has and what these are imagined as leading to. Thus, the transformational leadership theory, especially those which focus on "charisma," seems most appropriate in understanding how people decide if a prospect is the desired leader or not.

We used House's work to point to five qualities: being a role model, demonstrating competence, communicating strong ideological goals, communicating high expectations (for self and nation), and having and communicating important, noble motives for action. Communication is clearly important in exhibiting these qualities. The media might be able to tell voters enough so that they check off role model and competence. The voters have heard enough or read enough. But the latter three qualities seem tied to what a prospect communicates.

Of the several Maryland prospects we examined, Agnew, Delaney, O'Malley, and Ritchie, only the last communicated strongly enough to be a likely choice. Agnew, besides not being thought especially competent by many, also did not present a clear message that was his own. Delaney, besides only being a Congressman, offered a bland ideology and had limited expectations for government. O'Malley, besides being from a state perceived to be small, offered an inconsistent ideology and had some questioning if his rhetoric reflected more his ambition than what he wanted government and its people to aspire to. Albert Ritchie had the qualities the others lacked, but was not as personable as another candidate, Franklin D. Roosevelt. Ritchie also could assemble a coalition of supporters somewhat different from the one Roosevelt could assemble. Both had records that would attract progressives, but FDR, more so. To this, FDR could add more African Americans and some from organized labor. Ritchie arguably had more appeal to business interests and fiscal moderates, but those were more Republican groups than Democratic ones. And Ritchie, because of his strong states' rights stance, had more appeal to southern traditionalists, who were touting states' rights but not, like Ritchie, on the matter of prohibition. So, besides style, on which FDR's eloquence and affability beat Ritchie's more traditional eloquence, the deciding factor may well have been which coalition best fits the needs of 1932. The nation needed action, and action was favored by those lined up with FDR. As long as he could keep southern traditionalists content by seeming somewhat populist (and trying to not talk about civil rights), he fits the needs better than Ritchie. But Marylander Ritchie did have much more going for him than those mentioned as presidential prospects in the many years since.

NOTES

1. John Dugan, *Leadership Theory: Cultivating Critical Perspectives* (San Francisco: Jossey-Bass, 2017).

2. Peter G. Northouse, *Leadership: Theory and Practice,* 7th ed. (Los Angeles: Sage, 2016).

3. B. M. Bass, *Leadership and Performance* (New York: Free Press, 1985).

4. R. J. House, "A 1976 Theory of Charismatic Leadership," in *Leadership: The Cutting Edge,* edited by J. G. Hunt and L. L. Larson, 189–207 (Carbondale: Southern Illinois University Press, 1976).

5. Charles J. Holden, Zach Messitte, and Jerald Podair. *Republican Populist: Spiro Agnew and the Origins of Donald Trump's America* (Charlottesville: University of Virginia Press, 2019).

6. Charles J. Holden, Zach Messitte, and Jerald Podair. *Republican Populist: Spiro Agnew and the Origins of Donald Trump's America* (Charlottesville: University of Virginia Press, 2019).

7. Theodore F. Sheckels, *Maryland Politics and Political Communication, 1950-2005* (Lanham, MD: Lexington Books, 2006).

8. Angie Maxwell and Todd Shield, *The Long Southern Strategy: How Chasing White Voters in the South Changed American Politics* (New York: Oxford University Press, 2019).

9. Peter B. Levy, *Civil War on Race Street: The Civil Rights Movement in Cambridge,* Maryland (Gainesville: University Press of Florida, 2003); Justin Coffey, *Spiro Agnew and the Rise of the Republican Right* (Santa Barbara, CA: Praeger, 2015).

10. Sheckels, *Maryland Politics.*

11. Richard M. Cohen and Jules Witcover. *A Heartbeat Away: The Investigation and Resignation of Vice President Spiro T. Agnew* (New York: Viking, 1974).

12. Taylor Stephens, "With Nearly 3 Years Until 2020 Election, Deeply Red Utah Gets its First Visit from a Presidential Candidate—a Little-Known Democrat," https://www.sltribune/news/politics/2018/01/25/with-nearly-3-yearsuntil-2020-election-deeply-red-utah-gets-its-first-visit-from-a-presidential-candidate-a-little-known-democrat

13. Brett Locke, "Lawsuit Forces Maryland Democrats to Acknowledge the Obvious: Redistricting Was Motivated by Politics," *Baltimore Sun.* June 1, 2017.

14. The classic study of agenda setting, framing, and priming is Maxwell McComb and Donald L. Shaw, "The Agenda-Setting Function of Mass Media," *Public Opinion Quarterly* 36.2 (1972): 176–87.

15. Juddi S. Trent, Robert V. Friedenberg, and Robert E. Denton, Jr., *Political Campaign Communication: Principles and Practice*, 8th ed. (Lanham, MD: Rowman & Littlefield, 2016).

16. Robert J. Brugger, *Maryland: A Middle Temperament, 1634-1980* (Baltimore: Johns Hopkins University Press, 1988). See pp. 490–8.

17. Ibid., pp. 476–7.

18. Ibid., pp. 497–8.

Part III

POLICIES

Chapter 9

Race, Housing, and Segregation in Baltimore

Race is a complex issue anywhere and it's one fraught with difficulties for all involved. This nation's history of slavery has made race and any conversations about it especially difficult. Maryland poses a particularly interesting case since the positions of African Americans often shifted throughout its history. There were times when Black people had a substantial amount of freedom and the rights that went along with them. And there were times that slavery and then segregation restricted that freedom and those rights.

What makes Maryland so fascinating is that although conventional wisdom holds that the first Africans in Maryland were thirteen slaves who arrived in St. Mary's City in southern Maryland in 1642, that is not actually the case. The first colonist of African descent to arrive in Maryland was Mathias de Sousa, one of nine indentured servants brought by the Jesuits accompanying Lord Baltimore's expedition to Maryland in 1634.[1] De Sousa's indenture was finished by 1638, four years before the first enslaved Africans arrived in the colony.

Free of his indenture, de Sousa became a mariner and fur trader. In 1641, de Sousa commanded a trading voyage to the Susquehannock Indians. In 1642, he was master of a small cargo vessel owned by the Provincial Secretary.[2]

As a free man, de Sousa participated in elections held in the colony. In 1642, he served as a member of the legislative assembly of freemen.[3] He fell on hard times, disappeared from the historical record after 1643, and nothing more is known about him. It is possible that he died at about that time in battles between the colonists and Native Americans in 1643. But this was also about the same time that disease and famine affected the colony.

In the early days of slavery in Maryland, the status of Africans was not defined. Since they had been brought from Africa, they were not considered English subjects and were thus considered foreigners. In addition, courts at the time often ruled that anyone who became a baptized Christian should be freed. Given this situation, it did not take long for Maryland to institutionalize slavery.

In 1661, fewer than twenty years after the first enslaved Africans arrived, the Maryland Assembly made interracial marriage illegal. Three years later, in 1664, it passed a law that anyone who was a slave would be a slave for life. In addition, the law made the children of enslaved women slaves for life as well.[4]

Though interracial marriage was illegal, free families of color nevertheless developed, often through informal unions. These unions existed between white women and men of color regardless of status (free, indentured, or enslaved). Since the condition of slavery passed through the mother, if the mother were a free woman, the children were also considered free.

As the seventeenth century became the eighteenth century, parts of Maryland had developed plantation economies dependent upon the labor of enslaved Africans. By the mid-1750s, some 40 percent of the colony's population was Black. One result was the passage of increasingly harsher laws to institutionalize slavery. It even became illegal to free one's own slaves without permission from the legislature.

In the election to select the delegates who would write Maryland's 1776 constitution, those eligible to vote were, "freemen above twenty-one years of age being freeholders of not less than fifty acres of land or having visible property . . . to the value of £40 sterling at the least." The term "freemen" included free Black men and free men of color. About 55 percent of all heads of household were eligible to vote. In Annapolis, nearly all freemen could vote.

During the convention, an opposition group arose that wanted to expand the right to vote to include any free male over twenty-one with £5 of visible property.[5] Though the group's proposal was unsuccessful, the compromise final wording kept the 50 acres of land but reduced the alternative £40 of visible property to £30 of visible property.[6] This extended the right to vote to include about 63 percent of heads of household.[7]

Maryland was not alone in including free Black men and free men of color among those eligible to vote. State constitutions in Delaware, New Hampshire, and New York also included them among their voters. As a result, Baltimore and other early American towns sometimes had more Blacks voting in elections than white.[8]

Such were the conditions of free Blacks in Maryland that in 1792, Thomas Brown, a Black Revolutionary War veteran from Baltimore launched a campaign for election to a seat in the state legislature, albeit an unsuccessful one.[9]

The right to vote would not last long for non-white men in Maryland. Though an 1809 amendment to the 1776 constitution would repeal the property requirement as a qualification to hold office (Article XII), another 1809 amendment, Article XIV, changed the qualifications for voting to include only ". . . every free *white* male of this State" (Emphasis is mine).[10] What is important to understand is that slavery as an integral part of Maryland's economy had sharply declined between the first U.S. Census in 1790 and the 1860 census at the start of the Civil War. By 1860, slaves, who had been 32 percent of the state's population in 1790, comprised only 13 percent. As percentages of Baltimore's population, free Blacks had increased from only 3 percent in 1790 to 12 percent in 1860. The percentages of free Blacks in Maryland rose from 7 percent of the total Black population to 49 percent during the same period.[11] During that same period, Maryland alone accounted for 20 percent of all free Blacks in the United States.[12]

The numbers for Baltimore are more interesting. As percentages of the total population of Maryland, slaves and free Blacks represented 9 percent and 3 percent respectively in 1790.

By 1860, the percentages were 1 percent and 12 percent. By comparison, the percentage of free Blacks rose from 20 percent of Baltimore's total Black population in 1790 to 92 percent in 1860.[13]

All this is important for what it says about race relations and slavery in Baltimore. British journalist and social reformer James Silk Buckingham visited Baltimore in 1838. He wrote that while in Baltimore, he heard less about slaves and slavery than in any city he had thus far visited.[14]

In his book, *Baltimore: A Political History*, Matthew Crenson, professor emeritus of political science at Johns Hopkins University, wrote that Baltimore's geographical location as a city in a border state may explain some of its ambivalence toward slavery and discussions about it. Crenson goes on to write, though, that geography wasn't enough. He says Baltimore's orientation to the west had as much to do with that ambivalence as anything else did. A good deal of Baltimore's prosperity was due to the Western Maryland grain trade on which there was very little reliance on slave labor. That, combined with Baltimore's importance in manufacturing, ship building, and shipping meant there was far less need for slaves than was the case for the plantations of Southern Maryland and parts of the Eastern Shore.[15]

Crenson also writes that the nature of slavery in Baltimore was different as well. In Baltimore, slaves were fairly often "term slaves"; a variation on indentured servitude in which slaves served for a fixed period of time after which they were freed. About 20 percent of slaves in Baltimore were "term slaves."

Some of Baltimore's slave owners hired their slaves out to manufacturers or to the shipyards. Though such owners often kept all the slaves' pay, some permitted their slaves to save a portion of their salaries and to eventually buy

their freedom. Once free, these former slaves would often purchase the freedom of family members.[16]

An added factor to Baltimore's attitudes toward slavery involved the
increasing numbers of slave owners who were freeing their slaves. By the
early part of the nineteenth century, Maryland was experiencing very high
rates of manumissions either by deed or through wills at the deaths of the
owners.[17] The large numbers of manumissions created in Maryland the largest free Black population of any state in the United States. Free Blacks were
such a large part of the Black population that by the time of the Civil War,
Maryland had an almost equal number of slaves and free Blacks. And, as
already mentioned, free Blacks in Baltimore constituted 92 percent of the
city's Black population.

Another part of what made Baltimore so different from many other cities on the subject of race was the fast-paced growth of the city that blurred
social boundaries. As more and more people moved into the city, people had
to interact with those of widely divergent backgrounds and had to assess
each situation and person differently. The size of the city made generalizing
about others difficult. As Christopher Phillips points out in *Freedom's Port*,
Baltimoreans "defined and redefined their race relations according to need. In
this context economic status had everything to do with racial distinctions. . . .
Obsessed with economic expansion, white residents of Baltimore appear to
have grown at least marginally color-blind."

Phillips also writes that city directories did not separate black from white
householders until 1819. Tax directories did not do so until much later. He
maintains that this attests to "a relatively liberal racial atmosphere."[18]

According to Crenson, Baltimoreans' ambivalence toward slavery had at
least as much to do with *who* they were as a city as it did with *where* they
were. He named "conflict avoidance" as a motivation for how Baltimoreans
engaged the subjects of slavery and race.[19] Whatever the reason, free Black
Baltimoreans successfully forged cohesive communities. And they would
need that cohesiveness as the nineteenth century became the twentieth
century.

To a certain extent, this provides context for what eventually became the
flash point in the city's race relations—housing. Housing is really what created systemic segregation in Baltimore and served to exacerbate deteriorating
racial attitudes. These are things whose effects still deeply affect Baltimore
today—and things that clearly define the inequities seen in today's Baltimore.

The matter of housing and who lives where is a complex one—and
always a moving target. Between 1790 and 1830, Baltimore's white population quadrupled. But its Black population grew by 1,100 percent.[20] In those
early days, Baltimore expanded without much racial turmoil. Baltimore's
Black residents were scattered throughout the city. Streets were racially,

ethnically, and economically mixed. That began to change by the mid-1830s, though. By then, Blacks and White were separating themselves. Whites were largely living on the main streets while many Blacks were living in alley dwellings behind whites' houses.[21] The shift to main streets vs. alleys didn't mean that the neighborhoods themselves were segregating. That didn't happen yet.[22]

Prior to the Civil War, most city residents of all races lived in crowded neighborhoods near city centers. This was because people had to walk to go to work and to take care of daily needs. Blacks and whites were living in close proximity to one another, though there wasn't necessarily much social contact between them.[23]

At the end of the Civil War, thousands of former slaves and Black soldiers came to Baltimore. This placed a significant strain on the city's capacity to absorb them, house them, and care for those who needed help.[24]

Housing and public services in Baltimore were further strained by the doubling of its overall population between 1870 and 1900. The surge in population was fueled largely by the arrival of thousands of European immigrants, though there were also significant numbers of people still coming from rural areas looking for jobs.[25]

As is often the case in many cities, new arrivals to Baltimore tended to live in less desirable neighborhoods with poor housing stock that was available because the groups living in that area had moved on to something better made available when that area's previous residents had moved on to something better and so on.

Changes in the composition of neighborhoods owe at least some debt to new transportation technologies developed after the Civil War. Electrified trolley systems helped make suburbs possible. Baltimore's wealthier residents became increasingly mobile and moved to suburbs north and west out of the Oldtown center of the city.[26]

The attraction the suburbs had included the advantage of living in a less crowded, more country-like environment. The desire to move away from the city center was also partly fueled by industrialization, congestion, and the presence of social groups deemed inferior. Moderately priced homes in the suburbs were affordable for many middle-income blue- and white-collar workers. And they were almost exclusively white.[27]

As groups of people left various neighborhoods for the suburbs, other groups moved in.

When the "replacement groups" in turn moved to the suburbs, other groups took their places. The pattern repeated. As an example of these successive neighborhood replacements of one group by another, the area of Baltimore now called Little Italy didn't see Italians move in until after the neighborhood had seen in succession Germans, Irish, and Jews.[28]

A predominantly African American neighborhood didn't actually exist in Baltimore until about 1890. Until 1890, Black Baltimoreans were still widely distributed throughout the city. Although they constituted 10 percent or more of the population in three-fourths of the city's twenty wards, no single ward was more than one-third Black.[29]

Like other groups in Baltimore, African Americans were also looking for new and better homes. Migrants from rural Maryland and beyond exacerbated the already difficult and overcrowded housing situation for Black residents.[30] It was during this period that truly segregated African American communities first began developing. The first of these was Old West Baltimore. African Americans began moving there in about 1885 because of overcrowding in other areas of the city, especially in South Baltimore.[31]

In the first years of the twentieth century, 200 Black-owned homes in South Baltimore were demolished during the expansion of Camden Station, sending more Blacks into homes in West Baltimore.[32] Most Blacks bought or rented previously owned homes in areas left open by migrations of other groups to newer neighborhoods.

By 1904, half of Baltimore's African Americans lived in Old West Baltimore as they replaced the largely German community that had moved farther north.[33] Economically, too, Old West Baltimore was a diverse area and its residents ranged from the most prominent Black families to Black professionals to the Black working class. It featured both owner-occupied homes and various levels of rental units. The neighborhood of Old West Baltimore was bounded by North Avenue on the north, Franklin Street on the south, Madison Street on the east, and Fulton Street on the west.[34]

Until 1910, neighborhoods were fairly well-defined by custom and groups tended not to move into areas in which they "didn't belong." No legal mechanisms were needed. As whites left city neighborhoods for the suburbs, more and more houses were left vacant. Vacant houses in white neighborhoods began to be seen by the remaining white residents as a threat. As demand from potential white tenants and homebuyers declined some property owners sought to rent or sell to Black Baltimoreans. The remaining white residents felt that this was undermining their efforts to maintain the boundaries. In the summer of 1910, white Baltimoreans were not hesitant to share their feelings and they did so in letters to city officials and to the newspapers. The *Baltimore Sun* seemed especially invested in providing an outlet for white people upset at the gradual, but steady movement of African Americans into previously all white neighborhoods. An August 25 letter to the *Baltimore Sun* signed "Pure White" read in part, "When a man works and saves and buys a home thinking it will be his shelter in his old age, and wakes up some morning to find he has a negro neighbor, he feels hurt and aggrieved that he has to give up his home, but he moves."

Another letter writer demanded that the city protect his neighborhood from vacant homes in which the writer saw a threat that there would soon be Black neighbors. The letter said, "There are several vacant houses in the block, and this fear [of 'negro invasion'] may be the potent cause of non-rental or sale. Each vacant house is a standing menace to the rest."[35]

Legislative efforts to create and maintain legally segregated housing in Baltimore began in 1910 as a result of what today would be an innocuous real estate transaction. Margaret G. Franklin Brewer sold 1834 McCulloh Street to W. Ashbie Hawkins, a lawyer. The house was a three-story, 13-foot-wide, red brick rowhouse not unlike many such residences in that area of the city. After he purchased the house, he leased it to his law partner and brother-in-law, George W. F. McMechen, a Yale Law School alumnus who was also the first graduate of what was then Baltimore's Morgan College.

What made the transaction unusual is that Hawkins and McMechen were Black and no other Black families lived on the street. This "sensational" fact wasn't known until about three weeks after the purchase when the *Baltimore Sun* printed an article about the transaction. The headline warned of a "negro invasion."

The reaction in the neighborhood? Repeated vandalism to the house and the creation of the McCulloh Street-Madison Avenue Protective Association, which resolved that "colored people should not be allowed to encroach on some of the best residential streets in the city and force white people to vacate their homes."[36]

What followed was the first municipal ordinance in the nation requiring racially segregated housing on a block-by-block basis. In other words each block would be designated as either a white block or a Black block based on who was living there at the time of the ordinance. The very name of the ordinance was mouthful: An Ordinance for Preserving Peace, Preventing Conflict and Ill Feeling between the White and Colored Races in Baltimore City, and Promoting the General Welfare of the City by Providing so far as Practicable for the Use of Separate Blocks by White and Colored People For Residences, Churches and Schools.

The idea of the ordinance was presented at a meeting of the Madison Avenue, McCulloh Street, and Eutaw Place Improvement Association. Drafted by Milton Dashiell, a white lawyer who lived on McCulloh Street, the proposed ordinance on its surface sounded equal. African Americans would be barred from moving into blocks where the majority of residents were white and whites would be prohibited from moving into blocks where the majority of residents were Black. The justification for the ordinance was nothing if not interesting. Dashiell based it on the rationale for segregated schools. If white children could not be required to spend part of their days with Black children, then white adults should not have to live with Black neighbors.

The ordinance was introduced by Councilman Samuel West. It is not surprising that those who spoke at the hearings were white and overwhelmingly in favor. Two councilmen spoke out against it, though. One suggested that restrictive covenants in property deeds would achieve the same result and would not face the legal challenges which he said the ordinance was sure to face. The only Black councilman, Harry Cummings, raised a legal challenge and moved that consideration be tabled until the City Solicitor could be consulted. The motion was defeated.

The ordinance was passed and sent to Mayor J. Barrie Mahool. He referred it to the City Solicitor, who ruled that it was constitutional. To the delight and relief of many panicky white people, Mahool signed it on December 19, 1910. As Matthew Crenson puts it, "City officials were making an issue of race, in other words, to avoid the interracial friction that might compel them to address the issue of race."

The first version of the ordinance was ruled improper by two judges on Baltimore's Supreme Bench on the grounds that the title was too long. The city charter required that the title of any city ordinance specify a single subject. So it went back to Council for revision.

In its second iteration, currently racially mixed blocks were exempted from the law's provisions. Unfortunately, the language used was open to several interpretations. Though Dashiell tried to have the ambiguous wording removed, it passed anyway and Mayor Mahool signed it. This second version would not be the last, though. A month after the mayor signed it, the Council repealed it and reenacted it because there had been a procedural error in the approval of the second version.

Version three included new provisions that applied to the location of churches and schools belonging to the two races. This third version was signed on May 15, 1911.

The ordinance remained in place until in 1913, John Gurry, a "colored person," was charged with living in a house in a white block. The councilman who had first raised objections to the ordinance was right in saying that the city should expect legal challenges. The court challenge was led by W. Ashbie Hawkins, the attorney whose purchase of the McCulloh Street house let to the introduction of that initial ordinance. The court invalidated the ordinance because the law's provisions made no sense. The language that had been included to take racially mixed blocks into consideration effectively prevented *anyone* from moving into that block.

City Council was ready with a fourth version, though. When the law was invalidated, they passed the fourth version which included revisions to preserve the property rights in force before the ordinance was enacted. The 1913 version lasted until 1917.[37]

Residents of white neighborhoods persisted in their support of housing segregation legislation. A resident of Lafayette Square, a well-to-do neighborhood composed largely of the city's German merchant class, urged Mayor James H. Preston to put "an end to this hideous negro invasion" in "some way short of wholesale murder." Preston was sympathetic, but as he told another white resident, it was pointless to continue pursuing legislative remedies if they were only going to be struck down based on legal challenges from W. Ashbie Hawkins.[38]

Baltimore's housing segregation law inspired dozens of cities to pass their own versions. The version passed in Louisville, Kentucky was also challenged in court—but this case got all the way to the U.S. Supreme Court in 1917. In *Buchanan v. Warley*, the Court ruled that municipal segregation laws were unconstitutional. In that case, W. Ashbie Hawkins filed an *amicus* brief for the National Association for the Advancement of Colored People (NAACP).[39] Interestingly, however, the Court did not rule against the Louisville ordinance because it was racially discriminatory, but rather because it infringed on the right of a property owner to sell or rent to whomever he or she wanted,[40] even if that person were Black and local laws prohibited the transaction. This ruling effectively ended Baltimore's effort to enforce housing segregation through legislation.[41] Another way would have to be found.

With legislation to create and enforce segregated housing declared unconstitutional, the next method of keeping Black people "out of our neighborhoods" became the use of restrictive covenants that limited who could sell or rent a home. This was what the city councilman had encouraged the city do in the first place.

Some restrictive covenants were already in place in a Baltimore suburb as early as 1892 when the Roland Park Company's general manager Edward Bouton was planning and building what would eventually be the Baltimore neighborhood of Roland Park. Through legal deeds, Bouton was restricting how homeowners used their land. The restrictions at first were aimed at ensuring the quality of what would become one of Baltimore's exclusive neighborhoods. The Roland Park Company set the lot sizes; approved house plans; established minimum construction value for any new home and banned, "outhouses, cesspools, private stables, chickens, livestock and other nuisances." The covenants even limited the number of pets a homeowner could have. Restrictions were a condition of sale and if the home was sold the restriction transferred to any new owner.[42]

Bouton had wanted to prohibit, "negroes or persons of African descent" from the start but was advised against it by attorneys George Whitlock, president of the Maryland Bar Association, and Samuel Schmucker, who would later be a Maryland Court of Appeals judge, In their opinion, such a deed restriction would be unconstitutional.[43] Finally, in 1910, Bouton did explicitly forbid non-servant African Americans to live in Roland Park. He did this partly because of competition from other builders developing communities in nearby areas and because he wanted Roland Park and his new community of Guilford to be seen as the most exclusive communities in the city.[44] They were—and they still are among the most exclusive. In spite of the potential for legal challenges, Bouton used racially restrictive covenants when Guilford opened in 1913.[45]

The *Baltimore Sun* supported the idea of racially restrictive covenants at the time that the City Council was working on the 1910 housing segregation legislation. While the *Baltimore Sun* also supported the ordinance and its purpose, it believed that the city would be on firmer legal footing if binding private agreements were used instead.

Sometimes individual homeowners would agree as a neighborhood to include racially restrictive covenants as conditions of sale. Typically these covenants would prohibit selling or leasing the property to "negroes or people of African descent" though they were permitted to live in a home if they were employed there as servants. In order for that to happen, though, the homeowner/employer had to be living there as well.[46]

Baltimore's African American citizens were not the only group Bouton and his Roland Park Company targeted. Jews were prohibited, too, though several prominent and wealthy Jews had bought homes in Roland Park when the company was having financial difficulties. Jews were prohibited in Roland Park beginning with property sold from 1913 onward. They were also prohibited from Guilford, Homeland, and Northwood, Bouton's other developments. Unlike with African Americans, the prohibition against sales to Jews was never actually put in writing. Bouton was able to enforce this ban because the Roland Park Company had the right to approve all sales and resales in the communities it developed.[47]

Covenants were widely used, and not just by white to keep Blacks and Jews out. Some Jewish neighborhoods barred Blacks and, sometimes unofficially, Eastern European Jews. Some Baltimore neighborhoods even barred Roman Catholics even though Baltimore had a large and influential Catholic population.

There were even Black Baltimore neighborhoods that prohibited sales or leases to white people. One such neighborhood was Morgan Park, near what was then the new campus of Morgan College (now Morgan State University). Morgan faculty and administrators lived in Morgan Park as did notable figures such as W. E. B. Du Bois and Dr. Carl Murphy, founder of the *Afro-American* newspaper chain. It is still a largely Black neighborhood. Nearby Wilson Park, developed by Harry O. Wilson, Sr., a wealthy Black businessman and banker, was another such neighborhood. Wilson Park became an elite enclave whose homeowners included W. Ashbie Hawkins and George

W. F. McMechen as well as the Rev. Garnett Russell Walker, the national NAACP's first vice president.[48]

Though clearly discriminatory, racially restrictive covenants were supported at all levels of the judicial system. Sometimes the courts commented as they rendered their decisions as the Maryland Court of Appeals did in the 1938 case *Meade v. Dennistone.* "The large, almost sudden emigration of negroes from the country to the cities, with consequent congestion in colored centers, has created a situation about which all agree something must be done," the court wrote. It went on to say that the Fourteenth Amendment prohibited public action "to contain blacks and 'to solve what has become a problem,'" but found that private racially restrictive covenants were both legal and enforceable.[49] With the courts fully behind private covenants, Baltimore was able to enforce segregated neighborhoods with little trouble and without any real violence.

Racially restrictive covenants received a major boost when the Supreme Court upheld them in *Corrigan v. Buckley* in 1926. The case involved Irene Corrigan who had signed a racially restrictive covenant when she purchased her home. When she wanted to sell that home to a Black couple, John Buckley and other neighbors objected and fought the sale. Asked to decide whether such covenants were unconstitutional under the provisions of the Fourteenth Amendment, the Court said they weren't because that amendment applied only to actions of the state. Under *Corrigan* racially restrictive covenants were defined as actions by private citizens and not by the state.

The Court's *Corrigan* decision remained in place for another twenty-two years until the Supreme Court revisited racially restrictive covenants in the 1948 case of *Shelley v. Kramer* and its companion cases. The Court effectively dismissed the arguments presented by both sides. The defendants had argued that covenants were private agreements and not subject to the Fourteenth Amendment. The plaintiffs had argued that "the freedom to purchase and use property, regardless of race or color, was a fundamental and basic freedom that was protected by the Constitution."[50]

The Court found that bringing racially restrictive covenants to the courts had made them a state matter rather than a private one.[51] Judicial enforcement of racially restrictive covenants constituted discriminatory government action in violation of the Constitution. Therefore, the Court ruled that, "the state may not accomplish indirectly through the courts what it cannot constitutionally do directly through the legislature."[52]

Racially restrictive covenants first appeared in the late nineteenth century and their use was widespread through the first half of the twentieth. It is estimated that more than half of all residential properties built during that period were subject to such covenants.[53] Even with the Court's 1948 ruling in place, some new deeds were still written with racially restrictive language. Not until the *1968 Fair Housing Act* was *writing* racially restrictive covenants made illegal.[54]

Even though the Supreme Court had ruled racially restrictive covenants unconstitutional, there was already in place a federal program that effectively kept racially segregated neighborhoods very much a fact of life in the United States.

Trying to create and enforce segregated neighborhoods through legislation and racially restrictive covenants had been bad enough. More pernicious, however, were several federal programs that were supposed to help people gain access to housing but through official policy actually served to ensure that minority citizens, especially those with lower incomes, would be contained in neighborhoods well away from middle- and upper-class white neighborhoods.

The *1934 National Housing Act*, which ultimately created what became the Federal Housing Administration (FHA), was created "to encourage improvements in housing standards and conditions." Though the FHA helped millions of people, millions more were left out. At the same time the FHA was insuring mortgages for white suburbanites, it was refusing to insure mortgages in Black neighborhoods—and even in neighborhoods *near* where African Americans were living. This was a process known as *redlining*.

The origins of redlining can be traced to Homer Hoyt, chief economist for the FHA. Ostensibly the purpose was to improve the accuracy of real estate appraisals to reduce the federal government's risk in insuring mortgages. Hoyt believed ethnicity predicted value. Northern Europeans were rated highest. African Americans were almost at the bottom of the ratings scale. The only group getting a lower rating was Mexicans.[55]

Some 239 cities were surveyed and color-coded maps were produced. Neighborhoods were colored green for "best," blue for "still desirable," yellow for "definitely declining," and red for "hazardous." The redlined neighborhoods were those lenders considered riskiest. Most redlined neighborhoods were predominantly African American though depending on the prejudices of the individual city, neighborhoods composed primarily of Catholics, Jews, Asians, and southern Europeans might also be redlined. Baltimore was one of those cities with redline maps.

Loans in redlined neighborhoods were either impossible to get or were very expensive so that low-income minorities were unable to buy homes. Because owning a home is the most significant way for ordinary people to accumulate wealth, the inability of those living in redlined neighborhoods to obtain mortgages created a wealth gap that still disproportionately disadvantages people of color.[56]

In the redlining process, new construction and design were important considerations. Many of Baltimore's traditional working class neighborhoods of rowhouses were colored yellow on the maps. They were "definitely declining" because they were older neighborhoods, any racially restrictive covenants were either not present or about to expire and they were being infiltrated by "lower grade populations."[57] They would eventually be redlined.

Redlined neighborhoods had older homes in poor condition. Most of Baltimore's core was redlined as too hazardous for conventional lending. In addition to the age and condition of the properties, other determinants were the residents' race, national origin, religion, and economic and immigration status.

Redlining in Baltimore created a two-tiered lending system. Banks lent to white people at conventional rates. Baltimore's Black population had to go to speculators or predatory lenders who charged high interest rates.

All of Baltimore's Black neighborhoods were redlined except for two notable exceptions. They were the previously mentioned Morgan Park and Wilson Park. They were colored blue on the maps and were considered "still desirable," a rating they both shared with the white neighborhoods surrounding them. Morgan Park checked off all the FHA's boxes. It was new. It was still being developed. And it had racially restrictive covenants limiting those who could live there to educated Blacks. Whites were the "inharmonious element" that the FHA didn't like.[58]

The discriminatory policies that created redlining lasted well into the 1960s. Though the *Fair Housing Act of 1968* dismantled those policies, it didn't undo the damage they caused. A March 2018 article by Tracy Jan in the *Washington Post* reported that nearly every Baltimore census tract redlined in the 1930s remains low-to-moderate income today. Furthermore, nearly 70 percent of those communities are both minority and low-income. In addition, there were areas of West Baltimore that as white neighborhoods had received a green "desirable" rating in the 1930s but became predominantly minority and low-income when their white neighbors moved to the suburbs.[59]

The *1934 National Housing Act* was not the only federal program to exacerbate segregated housing patterns and disproportionately disadvantage those who lived in those neighborhoods. The *United States Housing Act of 1937* established the public housing system. The purpose was to provide financial assistance for "elimination of unsafe and unsanitary housing conditions, for the eradication of slums, for the provision of decent, safe and sanitary dwellings for families of low income." A major part of the *1937 Housing Act* was that it shifted the federal government's emphasis from building public housing to providing loans to state and local governments for building their own public housing. Many governments used the idea of eradicating slums as an excuse to bulldoze less affluent neighborhoods largely occupied by people of color.

The G. I. Bill was signed in 1944. Among its many provisions were low-cost mortgages and low interest loans. The return of millions of veterans from World War II needing homes for themselves and their families fueled an enormous construction boom as thousands of homes were built in hundreds of suburbs. The Veterans Administration guaranteed more than two million home loans in the six years between 1944 and 1950. African American veterans were routinely denied these and other benefits as a matter of policy. While home improvement and ownership became possible for millions of white veterans, the program also helped to maintain a system of racially segregated communities.

A corollary to redlining was blockbusting. Blockbusting was an unethical real estate practice of buying homes from white homeowners at below market value based on an implied threat that their property would be devalued if racial minorities were to move into previously segregated neighborhoods.

What this description doesn't mention is the other half of this process. After purchasing a house at below market value, real estate agents would "flip" the home, selling it at inflated prices to African Americans anxious to own better housing. Because of the two-tiered lending market described earlier, the only loans African Americans could obtain had to come from predatory lenders, often the blockbusters themselves, at high interest rates. When questioned about the ethics of these practices blockbusters would counter that they were providing a necessary service that others would not and that high interest rates were warranted because of the greater risk.

To understand what led up to blockbusting in Baltimore, it is helpful to have some historical context. Racial and class divisions were, and to a large extent still are, the basis of both neighborhood identity and neighborhood isolation in Baltimore. Periodically, the need for housing and the segregated housing patterns resulted in Black expansion into white neighborhoods. What followed was usually "white flight" and resegregation.

During the early 1880s, Fulton Avenue was the western edge of the city. In 1888, Baltimore added two miles to the city limits through annexation. Electrified trolley service made moving further out from the city's central core convenient. New developments of rowhomes were made possible through the annexation. These were attractive to middle-class whites who were looking for newer housing in less crowded environments. As white Baltimoreans began moving further west, Black Baltimoreans also moved further west. Fulton Avenue became an unofficial, yet distinct, racial dividing line. Whites lived west of Fulton. Blacks lived east of Fulton.

The 1950s saw challenges to the white way of life in what had been rowhouse suburbs. They had been safe from racial and social diversity. But their "safety" was about to end. World War II and the years just afterward brought increasing numbers of African Americans to Baltimore. This added pressure to an already pressured housing market. By the early 1950s, African Americans had begun moving westward again, crossing Fulton Avenue into what had previously been all white neighborhoods. The invisible color line had been broken and was now about a mile further west of Fulton to an area called Poplar Grove across the Edmondson Avenue Bridge from the white neighborhood of Edmondson Village.

W. Edward Orser writes in his chapter, "Flight to the Suburbs" found in *The Baltimore Book: New Views of Local History*, that conventional wisdom among whites was that African Americans would never cross the bridge. But by 1955, they had and were living in the area's southeastern corner.[60]

Edmondson Village is an extensive rowhouse community in West Baltimore. It began as a suburban enclave for the city's white middle class. Between 1955 and 1965, virtually its entire white population of some 20,000 was replaced very quickly by an equally sized population of African Americans. Given the strength of unofficial segregation in Baltimore, it is surprising that this racial change happened at all. That it happened so quickly came almost as a shock to Baltimoreans. This turnover in the population of Edmondson Village was the result of blockbusting.

Blockbusting occurred in other U.S. cities and in other Baltimore neighborhoods, but the racial shift in Edmondson Village was so large and so fast that it prompted a 1994 book entitled, *Blockbusting in Baltimore: The Edmondson Village Story*. Written by now University of Maryland Baltimore County Professor Emeritus of American Studies W. Edward Orser, the book is a fascinating case study of blockbusting, its processes, its effects on housing patterns, and its effects on the people, both Black and white, who were affected.

Real estate agents engaged in blockbusting used a variety of deceitful tactics to convince white homeowners that African Americans were beginning to move into the neighborhood. Tactics might include hiring Black women to push baby carriages in white neighborhoods, hiring Black youth to stage brawls in front of white-owned homes, selling a home to a Black family, or purchasing a home or homes and leaving them unoccupied.

These kinds of tactics preyed on white fears that if Black people moved in, the value of their homes would go down. They were implicit threats such as the neighborhood was no longer safe, that it was deteriorating, and might become a slum. Having stoked the fears, real estate agents then offered to buy the homes at below market prices. White residents became all too willing to sell up and move on. As people began to sell, the agents would leave business cards or flyers in the mailboxes of those remaining offering to buy their properties.

In his book about blockbusting Orser wrote that to induce what could be called panic selling, blockbusters might purchase one home on a block at an unusually high price assuming that even the rumor of a Black buyer would trigger a panic. They were usually right. Orser also wrote that in acute instances of heightened blockbuster-induced panic, white homes might be bought for as little as 50 percent below market value and sold to Black buyers for as much as 50 percent above market value. He called it ironic that the low prices whites received when they sold reinforced the perception that Black buyers depressed home values.[61]

New Black residents sometimes complained that commercial and governmental services declined as white residents left. Orser writes that the exploitative ways in which blockbusting works and the neighborhood instability caused by white flight and racial change caused both departing white residents and incoming Black residents to fear that the result would be new slums. Though such fears often proved true, Edmondson Village seemed to be a rare exception, managing the problems caused by blockbusting with a stability not seen in many communities.

In their social and economic status, the new Black residents of Edmondson Village more closely resembled than differed from the white residents who had left. But the segregated, two-tiered lending market created by redlining and continued during blockbusting made it less likely that Black residents would be able to maintain the middle-class lifestyles white residents had enjoyed. With overpriced older homes paid for with loans at high interest rates, Black residents who were able to pay for their homes were sometimes unable to maintain them as they might have wished.[62]

Blockbusting practices inflicted enormous harm on Baltimore's African Americans. Though they were able to purchase better homes in better neighborhoods to which they had previously been denied access, they did so at high financial cost. Most city banks would not lend to Black applicants so the alternative became the speculators and predatory lenders. Too often, African Americans were unable to keep up the payments resulting in loan defaults and foreclosures. High turnover rates caused neighborhood instability which then led to their general deterioration.

The *Federal Highway Aid Act of 1956* authorized the construction of the Interstate Highway System. On the surface, one wouldn't intuitively connect a federal highway construction program with segregation, but they are closely connected. While the Interstates did connect the nation's cities, it was when they arrived at those cities that the trouble began.

Interstate highways often encircled cities. When they went around cities, fewer people were inclined to drive into them. This encouraged the growth and development of suburban communities. As more and more (mostly) white and middle-class people moved out of the cities and into the suburbs, those who were left behind were mostly people of color with lower incomes. Making the problem worse was that amenities such as shopping and restaurants that grew up around the Interstate exits and their adjacent suburban communities gave those living in those suburbs even less incentive to go into the cities to shop or enjoy an evening out.

If Interstates going around cities caused problems for the cities, those that went through them caused even worse problems. In going through cities, blighted areas (i.e., areas in poor condition most often populated by people of color) were bulldozed. People displaced by these federal highway projects had few choices about where to move. Because it was all they could afford, they were often pushed into even poorer housing in even worse neighborhoods. Sometimes, though, neighborhoods that were bulldozed may have seen better days but were not in fact blighted. Communities that weren't bulldozed were often cut into pieces with residents becoming isolated and cut off from essential services.

Baltimore's "Highway to Nowhere" is a classic example of how destructive an Interstate through a city can be. Now called U. S. Route 40, it was originally to be called I-170 and was intended to connect the east/west I-70 coming out of Western Maryland to the north/south I-95. It would have cut a destructive swath through downtown Baltimore.

The "opening up" of areas west of Fulton Avenue had given many African Americans new housing opportunities. Unfortunately, the older homes east of the line began to deteriorate. One *Baltimore Sun* reporter wrote in 1944, "Homes are very badly in need of repair and paint; dead rats lie in the street where they are crushed by automobiles; alleyways are littered with debris and foul-smelling garbage; lots where homes formerly stood are covered with a thick layer of ashes."[63] Such descriptions gave city officials all the justification they needed for running the planned I-170 through there on its way to hook up with I-95.

I-170 never happened. An entire book could be written on how and why that was the case. But the 1.2 miles of what would come to be called the "Highway to Nowhere" that were built cost $50 million in the early 1970s. It took the form of a straight-line ditch with a four-lane highway in it. If the construction costs were high, the human cost was far higher. Clearing the way for I-170 cut several neighborhoods in two and required the demolition of 971 houses, 62 businesses, and a school. The residents, who were mostly Black, were resettled in nearby mostly Black neighborhoods. Today the areas adjacent to the "Highway to Nowhere" are 99 percent Black. Those who live there have average incomes about half of that of the city as a whole and substantial numbers of them live below the poverty line.[64]

The "Highway to Nowhere" was one of several such roads covered in a 2018 feature article Johnny Miller wrote for *The Guardian*. Miller quotes two Baltimoreans who provide a real indication of the impact the ditch has had. Denise Johnson, a community organizer who grew up in West Baltimore said, "We lost families, we lost homeowners, we lost businesses, and we lost churches. And we lost people. People who were stable. People who didn't plan to leave the community."

John Bullock is a city councilman representing the 9th District, which includes the "Highway to Nowhere." Bullock told Miller, "This was not a neighborhood that was struggling. We're talking about middle class neighborhoods, which were seen through the eyes of others as slums or ghettos because of the color of the people who lived there."

Bullock continued by referring to challenges faced by the marginalized citizens he represents; challenges such as redlining, lack of employment, and disinvestment. And, "Because if we say housing was lost, churches were lost, we have to remember also businesses were lost and oftentimes people have to go outside their communities to spend that money, which never gets recirculated in that community."[65]

There are proposals about what to do with the "Highway to Nowhere" ranging from making it into a park to removing it entirely and reuniting the divided neighborhoods. And for an interesting look at the coalition that stopped this project and another one as well, refer to chapter 10.

The final piece of federal legislation to mention in this chapter is the *Fair Housing Act of 1968*. Among its purposes was to dismantle the systemic racially driven policies that had helped create an increasingly racially segregated society in which too many people, mostly minorities, had been shoved as a permanent under-class. In addition to making discrimination when buying or leasing a home illegal, the *Fair Housing Act* also banned redlining, writing racially restrictive covenants, and blockbusting practices.

As previously mentioned, redlining had created a two-tiered system of lending. Over three decades, banks lent money to whites leaving cities for the suburbs while Black residents had to stay in deteriorating neighborhoods and were forced to borrow from predatory lenders. The situation was made worse as banks began closing branches in inner city neighborhoods. Those who lived there had no options but to go to check-cashing operations, payday loan offices, and similar services.

Subprime loans became an attractive, if dangerous, way for minority borrowers to get mortgages. When the housing bubble burst in 2007, thousands of mortgages were foreclosed. Antero Pietila, in his book, *Not In My Neighborhood*, wrote that between 2000 and 2008, more than 33,000 Baltimore homes were facing foreclosure. Pietila also wrote that race was such an overriding concern in lending that high-income African Americans living in Black neighborhoods were three times more likely to receive subprime home loans than low-income white borrowers in white neighborhoods.

Baltimore City sued Wells Fargo Bank under the *Fair Housing Act* alleging that two-thirds of its foreclosures were in census tracts having more than 60 percent African Americans while only 15.6 percent were in census tracts that had less than 20 percent African Americans. These practices had the result of intensifying segregation.[66]

Not much has changed in Baltimore. It remains one of the most segregated cities in the country. If you were to overlay a map showing Baltimore's mostly Black neighborhoods with one showing where poverty is concentrated, you would see a correlation.

According to the U.S. Census Bureau, 21.8 percent of Baltimoreans live below the poverty line. By comparison, the state's poverty rate is 9.4 percent and the three jurisdictions surrounding the city, Anne Arundel, Baltimore, and Howard Counties have poverty rates of 7.0 percent, 9.9 percent, and 5.2 percent, respectively. At 23.4 percent, only Somerset County at the extreme southern end of the Eastern Shore has a higher poverty rate than the city's. The Urban Institute reports that there are neighborhoods in Baltimore with poverty rates exceeding 35 percent.[67]

In Baltimore, the effects of segregation and poverty are clear. "The Racial Wealth Divide in Baltimore," a 2017 report from the Corporation for Enterprise Development showed that the median income of Black Baltimoreans was half that of whites. Further, 32 percent of Black households had zero net worth as compared with 15 percent of white households. The Black unemployment rate was 14 percent while that of whites was 4 percent. Only 14 percent of African Americans had finished a bachelor's degree or higher, but 51 percent of whites had. And there were 30,000 vacant homes in Baltimore, mostly in high-poverty areas.[68]

Neighborhoods with high levels of poverty are also neighborhoods that have suffered from a lack of capital investment. A 2020 study by the Urban Institute measured disinvestment in Baltimore's Black neighborhoods between 2004 and 2016. While its findings were shocking, they were not surprising. As reported by John Sankofa on the Institute's "Urban Wire" blog, by nearly every measurement, the disparities are alarming. Capital investment is uneven and driven by poverty and race. White neighborhoods received more than three times the investment than did majority Black neighborhoods.

Referring to the magnitude of the disparities, Brady Meixell, one of the study's authors, said that conditions in racially segregated neighborhoods are exacerbated by segregated capital markets. Brett Theodos, another of the study's authors, said that less investment results in even less investment. Without investments to upgrade housing and add amenities such as grocery stores, people with higher incomes are less likely to want to live and spend their money there thus perpetuating the problems faced by these neighborhoods.[69]

City government is limited in what it can do. Property taxes in Baltimore are double or more than those in the surrounding counties. The city is further disadvantaged by the amount of property in the city that is exempted from paying property taxes. Hospitals, universities, arts institutions, religious institutions, not-for-profit organizations, and federal and state government offices all have property. They all use city services, but they don't pay property taxes.

With high rates of poverty, entrenched segregated housing patterns, disinvestment in Black neighborhoods, systemic racism, stretched city resources, and other problems (including the police force), it is little wonder that in the spring of 2015, the city erupted in protest when a West Baltimore Black man named Freddie Gray suffered a fatal spinal injury while in police custody.

Even some years after those protests, little has changed. In a city that is 62 percent African American and in which the three main city elected offices are held by African Americans and in which ten of the fourteen members of the City Council are persons of color, too many African American Baltimoreans feel unheard. They feel neglected and overlooked, saying the city responds to service requests only if the neighborhood is white. While there hasn't been much positive change, there are glimmers of hope as will be seen in chapter 11.

NOTES

1. David S. Bogan, "Mathias de Sousa: Maryland's First Colonist of African Descent," *Maryland Historical Society Magazine* 96, no. 1 (Spring 2001): 071.

2. Ibid., p. 75.

3. Ibid., p. 78.

4. Archives of Maryland, "Proceedings and Acts of the General Assembly January 1637/8 – September 1664," https://msa.maryland.gov/megafile/msa/speccol/sc2900/sc2908/000001/000001/html/am1-533.html

5. Archives of Maryland, "The Maryland Constitutional Convention of 1776," July 2009. https://msa.maryland.gov/msa/speccol/sc2200/sc2221/000004/000000/html/00000004.html

6. Matthew A. Crenson, *Baltimore: A Political History* (Baltimore: Johns Hopkins University Press, 2017), p. 53.

7. Archives of Maryland, "The Maryland Constitutional Convention of 1776," July 2009. https://msa.maryland.gov/msa/speccol/sc2200/sc2221/000004/000000/html/00000004.html

8. David Barton, "This History of Black Voting Rights – From the 1700s to Present Day," *Original People*, 2004. https://originalpeople.org/the-history-of-black-voting-rights-from-the-1700s-to-present-day-2/

9. The Hopkins Diaspora ERG, *The Hopkins Diaspora ERG Celebrates 400 Years of African American History in Maryland.* Johns Hopkins Medicine, 2019 (website). https://www.hopkinsmedicine.org/diversity/_documents/400_Years_of_AfricanAmerican_Histor y_in_Maryland_FINAL.pdf

10. The Avalon Project, "Amendments to the Maryland Constitution of 1776," *Yale Law School Lillian Goldman Law Library*, 2008. https://avalon.law.yale.edu/17th_century/ma03.asp

11. Christopher Phillips, *Freedom's Port: The African American Community of Baltimore, 1790-1860* (Chicago: University of Illinois Press, 1997), p. 15.

12. Department of Planning, *City of Baltimore Comprehensive Master Plan* (Baltimore: City of Baltimore, 2006). https://planning.baltimorecity.gov/planning -master-plan/plan, p. 32.

13. Phillips, p. 15.

14. Crenson, p. 161.

15. Ibid., p. 163.

16. Ibid., p. 164.

17. Phillips, p. 36.

18. Ibid., p. 32.

19. Crenson, p. 163, 165.

20. Phillips, p. 58.

21. Antero Pietila, *Not in My Neighborhood: How Bigotry Shaped a Great American City* (Chicago: Ivar R. Dee, 2010), p. 8.

22. Karen Olson, "Old West Baltimore: Segregation, African-American Culture and the Struggle for Equality," in *The Baltimore Book: New Views of Local History*, edited by Elizabeth Free, Linda Shopes and Linda Zeidman, 57–80 (Philadelphia: Temple University Press, 1991), p. 57.

23. W. Edward Orser, "Flight to the Suburbs: Suburbanization and Racial Change on Baltimore's West Side," in *The Baltimore Book: New Views of Local History*, edited by Elizabeth Free, Linda Shopes and Linda Zeidman, 203–226 (Philadelphia: Temple University Press, 1991), p. 203.

24. Crenson, p. 277.

25. Olson, p. 61.

26. Department of Planning, *City of Baltimore Comprehensive Master Plan* (Baltimore: City of Baltimore, 2006). https://planning.baltimorecity.gov/planning -master-plan/plan, p. 37.

27. Orser, p. 36.

28. Department of Planning, *City of Baltimore Comprehensive Master Plan* (Baltimore: City of Baltimore, 2006). https://planning.baltimorecity.gov/planning -master-plan/plan, p. 36.

29. Olson, p. 57.

30. Department of Planning, *City of Baltimore Comprehensive Master Plan* (Baltimore: City of Baltimore, 2006). https://planning.baltimorecity.gov/planning -master-plan/plan, p. 37.

31. Olson, p. 59.

32. Ibid.

33. Department of Planning, *City of Baltimore Comprehensive Master Plan* (Baltimore: City of Baltimore, 2006). https://planning.baltimorecity.gov/planning -master-plan/plan, p. 40.

34. Olson, p. 59.

35. Eli Pousson, "Vacant Houses and Inequality in Baltimore from the Nineteenth Century to Today," in *Baltimore Revisited: Stories of Inequality and Resistance in a U.S. City*, edited by P. Nicole King, Kate Drabinski and Joshua Clark Davis, 52–66 (New Brunswick, NJ: Rutgers University Press, 2009), p. 56.

36. Pietila, p. 6, 8.

37. Crenson, pp. 340–42.

38. Pietila, p. 30.

39. Pousson, p. 56.

40. Crenson, p. 341.

41. Pietila, p. 31.

42. Ibid., p. 35.

43. Jacques Kelly, "1893 Letter Details Racially Restrictive Covenants in City Neighborhoods," *Baltimore Sun*, March 27, 2015. https://www.baltimoresun.com/maryland/baltimore-city/bs-md-ci-kelly-column-covenants-20150327-column.html

44. Pietila, p. 35.

45. Jacques Kelly, "1893 Letter Details Racially Restrictive Covenants in City Neighborhoods," *Baltimore Sun*, March 27, 2015. https://www.baltimoresun.com/maryland/baltimore-city/bs-md-ci-kelly-column-covenants-20150327-column.html

46. Pietila, p. 48.

47. Ibid., p. 36.

48. Baltimore Heritage, "Development of a Segregated Black Community: 1880s – 1900s," *Baltimore Civil Rights Heritage*, 2019 (website). https://baltimoreheritage.github.io/civil-rightsheritage/1885-1929/

49. Pietila, p. 49.

50. Welsh, p. 136.

51. Ibid., p. 134.

52. Melissa Holtje, "It's Not Over: A Historical and Contemporary Look at Racial Restrictive Covenants," *Homelight* (blog). https://www.homelight.com/blog/buyer-racialrestrictive-covenants/

53. Ibid., p. 134.

54. Ibid.

55. Pietila, p. 62.

56. Tracy Jan, "Redlining Was Banned 50 Years Ago. It's Still Hurting Minorities Today," *Washington Post*, March 28, 2018. https://www.washingtonpost.com/news/wonk/wp/2018/03/28/redlining-was-banned-50-yearsago-its-still-hurting-minorities-today/?noredirect=on

57. Pietila, p. 72.

58. Ibid., p. 70, 72.

59. Tracy Jan, "Redlining Was Banned 50 Years Ago. It's Still Hurting Minorities Today," *Washington Post*, March 28, 2018. https://www.washingtonpost.com/news/wonk/wp/2018/03/28/redlining-was-banned-50-yearsago-its-still-hurting-minorities-today/?noredirect=on

60. W. Edward Orser, "Flight to the Suburbs: Suburbanization and Racial Change on Baltimore's West Side," in *The Baltimore Book: New Views of Local History*, edited by Elizabeth Free, Linda Shopes and Linda Zeidman, pp. 203–26 (Philadelphia: Temple University Press, 1991), pp. 207, 209–211, 221.

61. W. Edward Orser, *Blockbusting in Baltimore: The Edmondson Village Story* (Lexington, KY: The University Press of Kentucky, 1994), p. 90.

62. Ibid., pp. 131–2.

63. W. Edward Orser, "Flight to the Suburbs: Suburbanization and Racial Change on Baltimore's West Side," in *The Baltimore Book: New Views of Local History*, edited by Elizabeth Free, Linda Shopes and Linda Zeidman, 203–26 (Philadelphia: Temple University Press, 1991), p. 211.

64. Ibid.

65. Johnny Miller, "Roads to Nowhere: How Infrastructure Built on American Inequality," *The Guardian*, February 21, 2018. https://www.theguardian.com/cities/2018/feb/21/roadsnowhere-infrastructure-american-inequality

66. Pietila, pp. 257–8.

67. United States Census Bureau. https://census.gov

68. Racial Wealth Divide Initiative. *Racial Wealth Divide in Baltimore*. Corporation for Enterprise Development, 2017. https://prosperitynow.org/files/resources/Racial_Wealth_Divide_in_Baltimore_RWDI.pdf, pp. 5–7.

69. Sankofa, John, "Disinvestment in Baltimore's Black Neighborhoods Is Foreboding But Reversible," *Urban Wire*, September 29, 2020, https://www.urban.org/urbanwire/disinvestment-baltimores-black-neighborhoods-foreboding-reversible

Chapter 10

Transportation Policy

Questions of Power, Questions of Identity

Gerrymandering, the subject of another chapter, involves the drawing of lines. Doing so has both political effects and identity effects. Transportation decisions also draw lines—lines on maps that represent connections (or their absence) and that signal importance (or its absence). Those who make transportation decisions may not think of them in this manner, but they should. This chapter will review a number of important transportation policy decisions in Maryland and highlight what messages they sent. The list begins from the 1950s and extends to (and beyond) the present. Fifteen projects are listed. They are not the only ones, but, together, they raise the issues we want to raise. In addition, they represent the range of projects most states face.

THE CHESAPEAKE BAY BRIDGE

When the two-lane span crossing the Chesapeake Bay near Annapolis was completed in 1954, most knew it would change Maryland's "Eastern Shore." What might have been less in view is how it would change the western one.

Maryland's "Eastern Shore" had long been a place unto-itself. Largely agricultural, dotted with small towns, it was politically much more conservative than the rest of the state. That conservatism exhibited itself in many ways, one of the most prominent ones being race relations. The region, with a sizeable African American population, saw more voter suppression than the rest of the state and also more lynchings. In many ways, setting foot onto the "Eastern Shore" was like setting foot in the Deep South.[1]

The region might have remained much that way if it weren't for, first, the influx of tourists the bridge brought and, second, the influx of new residents moving across the bay from metropolitan Baltimore and Washington, tolerating the longer commute in order to buy a lower-priced residence. The tourists largely passed through, en route to the oceanfront beaches, which would experience phenomenal growth after 1954, but they would stop for gasoline or lunch. They thereby came to know more about places such as Easton, Cambridge, and Salisbury. One result is that what was happening on the "Eastern Shore" was no longer invisible. Antisegregation demonstrators from colleges and universities on the western shore, as well as up into Pennsylvania, knew of Cambridge's discriminating record on race and public accommodations and were drawn to it in 1962 and 1963.[2] The demonstrators exacerbated already existing tensions, so did the new residents whose politics did not match well with what was the norm. Although the "Eastern Shore" retained its conservative bent, a few counties—for example, Talbot—became less reliably "red." And, as voter suppression diminished, some places—for example, Salisbury—developed reliably "blue" pockets. The bridge was if not the cause of changes at least a major catalyst.

The western shore featured a number of popular resorts. Just as an example, consider Chesapeake Beach.[3] It was one of the easier ones to reach from Baltimore or Washington. It was not far down the Chesapeake Shore like, for example, Point Lookout at southern Maryland's end. In addition, from Washington, D.C., one could access Chesapeake Beach by a railroad line, commemorated in the railroading museum in the town and, after it closed, a trolley line.[4] Before the bridge, getting to the ocean was possible only two ways. First, one could drive northeastwardly through Harford and Cecil Counties and, then, having reached the bay's northern extreme at the mouth of the Susquehanna and Elk Rivers, proceed down the Eastern Shore. That loop would add hours to the trip compared to a direct highway if such were to exist. Second, one could take a ferry across the Bay. This approach, although much more straight-line, still added hours. The consequence of the journey's length is that many settled for the likes of Chesapeake Beach. The bay was not as polluted or jelly-fish infested then as now, so it offered a very pleasant beach experience.

Once the Chesapeake Bay Bridge opened, decreasing numbers visited these western shore beaches. A steady decline began, with some communities transitioning to residential ones and others stuck with rotting boardwalks and rotting pavilions. The railroad ceased operating in 1935; the replacement trolley line lasted another decade or so. Highway money did not go to the widening of the roads leading to these beaches such as Central Avenue or Landover Road coming out of Washington; rather it went to U.S. 50, which led to the bridge. Meanwhile, on the Eastern Shore, Ocean City grew. In the late 1960s, development faded after 30th Street and disappeared after 45th, with a few structures, such as the infamous U.S. Senate aide Bobby Baker's Carousel Motel, close to the Maryland-Delaware border.[5] There was though a large gap between 45th Street and 110th, where the Carousel was. There was no convention center, no bridge crossing into Ocean City at 61st Street, and no mobile home developments along what would be called "Montego Bay." The Delaware beaches grew too, but Rehoboth Beach lacked space to grow and the beaches between Rehoboth and Ocean City—Dewey, Bethany, Fenwick Island—did not boom as Ocean City did. Some Delaware shoreline was also protected. And the boom there was different: whereas Ocean City saw a variety of commercial establishments built, Bethany saw condominiums and Dewey cottages. All the beaches changed, but Ocean City tripled in size.[6] Meanwhile, on the western side of the Bay Bridge, once-thriving resort communities struggled. The construction of a two-lane bridge (a second three-lane span was added in 1973) effected major changes on both sides of the Bay.

Were those who proposed and planned the bridge aware of what effects it would have? The rhetoric surrounding the bridge, rhetoric involving a few governors, was all positive. Giving urban dwellers easier access to the ocean was a bipartisan goal they embraced and most Marylanders supported. Did those who would be negatively affected in three Maryland counties—Anne Arundel, Calvert, and St. Mary's—protest? Only a bit, for they seemed to believe that there would be traffic for both the ocean beaches and the bay beaches.

In addition, the western shore had another industry propping it up—legal gambling. Early in the twentieth century, the dominant activity in southern Maryland was tobacco farming. A number of factors, including legislative action, made tobacco farming less and less lucrative. So, as a sop to four Maryland counties, the three mentioned above and Charles (which lacked bay frontage), the legislature legalized certain types of gambling in them—most prominently, slot machines.[7] So, as one crossed the line between Prince George's County and Charles County near Waldorf, there were slot machine "palaces" one might visit. And on the Patuxent River separating Charles and Calvert, there were large gambling pavilions in small towns such as Benedict and Hughesville. One did not need to go to the bay to find slots, but, if one did get to resorts such as Chesapeake Beach, one would find gambling a-plenty.

So, those on the western shore who might have objected to the bridge because it would mean less business thought that they had an ace in the hole with slot machines. Yes, you could cross the bay and go to Ocean City, but there was no legal gambling over on the Eastern Shore. Higher surf, yes; slots, no.

The legislated gift of legalized gambling unfortunately had an expiration date. Although intended to help southern Maryland transition from tobacco to some alternative, the gift actually helped the region transition from vacationland to something else. There were, as gambling ended, losses: properties in Waldorf, for example, went from prosperity to bankruptcy. But the overall transition was smoother than it might have been without "slots." That transition was aided by the region's slowly becoming Washington, D.C.—and, a bit less, Baltimore—exurbia.

Highways that once carried beach traffic and then gamblers now carried commuters. Also emerging at this point were pronouncedly different images for the four counties. Anne Arundel became more urbanized as the Baltimore area grew southward and the Annapolis area simply grew, both developments featuring more and larger roadways; Charles, with major highways running through it, became quite commercial; Calvert, with a less traveled highway running north-south through it, became residential; St. Mary's, still a tad out of the way, remained somewhat quaint.

Transportation, then, played a role in what these counties became. The roads were not rhetorically neutral; rather, they played a constitutive role. U.S. 301, which runs north-south through Charles County carries a good bit of interstate traffic including much truck traffic; Maryland routes 2 and 4, which run north side through Calvert, carry mostly cars heading to and from bayfront properties. A roadmap of Anne Arundel looks like any number of others from just outside cities whereas a roadmap of St. Mary's looks more rural. Anne Arundel has expressways radiating out from Baltimore as well as a number of cross-county limited access highways. The presence of Baltimore's airport in Anne Arundel adds major roads getting fliers north to Baltimore and south to Washington: the airport is "Baltimore-Washington International," although it is not convenient for much of the Washington, D.C. area. In St. Mary's, a four-lane road would be difficult to find. The roads, then, defined very different counties.

BELTWAYS

A feature of the interstate highway system was its circumferential highways, which were ways of bypassing cities designed for those not traveling to and from the affected cities. Some envisioned them as rather lightly traveled and heavily used by interstate trucking. The latter prediction proved true but not the former. These roads were heavily used, bringing commercial development along with them as well as new inter-suburb patterns. They also had unintended effects on the cities they bypassed.

Maryland had two of these circumferential roads: I-695 circling (eventually) Baltimore and I-495 circling Washington, D.C., the Baltimore Beltway, and the Capital Beltway.

One only needs to travel on either of these routes once to realize that they are not bypasses. That original intention quickly vanished as both beltways attracted commercial and residential development. That development was probably likely to occur, beltways or no beltways, but what the two highways did was pattern it. Most exits became mini-hubs, whereas, previously, the development was occurring along roads leaving the cities. In Prince George's County, for example, development was extending gradually out roads like Landover Road (Maryland Route 202), Central Avenue (Maryland Route 214), and Pennsylvania Avenue (Maryland Route 4). The beltway, however, quickly produced hubs at its intersection with these roads, altering the development pattern with construction now occurring farther out from the city. It is difficult to say what, if any, effect this change had, but it may well have exacerbated an already growing divide between city and suburb by pushing suburbia farther out.

Consider shopping patterns in Washington, D.C., for example. In the 1950s, suburbanites—to a large extent—traveled into the city for major shopping trips. By the end of the 1960s, where did they shop? At malls, almost all of which were near the beltway. Then came the urban rioting in the late 1960s, especially in 1968 in the wake of the King assassination, and the suburbanites stuck to their new shopping pattern out of fear of the inner city. These riots played a role in what some pointed to as the decline—if not death—of downtown shopping districts in both Washington and Baltimore, but the pattern of central city avoidance was already in place with shoppers going to Montgomery Mall, Wheaton Plaza, Prince George's Plaza, and Landover Mall (even Tyson's Corner Center, several minutes on I-495 into Virginia), not downtown Washington.

The downtown shopping areas did indeed suffer. In Baltimore, major development efforts such as the one that produced the Inner Harbor complex were needed to stop the downtown decline. In Washington, the reversal was a bit later when Abe Pollin built a large sports and concert arena where the Hecht Company once had its flagship store at 7th and F NW. Downtown decline was not, however, the only consequence of beltway development.

The two beltways also knitted together suburban communities that once were rather separate. In the 1950s, residents in Silver Spring in Montgomery County shopped in downtown Silver Spring (which had major stores) or traveled to downtown Washington. By the mid-1960s, driving up Georgia Avenue (Maryland Route 97) to Wheaton Plaza was an option. The drive took ten minutes. Then came the beltway and options in both directions became not that much farther. Residents of the different suburban communities became less strongly identified with those communities and more identified with "suburban Washington." The same phenomenon was occurring in the Baltimore area, as Catonsville and Pikesville and Towson formed into an arc on the city's west side.

Pockets of what we might term "town identity" remained, either because the identity was so strong (Takoma Park, Ellicott City) or because the place was removed from major transportation corridors (Garrett Park, Mt. Rainier), but, for the most part, a suburban identity was replacing a "town" one. This development compelled suburban places to assert, sometimes desperately, their identity. Some succeeded; some didn't.

Any loss was offset by a gain, for the suburban identity grew stronger and stronger. In the Washington, D.C. area, it embraced two states. Those in the Maryland jurisdictions of Montgomery and Prince George's Counties became allied with those in the Virginia jurisdictions of Arlington and Fairfax Counties and the independent cities of Alexandria and Falls Church. All were suburban with suburban problems, suburban identities, and a suburban relationship with the big city at the center. In Washington, D.C., one need only look at a map of the Metro subway system to see the center-periphery relationship. Then, draw the beltway onto it to see how the places at the periphery are joined in a transportation circle. Increasingly, Metro and the roads leading in were workday ones with the beltway leading suburbanites to many desirable sites, all advertised as "just off the beltway."

Arguably, this phenomenon was more pronounced in Washington than in Baltimore. Baltimore lacked the elaborate subway system; furthermore, for a long period, Baltimore's beltway was a horseshoe, not a circle. In both the northeast and the southeast, the highway petered out. The petering out was more pronounced in the northeast because it pushed further to the east and went into and through what had been major industrial areas. Along the western arc, then, the flow was much greater. And, even after the Francis Scott Key Bridge was completed to close the beltway circle, the western arc traffic exceeded the eastern. The western route seemed to be the faster one if one were trying to bypass the city and avoid the two tunnels that took traffic more directly through it (also avoiding tolls). Thus, the links along the Catonsville-Pikesville-Towson arc were stronger than any that might develop between Dundalk and Glen Burnie. The Key Bridge was perceived as liminal whereas, in the Washington area, the American Legion and Woodrow Wilson bridges across the Potomac were crossed without blinking.

All of this discussion may seem remote from communication; however, if one understands rhetoric as potentially constitutive, what we're talking about is how those living in these two urban areas understood themselves. What was their identity? And how was that identity formed? Our point is that transportation policy decisions are not just about getting people from point a to point b. Rather, those decisions affect who people are. The suburban identity has many sources. In both Baltimore and Washington, that identity as a trans-suburban one was advanced by the beltways. Once that identity emerged, there were two consequences. The identity strongly separated one from the city at the center of it all, creating various city-suburban tensions; and the identity, by connecting suburbs, diminished the identity that one might acquire from any particular suburban community. Residents of Chevy Chase in Montgomery County held on to their identity fiercely, but, just a few miles away, residents of Silver Spring couldn't tell you what the borders were, if any, among places such as Silver Spring, Wheaton, Aspen Hill, White Oak, and Colesville (all of which had Silver Spring Zip codes).

I-95, NORTHEAST OF BALTIMORE

U.S. 1, the Maine to Florida highlight of the national highway system, went North by Northeast out of Baltimore, but it did not trace the route most wanted to follow. The preferred route was that taken by U.S. 40. Coming out of Baltimore, it was Pulaski Highway. Then, it made its way through Aberdeen, Havre de Grace, and Elkton before passing into Delaware. Once in Delaware, its route was odd. It did not go into Wilmington and then onto Philadelphia; rather, it crossed the Delaware River and turned East to Atlantic City, New Jersey. After all, it was a West-East route. Crucially, before it turned toward the Atlantic, it junctioned with the New Jersey Turnpike.

So, U.S. 40 became the Baltimore to New York route, with its New Jersey portion, the Turnpike, not even having an official "U.S." designation.

As such, U.S. 40 was heavily traveled—more and more as the number of automobiles increased and leisure travel became possible after World War II. The road, therefore, had the amenities one would expect—service stations, a handful of Howard Johnson's, other restaurants, and a few fledgling motels. Unfortunately, into the 1960s, many of these establishments were "whites only." Yes, the stretch of highway we're talking about was North of Baltimore but, nonetheless, "Jim Crow" lived.[8] Baltimore County was not especially retrograde but Harford County and Cecil County were.

As African nations began achieving independence, beginning with Ghana in 1957, they were admitted to the United Nations. Unable to afford an embassy in Washington and a legation in New York, these new nations' diplomats would commute back-and-forth between the two cities along U.S. 40. The discrimination they experienced eventually became embarrassing to the president. Although John F. Kennedy, when confronted with the issue, did cavalierly suggest that they just fly, his administration eventually saw the need to bypass U.S. 40. Thus, the plans for the stretch of I-95, named the "John F. Kennedy Highway," were accelerated. A toll road, it—and the short but not cheap Delaware Turnpike—would carry traffic quickly from Baltimore's Harbor Tunnel to the southern outskirts of Wilmington. In traffic islands along the way, the highway would have all the amenities interstate travelers, white and black, needed.

Most probably saw the stretch of I-95 as simply a response to the heavy traffic on U.S. 40, but it was more than that. It represented a federal response to a Maryland issue that, rather than flag the issue down, government officials chose to bypass. Interestingly, the facilities along U.S. 40 had evoked protests—largely by college students from both Baltimore and Philadelphia schools. With many of the discriminating facilities now struggling to survive, the protests moved South and East. Just as they took on discrimination along U.S. 40, the student protesters would take on discrimination along U.S. 50, the highway that connected the Chesapeake Bay Bridge to the oceanside. Their focus would be the halfway point of Cambridge, which would see racial unrest from 1963 to 1967.

I-95 BETWEEN BALTIMORE AND WASHINGTON—AND IN THE CITIES

There undoubtedly were vestiges of racism along U.S. 1 between Baltimore and Washington. Prince George's County, now a largely African American jurisdiction, was at the time rather "southern" in its feel. There was a striking difference between the two Maryland counties that bordered the nation's capital: Montgomery to the North was more affluent; Prince George's to the East less so. Although both featured communities with different demographics and, therefore, different political attitudes, the two counties, as a whole, were strikingly different. In 1972, for example, the George Wallace campaign for the Democratic presidential nomination chose to hold a rally that proved to be the campaign's termination, when Wallace was shot, in Prince George's County. Less a segregationist and more a populist than in previous years, Wallace was still much more likely to have appeal in "PG" County than in the likes of Bethesda, Silver Spring, and Rockville. (Some thought it was ironic that, seriously wounded, he was transported to a hospital in Montgomery, not to a closer one in Prince George's.)

The traditional highway route from Baltimore to Washington was through Prince George's County, so some of the push behind the I-95 route might have been rooted in getting those who might be subject to discrimination riding through Laurel off U.S. 1. But there already was the Baltimore-Washington Parkway, a four-lane expressway managed by the U.S. Park Service linking the cities. So, one does not find the urgency to build I-95 here that there was in Northeast of Baltimore.

The controversy surrounding this stretch of I-95 concerned its route. There were sufficient open spaces to plow through a large highway along most of its route. At the North end, the proposed routes were through largely industrial areas, many of which were partially abandoned. So, controversy surrounded not the inter-city Baltimore-Washington path but the route through the cities. That controversy involved not just I-95 but other interstate routes.

At the southern end, a highway then known as I-70S (now I-270) entered the Washington suburbs in Bethesda in Montgomery County. Rather than take it further through affluent Bethesda, the plan was to run the route with the Capital Beltway a few exits and then take it into Washington through less affluent Silver Spring and Takoma Park. Much of this route—known as the "North Central Freeway"—would run overtop the Baltimore and Ohio tracks. Although some questioned both its cost and its visual appeal, the route did not affect residents except when the highway abandoned the railroad route just outside downtown Silver Spring and crossed through several neighborhoods to a proposed beltway junction in between Georgia Avenue (MD Route 97) and Colesville Road (U.S. 29).

One might wonder why the proposed highway did not just continue along the B & O right-of-way until it crossed the Capital Beltway. Two reasons might be cited. First, that would have created a major intersection at the beginning of the I-495 section referred to by locals as the "Rock Creek Roller Coaster," perhaps not the safest spot. Second, that would have taken the highway through the federally owned Walter Reed Army Hospital Annex. The annex, built to handle an overflow of patients after World War II, has an interesting history, much of it having nothing to do with the Army. Those living near it often wondered what would be done with it as its buildings gradually fell into decay. The Army and the federal government wondered too, making it a site without any clear plan.[9] Taking a highway through it might have disrupted a future use, but no one knew what that future use might be. So, rather than get tangled-up in the question of the Annex's use, planners steered the expressway westward and through neighborhoods.

These neighborhoods banded together to stop the highway. Interestingly, the neighborhoods were demographically quite different in both age and in social class. The range between lower middle class and upper might not immediately strike one reviewing the project, but Silver Spring residents were well aware that those on the one side of Georgia Avenue were finding common cause with those on the other as well as the newcomers in homes in the valley formed by Sligo Creek. The resistance was successful, but that success was probably due to, first, the parallel resistance in Northeast Washington and, second, the high cost of building a lengthy elevated highway.

If the "North Central Expressway" had been built, it would have intersected with I-95 in Northeast Washington. But the residents there—overwhelmingly African American—did not want either I-70S or I-95. So, they campaigned against the very idea of taking highways through poor urban areas that, though poor, were still strong communities. They not only helped stop I-70S but also stopped I-95, creating a gap in the I-95 plan. It was supposed to come into Washington, D.C. across what locals refer to as the "Fourteenth Street Bridge" (now multiple bridges with names locals don't use). Then, it would veer East along the Washington Channel waterfront, tunnel under the Mall, and proceed to the junction with I-70S. From there, it would continue through more Northeast Washington neighborhoods and into Prince George's County, Maryland. With the highway through Northeast Washington scrapped, I-95 was rerouted onto the Capital Beltway, creating a loop to the East of the city, changing what was going to be I-95 into I-395, and creating a rather awkward spot where the interstate just ends at a traffic light intersection with New York Avenue. Protesters had won the day without much protest, but the Baltimore story would be different.

There, the plan was to create a mega-interchange right in the center of the city. I-70N would come in from the West on a spur labeled I-170, I-83 would come in from the North, and I-95 would come in from the South and the East. The interchange was touted as being such an engineering marvel that tourists would come from all over to view it, filling downtown Baltimore's hotels and restaurants. But the I-170 route would do damage to African American neighborhoods West of downtown, and the I-95 route East of the city would do damage to ethnic (Italian, Polish) neighborhoods. So, parallel protests began, and, then, they merged in a dramatic "Stop the Highway" movement.

That movement, like the one in Silver Spring, crossed demographic lines, but that crossing was much more dramatic in Baltimore. The affected neighborhoods were not only racially different but racially divided. That divide reflected how tight the neighborhoods were and also the racism of the times. So, seeing African Americans from West Baltimore rallying with residents of Little Italy and Highlandtown was quite striking.

As noted in another chapter, among those protesting was a young, quite diminutive social worker named Barbara Mikulski. The "Stop the Highway" protest was the start of her political career.

The protesters were successful here as in the Washington, D.C. area. The path of I-83 was re-done so that the highway simply faded into city streets; the path of I-95 was re-done so that it went through industrial areas and under the harbor in the "Fort McHenry Tunnels"; and the path of I 70-N was terminated, pretty much, at the Baltimore Beltway, with a tail-like piece leading into the Social Security Administration office complex in Woodlawn and a curious vestige paralleling Franklin and Mulberry streets just West of downtown. The planned "grand" intersection, by the way, would have been at what is now the site of the Baltimore "Inner Harbor" complex. So, the protests not only save neighborhoods but made a genuine tourist draw in downtown Baltimore possible.

That vestige of I-170 figures in this story as well as in the discussion of Baltimore's red line. It also figures in a report just issued by the Urban Land Institute.[10] The report proposes largely re-purposing the highway stretch, making the expressway into a boulevard, adding in recreational facilities and a desperately needed grocery store, reconnecting the neighborhood to the south with the neighborhood to the north. The plan will require decades to execute, but still leaves space for the red line (more on that later) that many hope will still be built. The report notes the presence of an east-west divide in the city. The plan won't address that (although the red line might). However, the opposition to the merging of the interstates in the center of Baltimore did overcome that divide, at least for a moment. In communicating their opposition, different groups, east and west, did come together.

THE "OLD" U.S. HIGHWAYS: BYPASS, UPGRADE, NEGLECT

A tricky policy decision involved the national highway system that the interstate one was largely replacing. What does one do with U.S. 1, U.S. 40, and U.S. 50, as well as lesser known routes such as U.S. 219 and U.S. 220 in the western part of state, U.S. 11, U.S. 15, and U.S. 340 in the middle, U.S. 301 on the Chesapeake's shores, and U.S. 13 and U.S. 113 on the Eastern Shore. A number of options existed, and the decision among the options reflected not just transportation priorities but the relative importance of the state's regions and citizens to the state.

The western part of the state has occasionally threatened secession, the reason being its neglect.[11] Long-isolated, little was done (until the I-68 project) to connect this mountainous area to the state's "heartland." For a long time, the precarious two-lane U.S. 40 was the only way into the region, and U.S. 220 and U.S. 219, which passed North-South through it, were left pretty much as they had always been. Eventually, U.S. 40 was basically bypassed by I-68, which runs parallel to the older road. U.S. 220 and U.S. 219 have experienced very minor upgrades, although a limited access bypass for U.S. 219 around Oakland in Garrett County has recently been proposed. Locals have objected to the idea—not because they don't want better roads but because the current route brings commerce to the towns that dot them. The residents on the state's West might well want better roads linking them to the North and the South, but the I-68 link to the East and the West has given them the more desired links to Baltimore and Washington to the East and to Pittsburgh, PA and Charleston, WV to the West.

In the state's central region, I-81 did to U.S. 11 what I-68 West of Hancock and I-70 East of Hancock did to U.S. 40. In both cases, the interstate made the national highway irrelevant and drove many businesses along the old routes to closure. U.S. 15 eventually saw a series of improvements from Frederick North to the Pennsylvania line. South of Frederick, the story is different. For a short distance, U.S. 15 and U.S. 340 run together on a high-speed, four-lane road. South of their juncture, U.S. 340 continues in upgraded shape into West Virginia, where, after the few miles to the racetrack and casino in Charlestown, it reverts to its old two-lane version. South of the U.S. 15–U.S. 340 juncture, U.S. 15 immediately reverts to two lanes, despite ever-increasing volume. The problem is undoubtedly the old two-lane bridge across the Potomac at Point-of-Rocks. The bridge, long in need of replacement, serves as a bottleneck preventing U.S. 15 from serving much of an interstate purpose. The route could be significant, linking central Maryland to rapidly developing Loudoun County, Virginia. Maryland's neglect of the route— and the bridge—would seem to suggest that it is not interested in such a link-ing. Maryland owns the river: the state line is on the Virginia shore. So, any bridge-building is theoretically up to Maryland.

North of Baltimore, U.S. 1 also seems neglected. Like U.S. 40 to its East, it is no longer important. And, for a long time, U.S. 301, which runs through southern Maryland, suffered almost as much—until Washington, D.C.'s exurbs hit it. Then, it received the upgrades commuters needed, as did other routes connecting the growing southern Maryland counties to the nation's capital (MD Route 4 and MD Route 234). The economic interests of southern Maryland had not motivated transportation improvements but the mobility needs of the new commuting residents did. And, across the top of southern Maryland, U.S. 50 was dramatically upgraded, but the rationale for doing so had little to do with the area's residents or even the desire to establish a good link between Washington, D.C. and Annapolis. Rather, the rationale for the upgrade—as well as the construction of I-97 from Baltimore to just West of Annapolis—seemed to be getting vacationers to the Chesapeake Bay Bridge and onward to the beach.

U.S. 50 on the ocean side of the Bay was also gradually upgraded. Except for the stretch running through the outskirts of Easton and Cambridge, it is now a fast-moving four-lane highway. An expressway bypass sweeping traf-fic North of Salisbury and new bridges across the Choptank and Nanticoke Rivers reduced the time required to get to Ocean City. U.S. 13, running North-South from Delaware to Virginia, saw an upgrade, as—eventually— did U.S. 301, running North-South from Delaware to the eastern side of the Chesapeake Bay Bridge. Traffic volume seemed determinant in these cases, as it did in the case of U.S. 113, which did not receive any upgrade along its route until very recently.

Most Americans do not know the stories of the national highway system and then the interstate one. They also don't understand the numbering schemes used for both. For example, they don't know that the highways are (with the exception of U.S. 101) two-digits long, with the third digit in the front indicating a relationship to the two-digit road. For example, in the interstate system, an affixed 4 or 6 connotes a beltway-like route, so I-495 in the D.C. area and I-695 in Baltimore are circumferential routes associated with I-95. This use of an upfront third digit was borrowed by the interstate system from the national one. So, U.S. 113 on Maryland's Eastern Shore is a spur off U.S. 13, and U.S. 219 in far western Maryland is a spur of U.S. 19 and U.S. 301 (which runs on both sides of the bay) is a spur of U.S. 1. Arguably, in the national system, these spur routes were less important than the main roads numbered 1 to 101. So, the ultimate neglect of a road would be eliminating the spurs completely from the national system, and this happened to quite a few spurs.

Two examples. Long ago, there was a spur off U.S. 40 from Frederick, MD to Washington, D.C., U.S. 540. A few might recall signs to that effect along Wisconsin Avenue and then the Rockville Pike in Montgomery County. They're gone: with the completion of I-70S (now I-270), this national route (a spur of U.S. 40) was no longer necessary. Another U.S. 40 spur was U.S. 140. This highway, which heads northwestwardly out of the Baltimore area, is now MD Route 140. The number remains, although the national highway designation (and federal funds) is gone.

To most, a big road is a big road is a big road. U.S. 50 between Washington and the Bay is just as big—and just as important—as any interstate in the state. So, one should, in interpreting who got the attention, not get lost in the national vs. interstate distinction. Some highways get attention, signaling their importance and the importance of whom they serve; others get little attention with very different signals. So, I-68 in western Maryland signals the importance of getting through that region with speed. The somewhat unimproved conditions of U.S. 220 and U.S. 219, which run North-South through—note the preposition—the region, shows the relative unimportance of venturing into the region off the I-68 speedway.

Big highway decisions, such as where to plow I-95 through a city, are clearly rhetorical acts insofar as they usually signal who has power and who does not. Such decisions can also be rhetorical insofar as they constitute or de-constitute an area and its community. But even the smaller decisions involving the many pieces of the national highway system send messages. Transforming U.S. 50 into a superhighway signaled that the travel (to the beach) was important to the state; leaving U.S. 220 north and south of Cumberland as a two-lane road signaled that Cumberland was not a priority; demoting U.S. 140 to Maryland route 140 in Westminster signaled that that town was not even on most people's maps.

RAPID TRANSIT IN BALTIMORE

If one were to study the cities along the nation's northeast corridor, one would find different answers to their needs for rapid transit. New York has long relied on its subways, but it does have buses and trains. There is a logic in-place too (although with merged subway lines, sometimes difficult to see): certain modes are used for certain purposes. The other cities all seem inferior to New York. Boston merged together networks of underground trains and trollies, creating "The T," which requires some deciphering before a logic emerges. Philadelphia has a north-south line (under Broad Street) and an east-west line (under Market Street), but those two lines don't go everywhere people need to go. So, superimposed on it are two merged urban rail systems, the routes of which are difficult for city newcomers to understand until they're told that there were once two separate systems with three downtown stations. So, Boston and Philadelphia adapted what they had. But Baltimore and Washington had only buses—and, once, trollies.

There wasn't much to adapt.

Washington is, of course, the national capital. So, it was able to do it all "right," with the Metro system leading subway trains out of the city core in several different directions. Baltimore was not the national capital, so it had fewer resources to create a system. The city got only so far. It built an east-west subway line; then, it shifted to the less expensive alternative of light rail, creating a north-south corridor with branchings at both ends. But the city felt it needed at least one more piece, the "Red Line."

DC's Metro has a red line, but this one is in Baltimore. The red line was intended to be an addition to the existing mixed system, serving much the same function as the purple line in the Washington suburbs: transporting people from where they resided to where the jobs were. Furthermore, like the purple line but much more so, the Baltimore red line would benefit low-income residents more than the affluent because of who the workers were and where they lived. Upon being elected governor, Republican Larry Hogan killed the red line project. This killing in and of itself sent messages, but so did the fact that he funded the purple while nixing the red. Hogan's action struck many in the Baltimore area as a contradiction.[12] Was it?

The story of the defunct Baltimore red line is a complex one. Part of a six-line system imagined for the city, the red line gained the most support and plans for it moved beyond the conceptual stage. Communities that would be affected, positively and negatively, became involved in the process of making and revising plans, even though Republican Governor Robert Ehrlich tried, using his veto power, to minimize community involvement.[13] Eventually, what emerged was the LCA, the Locally Preferred Alternative. It would be a largely at-grade route from its western terminus near the Woodlawn Social Security

Administration's headquarters until nearing downtown. Then, it would be a genuine subway until it hit East Baltimore, where it would return to at-grade and end in the gentrified areas of Fells Point and Canton. The LCA arguably reduced negative impacts while maximizing the red line's positive features. Two positive features should be pointed to: how the red line somewhat eliminated an urban eyesore left over from the 1970s; and how the red line provided rapid transit service to some of the city's more impoverished neighborhoods.

We have discussed the plan to bring I-70 (on the I-170 spur) from its junction with the Baltimore beltway into downtown Baltimore. This plan was part of a larger one that would have brought I-70, I-83, and I-95 to a "grand" junction near where the current Inner Harbor complex stands. Community groups opposed it, and, as a result, I-83 peters out into city streets at its southern terminus and I-95 sweeps south of downtown through the Fort McHenry Tunnels and industrial areas on both of its sides. I-70 now ends at I-695 (beltway) with a short spur heading toward the Social Security complex, but, before the decision was made to end of highway here, a stretch of it had been built in an area of the city just west of downtown. The result was a four-lane expressway running in between and parallel to Franklin and Mulberry streets (see fig. 10.0; p. 206). It ended up an urban oddity: an approximately fifteen-block long superhighway that, if used, got traffic on U.S. 40 through a stretch of west Baltimore just a tiny bit faster than the regular roads. The expressway fragment also was heavily symbolic of the way the interstate highway system too often tore impoverished black neighborhoods apart. Ever since the abandonment of the I-170 plan, ways to deal with the expressway fragment had been discussed. As part of the CPA version of the red line, it would use this right-of-way, both the median that had been designed to accommodate rapid transit and some adjoining space. The red line, then, would turn an eyesore that symbolized indifference to African American neighborhoods into a corridor that met some of their transportation needs. Furthermore, the use of the superhighway fragment would prevent any further damage in the west Baltimore communities it passed through. A win-win. The second positive feature of the proposed red line is implicit in the story above: it would have heavily served the city's poorer residents, giving them a convenient link between where they resided and jobs downtown and to the east of downtown (e.g., the large Johns Hopkins University medical complex). Because of the line's ability to serve this population, Democrats in the state have generally supported it. Republican Governor Larry Hogan, however, canceled it. During Hogan's first gubernatorial campaign, he cited cost-benefit analyses as his basis for opposing both the red line in Baltimore and the purple line in the close-in Washington, D.C. suburbs. The projected ridership—and revenue—just did not justify the costs in his opinion. After his election, he changed his mind on the purple line. He insisted on cost-cutting modifications and, then, let the project go forward.[14]

This decision inserted variables into the controversy that muddle it a good bit. What might have been portrayed as an action directed against the African American community became also an action that seemed to prefer the DC suburbs to Baltimore and seemed to prefer the mixed African American and Latinx population (and white population) that would benefit from the purple line over the just African American population that would benefit from the red. What were Hogan's electoral calculations, people wondered. All indications are, however, that electoral calculations had little to do with Hogan's decision: it was based on cost-benefit analyses.

The Baltimore chapter of the NAACP did not see matters that way. It complained to the U.S. Department of Transportation that Hogan's action was in violation of Title VI of the *1964 Civil Rights Act*. The Department investigated the claim and, during Donald Trump's presidency, ended the probe, rendering no finding one way or the other on the claim that the cancellation represented discrimination against African Americans.[15] So, one might ask is the red line dead. Hogan will serve eight years as governor, so the earliest revival would come in early 2023 if a Democrat succeeds Hogan. It is, however, currently unclear as to whether there is still a desire on the part of Baltimoreans for the LPA version of the red line. Resentment against the governor, however, clearly lingers.

During the O'Malley years, one would have guessed the "Red Line" would be built. Hogan, however, campaigned against it—and other state spending, and, upon election, Hogan canceled the "Red Line," arguing—in purely financial terms—that the benefits did not justify the costs. The human terms did not enter into Hogan's calculations. The cancellation sent a message to Baltimore at-large and to specific Baltimore population groups that Hogan was not their friend. The message was made worse by Hogan's decision, despite campaign rhetoric, to go forward with the "Purple Line," which had a similar rationale and only slightly better cost-benefit data. Hogan significantly reduced state funding, requiring design alterations and requiring the two affected counties to pay more. These actions, however, were lost on some who saw the Washington area getting a "Yes" while Baltimore got a "No." The facts of the case—that is, that Hogan reduced state spending on purple significantly—mattered less than the rhetoric. The transportation decision as a rhetorical act signaled that the Washington, D.C. suburbs were important whereas the City of Baltimore was not.

THE ICC

Once upon a time, there was a plan to build an "Outer Beltway" around Washington, D.C. Some older maps even show the route, and, through the years, those buildings near the route have routinely been warned that a big highway "might" be on their doorstep. But, somewhere along the way, the plan was scrapped—except for a small piece of it. Many reasons led to the project's demise, among them ardent opposition in northern Montgomery County. (More about that soon.) Originally, the outer beltway's primary purpose was to route truck traffic away from Washington and its closer-in suburbs. That purpose was still somewhat relevant when the state decided to pursue, as a toll road, the "Inter-County Connector" or "ICC" along part of the outer beltway's path. Trucks from the West going North could bypass the DC area; so could trucks going West from the North. The highway would also facilitate cross-Maryland traffic by linking Montgomery and Prince George's Counties. Some questioned how much cross-Maryland traffic there was, but the desire to create traffic and commerce patterns that drew the two counties together informed the decision to build the ICC as well as the Purple Line. Those protesting both projects often seemed to not know this history. True, but the protesters did cause people to wonder about why the ICC was being built. That tolls would pay for it perhaps reduced taxpayers' concern. Still, the rationale for the highway was fuzzy.

Undoubtedly, the stretch of the Washington beltway between I-95 and I-270 was congested. And there is the "Rock Creek Roller Coaster." When the beltway was built in close-in Montgomery County, planners avoided destroying homes by taking the road along Rock Creek from just outside Silver Spring through Chevy Chase/Kensington to just outside Bethesda. To accommodate park-lovers, planners pledged to route the superhighway along a path that followed the meandering stream. Supposedly, the curving road would be visually more appealing than one that plowed straight through. Thus, the "roller coaster" nickname. An unforeseen consequence of that planning decision was a stretch of highway that saw a large number of accidents, many of which involved tractor-trailers that did not handle the curves as well as one would hope.

So, some felt that getting traffic off this beltway stretch, especially big truck traffic, was a good idea. The problem with the argument was that not all of that traffic was coming from the north to go west or coming from the west to go north. Much of it was north-south. So, there were many arguments about how much traffic the ICC would actually divert. Note that, if the ICC were indeed part of an outer beltway, it could divert the north-south traffic, but an extension into such a beltway, even an arc of it, seemed unlikely because of strong opposition (next section) to a new, farther out Potomac River crossing.

People questioned the rationale for the ICC that cited the desire to better connect the two Maryland counties. Perhaps, residents in Prince George's wanted to get to jobs in Montgomery, but the jobs were not where the ICC would take them. And, in Montgomery, residents questioned the desire to connect.

That questioning was rooted in the two counties' history. Montgomery, historically, was much more affluent. When both counties were predominantly white, there was a marked class division. Those in Montgomery thought white Prince Georgians were "rednecks"; those in Prince George's thought white Montgomerians were "elite snobs." Why would anyone want a stronger connection? Yes, the beltway had fostered cross-county links, but, as the ICC was being planned, on both sides of the county line, there were questions about the desire to connect.[16]

An examination of older maps is useful. Most roads radiate out of Washington. The farther they get, the farther they are apart. So, in downtown DC, Rhode Island Avenue and New Hampshire Avenue almost intersect. By the time they are out in the counties, there is a large gap between them. For a long time, not much was built in this gap, and down its middle ran the Montgomery County-Prince George's County line. Few roads crossed the gap. For the longest time, the only four-lane, relatively straight one was University Boulevard, very close in to DC.

Why did this connection exist? One, residents of Montgomery County wanted to travel to the University of Maryland's campus in College Park (in Prince George's); two, with liquor regulated and expensive in Montgomery, its residents wanted to travel to the "bargain" unregulated liquor stores just over the county line. Montgomery residents would drive over to "Tick Tock," buy their whisky, and quickly scoot back home—avoiding Montgomery County police who would stop residents who were trying to avoid the county surtax on alcohol. Neither the desire to go to the University nor the desire to buy cheaper liquor seemed to justify the ICC, and the traffic for those two purposes was miles away from where the ICC was going to go through the large inter-county gap.

The ICC, then, seemed to many to be a road without warrant. The ICC does not go very far into Prince George's County. It crosses the gap, intersects with I-95 and U.S. 1, and ends. So, since tolls would pay for it, residents of that county weren't bothered. The ICC's route in Montgomery rather carefully avoids many developed areas, cutting across the county north of them through land that was, to an extent, kept open for the "outer beltway." So, there was minimal concern in that county. People wondered why, but tolls would pay for the road, so it was not costing them as taxpayers anything. And, maybe, just maybe, they would use it on occasion.

The ICC actually drew more concern outside the two counties it affected because of what it symbolized. Thus, the ICC, which is a beautiful road, may be communicating more in Baltimore than in Bethesda or College Park. It suggested that the Washington area's needs were being preferred over those in Baltimore—even needs the Washington area was not sure it had.

There has for a long time been in Maryland a rivalry between the Baltimore area and the two counties that sit outside Washington. Those in the counties resented the domination of state politics by Baltimoreans; Baltimoreans thought those in the counties, given their affluence, didn't pay enough in state taxes. When candidates for statewide offices were assessed, the question of where they were from was always raised. If from the Baltimore area, there was always a risk that the vote in the DC suburbs would be lukewarm. If from the DC area, there was always a risk that Baltimoreans would stay home. Consider the following recent Democratic governors. Parris Glendening, from Prince George's County, has lukewarm Baltimore support, and voters in Montgomery County would frequently complain that William Donald Schaefer and Martin O'Malley were "Governors of Baltimore," not the state as a whole.

So, here, with the ICC, is something being done ostensibly to help the two suburban counties. Even though it would be paid for (eventually) by toll revenue, it represented something that was not being done for Baltimore area residents. Making matters worse was the argument that the need for the ICC was questionable. The two suburban counties were getting a beautiful highway project they neither needed nor wanted and Baltimore was getting nothing. Those in Montgomery's and Prince George's, if they had wanted a fight, might have pointed to a number of highway projects south of Baltimore that had been built while Montgomery's and Prince George's got nothing. Those in the two counties might have argued that it was their turn. Such interjurisdictional bickering, though, is largely beside the point. Yes, it exists, but the important thing is that it creates a context in which transportation projects are read as being for this jurisdiction or for that jurisdiction. Oddly, projects way in the state's west or way in the state's east might escape notice and not be read in this political context. But should Baltimore get a new subway line, DC suburbanites would see red, and should the DC suburbs get a new light rail line, Baltimore area residents would see, well, purple.

A NEW POTOMAC RIVER CROSSING

If the "Outer Beltway" had been built, there would have been a Potomac River crossing in between the American Legion Bridge on the Capital Beltway and the two-lane U.S. 15 bridge near Point-of-Rocks. The absence of such a bridge is a problem: traffic can back-up badly at the American Legion Bridge, and, in general, the need to come into the DC area as far as the American Legion Bridge delays trucking from West to South. That has resulted in some rerouting—for example, I-81 South to I-66 East to U.S. 17 South to I-95 just North of Fredericksburg, VA. The absence of a bridge has also miffed economic interests in Loudoun County, Virginia, which would benefit economically from a better route North and West than at present. Some in Loudoun have interpreted the refusal to build a bridge as a deliberate ploy by Maryland to thwart economic development in Virginia and thereby prompt it in Maryland. Again, it is important to note that Maryland owns the river and, therefore, Maryland controls what is built across it.

Maryland's economic rivalry with Virginia might well be part of the refusal to build a new Potomac River crossing, but the stronger reason would be the attitudes of residents in northern Montgomery County. This area is beautifully bucolic, with large homes, some farms, and much "unspoiled" land. In many ways, it is very unlike the rest of Montgomery County, which is "classic" suburbia. The residents in northern Montgomery County like the county the way it is and see a bridge—and the highway that would lead to it—as a threat. Residents of extreme southern Frederick County feel much the same way. The threat is posed less by the bridge itself than the development the highway connecting the bridge to I-270 would arguably prompt. If viewed objectively, the imagined problem might not exist: the distance from a bridge to I-270 is not great, and there are few needed intersections (maybe MD Route 28) in between. But residents—they say—have seen what highways have done elsewhere, and they resist. And, their wealth gives them influence in Maryland politics.

The need for this crossing was highlighted by the recent closing of White's Ferry. Many will say that there is no river crossing between the American Legion Bridge and two-lane U.S. 15 bridge. That's not entirely true, for a bit down the Potomac from Point-of-Rocks is White's Ferry, an old-fashioned barge that pulls a limited number of vehicles across the river. A public road leads to it in Maryland, but, in Virginia, both the landing and the road leading from it are on private property. Recently, the ferry's operators and the private land's owners could not come to terms on a lease, so the ferry shut down. Montgomery County and Loudoun County (Virginia) governments are trying to negotiate a compromise between two stubborn parties, and they will probably succeed. But the brouhaha over the closing of the ferry and the rerouting of traffic onto the U.S. 15 bridge suggests how much commuters would appreciate a new crossing. Truckers would appreciate it even more, for they could avoid the Capital Beltway entirely, although Virginia would most certainly need to find a way to connect the limited-access portion of state route 28 with the corridors (primarily Virginia Route 234) that would take traffic east to I-95. Not all of it will stay in booming Loudoun County.

Removing this truck traffic from the Maryland suburbs ought to be of interest to Montgomery County residents, and it probably is for those in the southern part of the county. However, those in the northern part have money and influence. So, this crossing, part of the planned "outer beltway" will likely never be built. The message is that money means influence and that influence trumps demonstrated need. The American Legion Bridge, even if widened, will remain a chokepoint, delaying interstate traffic, often dramatically.

THE PURPLE LINE

Washington, D.C.'s Metro system features lines colored red, blue, orange, green, yellow, and silver. Blue, orange, and green reach into different parts of Prince George's County—green at both ends. Red reaches into Montgomery at both ends. Arguably, the color left was purple, and, so, when the state of Maryland proposed a light rail line, they gave it that color. But it is important to know that it is not a part of Metro but, rather, its own animal.

The idea behind the purple line is much the same as the one behind the ICC—to link Montgomery and Prince George's Counties. But, rather than link them far out in the counties, the purple line links them close-in to Washington. The upshot is that, rather than serving trucks and cars and the commerce associated with them, the purple line serves residents who wish to get from the one county to the other. There may well be some Montgomery County residents who want to travel to the University of Maryland campus (which the purple line goes through), but the more important group envisioned using the light rail line will be workers in lower-income areas (predominantly in Prince George's) traveling to where the jobs are.[17] This pattern is more likely to be Prince George's into Montgomery, so the beneficiaries of the purple line may be more in the one county than the other.

The purple line has been rife with controversy. First, some Montgomery County residents have tried every legal maneuver possible to block it. In many cases, these residents bought homes with a delightful biking-hiking trail running along its backyard's boundary, a trail made possible when a railroad line linking Silver Spring and a coal-fired power plant in DC's Georgetown section was abandoned by the B&O. These residents were undoubtedly told that the right-of-way might be used by the state for other purposes, but they either didn't hear or believe, and, then, the purple line plan emerged. It would not eliminate the trail but would crowd it and create some unwelcomed noise. And, at one point, in downtown Bethesda, trail users would have to leave the trail, cross Wisconsin Avenue, and then reenter the trail because the avenue's bridge over the tracks is too narrow for both trail and light rail. Second, the cost of building the purple line kept increasing, making many wonder if its economic benefits justified the expense. Third, the newly elected Republican Governor Larry Hogan, after a campaign that questioned the expense, decided to go forward with the project but with some cuts in funding and presumably design features.[18] Many who voted for him questioned his decision. Fourth, the purple line was supposed to be a model public-private venture, but the partnership turned sour when delays continued and costs kept increasing, leading the private partner to abandon the project. The project will probably continue on different terms, but the idea of public-private ventures, which the governor intended to rely on for future projects, was significantly damaged.

The Purple Line, it should be noted, has been in the works for decades. One can cite several governors both approving and questioning it. And, although many civic groups lined up to support it, there was a persistent NIMBY group that mounted legal challenge after legal challenge. When Metro ridership fell and Purple Line projections had to be adjusted, this group went to court demanding a new environmental impact study that, again, compared the Purple Line to dedicated bus lanes. The court sided with the NIMBY group, but, on appeal, the group lost. And construction proceeded at a good clip—until issues arose between the state and the contractors, which brought work to a halt. Some then argued that the line should just be scrapped, but, almost certainly, the work will resume and the light rail line will run, but its completion date will be close to a decade after that originally announced.

A number of messages that are sent by the Purple Line's continuing saga are worth noting. They are tied to three questions: Why build the line? Why continue with the project under a Republican administration? What does the project say about the future of public-private partnerships? First, the purple line is a departure from the overall rapid transit plan in the Washington, D.C. metropolitan area. That plan sends lines out from the center to different points in the Maryland and Virginia suburbs. The purple line crosses from suburb to suburb, connecting with the subway lines at four spots. It is, therefore, designed to move people not along the traditional suburb-to-city path because that traditional path did not match the residence-to-workplace path for many people. These people, mainly low-income, needed to get from their homes, predominantly in Prince George's County to jobs in businesses and homes in Montgomery. The purple line might well serve other purposes—for example, getting Montgomery County residents to the University of Maryland campus, but the primary purpose was to provide a reliable, quick, relatively inexpensive commuting route. The line was less a response to either traffic congestion or bus overcrowding and more a response to a need to match lower-paying jobs in Montgomery with workers needing them living in Prince George's.

Serving low-income residents is typically a Democratic cause, so many expected Hogan, upon election, to scrap the purple line. It was increasing in cost—it seemed—daily, and it served a demographic not usually prominent in state GOP thinking.[19] But Hogan was not willing to dismiss Prince George's County as un-winnable for Republicans. He was from neighboring

Anne Arundel with some of the same demographics, so he felt he could relate to Prince George's County concerns; plus, his father, also Larry Hogan, had represented Prince George's County in Congress and, so, the new governor had deep roots in Prince George's. The county had changed since his father's days, but, still, there was an affinity. And, so, to demonstrate his and Republican interest in the county, Hogan decided to continue work on the purple line. He proposed some cuts to appease budget-conscious Republican legislators, but he prioritized the needs of low-income residents in Prince George's over fiscal austerity.

The purple line was also designed to send a message—to the public and to those involved in governing—about how major infrastructure projects should be tackled. Other states, including Virginia, had turned to public-private partnerships to reduce upfront state expense. These experiments had proven generally successful. So, the purple line was Hogan's message about how the state would now proceed with infrastructure projects which were becoming increasingly expensive. Beltway expansion in Maryland with an added toll lane (as in Virginia) and perhaps a new span across the Chesapeake, these and other very costly projects would follow the purple line model.

Unfortunately, the model has not proven to be one most Marylanders would want to follow. Problems have plagued the purple line from the outset. They can be put into three categories: first, under-estimates in the private company's bid; second, unanticipated land acquisition, environmental protection, and engineering costs; third, increases in material costs due to delays due to lawsuits. The first two categories could be addressed by better research and better contracting procedures. The purple line case could be then the foundation for better public-private partnerships. The third category is the nagging one, for lawsuits now seem to arise whenever there is a project announced. One almost needs to plan for a year in court fighting-off NIMBY legal challenges. In the case of the purple line, more than a year would have been needed for those opposed were relentless in filing suit, citing any rationale they could dream up, including the possible extinction of a microorganism that no one had ever heard of. Why? They wanted to maintain their grand estates, and they had the money to fight and fight in court. One could say to them that they should have known that the old railroad right-of-way might not always be just a green-lined biking-hiking trail, but saying that did not reduce their determination to use the courts to stop the purple line. They wanted the courts to either order a stop or the costs to continue up to the point that the state gave up on the light rail line.[20]

These suits could be described as the epitome of selfishness: residents putting their desires over the needs of many, many others. But there were also in this case the dimensions of power and wealth. Those with both were using it to block a commuting line needed primarily by those lacking both, the low-income residents in Prince George's County who would use the purple line to get to Montgomery County jobs. The suits, then, were not just suits but tools of hegemonic suppression. A major opponent of the line was Chevy Chase's Columbia Country Club, whose golf course bordered the line and even in one section straddled it.[21] The Club's involvement gave the suits a pronounced rich-and-elite vs. low-income quality in the eyes of the media and many citizens.

Some citizens are looking at the purple line case in just this manner—a benefit to low-income residents that the wealthy and powerful are blocking, but most Marylanders are seeing it as a costly mistake that should not be repeated. The negativity ought to be addressed toward those bringing lawsuit after lawsuit: they caused the delays, which led to the overruns; instead, the negativity is highly likely to scrap or significantly modify future public-private partnerships in the state. Privatizing government concerns and public-private partnerships—both ways to lower government expenses—are not without controversy. They can certainly be debated as good or bad ways of doing the state's business. But it is unfortunate that, rather than having that debate, Maryland may be scrapping an approach primarily because those with power and money made the approach look like a fiscally disastrous one.

The project that was supposed to be public-private was the widening of both Maryland's section of the Capital Beltway and the lower reaches of I-270, accompanied by a new, wider bridge replacing the American Legion Bridge across the Potomac. The new lanes would be toll ones, and, as in Virginia, a private concern would manage them and collect the toll. Already, the new lanes along most of the Maryland section of the beltway have been scrapped, and many residents in Montgomery County—and its County Executive—are lobbying against the remaining highway work. And it looks as if this lobbying may result in the scrapping of the entire project.[22] The objections focus mainly on property acquisition as well as the policy choice preferring automobiles over rapid transit. However, one cannot help but see the purple line debacle playing a role in what is, at the moment, a partial retreat from the next big Maryland transportation project.

The stories of the Red Line in Baltimore and the Purple Line in the Washington suburbs are different, but they have become intertwined. Both were designed to help low-income residents, more so in the case of the Red. However, once the rhetoric got going, many overlooked the low-income residents Purple would assist in getting to work and transformed into a light rail link for the affluent. That transformation is indeed ironic since many of the affluent in Montgomery County were suing to block it. Reality and rhetoric do not always coincide, however; thus, many read the defeat of Red and the triumph of Purple solely in socioeconomic political terms. There is some truth to that rhetorical reading, but the reality is that Purple was more like Red than the rhetoric suggested. Furthermore, Purple had additional rhetorical problems as it emerged as the proverbial "poster boy" for plagued public-private partnering.

A NICER NICE BRIDGE

We have already talked about two bridges across the Potomac—the existing U.S. 15 bridge near Point-of-Rocks; the desired one linking northern Montgomery County (or very southern Frederick County) to Loudoun County, Virginia. The first remains unimproved, thwarting interstate traffic; the second remains unbuilt, also thwarting traffic. A third Potomac River bridge that arguably needs upgrading is the Governor Harry Nice Bridge by which U.S. 301 crosses the wide Potomac from southern Maryland to King George County, Virginia. On both sides, U.S. 301 is four-laned, but the old bridge has only two. That can occasionally create bottlenecks but the real problem with the Nice Bridge is not its width but its age.

In this case, a new bridge is being built, prompted by the current bridge's age and by increasing traffic on U.S. 301. But the new bridge has been a long time coming. The sluggishness is due to the state's general neglect of this region—until the exurban Washingtonians arrived—and the unattractiveness to taxpayers and legislators of building a structure that will benefit Virginia as much as if not more than Maryland.

Twice, we noted that Maryland owns the river. This creates a curious dynamic, one that might well be true elsewhere. Since Virginia does not own the river, why—legislators there might ask—should Virginia contribute to the cost of a crossing. But, since Virginia will benefit from the bridge, why—legislators in Maryland might ask—should Maryland pay the total cost. These questions led to a stalemate. For a nicer Nice Bridge, the states overcame the stalemate, but it has been a barrier in the cases of the other crossings too.

Our federal system—that is, that the United States comprises fifty sovereign states (and the District of Columbia and other territories)—has many merits. But there have long been border issues. Traditionally, the question was where is the border and solved in most cases by careful surveying. The new problem, as illustrated by bridges over the Potomac, is who will pay so that people can cross the border. States, driven by self-interest and the state constitutional requirement of a balanced budget, tend to view this border-crossing problem from their perspective. Maryland does not want to pay for a crossing that will heavily benefit Virginia; Virginia does not want to pay for a crossing over top of a river Maryland owns. This communication deadlock is certainly a negative dimension of our federal system. And we would ask readers to think about how often rivers requiring bridges (or tunnels) are the borders. The Hudson between New York and New Jersey comes to mind as well as the Mississippi between multiple states—for example, Tennessee and Arkansas. Who owns the rivers? Who is in the position of Maryland? Who is in the position of Virginia? How does the interstate communication play out if a new tunnel out of New York City is needed or if a bridge out of Memphis is closed for safety reasons?

FAST RAIL, VERY FAST RAIL

Those who enjoy rail travel in the United States frequently note how, when it comes to speed and perhaps comfort, such travel is far, far better in Europe and Japan. We have nothing like France's TGV or Japan's bullet trains. But the idea of faster trains has inspired plans on both coasts. In the East, many envision high-speed rail eventually linking New York City and Charlotte. Maryland is, of course, in the middle of that route and has been the proposed site for some of the first steps in high-speed rail. One visionary scheme had train cars running in a tube between Washington and Baltimore in fifteen minutes. That scheme is indeed visionary. More realistic are the plans to upgrade the current AMTRAK line and to build a maglev line roughly parallel to it.

The AMTRAK upgrade is not especially controversial—largely because it has already been partially done. Acela trains can hit 150 miles per hour on most of the Maryland portion of the Washington-to-New York line. The major bottleneck is the series if tunnels east and west of Pennsylvania Station in Baltimore. Plans to address that bottleneck have been made, as well as plans to tweak stretches of track elsewhere in the state to accommodate high speeds.[23] Fortunately, in Maryland, the AMTRAK right-of-way is relatively straight. There are not major curves as there are, for example, with CSX-owned and Conrail-owned tracks in Pennsylvania that AMTRAK leases.[24]

A maglev line, however, cannot run on upgraded tracks, for it doesn't run on tracks at all. Rather, as its name suggests, it uses powerful magnets to levitate a train, which, then, zooms down a flume-like track without any friction. The vision is that a maglev line might connect New York and Washington. The proposed first leg would connect a site in Washington, D.C. (not Union Station) with a site in Baltimore (not Pennsylvania Station, maybe Camden Station). There were a number of proposed routes, but the preferred one would run for most of the line's miles along the right-of-way of the Baltimore-Washington Parkway. Some land on the one side or the other would be needed at points, but most of the land would be parkway land.

So, what is this Baltimore-Washington Parkway? Although it now bears what looks like an interstate highway number, it predates the interstate system. Then, in several urban areas, plans were made to build scenic high-speed roadways in cities and between cities. For whatever reason, the Washington, D.C. area featured three of them—the George Washington Memorial Parkway in northern Virginia—with a piece bearing the same name in Maryland; the Suitland Parkway in Prince George's County; and the Baltimore-Washington Parkway, which the city's New York Avenue fed into at the southern end and Baltimore's Russell Street fed into at the northern. The theory, back then, is that Americans would enjoy the very scenic drives along these limited-access, high-speed routes. Thus, the bridges were attractively designed, scenic overlooks were featured, and much greenery lined the roadways. One wonders today if these are features highway users appreciate, or are they simply trying to get from point a to point b as quickly as possible?

That question is relevant because the U.S. Park Service controls these parkways, not the state highway departments. And the U.S. Park Service is balking at the use of its corridor for a maglev line because that use would undermine the "B-W" parkway's scenic beauty. Also along the road are federal agricultural research facilities and Fort Meade. The maglev line would intrude a bit into the rather large footprints of these. Other maglev routes had NIMBY residents quickly up-in-arms, fearing both high-speed derailments and cancer-inducing magnetism. So as not to get into a battle with residents of Bowie and Crofton and experience delays such as those that affected the purple line, the planners preferred the parkway-hugging one.

Questions are also being asked about the maglev's two terminal points. Ending the line in Washington, D.C. near Mount Vernon Square would arguably serve the business district better, but, given Metro access to Union Station, one must ask if a Mount Vernon Square station is truly an advantage, especially since that route would be more disruptive of neighborhoods and would impede the inter-modal connections more possible at Union Station. The Baltimore terminus, if it is indeed Camden Station, brings the line closer to the business district (and tourist district) than Pennsylvania Station. But, if the terminus is in Cherry Hill, an area well South of downtown, the link to the desired destinations is lost. A Cherry Hill terminus is indeed being discussed, although strong objections are being raised not so much because of its remoteness as the effect a terminus would have on an area that is gentrifying along enlightened lines that recognize the need to sustain low-income housing in the city. The advantage of either Camden Station or Cherry Hill is that the routing from the South would not be extremely disruptive, proceeding through the MARC (commuter rail) right-of-way into Camden Station or proceeding through somewhat abandoned industrial areas into Cherry Hill. Washington has a huge rail yard area north of Union Station that a line could be woven through; presumably, a route to Mount Vernon Square would depart this area near where New York Avenue over-passes it and proceed through NE and NW Washington neighborhoods for a good twenty-some blocks (the precise number depending on the route).

So, the DC terminus poses a problem, much as did the I-95 scheme back in the 1960s. The Baltimore Cherry Hill terminus falls into the same category—disadvantaging low-income residents. In addition, either of the two Baltimore termini are a problem if the intent is to take the maglev line North to New York City. If one could route the maglev line into Pennsylvania Station (through improved tunnels), then it would have two rail right-of-ways (AMTRAK and Conrail) to follows toward New York. From Camden Station, the only possibility—besides plowing through much of the city—is to rehabilitate an old B&O tunnel underneath Howard Street that is currently used by freight traffic. Its rehabilitation is already planned: it is too short for double-decker freight cars, so, maybe, there is a way to widen as well as heighten and take a maglev line through. From Cherry Hill, there really is no route—except taking the line from Cherry Hill to Camden Station and then North through a dramatically improved Howard Street tunnel.

So, the maglev proposal then raises quite a few practical questions. To an extent, the answers are also practical ones involving such matters as land acquisition costs, the availability for expansion of existing corridors, and the feasibility of redesigning existing tunnels. The answers, however, also involve the same questions of community endangerment, perhaps along socioeconomic or racial lines that have come up with many of the transportation projects discussed in this chapter. Using Camden Station and the Howard Street tunnel and existing right-of-way East of the tunnel's northern end would allow Baltimore to escape major damage to neighborhoods, but, on the southern end of the line, considerable damage is likely unless the planners decide that Union Station is just fine as an endpoint.

As we write, the maglev story is evolving. Baltimore has officially objected; the private entity proposing the line has responded that all of the city's concerns can be addressed. By the time this book is in print, the project might be dead—or revised and approved. No matter what happens, the project is illustrative of not only the recurrence of previous transportation plans that had considerable disruptive potential, but the emergence of other questions.

The assumption is that a maglev train ticket will not be cheap; the assumption is that the line will have few stops, thereby serving primarily those who board in the city centers. The line, if it is to disrupt neighborhoods, will zoom through them while offering no economic benefit or service. The maglev line is thus perceived as something even better than Acela First-Class, catering to—perhaps even pampering—the rich who want to get from Washington to New York in just an hour. The questions then becomes should those less

privileged have their communities disrupted and should the general public, imagined to enjoy the pleasant parkway drives, lose their greenery and
scenery?

High-speed rail, whether it be an upgraded ACELA or maglev, has also
drawn objections from jurisdictions it will pass through. How often—if at
all—will trains on these lines stop between Washington, D.C. and Baltimore?
How often—if at all—between Baltimore and Wilmington, Delaware? On
the assumption that there will be no stops, are county residents' lives being
disrupted for no benefit? This is the rhetoric being heard. Truth be told, the
disruption is minimal. The lines being proposed are using either existing
right-of-ways or paths with fewer homes and businesses; the lines are safe;
the noise level is lower than for the trains the high-speed ones would be
replacing. These arguments for high-speed rail are, however, often falling on
deaf ears of those who are crying NIMBY—unless I get a station near-by.

The communication lesson is that, by this point in time, projects are presumed to be disruptive. The rhetorical burden is, then, on planners to convince
residents that a highway or a bridge or a railroad line will not adversely affect
them. This situation is, of course, far different than in the 1950s, when the
governments did what they wanted and most residents assumed that what was
happening was good for it represented "progress." Two things have changed.
First, projects have proven to be disruptive—in Maryland and elsewhere—
poisoning the well for future ones. Second, as demonstrated in this chapter,
activism directed against transportation projects has proven successful.

CONCLUSION

In discussing these transportation policy matters, we have glanced at the communication dimensions. But we need to make those explicit, for we are not
writing about transportation. Rather, we are writing about how transportation
decisions send political messages. Those decisions are too often perceived as
being practical ones. No one investigates the political implications, but they
are extremely important.

The political messages fall into three categories: identity, benefit, and
privilege.

Identity

The Eastern Shore had one identity; the opening of the Chesapeake Bay Bridge
slightly altered it by bringing more (and different) people into the region as
tourists and, eventually, as residents. The suburban towns around Baltimore
and Washington had separate identities, but the two cities' beltways, in

Figure 10.1   A Section of What Would Have Been I-170, Now Abandoned in the Middle of West Baltimore Neighborhoods. *Source*: Photo courtesy of Carl Hyden.

merging these towns, constituted a suburban identity that transcended that of a particular community. The new identity also assumed a greater separation from the city than had previously existed. Put another way: highway decisions were rhetorical insofar as they played a major role in constituting a suburban identity.

Benefit

The Chesapeake Bay Bridge brought prosperity to Ocean City but hurt resort towns along the Bay's western shore. The purple line may improve the lives of low-income residents in Prince George's County. Their lives are thereby "communicated" by the decision to be important.

Privilege

Building a maglev rail line will privilege the rich; not building the Baltimore red line failed to help poorer residents of color. Highway routing often not only fails to help but significantly hurts these residents. Not building a Potomac River crossing in upper Montgomery County privileges the supposed interests of the wealthy residents who live there but creates highway congestion for all and perhaps has a negative effect on interstate commerce.

All states have transportation policy decisions a-plenty to make. The thrust of this chapter is that such decisions communicate far more than what might be initially apparent. Such decisions can also have another communication effect. This one is more basic: a decision can evoke dissent. This dissent can bring people together. Thus, they acquire an identity. And, they may acquire—although maybe temporarily—an identity that transcends previous divides. The project involving I-70N, I-83, and I-95 in Baltimore united African American, Italian, and Polish communities; the project involving I-70S in Montgomery County united residents in three rather different neighborhoods in Silver Spring, all at the time white but socioeconomically separate. Such unity is arguably a good thing—on a number of counts. So, transportation policy decisions can do good as well as bad. Too often, they communicate messages that the policymakers are not fully aware of—and have effects that will surprise those policymakers.

NOTES

1. Robert J. Brugger, *Maryland: A Middle Temperament, 1634-1980* (Baltimore: Johns Hopkins University Press, 1988), pp. 159–60. A recent reflection of Eastern Shore identity is found in Jean Marbella, "'Silent No More': Eastern Shore Community Reckons with Lynchings in Its Past," *Washington Post*, June 10, 2021, p. B5.
2. Peter B. Levy, *Civil War on Race Street: The Civil Rights Movement in Cambridge, Maryland* (Gainesville: University Press of Florida, 2003).
3. Useful, although to some extent a "coffee table book," is *Memories of Chesapeake Beach and North Beach* (Atglen, PA: Schiffer Publishing, 2007).
4. "Old Railroad to Chesapeake Beach Due to Be Junked," *Washington Post*, October 11, 2016.
5. Robert A. Caro, *The Years of Lyndon Johnson: Master of the Senate* (New York: Vintage, 2002).
6. Brugger, p. 638, 791.
7. Brugger, p. 563.
8. Levy, p. x.
9. Justin M. Polk, "Fort Detrick to Take Over Forest Glen," *Frederick News-Post*, October 7, 2008.
10. Urban Land Institute, *From a Highway to Nowhere to the Road to Revival: Healing a Scar, Reconnecting Our City,* Issued June 26–27, 2018.
11. Michael S. Rosenwald, "Western Maryland Secession Seeks to Sever Ties with the Liberal Free State." *Washington Post*, September 8, 2013.
12. Michael Dresser, "Hogan Says No to Red Line, Yes to Purple," *Baltimore Sun*, June 25, 2015.
13. Add.
14. Dresser.

15. Katherine Shaver, "Federal Officials Close Civil Rights Complaint about Baltimore Light-Rail Project," *Washington Post*, July 13, 2017.

16. One should consider the peculiar status of Takoma Park. So close-in to Washington that a part of its business district was in the District of Columbia, Takoma Park, a town with a mayor, was in both Montgomery and Prince George's County. This split identity posed governing issues but also identity ones. In which county did Takoma Park fit? Eventually, the town petitioned the state to change the border between counties so that it could be entirely in Montgomery, in which, arguably, its residents fit better culturally.

17. Katherine Shaver, "Purple Line Foes Offer No Ideas, and No Names," *Washington Post*, July 12, 2008. https://www.washingtonpost.com/wp-dyn/content/article/2008/07/12/AR2008071200790_pf.html

18. Robert McCartney, Joshua Hicks, and Bill Turque, "Hogan: Maryland Will Move Forward on Purple Line, with Counties' Help," *Washington Post,* June 25, 2015. https://www.washingtonpost.com/local/2015/06/25/a255fe8c-1b4d-11e5-93b7-5eddc056ad8a_story.html

19. Katherine Shaver, "Purple Line Project Delays, Cost Overruns Reveal Long-Brewing Problems," *Washington Post*, July 18, 2020. https://www.washingtonpost.com/local/trafficandcommuting/purple-line-project-delays=costoverruns-reveal-long-brewing-problems/2020/07/18/debda6ae-c620-11ea-b037-f9711f89ee46_story.html

20. Andrew Metcaf, "Transit Agencies Say Metro's Woes Won't Impact Purple Line," *Bethesda Magazine,* December 19, 2016. https://www.bethesdamagazine.com/Bethesda-Beat/Web-2016/Transit-Agencies-Say-Metros-WoesWont-Impact-Purple-Line/; Katherine Shaver, "Federal Appeals Court Ruling Allows Purple Line Construction to Continue," *Washington Post,* December 19, 2017. https://www.washingtonpost.com/local/trafficandcommuting/federal-appeals-court-ruling-allows-purple-linrconstruction-to-continue/2017/12/19/4f0844d8-e4d6-11e7-a65d-1ax0f d7f097e_story.html; Katherine Shaver, "Judge Dismisses Third—and Final—Lawsuit Against Purple Line Project," *Washington Post,* April 14, 2020. https://www.washingtonpost.com/local/trafficandcommuting/judge-dismisses-third-and-final-lawsuit-againstpurple-line-project/2020/04/14/52add03a-7e6c-11ea-8013-1b6da0e4 a2b7_story.html

21. Katherine Shaver, "Fortunes Shift for East-West Rail Plan," *Washington Post,* January 15, 2005. https://www.washingtonpost.com/wp-dyn/articles/A12436-2005 .Jan15.html

22. Katherine Shaver, "Area Leaders Deliver Blow to Md. Toll Lanes Project," *Washington Post,* June 17, 2021, p. B1–B2.

23. Luz Lazo, "Light at End of Tunnel Logjam," *Washington Post*, June 19, 2021, p. B1, B6.

24. AMTRAK owns only two stretches of track in the United States, one at the core of the Northeast corridor and the other in California. Elsewhere, AMTRAK must lease track time from freight railroads. This arrangement, which has led to conflict and court cases, results in major delays for passenger trains when they are not on AMTRAK-owned tracks.

Part IV

PLACES

Chapter 11

Renewal, Revitalization, and Redevelopment across Baltimore from the Downtown Core to the Neighborhoods

It is tempting even for lifelong Baltimoreans to think that efforts to bring about the city's renewal began with Harborplace. It occupies an extremely visible place and was the centerpiece of the Inner Harbor. There have, in fact, been other efforts that predate Harborplace. Though this chapter could probably go back further, it will briefly go back only as far as the Great Baltimore Fire of 1904 as the first major opportunity for large-scale renewal.

The fire broke out on Sunday, February 7, 1904, in a dry goods store. At one point a box containing gun powder and cartridges exploded outside a hardware store. The fire was so intensely hot that it was difficult for firefighters to get close enough to pour water on it. By the time the fire was out the next day, some 140 acres of Baltimore were in ruins. Fortunately, no one was killed and only a few people were injured.[1]

With 140 acres of prime real estate now open, efforts to rebuild began. Buoyed by borrowing power authorized by the Maryland General Assembly, the city took advantage of this opportunity not just to rebuild destroyed buildings but to widen streets and to finally construct a long overdue sewer system.[2]

To accomplish this rebuild, the city condemned private property and seized it to repair the docks along the Inner Harbor, to widen the streets, and to create a new plaza on Saint Paul Street near City Hall.

Historian Samuel Roberts, cited in *Baltimore Revisited: Stories of Inequality and Resistance in a U.S. City*, described what he referred to as the city's "selective process of official neglect" in the Black neighborhoods north of City Hall. According to Roberts, the lack of sanitation to those areas was so pervasive that "site selection for redevelopment seemed the result of a self-fulfilling prophecy," a situation that in 1914 allowed Mayor James

211

Preston to condemn ten blocks of largely African American homes and replace them with redesigned roads and a park that would be named Preston Gardens.[3]

As is also mentioned in chapter 9, some 200 Black-owned or rented homes in South Baltimore were demolished at around the same time in order to make way for the expansion and renovations to Camden Station. The area was considered overcrowded and the sanitation was abysmal. African American residents had already been moving out of that area into Old West Baltimore. The seizure and demolishing of those homes exacerbated the exodus.[4]

Whether there were active efforts connected with renewal and revitalization in the city in the years after the post-fire rebuild may be open to debate. Beginning with the Charles Center project, urban renewal became a major factor in city policy in the late 1950s and early 1960s.

The years immediately following World War II were not kind to Baltimore. Some of its existing problems were aggravated by the federal government. The GI Bill supported suburban home ownership which served to increase white outmigration from city neighborhoods. Those with middle-class incomes were moving in large numbers to the suburbs.[5]

The widespread use of the Homeowner's Loan Corporation redlining maps by both public and private lenders effectively prevented African Americans from purchasing homes in certain areas of the city even when they could easily afford them. People of color were increasingly concentrated in deteriorating neighborhoods.[6] For more information on redlining and its effect on communities of color, see chapter 9.

Beginning with the Eisenhower administration in the early 1950s, the push to build the interstate highway system certainly increased the numbers of people traveling and the ease with which they could do that. The use of ring roads around cities allowed travelers to bypass many cities like Baltimore by driving around them. This, in turn, decreased the numbers of visitors coming into the downtown.

These factors pushed the creation of the Greater Baltimore Committee (GBC) in 1955, partly in response to slow decline in the numbers of people shopping in the city. Composed largely of Baltimore's major business leaders, the GBC's members were concerned about the potential for their own economic losses, to be sure, but they were also motivated by a desire to see a revitalized Baltimore. Their main purpose was to convince people to return to the city to live and shop. The primary focus of their attention was the city's downtown core. For the GBC to be effective, however, required the support of City Council and especially the support of the mayor. Two successive mayors, Thomas D'Alesandro, Jr. (father of Speaker of the House Nancy Pelosi) and Theodore McKeldin, and their administrations strongly supported the GBC's efforts, recognizing that almost no new office buildings had been constructed since the Baltimore Trust Building in 1929, the GBC's first project became the Charles Center.

Comprising some 22 acres, Charles Center would include three major public plazas (Charles, Center, and Hopkins) surrounded by mostly office buildings. Included in the plan was an extensive multilevel underground parking garage. The plazas would be connected by a series of elevated walkways, pedestrian bridges, and stairways (including stairways that took people to and from street level).[7]

To shepherd the plan, the city created the Charles Center Management Corporation, a public-private corporation. In addition, to make the project happen required passage by Baltimore voters of a $25 million bond question. Voters approved the question during the 1958 city elections and the project began.

Charles Center was innovative in two important ways. First, it used a public-private partnership model for financing infrastructure projects that would serve Baltimore (and other cities) well on future projects. Charles Center Management Corporation would be first of a number of such public-private entities that would eventually fuel redevelopment in Baltimore's downtown.

The second way the Charles Center project was innovative involved its approach to the building site. Until this project, major urban renewal efforts (often with substantial federal financial support) used a "raze-and-rebuild" approach to clear land that was occupied by buildings that had been declared blighted or were considered slums. This approach often displaced people, mostly people of color, who were forced to move to make way for the project. Building Charles Center did not do that. Rather than raze existing buildings, Charles Center incorporated them into the plan.[8] Five buildings were preserved. They included the previously mentioned Baltimore Trust Building (later the Maryland National Bank Building), the Fidelity and Deposit Trust Company Building, the Baltimore and Ohio Railroad Company Building, the Lord Baltimore Hotel, and the Baltimore Gas and Electric Company Building and its annex. The first building completed in this first Baltimore urban renewal project was the 24-story One Charles Center, which opened in 1962. Designed by Mies van der Rohe, the building was constructed using glass and a dark bronze-colored metal. The Charles Center complex would eventually also contain several office buildings, the hotel, apartment towers, retail spaces, and the Morris A. Mechanic Theatre.[9] As an interesting side note, this first of Baltimore's major urban renewal projects has been undergoing renewal itself. Though nothing has replaced it yet, the Mechanic Theatre has been demolished. And an office building constructed for Mercantile Bank and Trust at 2 Hopkins Plaza is now a luxury apartment building.

As part of the highway plan to join I-70, I-83, and I-95, some 200 historic properties were demolished and hundreds of others had been condemned and sat empty. Fortunately, those opposed to the project and its planned destruction of the harbor front and neighborhoods in several parts of the city won out and the highway project was scrapped. Unfortunately, however, it also resulted in the "Highway to Nowhere" in West Baltimore which is discussed in more detail in chapters 9 and 10.

By 1975, another neighborhood was facing destruction. In Otterbein, just south of the Inner Harbor, 108 houses had been scheduled for demolition. The city reconsidered, though, and rather than destroy them it chose instead to sell them for one dollar. Those who purchased them had to restore them and live in them for at least five years. For some, this program was the Urban Homesteading Program. For others it was the Dollar House Program. The program soon spread to other nearby neighborhoods, including Federal Hill. In a nearby area where houses had already been demolished new homes were built in a style reminiscent of the homes they replaced.[10]

THE INNER HARBOR

With the success of Charles Center, Baltimore officials decided to take its urban renewal efforts further, to the Inner Harbor. This next phase of Baltimore's transformation began under the leadership of Mayor Theodore McKeldin. It continued most notably under Mayor William Donald Schaefer. Schaefer would use a combination of public/private partnerships, federal urban renewal money, city bond issues, his connections with the business community, and more to get his many projects completed. To reflect the expansion of the urban renewal effort, the name of the Charles Center Management Corporation was changed to the Charles Center Inner Harbor Management Corporation. The result was a vision of a harbor encircled with new public spaces, office buildings, hotels, amphitheaters, marinas, piers for visiting ships, parks, and something new called a festival marketplace.

Before anything else could happen, though, the decaying warehouses and piers that had once been important to the prosperity of the harbor had to be cleared. Using federal urban renewal funds, the city demolished nearly all the buildings in the area proposed for redevelopment. It then built a new infrastructure of piers, bulkheads, roads, and utilities. A wide brick promenade was built along the water's edge.[11]

The first building to go up was the Maryland Science Center, which opened in 1976. There were three levels of exhibits along with a planetarium and an observatory. An IMAX theater was added in 1987. In 2004, the Center opened a large addition. Exhibits were modernized, including the addition of more hands-on experiences. More than two dozen dinosaur skeletons were added to the collection as well as an exhibit centered on the Chesapeake Bay and the Maryland blue crab.

The Science Center was followed the next year by the Baltimore World Trade Center, located diagonally across the harbor from the Science Center. Designed by I. M. Pei's architectural firm, it is the tallest regular pentagonal building in the world. It stands at the edge of the water and seems to rise from it. It is positioned so that a corner points toward the water, suggesting the prow of a ship. The building's Pratt Street façade faces a large open plaza.

The Baltimore World Trade Center is owned by the Maryland Port Administration which has its offices there. The Maryland Department of Business and Economic Development, the World Trade Center Institute, and the law firm of Ballenger and Roche, LLC, also have offices in the building.

On the building's twenty-seventh floor is "Top of the World," an enclosed observation level with a 360-degree view of the city. There is an exhibit focused on Baltimore history along with rotating art exhibits. The Baltimore World Trade Center is also home to the 9/11 Memorial of Maryland. In addition to an exhibit in "Top of the World," there is a large memorial piece made of steel from New York's World Trade Center and tablets that list the names of Marylanders who died in that day's attacks.

Tethered to the Center's waterfront bulkheads are several grassy floats which form a floating wetland in the harbor. It naturally extracts nitrogen from the water and provides a habitat for small marine life, including crabs, eels, and mussels. The next major piece of the Inner Harbor's transformation to open was Harborplace in 1980. Harborplace comprised two pavilions at right angles to one another. One is along Light Street and the other is on Pratt Street. Conceived by developer James Rouse, Harborplace was called a "festival marketplace." It opened on July 2, 1980.

Harborplace had both retail shops and restaurants, many with local roots. When it opened it was unique and people came. There were some seven million visitors in its first three months. It attracted visitors and local residents alike. It was the place to go after a day of visiting nearby attractions. It was even a destination of its own. The festival marketplace concept drew interest from around the world. Soon there were similar projects in other cities. It's been more than forty years since Harborplace opened and time has not been kind. Many of the locally based businesses are gone and a good portion of it is empty. The culprit (aside from changing tastes) is the businesses that caused the exodus of the smaller businesses are the kinds of national chains that you find in many suburban shopping malls. They priced the smaller businesses out. Harborplace has changed hands a couple of times and it's now in receivership.

There has been much talk lately about what to do with Harborplace. Should this product of redevelopment be redeveloped? Some are saying raze the pavilions and replace them with either green space or something else. Others are saying that Harborplace needs re-envisioning.

In an Ethan McLeod piece written for *Bloomberg*, Jimmy Rouse, James Rouse's son, said Harborplace should be re-envisioned and managed by someone Maryland-based. He believes that with so many people now living in new apartment buildings and in older buildings converted to apartments, the customer base is there, especially since attractions such as the Science Center and the Aquarium are still bringing lots of visitors from out of town.[12] The year after Harborplace opened saw the addition of two more pieces to the Inner Harbor. They were the National Aquarium on Pier 3 and Pier 6 Concert Pavilion on Pier 6.

The National Aquarium's construction was funded through a 1976 city bond referendum. It is arguably the crown jewel of the Inner Harbor. It draws more than 1.5 million visitors each year. Major exhibits include the Upland Tropical Rainforest, the Atlantic Coral Reef, an open shark tank, and a 4D immersion theater. There are also exhibits featuring animals native to Maryland.

In 1990, a second building was added on Pier 4. It houses a marine mammal exhibit which includes the aquarium's six remaining dolphins. While visitors can observe the dolphins' training and feeding and can watch them play, there are no longer performances. The dolphins are scheduled to be moved to a sanctuary sometime in 2023. The Pier 4 building also has a temporary exhibit featuring jellyfish.

In 2015, the Studio Gang, an architecture and urban design firm headquartered in Chicago, was commissioned to create a strategic master plan to re-envision the National Aquarium complex. The plan showed a reconfigured entrance. The Pier 4 building would house a Chesapeake Bay-themed set of exhibitions. The Pier 3 building would include "Hope Spots" exhibits featuring places around the world that are worth protecting. Between the piers would be an urban wetland based on the geometry of Chesapeake Bay tidal meanders.[13] So far, there has been no action to enact the plan.

Something that many people remember about the opening of the aquarium was the fact that its opening was delayed until August 8, 1981. It was supposed to open on July 1. Earlier that year, Mayor Schaefer had pledged that if the aquarium didn't open, he would take a swim in the outdoor seal pool. It didn't, so on July 15, the mayor kept his promise, dressed in a late nineteenth-century bathing costume and a straw boater hat and clutching a large inflatable plastic duck. When he emerged, he said he was a man of his word. The swim in the seal pool got international attention for Baltimore and the aquarium. In 2019, a mural commemorating the swim was unveiled at the aquarium.[14]

Also opening in 1981 was what was then called the Pier 6 Concert Pavilion. It is a music venue and has featured music of all times. There even been musical plays performed there on occasion. Since the space is covered by a large tent and its sides are open, performances are held there only from late spring until early fall. There were renovations in 1991 and in 2018. In 2018, naming rights were sold to the Municipal Employees Credit Union (MECU). The venue is now called the MECU Pavilion.

The last two parts of the Inner Harbor area include the Pier 5 Hotel Baltimore and the Pratt Street Power Plant. The former is part of the Curio Collection by Hilton. Built in 1900, the latter includes three buildings and was formerly a coal-fired power plant that provided electricity to the city's streetcar system. It later provided steam for the predecessor of the Baltimore Gas and Electric Company.

The Power Plant sat empty from its closure in 1973 until it was redeveloped in 1985. It has had several iterations and currently houses several restaurants and office spaces. It is part of the Power Plant Live complex which includes entertainment venues in the nearby Fish Market complex. Power Plant Live was developed by the Cordish Companies which also developed the Maryland Live Casino and Hotel in Anne Arundel County, Maryland. The Cordish Companies has offices in the main Power Plant building.

HARBOR EAST

Harbor East is a mixed-use development along the waterfront east of the Inner Harbor. Originally it was filled with decaying warehouses and other industrial buildings, some dating back to the years just after the Baltimore Fire of 1904.

Harbor East was intended to be another urban renewal area. In 1983, the city commissioned a planning team to create a plan for the Inner Harbor East Renewal Area. The plan stressed wide sidewalks and streets to connect residents and visitors to the waterfront. Though spurred by city action, the development in Harbor East has been largely privately undertaken. The developer was H&S Properties co-founded in 1995 by John Paterakis and Michael Beatty to develop and manage Harbor East, a 20-acre mixed-use development neighborhood with 6 million square feet of development worth more than $1 billion. In 2013, Beatty would form his own firm, Beatty Development Group, about which more will be seen later.[15]

Since 1995, Harbor East has become an important commercial core with office buildings, high-rise hotels, and luxury apartments and condominiums. Retail in the area includes Whole Foods, an Under Armour store, high-end retailers, restaurants, and a movie theater. Several major Baltimore firms have moved from the traditional downtown area to spaces in Harbor East.

Figure 11.1 Baltimore's Inner Harbor Area Stretching Eastward from the Original Structures toward Harbor East. *Source*: Photo courtesy of Carl Hyden.

HARBOR POINT

Harbor Point is a recent development located on a former brownfields site between Harbor East and Fells Point. It is being privately developed by Beatty Development Group, which is also the lead developer of a project to redevelop Baltimore's Penn Station and the area around it. The Harbor Point project received $107 million in tax increment financing (TIF) for infrastructure.

Between 1845 and 1972, the area was the site of Baltimore Chrome Works which produced chromium chemicals. The Works was purchased by Allied Signal which operated it until 1986 when it closed. Shortly before the plant closed, it was discovered that the site was seriously contaminated and was leaking chromium into the harbor. In 1989, the U.S. Environmental Protection Agency, the Maryland Department of the Environment, the U.S. Department of Justice, and Allied Signal entered into a consent decree which required Allied to clean up the site with an eye toward its eventual reuse. Cleanup took from 1990 through 1999. While the cleanup was proceeding, the Baltimore City Council passed a planned use development (PUD) ordinance for the site. In May 2004, Council approved a PUD for up to 1.8 million square feet.

Beatty Development Group has divided Harbor Point into eight parcels. Seven parcels will contain one or more buildings. The eighth will be a 4.5-acre park. So far, buildings have been constructed on four parcels. Three of those buildings are LEED certified either gold or silver. One building, 1405 Point, is residential. The Excelon Building houses Excelon Corporation's regional operations as well as residences. The Thames Street Wharf houses Morgan Stanley and Johns Hopkins Medical International, while Wills Wharf includes a hotel, a restaurant, and offices for Ernst and Young and Transamerica. A building on Parcel #3 will be the new home of T. Rowe Price and is in the design phase as of the writing of this chapter.[16]

PORT COVINGTON

While all the projects described so far are in Baltimore's downtown area, not all efforts at renewal and redevelopment are located there. The most ambitious and potentially the most impactful project is Port Covington, a 235-acre, $5.5-billion mixed-use development project expected to take up to twenty-five years to complete.

Located in South Baltimore on the Middle Branch of the Patapsco River, Port Covington is a former industrial area. It was once the home of Locke Insulators and a city bus garage. The printing plant for the *Baltimore Sun* is there as well. The site's first occupant was Fort Covington, one of a series of forts that defended Baltimore during the War of 1812. In the 1850s it was a rail hub to transport coal from Pennsylvania, West Virginia, and Ohio to other markets. By 1904, it was the Western Maryland Railway terminus with piers, warehouses, a grain elevator, and more. Port operations ended in the 1970s. The ruins of some of the piers are still there.

Largely abandoned, there had been some efforts to bring it back to life. Between 2002 and 2016, there was a Walmart and a Sam's Club there. Proposals to build a mixed-use development around them never went anywhere and they eventually closed. Locke Insulators closed in 2017 leaving behind the *Baltimore Sun* printing plant, rotting piers, and some decaying buildings.

The redevelopment of Port Covington is the brainchild of Maryland native and Under Armour CEO Kevin Plank and his real estate firm Sagamore Development Corporation (SDC). Included in the plan are some 18 million square feet of residential, retail, and commercial space, 2.5 miles of restored waterfront, and 40 acres of parks and green space for the city.

What the new Port Covington project does not include are new, existing or planned projects on land owned outright by Plank or by others. These include City Garage, an incubator for startups in a building that really once was a city-owned bus garage. Nor does it include two restaurants; Nick's Fish House and Rye Street Tavern. It doesn't include the *Baltimore Sun*'s print operations or the 26 acres owned by Locke Insulators which Sagamore Development is not now wanting to purchase. It also doesn't include the 5-acre parcel on which Plank has already built his Sagamore Spirit rye whisky distillery. And finally, it doesn't include the 50-acres Under Armour already owned and on which it will build its new world headquarters campus.

For the Port Covington project to be realized, substantial infrastructure expenditures are necessary for roads, water and sewer lines, among others. SDC asked the city to approve $535 million in TIF to pay for those needs. The request eventually hit $660 million. The City Board of Estimates approved the request in April 2016.[17]

The size of this TIF request raised eyebrows and some questions, including from people wondering why the city was subsidizing a private project. In a March 24, 2016 editorial, the *Baltimore Sun* editorial board explained what TIFs were and how they worked. The *Sun* pointed out that the things the TIF would finance would be the kinds of investments cities would finance through bonds anyway. The editorial support was crucial and helpful.[18]

An important aspect of the Port Covington project has been the involvement of residents of the six communities nearby to the site. Those neighborhoods, which collectively call themselves the South Baltimore Six Coalition (SB6), are Brooklyn, Cherry Hill, Curtis Bay, Lakeland, Mt. Winans, and Westport.

The June 2016 Port Covington Master Plan described the community outreach efforts Sagamore Development made.[19] An appendix to the Plan has a two-and-a-half-page list of groups and organizations with which SDC had contact during the community outreach process.[20]

The result of the outreach was a thirty-eight-page Community Benefits Agreement (CBA) and Memorandum of Understanding (MOU). SDC committed to local hiring and a $25 million workforce development initiative, along with supplier diversity, affordable housing, and funding for education programs, college scholarships, recreations facilities, and youth summer jobs. In all there would be more than $100 million in additional investments and upgrades.

So far, some $10 million have gone directly into the SB6 neighborhoods. As reported by WBFF-TV, Mark Broady, Vice President of Community Affairs for Weller Development, the lead developer for Port Covington, said that how those dollars are spent is up to the communities themselves.

Construction at Port Covington began in 2019. There was a several month delay in construction beginning in April 2020 to protect worker safety during the COVID-19 pandemic. Construction on the next phase of the project resumed in early 2021.[21]

What's happening as this chapter is being written is the simultaneous construction of five buildings along Cromwell Street, the main road of the complex. Among the things that are part of this phase is Rye Street Market, a 45,000-square-foot market and food hall. It will be physically connected to two buildings comprising 440,000 square feet of office and meeting space. There will also be local, regional, and national retailers in spaces mostly on the first level of multistory buildings.

There will be 456 apartments in three buildings. Of those, eighty-nine will be the first of the inclusionary housing units promised to SB6. One of the buildings with apartments will also have eighty-one extended stay units. Amenities include 10 acres of parks, promenades, roads and bike paths, and two marinas. Indoor and outdoor event spaces, some with water views, will be available for rental for corporate events, weddings, birthdays, fundraisers, and other events.[22]

OTHER LARGE-SCALE PROJECTS

There are three additional large-scale projects that are worth mentioning. One is already underway. A second is about to enter the design phase. The third is only a proposal for now.

Major redevelopment is already underway in the Park Heights area of Northwest Baltimore. Largely known for scores of vacant buildings, drugs, and crime, some 17 acres of Park Heights are slated for redevelopment. Ground was broken in September 2020 on an apartment building with eighty-four affordable units. Called Renaissance Row, it will have a variety of amenities, management offices, and offices that will be the headquarters of Park Heights Renaissance, a not-for-profit community development corporation that serves as the liaison between Park Heights residents, the city, and developers.[23] Other housing options are planned, including additional apartments (some for seniors) and single-family detached homes. Green space is also part of the plan. The development team is led by NHP Foundation, a national affordable housing not-for-profit, and includes two Baltimore-based real estate developers, Henson Development Co. led by Dan Henson and Marenberg Enterprises, Inc., led by Sandy Marenberg. The Henson Co. Vice President, Dana Henson, is a resident of Park Heights.[24] The projects are being funded by $100 million in public and private money.[25]

Part of the overall plan for the revitalization of Park Heights is a complete re-do of the Pimlico Racetrack, home of the Preakness Stakes. The clubhouse and grandstand will be demolished and the track rotated by 30 degrees which opens parcels for further development. A new clubhouse and an event center will be constructed, which will make the racecourse usable year round. The infield will have sports fields for use by the Park Heights community. The Pimlico redevelopment is funded by $375 million in state-issued bonds.[26]

Baltimore's Pennsylvania Station (a.k.a. Penn Station) is the eighth busiest railway station in the country. It sees more than 3 million Amtrak and MARC (Maryland Rail Commuter) passengers each year. Amtrak is planning to redevelop and improve Penn Station to prepare for the expected increases in passenger volume through 2040.[27]

There are plans to renovate and update the 1911 Beaux Arts-style station building. A high-speed rail platform is also planned, as is a glass-walled passenger concourse above it. Space will be renovated or added for shops and eateries on the ground floor and offices on the now-vacant two upper floors. Amtrak owns several other parcels along the track right of way which may also be developed.[28] If fully built out, mixed-use transit-oriented development could grow to encompass 10 acres and include up to 1.5 million square feet of offices, retail, residential, and hotel space.[29]

The development team for the project is Penn Station Partners. The lead developer is Beatty Development, which is also developing Harbor Point. Developers envision as much as $400 million in total investment over time.[30]

The most recent project is only a proposal for now. Stonewall Capital has purchased a 43-acre site in the Westport community of South Baltimore, adjacent to Port Covington. The property would be a dense mix of uses under a PUD. Stonewall developer Ray Jackson purchased the land from Weller Development, the lead developer for Port Covington.

Jackson proposes mostly housing in a scale that works well with the existing rowhome neighborhood and would offer affordability. Jackson has said he will work closely with the community as plans begin to develop.[31] The community has seen other development proposals in the past for that site and none have panned out.

Before the Westport proposal can get underway, Stonewall will have to go to court to stop a lawsuit filed by Baltimore-Washington Rapid Rail that if successful would condemn the 43 acres Stonewall wants to develop. The company, which has proposed a $10 billion high-speed maglev train line between Baltimore and Washington, wants the property for its Baltimore station.[32] Baltimore City has asked the federal government not to approve the maglev project over concerns about equity and its effect on the environment.

REDEVELOPMENT, RENEWAL AND REVITALIZATION
MOVES TO THE NEIGHBORHOODS

All the redevelopment projects described so far have been large-scale projects often involving many acres of land and millions (even billions) of dollars. Many have involved public money. Some received TIFs. Many of the most visible projects throughout the years have been in Baltimore's downtown. But these large-scale projects are not the only ones happening. There are smaller projects happening in or near downtown. But there is also much happening in the neighborhoods, sometimes through sheer grit and determination of people wanting to make something good happen.

What follows will be nowhere near an exhaustive list, but it does show that exciting things have happened and are happening.

In a January 2, 2021 commentary, *Baltimore Sun* columnist Jacques Kelly penned a piece called, "Baltimore Witnesses a Year of Stealth Change." There was an 1894 bank building on Howard Street that had been empty for decades that was converted into a Springhill Suites hotel. The city's famed Lexington Market was being renovated and revitalized. A loft apartment building opened with units for artists and those exiting homelessness. Small businesses opened in spite of the pandemic. Among others, they included a bakery, a bagel shop, and a shop specializing in pies. Two abandoned movie theaters are in the hands of neighborhood-based organizations working to preserve them and find new uses for them.[33]

These weren't the only new businesses that opened. Guilford Hall Brewery opened in an old Crown Cork and Seal building. During the renovations to the building, the owners gave Baltimore's artisan community a lot of work. Overhead lighting fixtures, the bars, the staircases, and tables and chairs were all commissioned from local artisans.[34]

The Arch Social Club at North and Pennsylvania avenues has sought zoning approval to install a marquee on the façade of the 109-year-old former movie theater that houses the oldest known continuously operating African American social club in the United States. The club received a $118,000 grant from the National Trust for Historic Preservation to restore the marquee and to make other improvements. The club is trying to raise $5 million for renovations. In 2019, the area around the club was designated the Pennsylvania Avenue Black Entertainment District, which made tax credits available to develop spaces where artists live, work, and perform.[35]

Also on North Avenue is the former O'Dell's Nightclub. Built in 1909, it has at various points been a dance academy and an auto showroom. The building is slated for a $7 million renovation. It will be the new home for two not-for-profit organizations: Young Audiences of Maryland and Code in the Schools. Renovations began in January 2021.[36]

The Baltimore Traction Co. Car Barn on Central Avenue, a relic of the city's cable car system, will undergo a $15 million renovation to house offices, retail spaces, and community programming. The renovation is a collaboration of Cross Street Partners and the Beatty Development Group. It has received $3 million in tax credits.[37]

An abandoned fire station on Oliver Street in East Baltimore will be renovated by the African American Fire Fighters Historical Society and will be a museum that honors the legacy of Black fire fighters. The location is near the

National Great Blacks in Wax Museum and is accessible by several public transit options.[38]

The Central Baltimore Future Fund has been active in purchase/renovation projects. The Fund, which is underwritten by the State of Maryland, has taken on several projects. Among those is the 1870 Waverly Town Hall at Greenmount Avenue and 31st Street. Though now located well within the city limits, the Waverly area was once a village in Baltimore County. This building served the village as a school, a library, a post office, and a drug store. More recently, however, it was a dive bar. The Town Hall and two contiguous properties will become seven apartments and five retail spaces. The project has a budget of $1.5 million.[39]

The Fund purchased the 1921 Boulevard Theatre in Waverly for $1.2 million with the intent to overhaul it. The Fund also helped the owner of the Voxel Theatre on Charles and 25th streets.[40]

An old burlap bag factory in the Washington Hill section of East Baltimore is now called City Springs Lofts and will contain fifteen apartments and two retail shops. After the factory closed, the building was a used car dealership and then Reece Chairs, a furniture maker.[41]

An abandoned rowhouse in West Baltimore will be a center for the arts. It will have some living spaces for the homeless, areas to explore different art forms, and a skills-based training program. The project is independently funded.[42]

Baltimore City has approved the sale of the Upton Mansion at 811 West Lanvale Street to the *Afro* newspaper and its charity arm. The 1838 Greek Revival-style mansion was the country home of Baltimore attorney David Stewart. It is the last surviving Greek Revival country house in Baltimore.[43] The $7 million project will be funded through a combination of grants, federal and state tax credits, city funds, and some equity from the *Afro*.[44]

Pigtown Main Street, a West Baltimore organization, is spearheading an effort to bring the area back to life. Parts of Pigtown are still fairly rough places, but other parts have seen a resurgence. Twelve new small businesses opened in just eight months in 2019. Kim Lane, Pigtown Main Street's executive director, aims to expand that success to more blocks.[45]

A not-for-profit organization called Parks and People is demolishing abandoned buildings and building parks in their places. In seven years, the group has created 27 acres of park space in several areas of the city. It gets both public and private funding for its projects.[46]

A skateboard park in Easterwood in West Baltimore was the product of a collaboration between seventy-year-old civil rights activist Marvin "Doc" Cheatham, who is African American, and thirty-eight-year-old Stephanie Murdoch, founder of the not-for-profit volunteer group Skatepark of Baltimore, who is white. They spent months scouting vacant blocks in the Easterwood section for the right place. The project caught the attention of the Department of Recreation and Parks which allocated $300,000 for it in 2019. A GoFundMe effort raised enough money to buy several hundred skateboards and helmets which will be given to kids. When the park opens, experienced skateboarders from mostly white Hamden will go to mostly African American Easterwood to help teach kids how to skateboard.[47]

CONCLUSION

Renewal, revitalization, and redevelopment in our nation's cities have too often been top-down government-driven projects primarily focused on city downtowns. Little benefit comes to the neighborhoods, especially those that are mostly people of color. While that approach has certain efficiencies and has resulted in many worthwhile projects, it does little for city residents.

Indeed, too many of these projects have clearly demonstrated who has influence and who does not. That can be seen with the "raze and rebuild" attitude that many of these projects adopt. The goal has often been to get rid of "blight" without considering those for whom what some call blight might actually be a home in a vibrant, tightly knit neighborhood. The infamous "highway to nowhere," described in chapters 9 and 10, cut several lower-income, yet vibrant, tightly knit communities in half, an action from which none have actually recovered.

With large-scale, high-visibility projects, there is little incentive to consult regular citizens. When citizens raise objections, they are often ignored. Even when a major project requires a bond issue referendum, little effort is made to find out what the citizens actually want. The bulk of the effort is made toward convincing voters that the proposed project is what they want and need. This creates a situation in which those who may be most affected are essentially voiceless.

Renewal in Baltimore has had an uneven history. Early projects were those designed to bring business and visitors to the city rather than to bring people back to the city to live. These projects were centered in Baltimore's downtown core. Generally, they successfully lived up to the vision the city had for them. Since, as has been seen, some of these projects depended upon successful bond referenda and government money if they were to happen, convincing voters became important.

More recently, however, voter approval isn't even sought. Redevelopment projects such as the $1 billion Harbor East and the $5 billion Port Covington project, though largely privately funded, required TIFs for the infrastructure improvements needed. These were done with remarkably little community outreach.

The communities surrounding Port Covington weren't really consulted about the $660 million in TIFs. But to give the developers their due, those communities were consulted about the project and its vision. Their input was actively sought. Communication occurred in this case in a manner not seen with most of the earlier developments. The result of that consultation process was an extensive CBA that guaranteed in writing the communities' wants and needs. That agreement is already providing direct benefits to the communities.

The Park Heights redevelopment project is not a single large project, but rather several related projects, many of which are privately funded. To ensure that the community's needs are met, the Park Heights Renaissance organization makes sure that it is very involved in any proposed project.

Historically, little attention has been paid to renewing and revitalizing the neighborhoods where people live. If a renewed, revitalized Baltimore is to happen, it requires a focus on those neighborhoods. That's beginning to happen with exciting smaller projects spearheaded by not-for-profits and by the people who live there. While these one- or five- or ten-million dollar projects are very small in comparison with Harbor East and Port Covington, those projects are making an enormous difference to the communities. And these smaller-scale projects are proving successful.

If renewal and revitalization are to be successful across the city, it will take a drastic re-imagining of the city; a new vision that pays attention to neighborhoods as well as to the important city core. And apparently there is renewed interest in seeing that happen. In the space of just five months in early 2021, no fewer than eight commentaries appeared in the *Baltimore Sun* advocating just such re-imagining. These included a January 1 commentary urging area residents to "Resolve to sing Baltimore's praises in the new year." Just four days later, another commentary asked that readers re-imagine Baltimore as a city for children.

In March, a third commentary wanted Baltimore's Inner Harbor re-imagined as a place for the city's residents rather than a place just for tourists. There were four commentaries in April. One suggested that it was time for the city to engage in some shameless self-promotion (like Mayor Schaefer's swim in the aquarium's seal tank). Another suggested that the infamous "road to nowhere" could be turned into a mile-long city park. A third thought the park was a really good idea.

The fourth April commentary came from *Baltimore Sun* columnist Dan Rodricks. It advocated two things. One was to tear down the Jones Falls Expressway (a.k.a. the JFX) from Penn Station to its end at Fayette Street near City Hall and replace it with a tree-lined boulevard. In that commentary, he, too, suggested that the "road to nowhere" could be a park, which he suggested could be called the Westside Greenway.

In Mayor Brandon Scott, Baltimore now has a young, energetic mayor with the willingness, the drive, and the energy to take on that re-imagination. Scott had already been a strong proponent of the renewal and revitalization of Park Heights, the neglected African American neighborhood in which he grew up. In a WBAL Channel 11 interview, Scott said that he was also committed to a total re-imaging of downtown Baltimore.[48] That interview and that commitment engendered a May commentary whose headline read, "Total re-imagining of downtown Baltimore? Yes, please." The commentary was penned by one of the thousands of people who, in recent years, have taken up residence in Baltimore's downtown. Although not expressed in rhetorical terms, what is being called for is new constitutive rhetoric—rhetoric that hails those in the city—and the city itself—into new identities.

In addition to those community-level projects described in this chapter, there are dozens more happening in neighborhoods across Baltimore. Those covered in this chapter provide just a taste of what's going on. What makes them interesting is that many of them are revitalizing existing parts of communities and putting them to uses wanted by those communities.

Because much of the excitement is being driven by not-for-profits and by regular Baltimoreans taking things into their own hands, much more attention seems focused on making Baltimore a better, greener, safer, and more vibrant place to live, work, and visit. This time the critical mass just might be there to make it happen—and not just in the downtown, but across the entire city. And I find that a very hopeful sign.

NOTES

1. Matthew A. Crenson, *Baltimore: A Political History* (Baltimore: Johns Hopkins University Press, 2017), pp. 332–33.

2. Ibid., p. 333.

3. Eli Pousson, "Vacant Houses and Inequality in Baltimore from the Nineteenth Century to Today," in *Baltimore Revisited: Stories of Inequality and Resistance in a U.S. City*, edited by P. Nicole King, Kate Drabinski and Joshua Clark Davis (New Brunswick, NJ: Rutgers University Press, 200), p. 57.

4. Karen Olson, "Old West Baltimore: Segregation, African-American Culture and the Struggle for Equality," in *The Baltimore Book: New Views of Local History*, edited by Elizabeth Free, Linda Shopes and Linda Zeidman (Philadelphia: Temple University Press, 1991), p. 59.

5. Mary Rizzo, "Image and Infrastructure: Making Baltimore a Tourist City," in *Baltimore Revisited: Stories of Inequality and Resistance in a U.S. City*, edited by P. Nicole King, Kate Drabinski and Joshua Clark Davis (New Brunswick, NJ: Rutgers University Press, 2009), p. 260.

6. Ibid.

7. Department of Planning, *City of Baltimore Comprehensive Master Plan* (Baltimore: City of Baltimore, 2006). https://planning.baltimorecity.gov/planning -master-plan/plan, p. 42.

8. Rizzo, p. 261.

9. Department of Planning, pp. 42–3.

10. Ibid., p. 43.

11. Ibid., p. 44.

12. Ethan McLeod, "What Happened to Baltimore's Harborplace," *Bloomberg*, January 16, 2020. https://www.bloomberg.com/news/articles/2020-01-16/what-hap-pened-to-baltimore-sfestival-marketplace

13. Studio Gang, "National Aquarium Strategic Plan." https://studiogang.com

14. Chris Kaltenbach, "National Aquarium to Unveil Mural of Former Baltimore Mayor's Seal Pool Swim," *Baltimore Sun*, April 9, 2019. https://www.baltimoresun.com/opinion/editorial/bs-ed-0418-downtown-baltimore-future-20210416-pifapkm oybcnhfkosglx5gohqi-story.html

15. Beatty Development Group, "About." https://beattydevelopmentgroup.com

16. Beatty Development Group, "Harbor Point." https://beattydevelopme ntgroup.com

17. Daniel Kravetz, "Who Will Benefit from Port Covington," *Shelter Force*, October 2016. https://shelterforce.org/2016/10/21/who-will-benefit-from-port-covington/

18. Editorial Board, "What Kevin Plank's Plan Means for Baltimore," *Baltimore Sun*, March 24, 2016. https://www.baltimoresun.com/opinion/editorial/bs-ed-saga-more-20160324story.html

19. Department of Planning, *Port Covington Master Plan – Draft* (Baltimore: City of Baltimore, June 6, 2016). https://planning.baltimorecity.gov/sites/default/files /PORTCOVINGTONMASTERPLANJune16.pdf, p. 7.

20. Ibid., pp. 58–60.

21. Hallie Miller, "Construction on Baltimore's Port Covington Development to Resume After Financing Next Phase," *Baltimore Sun*, January 5, 2021. https://www .baltimoresun.com/business/real-estate/bs-bz-port-covington-moves-forwardfinanc-ing-20210105-72olijelbzgxxkz5e6qfhuofxi-story.html

22. Ed Gunts, "What to Expect From Port Covington's Next Development Phase," *Baltimore Magazine*, March 31, 2021. https://www.baltimoremagazine.com/section/community/what-to-expect-from-port-covingtonsnext-development-phase/

23. Hallie Miller, "Renaissance Row Apartment Building to Provide 'Affordable' Units in Baltimore's Park Heights," *Baltimore Sun*, September 22, 2020. https://www.baltimoresun.com/business/real-estate/bs-bz-renaissance-row-park-heights -20200922-ingnztxm4zhbjfmzgggmowix6u-story.html

24. Hallie Miller, "Plans for Park Heights Redevelopment Show Mix of Housing Types, Public Park Improvements," *Baltimore Sun*, February 27, 2020. https://www .baltimoresun.com/business/real-estate/bs-bz-apartment-next-to-metro-baltimorepark -heights-20200227-2j6hagku7rbftbosyo4pnv3myq-story.html

25. Catherine Rentz, "Baltimore Invests $100M to 'Revitalize' 17 Acres of Park Heights; City Presents NHP Foundation as Developer," *Baltimore Sun*, September 18, 2019. https://www.baltimoresun.com/maryland/baltimore-city/bs-md-park-heights -vacants-20190918a2ryyin3vjfc7bik6q3dttn6qe-story.html

26. Jean Marbella, Childs Walker and Daniel Oyefusi, "As Preakness Approaches, the Real Winner Could Be Pimlico and the Surrounding Neighborhoods. Here's

Why," *Baltimore Sun*, May 6, 2021. https://www.baltimoresun.com/maryland/bs-prem-md-pimlico-redevelopmentpreakness-20210506-vpt7v57sjbcbfcwrcbm rx3iqcq-story.html

27. Beatty Development Group, "Baltimore Penn Station," https://beattydevel opmentgroup.com

28. Lorraine Mirabella, "Amtrak and Developers Push Ahead with Multimillion-Dollar Transformation of Baltimore's Penn Station," *Baltimore Sun*, March 18, 2021. https://www.baltimoresun.com/business/bs-bz-penn-station-redevelopment-2021031 8fuen4cjidvh6reaozmsr3sttoi-story.html

29. Beatty Development Group, "Baltimore Penn Station." https://beattydevel opmentgroup.com

30. Lorraine Mirabella, "Amtrak and Developers Push Ahead with Multimillion-Dollar Transformation of Baltimore's Penn Station," *Baltimore Sun*, March 18, 2021. https://www.baltimoresun.com/business/bs-bz-penn-station-redevelopment-2021031 8fuen4cjidvh6reaozmsr3sttoi-story.html

31. Lorraine Mirabella, "Developer Plans Mixed-Use Project on Westport Waterfront Formerly Owned by Kevin Plank," *Baltimore Sun*, October 6, 2020. https://www.baltimoresun.com/business/real-estate/bs-bz-westport-development -20201006-

32. Colin Campbell and Lorraine Mirabella, "Maglev Company Sues to Condemn Land Planned for Westport Development, Setting Up Showdown Between Projects in South Baltimore," *Baltimore Sun*, June 30, 2021. https://www.baltimoresun.com/ business/bs-bzmaglev-westport-20210630-hetpya4vtjfbhgsskh5fode7he-story.html

33. Jacques Kelly, "Baltimore Witnesses a Year of Stealth Change," *Baltimore Sun*, January 2, 2021. https://www.baltimoresun.com/maryland/baltimore-city/bs-md -kelly-2020-20210102bqolhvcyuzh7zij3wu77lqea6q-story.html

34. Jacques Kelly, "Guilford Hall Brewery Arrives at Old Crown Cork and Seal Location in Baltimore's Greenmount West Neighborhood," *Baltimore Sun*, April 17, 2021. https://www.baltimoresun.com/maryland/baltimore-city/bs-md-kelly-guilford -20210417yf26intvnvhphjjw2szptkq5bm-story.html

35. Mary Carole McCauley, "'Everything Was Lit Up': Arch Social Club Seeks Zoning Approval for New Marquee Signaling Rebirth of Pennsylvania Avenue," *Baltimore Sun*, March 2, 2021. https://www.baltimoresun.com/entertainment/arts/bs -fe-arch-social-club-marquee-20210302-vxxn4lhopfh2bm4ltlps65py7a-story.html

36. Jacques Kelly, "Another Act Comes to the Former Odell's Nightclub on North Avenue," *Baltimore Sun*, January 16, 2021. https://www.baltimoresun.com/maryland/baltimore-city/bsmd-kelly-odell-20210116-xsyanvvhd5fzjl7bcote22ymfq-story.html

37. Christine Tkacik, "Retro Baltimore: Central Avenue Car Barn, a Relic of City's Cable Car System, to Get Overhaul," *Baltimore Sun*, January 14, 2021. https://www.baltimoresun.com/features/retro-baltimore/bs-fe-retro-central-ave-car-barn -20210114-srt4hlqp5bcztfbxvl3ub25sla-story.html

38. Hallie Miller, "Abandoned Baltimore Fire Station to Get New Life as Museum Honoring Black Firefighters," *Baltimore Sun*, September 16, 2020. https://www.baltimoresun.com/business/real-estate/bs-bz-oliver-fire-fighters-museum-20200916-p6i b7lba6beljkc5c4dat4zo4m-story.html

39. Jacques Kelly, "Life Anew Is Coming for Waverly's Long-Neglected Town Hall," *Baltimore Sun*, January 9, 2021. https://www.baltimoresun.com/maryland/baltimore-city/bs-mdkelly-waverly-20210109-7x3wjvlrwvbgrguekib63sqfuu-story.html

40. Jacques Kelly, "The Boulevard Looks Forward to a Second Century in Baltimore's Waverly," *Baltimore Sun*, July 25, 2020. https://baltimore.cbslocal.com/2021/02/10/abandonedbuildings-being-torn-down-to-make-way-for-new-park-in-west-baltimore/

41. Jacques Kelly, "Old Burlap Bag Factory Becoming Loft Housing in Baltimore's Washington Hill," *Baltimore Sun*, September 9, 2020. https://www.baltimoresun.com/maryland/baltimore-city/bs-md-kelly-citysprings-20200919cj4ppao2xrhkbnee4yozqeqk3e-story.html

42. Hallie Miller, "City Spending Board Approves Sale of West Baltimore's Upton Mansion to Afro Charities," *Baltimore Sun*, May 19, 2021. https://www.baltimoresun.com/politics/bsmd-ci-afro-charities-upton-mansion-20210519-p4gvswaiajg2nnjobpzyxgxmgu-story.html

43. Abigail Matthews, "Abandoned Row Home in West Baltimore Set to Become a Home for the Arts," *Baltimore Sun*, May 18, 2021. https://afro.com/abandoned-row-home-in-westbaltimore-set-to-become-a-home-for-the-arts/

44. Hallie Miller, "The Afro Newspaper to Move to Former Upton Mansion, Revitalize Historic West Baltimore Building," *Baltimore Sun*, February 20, 2020. https://www.baltimoresun.com/business/real-estate/bs-bz-afro-returns-to-west-baltimore-uptonmansion-20200226-cslog5cnvfdypo36z4sfzx63be-story.html

45. Dan Rodericks, "In Pigtown, Building Stability and Pride in the Neighborhood Block by Block/Commentary," *Baltimore Sun*, June 24, 2021. https://www.baltimoresun.com/opinion/columnists/dan-rodricks/bs-md-rodricks-0625-20210624-c5vjawk24zecph52urxzzlqab4-story.html

46. Sean Streicher, "Abandoned Buildings Being Torn Down to Make Way for New Park in West Baltimore," *WJZ-TV*, February 10, 2021. https://baltimore.cbslocal.com/2021/02/10/abandoned-buildings-being-torn-down-to-make-wayfor-new-park-in-west-baltimore/

47. Tatyana Turner, "Two Neighborhoods, One Black and One White, Team Up to Bring a Skatepark to West Baltimore," *Baltimore Sun*, June 4, 2021. https://www.baltimoresun.com/maryland/baltimore-city/bs-md-skateboard-park-west-baltimore-

48. Deborah Weiner, "Baltimore Is Better Than Everyone Else and We're Going to Show You Why: Interview with Baltimore Mayor Brandon Scott," *WBAL-TV Preakness Coverage*, May 15, 2021. https://www.youtube.com/watch?v=40PuXpQKgH8

Chapter 12

Gerrymandering

Questions of Power, Questions of Identity

Gerrymandering is far from a new political tradition. For many decades, when the time came to draw the lines separating one Congressional district from another, the party controlling the process would sometimes skew it to give that party political advantage. Sometimes, the skewing was egregious; sometimes, subtle. As time has passed, the former has come to dominate. The frequency of gerrymandering has also increased. Furthermore, what began as an attempt to increase a political party's sway has become a tool in racial politics—to suppress minority influence as well as to ensure it or even increase it.[1] There is a tendency in recent commentary on gerrymandering to associate it with the Republican Party's efforts to suppress the vote prior to 2016 and after 2020. Whereas many examples support this commentary, gerrymandering has been practiced down through the years by both political parties. In Maryland, as we will see, it has been used by the Democrats because, as the controlling party, they wanted to increase that control.

In Maryland, gerrymandering has been used in service of both political and racial purposes (i.e., increasing minority involvement on government), and this chapter will investigate both. But the chapter will also raise an important matter not often discussed: how gerrymandering affects political identity, for the practice can be a definitive step in constitutive rhetoric. That rhetoric can reinforce identity, create identity, or obliterate identity, all depending on where the lines are drawn. The drawing of lines can, then, be a rhetorical act.

Rhetoric has traditionally been focused on persuasion. Then, theorists made a critical turn, asking important questions about how rhetoric was used to reinforce power and privilege or, perhaps, to undermine them. Then, theorists made a constitutive turn. Inspired by the work of French philosopher Louis Althusser and encouraged by the work of Canadian communication scholar Maurice Charland, rhetorical scholars began asking how communication might call an identity into being, undoubtedly layering a rhetorically inspired identity over others that a group might have.[2] Both critical rhetoric and constitutive rhetoric are very relevant in "reading" the results of gerrymandering. The drawing of lines is quite often about power and privilege; the drawing of lines is also quite often a major part of what interpellates (Althusser's term) an identity into political existence.

PROMOTING THE DEMOCRATIC PARTY

Gerrymandering most often has been a tool to give the political advantage to the party in control at the point in time redistricting occurs. Maryland's efforts have followed this tradition, but Maryland took a while to get to such partisan line drawing.[3] For the longest time, Maryland's Congressional districts followed a loose geographical logic, as was true nationwide. Baltimore City would be a district, so would Montgomery County and Prince George's County. Baltimore County, which surrounds the city (which is not a part of the county), might be split, with the northern part aligning with other counties in that direction and the southern part aligning with other counties in that direction. Southern Maryland, Western Maryland, and the state's Eastern Shore would be regional districts. That's seven. With eight, there was some realignment but geography was still the primary factor in defining districts. In fact, the growth from seven to eight proved difficult in the state because the existing seven made so much geographical sense. So, for a short period in the 1960s, the state had a "Congressman At-Large," who represented the entire state because it could not figure out how to alter the seven-district pattern.

Geography—it should be noted—is not just a matter of either mountain and rivers or lines drawn long ago by a legislature. Geography involves culture. And even in a state as geographically small as Maryland, there are distinct cultures in the different areas. The Eastern Shore had a pronounced southern feel, and the western part of the state was both very ethnically German and, in looks, more like Pennsylvania than the areas to its East. Baltimore, both the city and its suburbs, was very different from the bedroom counties of Washington, D.C. It was as much this set of cultural differences as any physical features or legal demarcations that the state's traditional stress on geography in creating districts honored. Those on the Eastern Shore were culturally bound as were those in Western Maryland and the other regions that were also Congressional districts.

REDUCING REPUBLICANS IN CONGRESS

Then, perhaps, partisanship increased, and the Democrats, holding the majority of the state's Congressional seats, wanted them all. Unable to achieve that goal, they wanted to reduce the Republicans to just one. They also wanted to rid the delegation of long-serving but arguably over-the-hill Roscoe Bartlett.[4] The way was to make his Western Maryland district competitive by moving Democrats in from the Montgomery County district. This shrank the Montgomery County district, which then had to acquire parts of Prince George's. That shrank Prince George's a bit, requiring inroads into Howard, Anne Arundel, and Charles. Enlarging the Montgomery County district was not, however, just a response to its shrinking as residents joined jurisdictions to the west. It was also a response to the desire to transform Montgomery (and whatever else might be added in) from a blue district that too often elected moderate Republicans to a blue district that reliably elected Democrats. No more Gilbert Gude or Connie Morella, who served Montgomery County quite well but were members, albeit it moderate ones, of the GOP.

Geography went out the window as the Democrats tried to turn everything but the Eastern Shore blue. They ceded that area, but decided to enlarge it—moving more Republican voters into it and thereby strengthening the Democratic hold on everything else. This move did not undermine the Eastern Shore identity of the district but did create oddities—that is, people with little culturally in common with the Eastern Shore all of a sudden finding themselves allied in a district with that region.

ENSURING MINORITIES REPRESENTATION

Another agenda also was involved in gerrymandering nationally, and it involved race. In some states, gerrymandering was practiced to create minority districts because, otherwise, African Americans would likely not be elected to Congress. One might characterize the motive in that case as nobly promoting diversity. But closely connected was gerrymandering to make sure there was only one minority district. African Americans got their representative but they lost the opportunity to have two at a time when African American candidates were attracting white voters. A district with a white majority but a sizeable African American population might elect an African American, but probably not if a large number of the African Americans were packed, via gerrymandering, into a single district. The motive in this case would be ignoble. Often, especially in the South, the desire to disadvantage Democrats also may have reflected the desire to disadvantage racial minorities. So, in many cases, partisan gerrymandering was also the ignoble sort of racial gerrymandering.

In Maryland, the noble motive prevailed. Maryland's 7th Congressional District, dominated by Baltimore City's African American neighborhoods would send Kwesi Mfume and Elijah Cummings to the House; Maryland's 4th Congressional District, dominated by the increasingly African American Prince George's County, would send Al Wynn, Donna Edwards, and Anthony Brown to the House.

Here, we need to avoid getting into the proverbial weeds, but to accomplish this goal, population groups had to be moved among districts without much reference to physical or cultural geography. The result was some of the most bizarre Congressional districts in the nation. Until 2022, Maryland's 3rd District, for example, consisted of several barely contiguous spots, giving it the shape of a praying mantis.[5] In general, Maryland's absurd use of gerrymandering ought to prompt federal legislation establishing requirements for a district, such as that the land be a contiguous mass, not loosely connected pieces, although even that requirement would not have prevented the westward extension of the 1st District along a narrow strip across northern Maryland in an attempt to move more GOP voters into the 1st (and out of the 6th). If the Eastern Shore were an elephant, that strip might be its outstretched trunk. It was contiguous but geographically and culturally remote from the bulk of the district.

UNDERMINING REGIONAL IDENTITY

Many will lament the partisan use of gerrymandering, and many will debate its use to achieve— and limit—minority representation. But what is often overlooked are the negative effects gerrymandering has on identity. Following the theory of Louis Althusser and the excellent analysis of the Parti Quebecois by Maurice Charland, rhetoricians now recognize that rhetoric has a constitutive dimension. When speaking of how rhetoric can hail people into an identity, which will be layered on previously held ones, Althusser had discursive elements in mind, things like narratives or rituals. He most certainly did not have in view the arbitrary lines those in government might draw on paper, but they have long had constitutive effects. In Spain, for example, there are strong Basque and Catalan separatist groups. One is constituted as a member of those groups by several means, but one is most certainly where one lives, whether one is over the line into the Basque region or into Catalonia.[6] One therefore should not be surprised that the lines defining longstanding Congressional districts had something of a constitutive effect. In the case of Catalonia, one determinative factor is which football (or soccer) team one supports; another is what holidays one observes. Matters one might think trivial can be both determinative and/or reflective of identity.

Maryland's 1st District, despite some gerrymandering that extended it westward across the Bay along the state's border with Pennsylvania, has retained an identity as "The Eastern Shore." The region would still be "The Eastern Shore" if it were divided among Congressional districts, but being a single district strengthens that identity. Once Maryland's 8th District was synonymous with Montgomery County, and, as a district, it acquired an identity as somewhat non-partisan despite having far more registered Democrats than registered Republicans. Voters supported good people who they thought would serve them well, and the party label did not matter as much as in other districts. Thus, the 8th District was represented for long stretches by Republicans Gilbert Gude and Connie Morella. The 8th District had other traits as well—a fair measure of affluence, a high level of education, and a very positive evaluation of its public schools. Those from the 8th saw these and other traits distinguishing them from residents of other districts such as the near-by 4th. There was once a striking difference between how 8th District residents and 4th District residents saw themselves and each other. Those in the 8th saw many in the 4th as "rednecks"; those in the 4th saw many in the 8th as effete snobs. These negative views each had of the other had, as a corollary, the positive view of themselves. Those in the 8th were most decidedly not "rednecks." Although it is perhaps a silly indicator of the difference, in the traditional 8th, liquor was county-regulated and available only at government-run stores whereas, in the traditional 4th, there were private, rather garish liquor stores galore. The 8th was a tad "prim and proper"; the 4th drank hard and drove pick-up trucks. And the districts were adjoining.

But gerrymandering has altered the 8th and the 4th. Part of the 8th was "moved" westward in order to make the 6th less Republican; and another part (with a sizeable minority population) was merged in with the 4th in order to create a second heavily minority district (then a part of that part was moved back into the 8th during the next redistricting). Parts of the traditional 4th and 5th were played with to both create the heavily minority 4th and make sure the 5th would reelect Steny Hoyer. Doing so involved adding in pieces of the once 3rd here and there, making the current 3rd District an absurd collection of scattered spots.

Gerrymandering is usually understood in party terms or racial terms, but, when focusing on those two variables, other things can happen. And they did in Maryland. Traditional regions and traditional identities were undermined. Now, perhaps, it is a bad idea for identities to be so tied to counties, but it has been "the way" in the nation for states to have and try to hold onto particular identities, and one can argue that what's good for the states is good for its

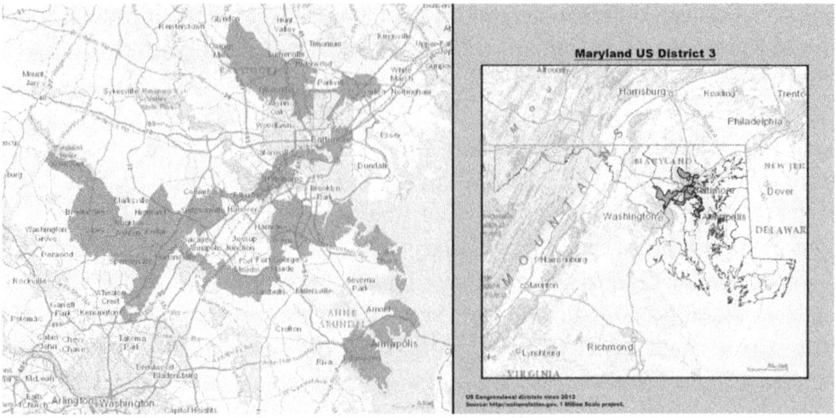

Figure 12.1   One of Maryland's Most Gerrymandered Congressional Districts. *Source*: Data created by the United States Department of the Interior and rendered using ArcGIS® software by Esri. File provided by Wikimedia user 7partparadigm. Public domain.

counties. If Missouri can distinguish itself from Illinois, why can't two counties in a state do the same thing?

Consider metropolitan Philadelphia: there is an identity difference among Chester, Delaware, Montgomery, and Berks Counties; consider metropolitan Atlanta: there is an identity difference among Fulton, Clayton, DeKalb, and Cobb. So, the way Maryland features—or once featured—strong county identities is not unique to Maryland. But identity is a tricky matter. Are identities based on geography inherently superior to ones tied to other demographics? Have we reached the political point where a district identified by being heavily Hispanic trumps a district identified by its traditional physical and cultural geography?

The question is certainly an open one, but the point here is that, by redrawing lines, state officials performed a rhetorical act that reconstituted an identity tied to geography in many parts of the state. In general, this means that the traditional identity was weakened—presumably (but not necessarily) a negative occurrence.

Thus far, attention has been focused on lost identity. Let's consider the opposite.

CREATING NEW IDENTITIES?

Consider Maryland's 6th District, which encompasses the western part of the state. Traditionally, it has been a Republican region, although moderately so. With gerrymandering designed to switch it from red to blue, what has happened to its identity? Is it, as a whole, more progressive now? Or, because it does mix the parties well, is it a model of bi-partisanship? Neither of these changes has occurred. Rather, it is a region with increasingly redder areas whose residents deeply resent the blue spots within and the blue areas that were added in the southeastern corner so as to tilt the balance to the Democrats. It is, then, a much more divided region than it was with, arguably, an emerging identity as deeply, hotly divided. Gerrymandering is very much a "dirty" word among conservatives in this district, for they feel that the limited political voice they had has been taken away from them. They are bitter—even proposing secession from the state.

Meanwhile, in the same district, are those who feel they are ably represented by Democrat David Trone, but these residents (in upper Montgomery County) are not at all politically or culturally in sync with many in the district, whom they have a negative opinion of, reflected in negative comments about all of the pro-Trump signs one still sees as one travels westward in District 6. A harmonious region, defined by its Congressional district, has become sharply divided, perhaps now mirroring the state of the nation.

Consider Maryland's 4th, now a heavily minority district. It is more Democratic than once (when Republican Larry Hogan, Senior, represented it), but there are pockets where the "heavily minority" label is not appreciated. Some, once in the 8th, say they never asked to be in a "heavily minority" district and they believe their political interests to be not especially aligned with those of the new district's minority voters. The new district also blended together African American populations that, while united by skin color, are divided on several issues. The homogeneity of the 4th District may then be an illusion, especially when one recognizes that "majority minority" still leaves pockets of middle-class white voters (not as affluent as those in the 8th) who find little in common with an African American majority now dominating the political scene.

The tension is very evident if one considers the composition and the conduct of the Prince George's County police. Although the force is now racially diverse, it is dominated by a lower-middle-class white population—as it long has been. Thus, the police force has a long-standing reputation in the Washington, D.C. area for overly aggressive behavior toward people of color. The police force is changing, but its present state reflects what the area was, not the black-majority area that redistricting supposedly reflected or created. A new identity here is illusory upon close examination. One might argue that one is forming, but a closer examination suggests that the election of African American federal and county officials hides lingering racism.

Consider Maryland's 5th, House Majority Leader Steny Hoyer's district. It was once "Southern Maryland," and although the counties that comprise that region have long had different cultures, there did exist a "Southern Maryland" identity oddly mixing the Chesapeake Bay and gambling. But that "Southern Maryland" was too politically volatile—too many Republicans in St. Mary's County and Calvert County who could, if the candidates were "right," put a Republican in the House. Elections might be close for Steny Hoyer, so, some population trading took place at the district's northern edge. Republicans were moved North to the heavily Democratic 3rd and 4th (where they would be irrelevant) while Democrats from Anne Arundel and Prince George's Counties were moved South. As that northern edge became less well-defined, the "Southern Maryland" identity began to fade. Replacing it was more of mishmash.

Then, there's Maryland's 3rd, the bizarre collection of a slash here and a spot there that supposedly formed the shape of a praying mantis. Put together, they did guarantee a Democrat in the House, but did these random slashes and spots even have the possibility of an identity? Once, the district was a few sections of Baltimore City; the area to the South of the city—a mix of working-class suburbs and a few more affluent ones; and a handful of places that go "way back" (see fig. 12.1; p. 236).

The mix worked, and, although Fell's Point, Catonsville, Glen Burnie, Pasadena, and Severna Park were certainly different communities, they were united in being Baltimore's southern reaches. And they were contiguous in the 3rd District, not widely spread-out sections.

AN UNFORESEEN POLITICAL CONSEQUENCE

Gerrymandering can create a political mishmash as in the case of the 5th District or crazily separated stretches as in the case of the 3rd. Homogeneity is unlikely in either case, but gerrymandering can create that homogeneity. A very blue district; a very red district; a heavily minority district. That creation could well have a negative political effect.[7]

The effect is much like the two sides of a coin.

Might those elected in these districts thereby acquire a reputation that is so dominated by a single political ideology or by a racial demographic that they lose traction when running for a statewide office? Is, for example, a 4th District representative so blue and so black that he or she would not receive a warm political welcome in other districts? The theory here is that, although gerrymandering has helped minorities gain representation, the process may have inadvertently limited their ability to move beyond the district that elected them. Their identity has been rhetorically defined by their district so that it is difficult for those in other districts to identify with them, that identification, in Burkean terms, being required for a vote.

The flip side is that they may have become so attuned to their district's prevailing views that they have a difficult time campaigning outside that district. They find that a message that resonates well in the 4th or the 7th falls on deaf ears or, worse, evokes hostility elsewhere. Let's consider the ideology of "Black Lives Matter." A Congressional representative might not only embrace the ideology but believe that, at its core, is systemic racism that the white population may not see. In other words, in that representative's mind, the ideology reflects the truth. Might that man or woman, then, have difficulty campaigning—communicating—with those who are skeptical about "BLM"? In Maryland, there might well be pockets of skepticism in the 5th, and there might well be large pockets of opposition in the 1st and 6th. Has then being gerrymandered into office imprisoned an elected representative in views that he or she has a difficult time seeing as matters on which voters (some arguably unenlightened) might disagree?

COMMUNICATION DIMENSIONS

This chapter could well have gone into more detail than it did about the gerrymandering increasingly involved in Maryland's redistricting efforts. Many maps would have been necessary, but, even with these visual aids, it is doubtful that the maneuverings would have been totally clear. One would have to know Maryland quite well to understand that Langley Park, College Park, Greenbelt, and Hyattsville—jurisdictions that surround the University of Maryland's campus—are demographically strikingly different—so much so that moving any of them out of a Congressional district, such as Maryland's 4th, might significantly change how that district votes. That detail would have been necessary if this chapter was about the politics of gerrymandering, but, rather, it is about gerrymandering as rhetorical, as communicative.

A critical rhetoric perspective alerts one to how gerrymandering involves messages of power and privilege. A Democratic majority in the state legislature can disempower Republicans through redistricting, or a Republican majority can disempower Democrats. The first occurred in Maryland; the second has occurred in many parts of the nation. In many cases, the second was also an attempt to disempower people of color. Emory Professor Carol Anderson outlines many techniques Republican governors and legislatures have used to suppress people of color in *One Person, No Vote* (2018).[8] Among them is gerrymandering carefully designed to dilute the power of their voting.

A constitutive rhetoric perspective alerts one to how gerrymandering might create identities, although it is far more likely that is destroys identities by running contrary to the geographical and cultural realities in a state. Once, in

Maryland, one could go county-by-county and point to its identity in many areas. Montgomery and Prince George's were distinct from each other, as were Baltimore and Harford. There was a county identity. And even in areas where several counties were merged into a district, there was still a measure of county identity. In southern Maryland, Anne Arundel, Charles, Calvert, and St. Mary's were different; in western Maryland, Frederick, Washington, Allegany, and Garrett were different. The shared Congressional district gave them an identity as a region but did not totally undermine the county ones. Only on the "Eastern Shore" did the county identities vanish somewhat, but those in Talbot still insisted that they weren't like those in Dorchester, and those in Wicomico felt they weren't like either Talbot or Dorchester to their west. Districting, at this point, reinforced or at least kept alive traditional political-cultural identities.

Now, they often do the opposite, undercutting identity while not adequately constituting a new one. One can forecast a Western Maryland where divisiveness replaces the identity once dominant; one can forecast a Prince George's County where multiple identities emerge depending on what district you're placed in—an identity for this part of the county and an identity for that part—or, more likely, a situation where, with the bulk of the county in a majority-minority district (the 4th), a white minority, with the feeling that it has been disenfranchised, develops. Either way, identity is not as stable as it once was.

To some extent, any creation of a political entity is arbitrary, even if it follows such geographical features such as mountains or rivers. However, over time, entities develop a culture, which provides its residents with an identity. Much of this process is rhetorical, but, because it occurs over time, it may be difficult to see it as such. Redistricting, because abrupt, makes the constitutive rhetoric more noticeable. Lines are redrawn, and, suddenly, people who defined themselves in one way find that identity challenged by no longer being in the district that corresponded with and reinforced it.

Critical rhetoric alerts us to how gerrymandering is a textual (i.e., putting marks—lines—on *paper*) practice that allocated power and privilege. It is difficult to deny the importance of power and privilege. But one might ask why the insights that constitutive rhetoric leads us to are important. They are important because identity is important: it gives meaning to one's life; it links one with others. Whereas it is indeed true that the identities imparted by physical and especially cultural geography might be objectionable, it is far better to have identity and links with others than to just be an isolated voter id number moved here and moved there for political reasons. Let's imagine the residents of the 3rd District in Maryland. Once, this was the proud district that sent Paul Sarbanes and Barbara Mikulski to Congress; once, this was a socioeconomically diverse area that was united as Baltimore's southern and eastern reaches. Now, consider the pre-2002 3rd. It was a collection of many separate spots. If you lived in these southern and eastern reaches, you probably didn't know if you were even in the 3rd. You might have been, but the person down the street might not have been. The district thus did nothing to affirm the area's identity and a political linkage among its residents, and, left somewhat adrift, that identity and that linkage might well have weakened (see fig. 12.1; p. 236).

Gerrymandering, then, is a not just the drawing of lines. It's a rhetorical practice with material and identity consequences. One can denounce it as partisan politics at their worst, but one should also be alert to what a communicative or rhetorical critique reveals. Power is in play; identity is at stake. One cannot say it's "just politics." Certainly, what Congressional district one resides in is not the only determinant of identity: there are many. In most cases, districting reinforces rather than creates an identity from scratch. But, even though districting may not be the factor in creating—let's say—a western Maryland identity, it does sustain it. One from that region might well say that "We here think a certain way," and be correct. If districting matched, then one would see in her or his representative in Congress someone who thought that "certain way." If districting does not match, then political identity is disrupted. Tension can result; a weakening of identity can result. Currently, in the 6th District, many residents do indeed feel that the person in Congress representing them does not think their way, that he (and his predecessor) got elected because Democrats added-in Democrats way down in the southeastern corner.[9] Thus, the secessionist sentiment referred to earlier in this part of the state. It won't lead to anything, but the fact that it exists illustrates how redistricting, by threatening identity, can lead to tension. Critical rhetoric calls our attention to matters of power; constitutive rhetoric to matters of identity. They are not separate matters. As Maryland's redistricting shows, exercising power can have effects on identity. The two matters are interrelated.

One might wonder, after reading this chapter, if gerrymandering has increased. Evidence is it has. It most certainly has in Maryland. Advances in data analysis and modeling, both aided by computer technology, have played a major role in this increase.[10] They also can play a major role in solving the gerrymandering problem. Several states have turned redistricting over to commissions. The jury is still out on them. Some solutions use mathematics modeling and computer technology to flag down egregious gerrymandering.[11] Both commissions and this application of modeling are addressing the partisan way gerrymandering has been used, but it is unclear whether the identity issues raised in this chapter are even being considered. They need to be, for districting is not just a matter of balancing out the red and the blue. Another problem with commissions is that they are often advisory. Such is the case in Maryland, where the legislature ignored a commission's recommendations and approved a redistricting plan very much in line with previous attempts to make the state's Congressional delegation as blue as possible. Governor Hogan vetoed the legislature's first map, but the General Assembly overrode the veto. A court challenge resulted in a compromise map.

A comment on gerrymandering and the courts might be in order here. We have focused on the critical and constitutive dimensions of the practice because we are looking at gerrymandering rhetorically. But gerrymandering is a political practice. As such, the courts have been very reluctant to interfere with it. There is nothing in the Constitution that says that state legislatures, dominated by a particular political party, must be fair to other parties. (In fact, there is nothing about political parties, which, as we all know, George Washington feared.) Discrimination based on political party membership is not prohibited. Jurists might privately lament its existence, but they have long felt they had no basis for involvement. Only when the discrimination seemed to be based on race, not party, did they see fit to consider intervention. The fourteenth amendment gave them the basis they needed. But the courts have been quite cautious. If one reads the few relevant decisions, one concludes that justices have found it difficult to disentangle districting designed to disadvantage a race from districting designed to disadvantage a party and have, so as not to enter into matters of party politics, backed-off. With gerrymandering seemingly on the increase and given the ways modeling and computer technology can be used to accelerate and fine tune the process, the courts' concerns may be increasing. At least, decisions and the preceding oral arguments suggest as much. So, the political dimension of gerrymandering may soon be getting long-overdue attention from the judiciary.

Should that occur, one should not disregard the rhetorical dimensions we have explored. Gerrymandering is a rhetorical practice. It sends messages about who has power and who does not. It also plays a role in constituting political identity. It is easy—too easy—to focus on the bizarre shapes some districts have acquired and laugh. One needs, however, to remember that these shapes, whether dragons or praying mantises, contain people, people who may be disempowered or have their identities undermined. Rhetoric draws attention to these important effects.

NOTES

1. See Anthony J. McGann, Charles Anthony Smith, Michael Latner, and Alex Keena, *Gerrymandering in America: The House of Representatives, the Supreme Court, and the Future of Popular Sovereignty* (New York: Cambridge University Press, 2016).

2. Louis Althusser, "Ideology and Ideological State Apparatuses," *Lenin and Philosophy and Other Essays,* trans. Ben Brewster (New York: Monthly Review

Press, 1971); Maurice Charland, "Constitutive Rhetoric: The Case of the People Quebecois," *Quarterly Journal of Speech* 73.3 (1987): 133–50.

3. "How Maryland Democrats Pulled Off Their Aggressive Gerrymander," *Washington Post*, March 28, 2018.

4. Robert Barnes, "Supreme Court Will Take Up a Second Gerrymandering Case This Term," *Washington Post*, December 8, 2017.

5. Christopher Ingraham, "America's Most Gerrymandered Congressional Districts," *Washington Post*, May 15, 2014.

6. Raphael Minder, *The Struggle for Catalonia: Rebel Politics in Spain* (London: C. Hurst and Company, 2017).

7. Ed Kilgore, "African-Americans and Statewide Offices," https://washingtonmonthly.com/2012/03/16/africanamericans-and-statewide-offices/; Jamelle Bouie, "The Other Glass Ceiling," March 14, 2012, https://prospect.org/power/glass-ceiling/

8. Carol Anderson, *One Person, No Vote: How Voter Suppression is Destroying Our Democracy* (New York: Bloomsbury Publishing, 2018). See pp. 96–120.

9. Maryland law does not require an elected representative to live in the district he/or she represents. So, in the case of Maryland's 6th District, the feeling many have that they've been silenced by gerrymandering has been enhanced by the fact that neither Democrat elected by the new district lives there.

10. Kevin Drum, "Computers Have Revolutionized Gerrymandering: The Supreme Court Should Take Notice," *Mother Jones*. February 26, 2017, https://motherjones .com/kevin-drum/2017/02/computers-have-revolutionizedgerrymandering-supreme -court-should-take-notice. Both amicus briefs and oral arguments in the Supreme Court case Gill v. Whitford (2017) frequently noted the role of computer technology. The situation in question was in Wisconsin where Republicans spent four hours in a closed-door session running redistricting model after model on the computer to find the one that would maximize party advantage.

11. Sam Wang and Brian Remlinger, "Can Math Stop Partisan Gerrymandering?" *Los Angeles Times*, May 5, 2017, https:///www.latimes.com/opinion/op-ed/la-oe-wang-remlinger-gerrymandering-20170505-story.html. The Supreme Court in Vieth v. Jubelirer (2004) refused to rule on gerrymandering because the majority thought there was no definitive way to determine if gerrymandering went far enough so as to violate the 14th Amendment. In oral arguments on Gill v. Whitford (2017), the justices seemed intrigued by the possibilities math modeling offered, but remanded the case to a lower court based on jurisdictional concerns.

Chapter 13

Has Change Come to Maryland's Eastern Shore?

Maryland's geography is, in many ways, quite strange. The bulk of the state's landmass and population and a significant portion of its economy are in the center. There is a panhandle to the west sandwiched between Pennsylvania and West Virginia, which at one point is only about 10 miles wide. The third piece is called the Eastern Shore. It is called that because of its location on the eastern side of the Chesapeake Bay. It is the Eastern Shore that is the subject of this chapter.

The Eastern Shore (often called just "the Shore" by many Marylanders) comprises about one-third of Maryland's land mass. There are nine counties on the Shore: Caroline, Cecil, Dorchester, Kent, Queen Anne's, Somerset, Talbot, Wicomico, and Worcester. Of these, some maintain that Cecil County should not be considered a true Eastern Shore County. This is based on two things. One is geography. Because of the way its borders are drawn, roughly half the county is actually west of the Chesapeake Bay. The other reason is the presence of I-95. The fact that the county is bisected by I-95 places it within easy travel of Baltimore, Philadelphia, and Wilmington and therefore more easily subject to urban influences than other parts of the Shore.

Maryland's Eastern Shore is located on the Delmarva Peninsula, a landmass it shares with most of Delaware and with Virginia's eastern shore counties.

POPULATION

Although the Eastern Shore includes about one-third of Maryland's landmass, it is home to only about 8.6 percent of the state's population (based on 2020 census estimates). That has remained remarkably stable. In the 2010 census, the Eastern Shore accounted for about 8.1 percent of the state's population. With its population at some 524,121, Baltimore City and several individual counties in Maryland each have more people than all of the Eastern Shore counties combined.

There is little diversity on the Eastern Shore overall. All nine counties are majority white, and substantially so. Only three counties have any significant African American populations. These include Wicomico County with 27.3 percent, Dorchester with 29.0 percent, and Somerset with 41.5 percent. African American populations in the other counties range from the low to mid-teens, with Cecil and Queen Anne's Counties having less than 10 percent.[1]

African American populations in both Wicomico and Dorchester Counties rose between 2010 and 2019. The rise in Wicomico County's African American population coincides with a Jeremy Cox report in the Salisbury *Daily Times* on January 12, 2018. In that story, Cox reported that the population of Salisbury had become majority-minority according to figures released by the U.S. Census Bureau. Hispanic numbers had risen by 30 percent since 2010. African American numbers had risen by 21 percent in the same period. Minorities account for 51 percent of Salisbury's population.[2]

The change in Salisbury is being attributed at least in part to declining numbers of agricultural jobs spurring moves to more urban areas. Two other Eastern Shore incorporated communities are also majority-minority. They are Pocomoke City in Worcester County, which is 55 percent minority and Princess Anne in Somerset County, which is 65 percent minority. Princess Anne is home to the historically Black University of Maryland Eastern Shore. The majority-minority status has yet to translate into genuine political power in Salisbury. African Americans are still underrepresented on the Salisbury police force and there's always been a white mayor. But for the second time in the city's history, there are two African Americans on the five-person city council.

It may or may not be significant to note that historically the three counties with the highest African American populations, Wicomico, Dorchester, and Somerset, are all counties with more registered Democrats than Republicans. The only exception is Somerset in the 2020 election cycle when registered Republicans outnumbered registered Democrats by just nine registered voters.[3]

POLITICS

Politically, the Eastern Shore is largely conservative and tends to vote Republican. During the last four election cycles (2014, 2016, 2018, and 2020) registered Democrats outnumbered registered Republicans in only three counties: Dorchester, Kent, and Wicomico.

Dorchester and Wicomico Counties have significant population centers in Cambridge and Salisbury, respectively. And Kent and Wicomico Counties both have important institutions of higher education: Washington College (in Chestertown in Kent County) and Salisbury University (in Salisbury in Wicomico County).

In three of the last four cycles, Somerset County had more Democrats than Republicans. The exception was the most recent one in 2020. In 2014 Worcester County showed up on this list, but not by much.

Overall, however, Republicans have a numbers advantage. What they do not have is a majority of registered voters, though the percentages are rising. In 2014, Republicans were 43.4 percent of registered voters. In 2020, they represented 45.6 percent. By contrast, the number of Democrats declined from 37.3 percent in 2014 to 33.6 percent in 2020. The number of those registered in other parties or as unaffiliated rose from 17.8 percent to 19.3 percent during the same period.[4] While still voting reliably Republican, it is interesting that one-fifth of the registered voters on the Eastern Shore are neither Republicans nor Democrats. (Note: The numbers used in the preceding paragraphs are those of only the nine Eastern Shore counties and not of the entire 1st Congressional District.)

The Eastern Shore is the largest part of the state's 1st Congressional District. In addition to those nine counties, the district also includes small pieces of Baltimore, Carroll, and Harford Counties. Interestingly, unlike Maryland's other congressional districts (which have often been quite bizarrely configured and have changed radically from time to time), the map of the 1st District has remained relatively stable since at least the redistricting after the 1970 census. With only minor differences, the maps available for the 1972 and 2002 elections look remarkably similar to that for the 2012 election.[5]

All three maps included all nine Shore counties. What makes the district interesting is that in the elections since that 1972 map, the 1st District has twice been represented by Democrats. Frank Kratovil lasted only one term (2009–2011) before he was beaten by the incumbent, Andy Harris. Roy Dyson, on the other hand, represented that district for a decade (1981–1991).

As this chapter is written, the 1st District is represented by Andy Harris, a physician from Cockeysville in Baltimore County. A far-right Republican, he is in his sixth term. He had promised to serve only six but has already declared that he will run for a seventh. His election percentages have always been very high, ranging from 54.8 percent in 2010 to 70.42 percent in 2014.[6.]

THE CHESAPEAKE BAY BRIDGE

The first settlement on the Eastern Shore was on Kent Island in 1631 and predated the arrival of Lord Baltimore to Maryland in 1634. Other towns gradually came and thriving economies developed. Though politically part of Maryland, the Eastern Shore was physically isolated from the rest of the state except for its northernmost county. Travel between the Eastern and Western shores was difficult, time consuming, and most generally by cross-Bay ferry service.

That all changed in 1952 with the opening of the William Preston Lane, Jr. Memorial Bridge, which is more popularly known as the Chesapeake Bay Bridge. The idea of a bridge connecting the two sides of the Bay apparently first surfaced in the 1880s. In 1907, concerned about the Eastern Shore trade going north by road and by railroad to Philadelphia and Wilmington instead to Baltimore by boat, a group of businessmen commissioned a feasibility study for a bridge. Talk of a double-deck bridge to carry both railroad and trolley lines surfaced in 1919. In 1927, a group of Baltimore businessmen was authorized to raise funds to build a bridge. Although detailed plans were developed, the 1929 stock market crash put an end to that effort. There were several commissions exploring the idea of a bridge in the early 1930s.

There was regular cross-Bay ferry service but the trip took two hours and the number of people and vehicles each ferry could carry was limited. Pressure for a bridge mounted and in 1938, the Maryland General Assembly passed legislation authorizing one. World War II put plans on hold, though. Several locations had been proposed but the network of highways and the need to take safe navigation of the Bay into consideration resulted in the choice of Sandy Point not far from Annapolis on the Western Shore and the Matapeake area of Kent Island on the Eastern Shore as the points of crossing.

In 1947, under the leadership of Governor William Preston Lane, Jr. during both the regular session and an extraordinary session of the General Assembly, the State Roads Commission was directed to proceed with the bridge. Construction began in 1949. The bridge was finished in 1952 under the administration of Governor Theodore McKeldin. The span that opened in 1952 had two lanes, but by the early 1960s it was clear that two lanes would not be enough and that another bridge would be needed. The Maryland General Assembly authorized its construction in 1967. Although three locations were examined, it was determined that the best place to build the second bridge was next to the first one. The U.S. Coast Guard granted a permit in 1968. The second span, with three lanes, was opened in 1973.

The first bridge now carries eastbound traffic and the second carries westbound traffic. The presence of three lanes on that second span provides the flexibility to allow one lane to be eastbound during peak times (especially

Figure 13.1   The First Two Spans of the Chesapeake Bay Bridge, which Connected the "Eastern Shore" to the Bulk of the State. *Source*: Photo courtesy of Carl Hyden.

during the summer as people are heading to the beach). Shore to shore, the bridges are about 4.3 miles long. At the tallest point, the vertical clearance is nearly 380 feet to accommodate ships sailing to and from Baltimore. All lanes of the bridges have the capacity to carry 1,500 vehicles per hour. The annual traffic volume is nearly 30 million vehicles.[7] (Note: All information about the history and construction of the Chesapeake Bay Bridge was drawn from the webpage of the Maryland Transportation Authority.)

In recent years, traffic crossing the Bay has increased exponentially and it has become increasingly clear that another bridge is needed. The state has been studying the feasibility of five potential points of crossing, including a third span at or very near the current two. There appear to be advantages and (if you listen to those potentially affected) many disadvantages to all five proposed locations. So far, no decision has been made about whether to build another bridge much less where such a bridge might go.

The Chesapeake Bay Bridge has allowed easy passage across the Bay. Thousands of people cross from the Western Shore to the Eastern Shore every day for work or recreation. And the reverse is true as well. The ease with which people can access the Eastern Shore has made Kent Island and nearby parts of the Shore increasingly popular as bedroom communities for people working in Baltimore and Washington. I can personally attest to this since for some months in 2013, I made a daily commute from Kent Island to

Baltimore while staying with my daughter as I waited for my new house to be finished.

The huge number of people crossing the Bridge to the Eastern Shore has brought change to what had once been an isolated, sleepy part of Maryland. To try to cover how all of the Eastern Shore has been affected would be impossible. I have chosen to focus attention on five specific places: Kent Island, Easton, Cambridge, Salisbury, and Ocean City. I chose these because all five are on U.S. 50 and are the places that may have been most directly affected by the opening of the Chesapeake Bay Bridge. Anyone coming from the Baltimore/Washington region and using U.S. 50 will travel through the first four places (in that order) on their way to the fifth, which to be honest is most peoples' destination.

THE EASTERN SHORE—KENT ISLAND

Kent Island (which many locals call simply, "the Island") is part of Queen Anne's County. It is the largest island in the Chesapeake Bay and is only barely separated from the rest of the Eastern Shore by the Kent Narrows. Kent Island is the first piece of land on which one drives after coming off the eastbound span of the Chesapeake Bay Bridge.

The Island was first settled in 1631 by William Claiborne of the Virginia Colony who named it after his home county, making it the first English settlement in what would become Maryland. It is sometimes not "officially" recognized since the settlement was directed by someone from Virginia and not by Cecilius Calvert, 2nd Lord Baltimore to whom the English crown had given Maryland.

Nevertheless, the 1631 date is real. That date also makes Kent Island the third oldest permanent English settlement in what became the United States. Jamestown in Virginia (1607) and Plymouth in Massachusetts (1620) were older.

From its establishment (at least under the Calverts) until the early nineteenth century, Kent Island's economy was based mostly on farming tobacco and corn, until depleted soil made farming unprofitable. The economy went into decline.

The town of Stevensville was founded in 1850 and became a hub for steamboat travel across the Bay. There was also a railway station from which travelers from the Western Shore could catch a train to other parts of the Eastern Shore.

Later in the nineteenth century and through the twentieth, farming was again important with farmers growing corn, wheat, berries, and melons. In addition, a substantial percentage of Kent Islanders were watermen fishing for blue crabs, rockfish, and oysters.[8]

When the Chesapeake Bay Bridge opened in 1952, the changes for Kent Island were at first quite jarring for residents. Travelers came off the bridge onto the only highway that went across the Island to the Eastern Shore proper—and it was the highway the local residents had to use to go about their daily business. Things got very difficult and inconvenient. It only got worse as traffic increased and the second span opened in 1973. U.S. 50 was converted to a freeway across the Island, something completed in the early 1990s. Daily business for residents now happens on local roads running parallel to U.S. 50.

Things have indeed changed in several ways for Kent Island. On some parts of the Island, condominium complexes appeared catering to those who wanted a getaway but weren't interested in a beach vacation. Other condominiums and housing developments also grew up to accommodate new residents of what was becoming a Baltimore/Washington bedroom community.

To avoid the impacts of too much development, there are limits to how tall buildings may be built. There are also limits on the sizes of commercial buildings so that "big box" stores on Kent Island are not as big as they might be elsewhere.

There are still pieces of the past, though. Farming is still important and those who get off U.S. 50 and drive around the Island will see that. And watermen are still integral to the Island's life.

So change on Kent Island has been a mixed bag. The jarring changes initially brought by thousands of people speeding across the Island have largely been ameliorated by preventing that traffic from interfering too much with the Island's residents. Because the freeway prevents through traffic from venturing off U.S. 50 (unless deliberately planning a visit to the Island), there is enough of the past remaining for the longtime residents to still feel like the Island is home.

THE EASTERN SHORE—EASTON

A bit less than 30 miles east and south of Kent Island is Easton, the second "stop" on our journey to the ocean. The area that would be Easton was first settled by Quakers in 1682. Its meeting house is one of the oldest frame structures built for worship in the United States. Talbot County's official website says it is the oldest house of worship still in use and the earliest dated building in Maryland.

Easton was formally established as a town in 1710 when it was selected as the seat for the Talbot County Courthouse, being roughly in the middle of the county and relatively easily accessible for all.

Easton was an agricultural center trading tobacco and other goods. There was also an active slave trade, complete with an auction block in front of the courthouse. Easton's location on the Tred Avon River made it usable as a port. The port allowed it to serve as a center for moving coal. Capital and investment came to Easton and in the 1830s and 1840s it was one of the largest manufacturing centers in the United States.

Agriculture and light manufacturing are still important to Easton's economy today. The latter include the manufacture of power tools, distillation equipment, and highway flares.[9]

Tourism is equally important in today's Easton, made possible in part by the Chesapeake Bay Bridge, making it easily accessible from other parts of Maryland. Easton has art galleries, antique shops, and a theater for live performances. Easton is home to the Waterfowl Festival which draws thousands of visitors to Easton every year. Maryland's tourism website refers to Easton as the "cultural capital of the Eastern Shore" and it has become widely known for those cultural amenities.

Unfortunately, Easton (and Talbot County) has become well known around the country for another reason. The Talbot Boys monument stands on the grounds of the Talbot County Courthouse. It was installed there by city leaders in 1916.

Like many areas of Maryland, Easton was conflicted about the Civil War. Some people sided with the Union; others with the Confederacy. Because of the county's dependence on slave labor for the tobacco fields, the numbers of the latter were quite significant. The Talbot Boys statue memorializes the eighty-four men from Talbot County who fought for the South. Their names are inscribed on the pedestal on which the sculpture stands. The Talbot Boys is believed to be the last statue to Confederates still standing on public land in Maryland.

That conflict is still very much present. Some in Easton call the sculpture historically significant and say it should remain. Others say it glorifies slavery and its location on the Courthouse grounds clearly says that justice isn't for everyone. Each side has an organization; "Save the Talbot Boys" for those who want it to remain and "Move the Monument" for those who want it removed from the Courthouse grounds. Both also have Facebook pages. The one for "Save the Talbot Boys" has twice as many followers.[10]

At one point, there was a successful movement to install a monument to Frederick Douglass at the Courthouse. Douglass was born a slave on the Wye Oak Plantation near Easton, which is still owned and occupied by the eleventh-generation descendants of its builder. The Douglass sculpture was installed in 2011.

Over the years, there have been several unsuccessful attempts to have the Talbot County Council vote to remove the Talbot Boys sculpture from the

Courthouse grounds. Some previous votes have been unanimous for keeping it where it is. The most recent vote, in 2020, was 3 to 2 to keep it.

In 2021, the NAACP, the ACLU, and others filed a federal lawsuit seeking removal of the statue. Talbot County officials have asked the court to dismiss the suit on the grounds that the plaintiffs had not done enough to prove the statue's presence was discriminatory. They also argue that the court lacks subject matter jurisdiction.[11]

So, has change come to Easton? I suppose the answer to that is probably yes and no. Yes, because increased tourism to Easton has brought shifts in its economy. Agriculture and manufacturing are still there, but there is a growing sector more focused on cultural attractions such as art galleries and live performances.

Unfortunately, the answer is also no. The divisions caused by the Civil War remain and still go very deep. That a symbol honoring a racist past remains is bad enough. That it stands on the grounds of a building that is supposed to represent equal justice under the law is appalling to many.

Many votes to remove the Talbot Boys have been 5 to 0 to keep it. Another vote was 4 to 1. Then it was 3 to 2. Change was coming, but it was coming very slowly. We couldn't say that change was actually arriving until the vote to remove the Talbot Boys picked up at least one more vote for its removal. And on September 14, 2021, the Talbot County Council voted to remove the Talbot Boys statue from the grounds of the county courthouse in Easton. It was finally removed on March 14, 2022, and taken to Cross Keys Battlefield in Harrisonburg, Virginia, a private park in the care of the Shenandoah Valley Battlefield Foundation.

THE EASTERN SHORE—CAMBRIDGE

Having traveled some 30 miles from the Bay Bridge to Easton, we now travel south for another 16 miles to Cambridge. Cambridge was settled in 1684, which makes it one of the oldest cities in Maryland.

Like Easton, the early economy of Cambridge focused on agriculture; first tobacco and then mixed types of farming. And like Easton, the farms around Cambridge had depended a great deal on the labor of enslaved Africans. And also like Easton, Cambridge was a trading center, including the trafficking in slaves. Though the Cambridge area depended on slave labor, or perhaps because of that, Cambridge became an important stop on the Underground Railroad. Other parts of the economy focused on the water. Boatbuilding was important. Crabs, oysters, and other seafood were as well. Near the end of the nineteenth century, food processing became a major employer in Cambridge. The Phillips Packing Company processed things such as oysters, tomatoes (for which the Eastern Shore is particularly famous), and sweet potatoes.

Phillips employed as many as 10,000 people during and between the World Wars. The postwar era saw the beginning of a decline in food processing, especially during the 1960s. Eventually, Phillips closed the processing plant resulting in high unemployment. People of color were the worst hit.

Between 1962 and 1967, Cambridge saw a series of civil rights protests that have become known as the Cambridge Movement. Schools and most public accommodations in Cambridge were segregated. African Americans did not have equal access to either employment opportunities or to housing.

Led by Gloria Richardson, the 1962 protests included marches, sit-ins, and boycotts of white-owned businesses. At one point businesses were burned and gunfire erupted. The governor declared martial law and sent in the National Guard, which stayed for nearly a month. After the Guard left, further clashes occurred and the Guard was sent in again. This time, they stayed for a year. Some people have referred to this as an occupation.

There were further disturbances in 1967 as little progress had been made on the issues that sparked the 1962 riots. Black Power leader H. Rap Brown came to Cambridge to speak and lead a march. During the march, the Deputy Sheriff twice fired his rifle and Brown was slightly wounded by a ricocheted bullet. He was treated and moved out of Cambridge. Riots broke out after the crowd learned Brown had been wounded. During that riot a Black elementary school was burned to the ground, largely because the all-white Cambridge Fire Department would not put it out. Some seventeen other buildings were destroyed.

It took two more years, but Cambridge schools were finally desegregated in 1969, followed by movie theaters, restaurants, and the skating rink.

What has happened in Cambridge since then? The population of Cambridge is about 48 percent African American and 46 percent white. Cambridge elected a Black mayor, Victoria Jackson-Stanley, to three successive terms. She served from 2008 until 2020.

The economy has largely recovered from the closing of the Phillips plant. Like Easton, tourism has become important, fueled partly by the Hyatt-Regency Chesapeake Bay Resort, which has provided jobs and brought business to Cambridge. There are art galleries and restaurants in the historic downtown area. There are also plans to develop the old Phillips cannery building into a mixed-use space.[12]

In addition, according to the official website, Cambridge and Dorchester Counties have embraced the idea of heritage tourism. Although this effort focuses a great deal of attention on Harriet Tubman, who was born into slavery in Dorchester County, there is also attention paid to the area's Native American heritage as well as to its agricultural and maritime past. The Harriet Tubman Trail is a thirty-stop driving tour that includes sites associated with

Tubman in Dorchester and Caroline Counties in Maryland and in Delaware. About twenty minutes outside Cambridge is the Harriet Tubman Underground Railroad State Park and Visitor Center.

And Cambridge seems to be trying to come to grips with its past—especially the events of 1962 and 1967. An organization called Eastern Shore Network for Change convened a community meeting in 2012 to allow residents to share their feelings about the 1967 fire. Some 150 people came. About half of them were Black and about half were white. Afterward, the organization decided it needed to do something for the fiftieth anniversary.

In 2017, the Network worked with a local radio station and a film company to produce a documentary in which local residents shared memories of the fire. It was screened at an event honoring the anniversary.[13]

So, have things changed in Cambridge? It would seem so. Is the change driven by the connections with the Western Shore made possible by the Chesapeake Bay Bridge? Perhaps a little since some of the surface changes are things that would appeal to tourists. In Easton, change appears to be superficial and dealing solely with things like its economy. But in Cambridge, the most significant changes seem to go deeper and come from within and from a desire to be better.

THE EASTERN SHORE—SALISBURY

Some 32 miles southeast of Cambridge is Salisbury. It is the largest city on the Eastern Shore and is the next-to-last stop on the journey to the Atlantic Ocean. Salisbury began as a small colonial outpost established by Lord Baltimore. It became a town in 1732.

Salisbury's location at the head of the Wicomico River made it a good location for a trading port. It became the second port after Baltimore.[14] A major part of the economy was agriculture, as it was for much of the Eastern Shore. Like Easton and Cambridge, the principal crops were tobacco and corn. And like Easton and Cambridge, those crops were tended by enslaved Africans.

Salisbury was also an active center for the slave trade. Byrd Tavern was the site of that trade—and other trade as well. The slave pens were located in the tavern's basement and at the rear of the building. Interestingly, the tavern was torn down in 1878 to be replaced by the courthouse for the newly established Wicomico County.[15]

With the prevalence of slavery and the slave trade, Salisbury had a large number of people who supported the Confederacy. During the Civil War, Salisbury was the site of a Union encampment whose forces had two charges. One was to search for Southern sympathizers. The other was to inhibit movement of contraband to the South.

Fires in 1860 and again in 1886 burned substantial parts of Salisbury. The town rebuilt after both fires.

The end of the Civil War did not bring an end to the uneasy relations between Salisbury's African American and white residents. At least three lynchings of African Americans are known to have taken place. Garfield King was lynched on May 25, 1898, after allegedly shooting a white man after an argument. Matthew Williams was lynched on December 4, 1931, after being accused of murdering his white employer. A third unidentified man was found dead on railroad tracks outside Salisbury in the days after Williams was lynched. Though the cause of death was reported as a railroad accident, it is widely believed that he was lynched by a part of the mob that lynched Matthews. According to the Maryland Lynching Memorial Project at least thirty-nine African Americans were lynched in Maryland. Fully half those lynchings were on the Eastern Shore.[16] Today, Salisbury's economy is fairly broad-based. The Delmarva poultry industry plays a large role. Salisbury is home to the headquarters for Perdue Farms, Inc. Perdue, with 22,000 employees, is the city's largest single employer.

There is, however, a significant light industry sector. Products such as petroleum-handling equipment, electronic products, pharmaceuticals, plastic film and sheet, and manufactured homes are all important contributors. Healthcare is important as well. Salisbury is home to Peninsula Regional Medical Center. Other jobs include those in foodservice, boatbuilding, and agriculture.

Salisbury is also home to Salisbury University. Founded in 1925, Salisbury is part of the University of Maryland System and has some 8,600 students. The university is one of the city's larger employers.

Tourism also has an economic impact, primarily with fishing and duck hunting. The Ward Museum of Wildfowl is renowned for its collection of hunting decoys and paintings of wildfowl. A variety of arts and cultural events also bring tourists to Salisbury.

Has change come to Salisbury? And is any change the result of the Chesapeake Bay Bridge? While some change may have resulted or grown from the opening of the Bridge (tourism for example), Salisbury's largest employer, Perdue Farms, was established in 1920, long before the Bridge. And another large employer, Salisbury University, was established in 1925. Salisbury has had a fairly broad-based economy and didn't suffer the kind of economic collapse Cambridge did when the Phillips cannery closed. This may have helped keep Salisbury stable when Cambridge was not.

The most significant changes have come with race relations, as noted elsewhere in this chapter. Salisbury is now a majority-minority city. Two members of its current city council are people of color.

Of greater importance, perhaps, is that Salisbury seems determined to find reconciliation with its troubled past of slavery, the slave trade, and lynching.

The City of Salisbury has established the Salisbury Lynching Memorial Task Force, which is dedicated to memorializing the victims of lynching in Salisbury and to promoting reconciliation throughout Wicomico County.[17]

So, yes, change has come to Salisbury, but it much of that appears to be self-driven and not the result of outside forces.

THE EASTERN SHORE—OCEAN CITY

Our final stop on U.S. 50 is Ocean City, about 30 miles east of Salisbury. Ocean City is the final destination for most of the people crossing the Chesapeake Bay Bridge heading east. It's where many Marylanders go to spend vacations or weekends, mostly between Memorial Day and Labor Day.

One often doesn't think of a beach resort as having a long history, but Europeans first set eyes on the land that would be Ocean City in 1524 when Giovanni da Verrazano surveyed the eastern coast of North America. By the seventeenth century, British settlers from Virginia had moved to the area. Because Ocean City is on a barrier island, it remained a small, isolated fishing village until about 1875, when the Atlantic Hotel opened.

Ocean City's history as a resort goes back a few years earlier than that 1875 hotel opening to 1869, when Isaac Coffin opened the first beachfront cottage to paying guests. A few other boarding houses opened and the activity spurred the interest of some Philadelphia businessmen. They created 250 lots to be sold. They also sold 4,000 shares in a corporation that would develop the area.

The Atlantic Hotel had 400 rooms and offered dancing and billiards along with the natural beauty of the beach and the ocean. People also liked to fish off-shore. Railroad access helped as the resort slowly developed.

In 1933, a major hurricane separated Ocean City from Assateague Island, creating an inlet that allowed passage from the ocean to the area behind the island. The Army Corps of Engineers saw the benefits of the newly created inlet and reinforced it. Today, the inlet allows easy access to the Atlantic Ocean for fishing and boating.[18, 19, 20]

For Ocean City, 1952 was a pivotal year. As we have seen, that was the year that the first span of the Chesapeake Bay Bridge opened providing quick, direct access from the Western Shore of the Bay. Previously, anyone from Baltimore or Washington wanting to go to Ocean City had to either cross the Bay by ferry or drive up to the northeastern corner of Maryland, cross the Susquehanna River and drive south to Ocean City. With the opening of the bridge, summer tourism began a large and rapid expansion.

It was when the 1970s arrived that the tourism industry really exploded. Ocean City expanded north all the way to the Delaware state line and is now nearly 10 miles from end to end. At Ocean City's south end is the 2.25 mile long board-walk, which features amusement parks, arcades, and food and souvenir shops. As one travels further north, the scene changes to high-rise hotels and condo-minium buildings. The ocean front is where most of those are. It's across the highway that one finds grocery stores, restaurants, and the like. The first board-walk was installed in 1902. Shortly after, the first amusement park, Trimpers, opened. Trimpers is still a fixture in Ocean City and now has two locations. The Boardwalk was damaged by a storm in 1962, again in 1985 by Hurricane Gloria, and a third time in 2012 by Hurricane Sandy. Each time it has been rebuilt.

In addition, the beach has several times undergone beach replenishment to replace sand that is moved around by the natural activity of the ocean. These replenishment efforts have included reestablishment of the dune lines along the building line.

But Ocean City is more than beach activities. Commercial and sport fish-ing are important to its economy. Ocean City calls itself the "White Marlin Capital of the World." Throughout the summer, charters and private boats fish for a variety of game fish. In early August, the city hosts the White Marlin Open, one of the largest fishing tournaments in the world.

Ocean City is also home to a number of special events such as the annual OC Air Show, the July 4 Celebration, and Sunfest. There are events that hap-pen during the off-season, as well. Ocean City also has a convention center which plays host to smaller-scale conventions throughout the year.

Of the major stops on our journey from the Chesapeake Bay Bridge to the Atlantic Ocean, Ocean City is, without doubt, the most strongly affected by the opening of the Bay Bridge. While it was growing as a summer resort during the pre-Bridge era, any growth was necessarily slow because Ocean City remained relatively isolated and was a place to which it was difficult and time consuming to travel. The Bridge changed all that and the resort's growth post-Bridge has been very fast.

The people on the Eastern Shore who have been most affected by the changes the hordes of summer visitors have brought to the Shore are the 7,000 or so permanent residents of Ocean City. They seem to cope quite well, especially since on any given summer weekend there may be as many as 350,000 tourists in town. During the summer season, Ocean City is actually the second most populous town in Maryland after Baltimore.

CONCLUSION

This chapter began as I was wondering what changes had happened on Maryland's Eastern Shore. For most of its history, the Shore had remained fairly isolated from the rest of the state. The Chesapeake Bay was a formidable

barrier to easy travel from one shore to the other. The only geographical connection was the tip of the northernmost Shore county. To go from Baltimore
to Ocean City by land required one to travel north, then east, then south. That
took a long time. That isolation helped create a group of fairly conservative
people who had to depend on one another.

Agriculture was a major pillar of the economy of the Eastern Shore.
People farmed a variety of crops, but notably, tobacco. Tobacco plantations
used the labor of enslaved Africans—lots of them. At its height, one important plantation, Wye House, near Easton in Talbot County where Frederick
Douglass was born into slavery, used 1,000 slaves to farm some 42,000
acres. Dependence on slaves caused many on the Eastern Shore to side
with the South during the Civil War. The legacy of slavery was still seen
in things like the continued resistance of many Talbot County residents to
removing the Talbot Boys sculpture from the grounds of the Talbot County
Court House.

Ultimately, change is inevitable, but how quickly it may come and what
form it takes are other matters. The opening of the Chesapeake Bay Bridge
certainly brought with it the potential for very large and very rapid change for
the Eastern Shore. For the first time, the Shore wasn't isolated and thousands
of people could visit.

Because it's the main route from the Chesapeake Bay Bridge to the
Atlantic Ocean, I chose to look at five locations along U.S. 50. I did find
changes had occurred—uneven changes—and not all of them the result of
the opening of the Bridge.

Kent Island first had life upended. Traffic across the Island sometimes
made conducting the business of everyday life extremely difficult and frustrating. That problem was solved by making U.S. 50 a freeway and having
local businesses on local roads often running parallel to U.S. 50. In a way
that stopped many of the negative types of change the Island experienced at
first. But the one change that can't be stopped is the Island's attractiveness
as a bedroom community for people working in Baltimore and Washington.

Easton has changed and not changed. Its change has been economic in
that there is greater reliance on tourism. The opening of art galleries, antique
shops, and restaurants is more attractive to visitors than to many residents.
But Easton has not changed because it still has not effectively come to grips
with its legacy of slavery. That the Talbot Boys remained on the courthouse
grounds for so long is evidence of that. In Easton, there has not been enough
change, but what changes there have been may have been fueled at least
partly by the Bridge.

Cambridge also had a legacy of slavery that created a segregated society
with African Americans as an underclass. The closure of Cambridge's largest
employer exacerbated things. The result was a series of protests and riots. The

city had some other employers, but there has been a shift to a more tourism-oriented local economy. Unlike Easton, Cambridge chose to confront its legacy of slavery and discrimination in an effort at reconciliation. Change in Cambridge has been partly driven by the opening of the Bridge, but mostly, it's been self-driven in an effort to be a better place.

Salisbury has been fortunate to have had a broader-based economy than many other places on the Shore. The presence of a university and a large medical center along with more blue-collar jobs has meant a wider variety of jobs requiring a wider variety of educational levels. But Salisbury does have the post-slavery legacy of lynchings. Salisbury chose to confront that legacy as it looked to achieve reconciliation. And Salisbury has become a majority-minority city. Change in Salisbury seems mostly driven from within rather than happening as a result of outside forces.

Ocean City is the most changed by the Chesapeake Bay Bridge. A town of only about 7,000 permanent residents, it was, until the Bridge opened, a small community that became a small, quiet resort. The opening of the Bridge allowed thousands of people access to a part of Maryland that had previously been practically inaccessible. Though on summer weekends, Ocean City is the second most populous town in Maryland its residents have coped well with all that change.

So, where can we come down with the idea of change on the Eastern Shore? In some ways, there hasn't been much. The Eastern Shore is still mostly conservative. It still usually votes Republican. Except for some areas, it's still mostly white. And in many places, the economy is still mostly what it has been historically; focused on agriculture and on the water. Along U.S. 50, changes have been uneven and not necessarily driven by the access made possible by the Bridge: Kent Island, yes and no; Easton, some changes but not where it counts; Cambridge, changes, but not largely driven by the Bridge and Salisbury, but largely self-driven. The exception really is Ocean City which almost certainly would not be where it is except for the Chesapeake Bay Bridge.

Change will continue on the Eastern Shore. Some of that will certainly be driven by the existence of the Bridge as even more people look for vacations at the beach and as those working in Western Shore cities look for less expensive housing and a different kind of lifestyle. Other changes will be driven by changes in the demographics on the Shore and by changes in attitudes.

But change *will* continue. It's inevitable.

NOTES

1. United States Census Bureau. https://census.gov

2. Jeremy Cox, "Salisbury Undergoes Major Shift as Black, Hispanic Populations Surge," *The Daily Times*, January 12, 2018. https://www.delmarvanow.com/story

/news/local/maryland/2018/01/12/salisbury-shiftdemographics-black-hispanic/995772001/

3. Maryland State Board of Elections, "Elections." https://elections.maryland.gov/elections/2022/index.html

4. Maryland State Board of Elections, "Elections." https://elections.maryland.gov/elections/2022/index.html

5. Maryland Department of Planning, *Maryland Citizens Redistricting Commission Website.* https://planning.maryland.gov/Redistricting/Pages/default.aspx

6. Maryland State Board of Elections, "Elections." https://elections.maryland.gov/elections/2022/index.html

7. Maryland Transportation Authority, "William Preston Lane, Jr. Memorial (Bay) Bridge (US50/301)." https://mdta.maryland.gov/Toll_Facilities/WPL.html

8. Kent Island Heritage Society, "Kent Island History." https//kentislandheritagesociety.org/kent-island-history/

9. Britannica, T. Editors of Encyclopaedia. "Easton," *Encyclopedia Britannica*, December 15, 2011. https://www.britannica.com/place/Easton-Maryland

10. Jonathan M. Pitts, "Activists Vow to Continue Fight Against 'Talbot Boys' Confederate Monument in County Seat on Maryland Eastern Shore," *Baltimore Sun*, January 21, 2021. https://www.baltimoresun.com/maryland/bs-md-talbot-boys-controversy-20210103iwqle7gj5nfhlfeu2r64h4ykiy-story.html

11. Bennett Leckrone, "Talbot Officials Ask Court to Dismiss Lawsuit Seeking Removal of Confederate Monument," *Maryland Matters*, July 2, 2021. https://www.marylandmatters.org/2021/07/02/talbot-officials-ask-court-to-dismiss-lawsuit-toremove-confederate-monument/

12. Jonathan M. Pitts, "Half a Century After Rioting Ravaged Cambridge, Town Seeks to Embrace History – So As to Transcend It," *Baltimore Sun,* February 12, 2017. https://www.baltimoresun.com/maryland/bs-md-cambridge-riot-1967-20170212-story.html

13. Ibid.

14. Britannica, T. Editors of Encyclopaedia. "Salisbury," *Encyclopedia Britannica*, January 12, 2018. https://www.britannica.com/place/Salisbury-Maryland

15. Linda Duyer, "Salisbury's Slave Pens," Delmarva African American History website. Posted December 2, 2013. https://aahistorydelmarva.wordpress.com/2013/12/02/salisburysslave-pens/

16. Maryland Lynching Memorial Project – Wicomico County. https://mdlynchingmemorial.wixsite.com/wicomico

17. Ibid.

18. Ocean City History, https://www.beach-net.com/delaware-maryland-beach-towns/oceancity-maryland-history.php

19. Ocean City History, https://www.oceancity.com/history/

20. Ocean City History, https://www.ococean.com/oc-history

Chapter 14

Conclusions

The Communication Realities of State and Local Politics

The twelve chapters in this case study may, at first glance, seem to focus on rather random topics. However, the framework we've imposed on them—people, politics, policies, and places—not only is alliterative but also points to what we think should be the entry points for any study of state and local political communication. Let's consider each one.

PEOPLE

Political communication studies presidents after they've risen to the high office. It also looks back on how they got there with a focus on the various communicative acts they performed. This process, however, neglects those who never quite made it to that pinnacle, be they U.S. senators, governors, Congressional representatives, or mayors. Their communication is also of interest for at least three reasons: how it helps them successfully do their immediate jobs, how it suggests a capacity for higher office, and how it points to perhaps generalizable rhetorical limitations leaders at these different levels have. By studying state and local people, we learn how different members of Congress perform different tasks, how those a state resident would know about (but not a national audience yet) rise to national prominence, and why names that surface on the state (or local) level as having national potential don't always fulfill that potential.

POLITICS

The political communication researchers typically explore is that during elections and that during governance. More attention is paid to former—understandably since elections are a better story than getting a bill through a legislature and into law. Sometimes, it seems as if the story is all the researchers are interested in, not what the particular story says about how to successfully conduct a campaign. We have tried to focus on that. And, nationally, there are many state and local stories to explore, some success stories but some failed ones. Doing so is essential if we are to have a full understanding of how campaign communication works—or does not. We cannot assume that what's true of a presidential election is true of a statewide one, just as we cannot assume that what's true of a statewide election in Maryland is true of a statewide one just to the North in Pennsylvania or just to the South in Virginia. We need to investigate to acquire the full picture.

And the same is true of the political processes of government. Although they are less "sexy," they need to be grasped. Furthermore, how they may differ among the levels of government or among the states is well-worth knowing. All fifty states have a legislature, but it is unlikely that they are the same as far as communication is concerned. Some might be quite raucous; others, not. It's also unlikely that any of the fifty matches the U.S. Congress exactly.

Governors must have a balanced budget. Not so the president. That difference affects a great deal, affecting how governors must proceed. But they don't proceed the same way, for, personality aside, the governor's office is defined differently in different states. Some have strong governors; others, weak—based on different state constitutions and political traditions.

The bulk of the political science work on state and local government can be turned to discern what the structures and the processes are, in individual states and collectively. This work is largely descriptive, with data a-plenty. Often, the work will reflect on how structures and processes allocate power, for that is of course a major concern of the political science discipline. This work, however, rarely explores communication, and it most certainly does not consider the communication in rhetorical terms, whether traditional ones focused on persuasion or more recent ones focused on matters of power and identity. So, much work is needed to understand both campaign communication and that involved in governance.

POLICIES

This topic might seem to take one away from communication into matters more the business of the political scientist. That's true only if one's conception of political communication is limited to the most traditional kinds of texts such as speeches and debates and advertisements. We posit here that a policy is a rhetorical act—a "text," in the broadest sense. As such a policy has a critical dimension, a related material dimension, and a constitutive dimension. Housing policies assign privilege, determine who will live well and who not, and create identities tied to where one can live. Broader urban redevelopment polices, transportation policies, and other kinds of policies are similarly rhetorical. Urban redevelopment can help a part of a city thrive; a new bridge can cause a once-thriving region to wither. A "tight" neighborhood can be destroyed by a bisecting superhighway; how one gentrifies an economically depressed area can determine, for decades, that area's identity.

The rhetorical implications of policy, we suggest, can be seen better at the state and local levels. The matters at stake are closer to the people, and the policy effects do not get lost in the proverbial "big picture." So, examining state and local policies as rhetorical should alert the researcher to the fact that national policies are comparably so.

PLACES

Rhetorical study has, of course, devoted a great deal of attention in the past two decades to public places—to memory sites and to other kinds of spaces such as parks and stadia. Gradually—we would suggest—the insights of critical rhetoric and constitutive rhetoric were brought to bear on this study. Early, rich readings attentive to matters such as context and affect dominated the research, but, then, questions of privilege and questions of identity arose.

States consist of many places; so do cities. These can be studied as if static. More fruitful, however, is asking how they with their associated identity came into being and what forces are changing—or trying to change—that identity. Invariably, how that identity relates to power—or its absence— becomes an important, related concern. Consider the City of Baltimore. It has memory sites such as the restored Fort McHenry or a monument to George Washington. It has structures rich in meaning because of their history—for example, the Bromo Seltzer Tower, the Domino Sugar sign; and it has structures to which meaning was given when they were designed—for example, the Baltimore Orioles' Camden Yards ballpark. Baltimore also has multiple redevelopment projects as well as numerous neighborhoods. If a city has so much to study, imagine what an entire state must have.

THE THEORIES THAT EMERGE

So, we suggest that a framework of people, politics, policies, and places is a quite useful one to guide case studies of state and local political communication. (It may even be a useful one for national political communication, but, as one zooms out to take in the nation, the particulars possible when looking at a state or a locality do get lost.)

Beyond suggesting a framework, we want to suggest seven theories about state and local political communication that further researchers can investigate.

Number 1

State and local elections proceed as national ones do, but with some important exceptions.

The research on national campaign communication is substantial. We know how a campaign proceeds through phases, and we know how communication should proceed if it is to be successful at the different points. We know a lot about advertisements and about debating, about stump speeches and managing convention messaging. We don't know as much as we should about polling, as recent poor predictions have demonstrated, but research is on-going.

What we know, though, is almost always about national campaigns.

There is naturally a tendency to apply this research to state and local elections. We know that, nationally, negative ads are disliked but work, so we assume the same to be true if the election is a Maryland one or a Baltimore City one. To a large extent, this assumption is valid. However, there do seem to be some noteworthy differences between the large arena and the smaller ones.

At all levels, voters do use the kind of shortcuts that Samuel Popkin noted long ago in *The Reasoning Voter* (Chicago: University of Chicago Press, 1991). They vote for a party; they vote based on a single issue; they follow the advice of opinion leaders. In processing ads, they often engage in the kind of peripheral processing the Elaboration Likelihood Method (ELM) developed by Richard Petty and John Cacioppo in *Communication and Persuasion* (New York: Springer-Verlag, 1986) has pointed to. (Thus, negative ads still use grainy photos and scary music when depicting an opponent.) But state and local voters do not seem to behave this way as much as in a national race. Perhaps because the issues are both more immediate and easier to grasp, the voters in state and local elections seem to dig into matters a bit more. And, more importantly, they dig into who the candidates are, often voting based on the perceived characteristics of the candidate more than any platform positions. In 2018, for example, one might argue that voters liked Larry Hogan but did not care for Ben Jealous or voters thought Hogan was competent but Jealous insufficiently knowledgeable about how state government worked. These assessments are tied to candidate traits, not policy positions.

Recognizing this tendency, campaigns need to stress who the person is a great deal. One way to do so is advertising; another is getting the candidate out campaigning, particularly among those voters who would be considered a candidate's core constituencies.

Voters appreciate personable candidates, but they appreciate even more candidates who seem to know the state (or city) and its people. Candidates perceived as outsiders will not thrive; candidates too reliant on outside advisors or outside money may be viewed with suspicion. There seems to be an insistence that candidates project a connection with the state (or city) they are running in. New York might elect Bobby Kennedy and Hillary Clinton as their U.S. senators, but these are exceptions to what seems to be the rule.

Successful candidates, in Maryland at least, seem to have a clear, strong identity, created by either who they are or what they communicate. Barbara Mikulski, for example, won election after election, not because of her policy positions but because she was "Baltimore's gal." Martin O'Malley perhaps began his political career with a clear, strong identity, but he let it fade, resulting in a poor image as his second term as governor ended that played a role in his lieutenant's failure to keep the governor's office in Democratic control. Larry Hogan, arguably without a clear image as his gubernatorial campaign began in 2014, crafted one and has sustained it into a second term.

Many have said that state and local elections will feature more "retail" politics than national ones. True. But it is crucial to understand what the dimensions of the "retail" politics should be. In Maryland at least those dimensions include having a strong identity, connecting with the people (especially those crucial to winning), and signaling that one "gets" Maryland.

These may well be the crucial "retail" dimensions in many other—if not most—states.

Number 2

A state or local official's political future has less to do with the state or locality (or even the office held) and more to do with a mix of leadership qualities and message control.

One's advancement—at least to presidential consideration—might be affected by the perceived size of the state or the offices one has held, but leadership qualities seem to matter more. The public wants a president to exhibit the qualities associated with transformational leadership.

Seeking to advance, not to the presidency but within bodies such as the U.S. Senate and the U.S. House of Representatives may involve other qualities. (See Number 3.) There is—we hope we've shown—a large body of leadership research and theory that a political communication scholar should tap in trying to understand why certain political figures gain prominence and others do not. This work is often not by communication scholars; rather, it is conducted in cognate areas such as social psychology. Nonetheless—and ignoring how the conclusions are phrased as nouns (qualities or behaviors) not action verbs—this work deals heavily with how leaders communicate effectively or do not.

Number 3

Leadership comes in many forms, each requiring a different mix of communication traits.

Maryland has never put a person in the White House, but, at present, the two top figures on the majority side in the House are Marylanders, Hoyer because he represents the state's 5th District; Pelosi because she learned many of her political skills growing-up in the state with her father being Baltimore's mayor. Other Marylanders have achieved prominence in the Congress, but it is striking that the people we might cite have achieved prominence for different reasons—some for legislative skill, some for constituency service skill, some for interrogating skill, some for fund-raising skill, some for insisting on a politics founded into morality. There are then many different types of leaders.

The body of leadership research and theory is sometimes thought of as a progression—moving from no longer popular trait theories to in-vogue social justice ones. We would suggest that this is an inaccurate way to assess this work. Rather than a progression, we see descriptions of the different skill sets needed by the different types of leaders. A legislative leader is aptly described by a skills approach; the person you'd want leading an investigative committee by the authentic leadership approach.

Every state has produced leaders, but they are of different sorts. Examining the Maryland arena reveals that, but parallel examinations of other states would probably reveal the same picture. The varied leadership communication lenses offer a way to parse this picture.

Number 4

There should be no hierarchy among types of leadership, with mentoring a valuable (although underrated) type.

One might think that the transformational leader we seek when choosing a president is the "top dog" leader. Well, no. All types are important because government will not work well without all types, politics will not work well without all types. There should therefore be no hierarchy among them.

A case in point is that of Maryland's long-serving U.S. senator Barbara Mikulski. She very, very slowly rose to party leadership; she was also slow to achieve leadership positions on committees. Some important legislation is associated with her, but no one would claim that she was a talented and prolific writer or negotiator of laws. So, was she less than successful? Only if one ignores the leadership she demonstrated in mentoring the steadily increasing number of women in the U.S. Congress. She stood up for women on a number of legislative matters: she showed leadership in these instances, but she showed even more in the outside-the-limelight work she did and inspired others to do to help make women successful once they got to "The Hill."

Mikulski's mentoring efforts gained some attention. But one must ask who is mentoring the men. We should not assume that they don't need it, for they do, although how it is conducted and what it covers will probably be different. Who, though, is providing that mentoring? It is an important type of political communication, and we should discover the answer and, then, explore precisely how that mentoring is being conducted. And we should ask how it might have changed through the decades. Thanks to Robert Caro's multivolume biography of Lyndon Johnson, we know how Sam Rayburn in the House and Richard Russell in the Senate mentored the Texan who aspired to leadership. Do the kinds of late-afternoon whisky-sipping gatherings Rayburn and Russell convened still exist? If so, who leads them? If not, what has replaced them? And are they still male-only?

Number 5

Policies are rhetorical with critical, material, and constitutive consequences. Political communication studies twenty years ago dealt narrowly with communication. Thanks largely to new developments in rhetorical theory, that should no longer be the case. Critical rhetoric has drawn our attention to how many, many acts are inherently rhetorical with crucial power/privilege dimensions and important material consequences. Thus, we spent time discussing housing policies, urban redevelopment efforts, and transportation projects. Doing so may seem to take us far-afield, but not really, for these political decisions sent powerful messages to different groups in the state. Allowing racially exclusive covenants for neighborhoods communicates who is privileged and who isn't; shifting urban redevelopment efforts so that they are more community-based and community-led communicates who is and who isn't; deciding to plow a highway through one area but not another communicates who is privileged and who isn't. And ask African American residents of West Baltimore if the stretch of I-170 that was built (before the project was scrapped) did not affect their material circumstances when it knocked down blocks of low-income housing and divided neighborhoods in two.

Constitutive rhetoric (indebted to Althusser and Charland) also pushes one to consider policies. Highways, bridges, and the like can change a region's identity (i.e., how residents constitute themselves). Gerrymandering, of which Maryland has been quite guilty, can as well. A region, held together somewhat by being a Congressional district, can lose its identity when, all of a sudden, it is no longer so united. Conversely, a Congressional district can push an identity on a region. Both have happened in Maryland—and, most assuredly, elsewhere. Politicians rarely think of redistricting as having identity consequences, but it can.

Number 6

Place—not so much the state as where within a state—is rhetorically important and can be influenced by policy.

Implicit above is the importance of place. There may well be something of a state identity—stronger in some places (e.g., Texas) than others, but we would argue that the stronger identities are within a state. Northern California is quite different than Southern; Eastern Colorado is quite different from Western; the Chicago metropolitan area is quite different from down-state Illinois. And we could go on. The regional identities, as shown in Maryland, need not be tied to land masses this large. In Pennsylvania, for example, the counties that surround Philadelphia are quite different from each other; in Georgia, the counties that surround Atlanta are not only quite different from each other but strikingly different than most of the counties in the state.

These identities did not just happen, and they weren't created just by rivers, mountains, and the like. People drew lines; people routed roadways; people enacted policies such as legalizing slot machines in just four Maryland counties. These are all rhetorical acts and, over time, create identities. Or the acts may undermine existing identities. All Marylanders know that the "Eastern Shore" is different from the rest of the state. Isolated, the region developed along different lines with an identity strikingly unlike that in other parts of the state. Did the act of building a bridge across the Chesapeake Bay in the 1950s change the identity? Did the influx of tourists passing through it change the identity? Did embarrassment over its racist past (finally) change the identity?

Number 7

Political communication, especially on the state and local level, cannot be accurately understood without grasping state and local history.

This may well be true nationally as well, but studying a state makes it abundantly clear. Let's just focus on election politics. To understand why things play out as they do in Maryland, one needs to understand that Western Maryland and the "Eastern Shore" will probably behave differently than the bulk of the state. That's geopolitics. But why might Baltimore City and the Washington suburban counties be at odds? Why might a Baltimore candidate get a lukewarm response in the DC area? Why might a DC area candidate (let's say a county executive) get a lukewarm response in Baltimore? Why might the two Washington suburban counties be at odds?

Why might the county executive from one not be appealing to the residents of the other?

Why, if the state is so, so blue, does it elect Republican governors such as Harry Nice, Theodore McKeldin, Spiro Agnew, Robert Ehrlich, and Larry Hogan? How did a minority-dominated district (the 4th) emerge, not just through gerrymandering but through major shifts in demographics? Why are there blue pockets in Cumberland, Hagerstown, and Salisbury?

To these election-related questions we could add many related to governance. To answer them, we would have to know a good bit of history. Political communication conclusions, when it comes to the state and local scene, cannot be drawn by just looking at polling results or conducting focus groups to view candidates' ads. One needs to know how Maryland developed over time along paths that are both predictable and quirky. And much could be said about any state. The paths, it should be noted, parallel, but not perfectly, national ones. In 1966, the three Democrats seeking the nomination for governor agreed on little: they were liberal, moderate, and conservative. By 1980, the conservative wing had vanished, changing their political affiliation from blue to red. Then, the Republicans had to figure out their identity. Were they still the party of Theodore McKeldin? Had they become the party of Spiro Agnew, not the moderate Agnew who led the charge for Rockefeller in 1968 but the "law and order" Agnew who courted "the silent majority" during the Nixon years? These are the Maryland stories, matching up reasonably well with the national ones. One needs to know the state story in whatever state is selected for examination, but one also needs to put the state story into the national one while being ever-ready to say "but Republicans in Pennsylvania are different" or "Democrats in Virginia are different."

These seven suggestions should indeed be tested in other states. As explained in the preface to this book, the authors know a great deal about Maryland from personal experience.

But we know enough about Pennsylvania and Virginia to see that what we say here about Maryland is true there as well. But what we offer as conclusions are a mixed bag. Some are generalizations about state and local political communication that one can test, but others are guiding principles. We suspect that colleagues studying Pennsylvania and Virginia will find election dynamics there much as we describe them in Maryland, and we suspect that these colleagues will find leaders there who are indeed of different types. But we also suspect that the rhetorical consequences of policies there will merit attention, as will the many regions and how they were rhetorically created or changed.

So, we hope others will look at other states—their people, politics, policies, and places. We hope that these seven conclusions, be they observations that can be tested or guidelines that should be observed, will influence these explorations.

Works Cited

"A Brief History of Housing Policy in the U.S." *Housing is Health* (blog), October 29, 2019. https://nurseledcare.phmc.org/advocacy/policy-blog/item/641-a-brief-history-of-housing-policy-in-the-u-s.html

Althusser, Louis. "Ideology and Ideological State Apparatuses." *Lenin and Philosophy and Other Essays*. Trans. Ben Brewster. New York: Monthly Review Press, 1971.

Anderson, Carol. *One Person, No Vote: How Voter Suppression is Destroying Our Democracy*. New York: Bloomsbury Publishing, 2018, 96–120.

Archives of Maryland. "The Maryland Constitutional Convention of 1776." July 2009. https://msa.maryland.gov/msa/speccol/sc2200/sc2221/000004/000000/html/00000004.html

Archives of Maryland. "Proceedings and Acts of the General Assembly January 1637/8 – September 1664. https://msa.maryland.gov/megafile/msa/speccol/sc2900/sc2908/000001/000001/html/am1--533.html

Austermuhle, Martin. "Ben Jealous Has Big Ideas for Maryland. But, First He Needs People to Know He's Running for Governor." *WAMU*, November 1, 2018. https://wamu.org/story/18/11/01/ben-jealous-has-big-ideas-for-maryland-but-first-he-needs-people-to-know-hes-running-for-governor/

Babbington, Charles. "Cerebral Sarbanes Aloof into Limelight." *Washington Post*. March 12, 2005.

Bachelor, Tom. "Steny Hoyer Viral Speech Denouncing Marjorie Taylor Greene Viewed Two Million Times." *Newsweek*, February 5, 2021. http://www.newsweek.com/steny-hoyer-speech-marjorie-taylor-greene-1567062

Ball, Molly. *Pelosi*. New York: Henry Holt, 2020.

Baltimore Heritage. "Deed Restrictions and Exclusion by Design: 1980s – 1920s." *Baltimore Civil Rights Heritage*, 2019 (website). https://baltimoreheritage.github.io/civil-rights-heritage/1885-1929/

Baltimore Heritage. "Development of a Segregated Black Community: 1880s – 1900s." *Baltimore Civil Rights Heritage*, 2019 (website). https://baltimoreheritage.github.io/civil-rights-heritage/1885-1929/

Barker, Jeff. "Maverick Michael Steele Says He's Seriously Considering a Run for Maryland Governor and Won't Leave the Republican Party: 'It's My House, Too.'" *Baltimore Sun*, April 22, 2021. https://www.baltimoresun.com/politics/bs-md-pol-michael-steele-20210422-h7ruh6cevrbexcubebwav4zm44-story.html

Barnes, Robert. "Supreme Court Will Take Up a Second Gerrymandering Case This Term." *Washington Post*. December 8, 2017.

Barton, David. "This History of Black Voting Rights – From the 1700s to Present Day." *Original People*, 2004. https://originalpeople.org/the-history-of-black-voting-rights-from-the-1700s-to-present-day-2/

Bash, Dana. "Mikulski Makes History While Creating Zone of Civility for Senate Women." *CNN*. http://www.cnn.com/2012/03116/politics/mikulski-history/index.html?hpt=hp_t3

Bass, B. M. *Leadership and Performance*. New York: Free Press, 1985.

Beatty Development Group. "About." https://beattydevelopmentgroup.com

Beatty Development Group. "Baltimore Penn Station." https://beattydevelopmentgroup.com

Beatty Development Group. "Harbor Point." https://beattydevelopmentgroup.com.

Becker, Jo. "Van Hollen Ousts. Morella." *Washington Post*. November 6, 2002. "The Best and Worst of Congress 2014." *Washingtonian*. http://www.washingtonian.com/article/people/the-best-worst-of-Congress-2014

Blankenship, Jane and Debrah C. Robson. "A 'Feminine Style' in Women's Political Discourse: An Exploratory Essay." *Communication Quarterly* 43.3 (1995): 353–66.

Bogan, David S. "Mathias de Sousa: Maryland's First Colonist of African Descent." *Maryland Historical Society Magazine* 96.1 (Spring 2001): 68–85.

Briggs, Johnathon E. and Laura Vozzella. "Clarence H. Du Burns, First Black Mayor of Baltimore." *Baltimore Sun*, February 21, 2007 (originally published January 13, 2003). https://www.baltimoresun.com/features/bal-blackhistory-burns-story.html

Britannica, T. Editors of Encyclopaedia. "Easton." *Encyclopedia Britannica*, December 15, 2011. https://www.britannica.com/place/Easton-Maryland

Britannica, T. Editors of Encyclopaedia. "Salisbury." *Encyclopedia Britannica*, January 12, 2018. https://www.britannica.com/place/Salisbury-Maryland

Broadwater, Luke. "Despite Lawsuit, Hogan Says He's Relocating Workers, Moving Forward with State Center Project in Baltimore." *Baltimore Sun*, November 26, 2019. https://www.baltimoresun.com/politics/bs-md-pol-hogan-state-center-20191126-7ucinlgbcjf77pl47xylm6utmu-story.html

Brown, Travis. "When It Rains, It Pours Tax Dollars in Maryland." *Forbes*. https://www.forbes.com/sites/travisbrown/2014/01/03/when-it-rains-it-pours-tax-dollars-in-Maryland/?sh=360b223f7c69

Bouie, Jamelle. "The Other Glass Ceiling." March 14, 2012. https://prospect.org/power/glass-ceiling/

Boutler, Brian. "Pelosi Power Play Doomed Towns on Oversight Committee." https://tpmdc.talkingpointsmemo.com/2010/12/pelosi-power-play-doomed-towns-on-oversight-committee.php

Brugger, Robert J. *Maryland: A Middle Temperament, 1634-1980*. Baltimore: Johns Hopkins University Press, 1988.

Bzdek, Jeff. *Woman of the House: The Rise of Nancy Pelosi*. New York: St. Martin's, 2009.

Campbell, Colin. "Baltimore City Recommends Against Building Proposed $10 Billion High-Speech Maglev Train to Washington." *Baltimore Sun*, June 23, 2021. https://www.baltimoresun.com/politics/bs-md-ci-baltimore-says-no-maglev -20210623-itzlcpa7tnbi3d7ty6p2vpfx4a-story.html

Campbell, Colin and Lorraine Mirabella. "Maglev Company Sues to Condemn Land Planned for Westport Development, Setting Up Showdown Between Projects in South Baltimore." *Baltimore Sun*, June 30, 2021. https://www.baltimoresun.com /business/bs-bz-maglev-westport-20210630-hetpya4vtjfbhgsskh5fode7he-story .html

Caro, Robert A. *The Years of Lyndon Johnson: Master of the Senate*. New York: Vintage, 2002.

Cashin, Sheryll. "How Larry Hogan Kept Blacks in Baltimore Segregated and Poor." *Politico*, July 18, 2020. https://www.politico.com/news/magazine/2020/07/18/how -larry-hogan-kept-black-baltimore-segregated-and-poor-367930

Cassie, Ron. "Former Baltimore Mayor Thomas D'Alesandro III, Brother of Nancy Pelosi, Dies at 90." *Baltimore Magazine*, October 21, 2019. https://www.baltimo-remagazine.com/section/community/former-baltimore-mayor-thomas-dalesandro -iii-nancy-pelosi-brother-dies/

Cassie, Ron. "Likable Larry." *Baltimore Magazine*. October 2018. https://www.bal-timoremagazine.com/section/historypolitics/how-did-larry-hogan-become-second -most-popular-governor-in-the-country/

Charland, Maurice. "Constitutive Rhetoric: The Case of the People Quebecois." *Quarterly Journal of Speech* 73.3 (1987): 133–50.

"Christopher Van Hollen, Jr. Biography." https://msa.maryland.gov/megafile/msa/ speccol/sc3500/sc3520/0/2100/012178/hyml/12178bo.html

"Clemens Pressed by Congress, Denies Accusations." https://www.starnewsonline .com/article/NC/200802131/News/605128348/WM/

Coffey, Justin. *Spiro Agnew and the Rise of the Republican Right*. Santa Barbara, CA: Praeger, 2015.

Cohen, Rachel. "Why Ben Jealous Lost the Maryland Governor's Race." *The Seventh State*, November 7, 2018. https://theintercept.com/2018/11/07/maryland-governor -election-ben-jealous-larry-hogan/

Cohen, Richard M. and Jules Witcover. *A Heartbeat Away: The Investigation and Resignation of Vice President Spiro T. Agnew*. New York: Vintage Press, 1974.

Cohn, Meredith. "Report Shows Investment in Baltimore African-American Neighborhoods Hasn't Overcome Racist Policies of Past." *Baltimore Sun*, February 7, 2019. https://www.baltimoresun.com/business/bs-bz-urban-institute -report-20190206-story.html

Comia, Catalina. "Democrats Hoyer, Clyburn Fight for Leadership Post." *U.S.A. Today*. November 8, 2010.

Cox, Erin. "Ad Watch: Maryland Gov. Larry Hogan Inflates Tax Relief Claims in Campaign Commercial." *Baltimore Sun*, May 30, 2018. https://www.baltimoresun .com/politics/bs-md-hogan-ad-watch-20180529-story.html

Cox, Erin. "Brown on a Deliberate March Toward Goal Years in the Making." *Baltimore Sun*, October 18, 2014. https://www.baltimoresun.com/politics/bs-md -brown-profile-20141018-story.html

Cox, Erin and Michael Dresser. "Hogan Defeats Brown." *Baltimore Sun*, November 5, 2014. https://www.baltimoresun.com/maryland/anne-arundel/bs-md-governor -20141105-story.html

Cox, Jeremy. "Salisbury Undergoes Major Shift as Black, Hispanic Populations Surge." *The Daily Times*, January 12, 2018. https://www.delmarvanow.com/story /news/local/maryland/2018/01/12/salisbury-shift-demographics-black-hispanic /995772001/

Cox, Ramsey and Alexander Bolton. "Senate GOP Blocks Paycheck Fairness Bill." *The Hill*, April 9, 2014, http://thehill.com/blogs/floor-action/Senate/203064-senate -gop-blocks-paycheck-fairness-bill/2199/all-archives/

Crenson, Matthew A. *Baltimore: A Political History*. Baltimore: Johns Hopkins University Press, 2017.

Dance, Scott and Ian Duncan. "Gov. Hogan Issues Call for New Developer to Take Over Stalled State Center Project in Baltimore." *Baltimore Sun*, June 14, 2018. https://www.baltimoresun.com/politics/bs-md-hogan-state-center-20180614-story .html

Department of Planning. *City of Baltimore Comprehensive Master Plan*. Baltimore: City of Baltimore, 2006. https://planning.baltimorecity.gov/planning-master-plan/ plan

Department of Planning. *Port Covington Master Plan – Draft*. Baltimore: City of Baltimore, June 6, 2016. https://planning.baltimorecity.gov/sites/default/files/POR TCOVINGTONMASTERPLANJune16.pdf

DiMargo, Carissa. "Maryland Governor: Larry Hogan Defeats Anthony Brown." *NBC Washington*, November 5, 2014. https://www.nbcwashington.com/news /local/maryland-governor-republican-larry-hogan-democrat-anthony-brown /67640/

Donovan, Doug and Michael Dresser. "No Coattails: Maryland Voters Backed Republican Gov. Hogan, But Also Showed Their Disdain for Trump." *Baltimore Sun*, November 7, 2018. https://www.baltimoresun.com/politics/bs-md-hogan -coattails-20181107-story.html

Dresser, Michael. "Ads in Governor's Race Are Narrow, Negative." *Baltimore Sun*, September 25, 2014. https://www.baltimoresun.com/maryland/bs-md-governor -ads-20140924-story.html

Dresser, Michael. "Baltimore Lawmakers Press Hogan to Get State Center Project on Track." *Baltimore Sun*, April 7, 2017. https://www.baltimoresun.com/maryland/ baltimore-city/bs-md-state-center-delegation-20170407-story.html

Dresser, Michael. "Gov. Larry Hogan Blankets Maryland with Positive TV Ads as Ben Jealous Watches." *Baltimore Sun*, August 27, 2018. https://www.baltimoresun .com/politics/bs-md-hogan-ad-campaign-20180824-story.html

Dresser, Michael. "Hogan Says No to Red Line, Yes to Purple." *Baltimore Sun.* June 25, 2015.

Drum, Kevin. "Computers Have Revolutionized Gerrymandering: The Supreme Court Should Take Notice." *Mother Jones.* February 26, 2017. https://mother-jones.com/kevin-drum/2017/02/computers-have-revolutionized-gerrymandering -supreme-court-should-take-notice

Dugan, John. *Leadership Theory: Cultivating Critical Perspectives.* San Francisco: Jossey-Bass, 2017.

Duyer, Linda. "Salisbury's Slave Pens." Delmarva African American History website. Posted December 2, 2013.https://aahistorydelmarva.wordpress.com/2013/12 /02/salisburys-slave-pens/

Editorial Board. "Amtrak's Future Still Runs Through Baltimore." *Baltimore Sun*, November 10, 2020. https://www.baltimoresun.com/opinion/editorial/bs -ed-1111-amtrak-cutbacks-baltimore-20201110-wgdeqlyapfcalf63s4wygmggoy -story.html

Editorial Board. "Gov. Hogan Washes His Hands of Coronavirus Decision-Making/ Commentary." *Baltimore Sun*, May 14, 2020. https://www.baltimoresun.com /opinion/editorial/bs-ed-0517-stage-one-hogan-20200514-nob6y6ffrnbh3pdcgor hm66x54-story.html

Editorial Board. "Maryland's Next Governor Doesn't Have to Be from Baltimore, But Must Care About It." *Baltimore Sun*, July 12, 2021. https://www.baltimoresun .com/opinion/editorial/bs-ed-0707-maryland-governor-race-20210709-ystqvarmtrf 7vkqpbbb7yhg2ui-story.html

Editorial Board. "On School Reopening, Hogan Does Not Work Well With Others/ Commentary." *Baltimore Sun*, January 22, 2021. https://www.baltimoresun.com /opinion/editorial/bs-ed-0125-hogan-schools-reopening-20210122-3jy2a63uaza f3fp26y6gnvxvty-story.html

Editorial Board. "Theodore R. McKeldin Modernized Maryland; Governor and Mayor; Baltimorean Envisioned Today's Airport and Inner Harbor; Practice Racial Equality; Marylanders of the Century." *Baltimore Sun*, August 31, 1999. https:// www.baltimoresun.com/news/bs-xpm-1999-08-31-9909010432-story.html

Editorial Board, "What Kevin Plank's Plan Means for Baltimore." *Baltimore Sun*, March 24, 2016. https://www.baltimoresun.com/opinion/editorial/bs-ed-sagamore -20160324-story.html

Enten, Harry. "Flying Blind Toward Hogan's Upset Win in Maryland." *Five Thirty Eight*, November 7, 2014. https://fivethirtyeight.com/features/governor-maryland -surprise-brown-hogan/

Farrell, Greg. "The Men Behind the Sarbanes-Oxley Act." *U.S.A. Today.* July 30, 2017.

Fenton, Justin. "How the Feds Investigated 'Healthy Holly': Prosecutors Share New Details of Case Against Former Baltimore Mayor Pugh." *Baltimore Sun*, March 18, 2021. https://www.baltimoresun.com/news/crime/bs-pr-md-ci-cr-healthy-holly -investigation-backstory-20210318-rwd5w3xsuzczrhnkj27uw4lce4-story.html

Fisher, Marc. "Mikulski, a Role Model for Generations of Women in Politics, to Retire in 2016." *Washington Post.* March 2, 2015. https://www.washingtonpost

.com/local/dc-politics/mikulski-a-role-model-for-generations-of-women-to-retire
-in-2016/2015/03/02/c6770396c0e4-9ec2-b418f57a4a99-story.html

Foucault, Michel. *Discipline and Punish: The Birth of the Prison.* Trans. Alan Sheridan. New York: Pantheon Books, 1978.

George, B. *Authentic Leadership: Rediscovering the Secrets to Creating Lasting Value.* San Francisco: Jossey-Bass, 2003.

George, B., and P. Sims. *True North: Discover Your Authentic Leadership.* San Francisco: Jossey-Bass, 2007.

Gonzales Maryland Poll. *Gonzales Maryland Poll: October 2020.* Gonzales Research and Media Services, October 2020.

Gonzalez Research & Media Services. *Gonzalez Maryland Poll: October 2020.* Gonzalez Polls, Inc., October 2020.

Goucher College Poll. *Goucher College Poll: October 2020.* Sarah T. Hughes Field Politics Center, October 2020.

Goucher College Poll. *Goucher College Poll: March 2021.* Sarah T. Hughes Field Politics Center, March 2021.

Grimes, Seth. "Nancy Floreen Split the Republican Vote, Not the Democratic!, And Three Other 2018 Lessons Learned." *The Seventh State*, November 7, 2018. http://www.theseventhstate.com/?paged=50&ref=xranks

Gring-Pemble, Lisa. "Are We Going to Govern by Anecdote? Rhetorical Constructions of Welfare Recipients in Congressional Hearings, Debates, and Legislation, 1992-1996." *Quarterly Journal of Speech* 87.3 (2001): 341–65.

Gunts, Ed. "What to Expect From Port Covington's Next Development Phase." *Baltimore Magazine*, March 31, 2021. https://www.baltimoremagazine.com/section/community/what-to-expect-from-port-covingtons-next-development-phase/

"High Profile Democrats Back Hoyer in Whip Race." http://tpmdc.talkingpoints-memo.com/2010/11/high-profile-democrats-back-hoyer-in-whip-race.php

Hogan, Larry and Ellis Henican. *Still Standing: Surviving Cancer, Riots, A Global Pandemic and the Toxic Politics That Divide America.* Dallas: BenBella Books, Inc., 2020.

Holden, Charles J., Zach Messitte, and Jerald Podair. *Republican Populist: Spiro Agnew and the Origins of Donald Trump's America.* Charlottesville: University of Virginia Press, 2019.

Holtje, Melissa. "It's Not Over: A Historical and Contemporary Look at Racial Restrictive Covenants." *Homelight* (blog). https://www.homelight.com/blog/buyer-racial-restrictive-covenants/

House, R. J. "A 1976 Theory of Charismatic Leadership." *Leadership: The Cutting Edge.* Edited by J. G. Hunt and L. L. Larson, 189–207. Carbondale: Southern Illinois University Press, 1976.

Householder, Mike. "Morella Votes Present on Speaker Matter, Avoids Taking Position." *CNS Maryland.* https://cnsmaryland.org/1997/01/07/morella-votes-present-on-speaker-matter-avoids-taking-position/

"How Maryland Democrats Pulled Off Their Aggressive Gerrymander." *Washington Post*, March 28, 2018.

"Hoyer Seeks to Change Obama's Tax Compromise." https://wamu.org/story/10/12/13/hoyer_seeks_to_change_obamas_tax_compromise

Ingraham, Christopher. "America's Most Gerrymandered Congressional Districts." *Washington Post.* May 15, 2014.

Jacobs, Ben. "Martin O'Malley, Tommy Carcetti, and 2016." http://www/thedaily-beast.com/articles/203/05/09/martin-o-malley-tommy-carcetti-and-2016.html

Jacobson, Joan. "The Sheila Dixon Story: It Wasn't Just About the Gift Cards." *Baltimore Sun,* May 18, 2020. https://baltimorebrew.com/2020/05/18/the-sheila -dixon-story-it-wasnt-just-about-the-gift-cards/

Jan, Tracy. "Redlining Was Banned 50 Years Ago. It's Still Hurting Minorities Today." *Washington Post,* March 28, 2018. https://www.washingtonpost.com /news/wonk/wp/2018/03/28/redlining-was-banned-50-years-ago-its-still-hurting -minorities-today/?noredirect=on

Jentleson, Adam. *Kill Switch: The Rose of the Modern Senate and the Crippling of American Democracy.* New York: Liveright Publishing, 2021.

Kaltenbach, Chris. "National Aquarium to Unveil Mural of Former Baltimore Mayor's Seal Pool Swim." *Baltimore Sun,* April 9, 2019. https://www.baltimore-sun.com/opinion/editorial/bs-ed-0418-downtown-baltimore-future-20210416-pif apkmoybcnhfkosglx5gohqi-story.html

Kane, Paul. "In Race for Whip, Hoyer Gets Liberal Support." *Washington Post.* . November 10, 2010.

Kelly, Jacques. "1893 Letter Details Racially Restrictive Covenants in City Neighborhoods." *Baltimore Sun,* March 27, 2015. https://www.baltimoresun.com/ maryland/baltimore-city/bs-md-ci-kelly-column-covenants-20150327-column.html

Kelly, Jacques. "Another Act Comes to the Former Odell's Nightclub on North Avenue." *Baltimore Sun,* January 16, 2021. https://www.baltimoresun.com/mary-land/baltimore-city/bs-md-kelly-odell-20210116-xsyanvvhd5fzjl7bcote22ymfq -story.html

Kelly, Jacques. "Baltimore Witnesses a Year of Stealth Change." *Baltimore Sun,* January 2, 2021. https://www.baltimoresun.com/maryland/baltimore-city/bs-md -kelly-2020-20210102-bqolhvcyuzh7zij3wu77lqea6q-story.html

Kelly, Jacques. "Guilford Hall Brewery Arrives at Old Crown Cork and Seal Location in Baltimore's Greenmount West Neighborhood." *Baltimore Sun,* April 17, 2021. https://www.baltimoresun.com/maryland/baltimore-city/bs-md-kelly-guilford -20210417-yf26intvnvhphjjw2szptkq5bm-story.html

Kelly, Jacques. "Life Anew Is Coming for Waverly's Long-Neglected Town Hall." *Baltimore Sun,* January 9, 2021. https://www.baltimoresun.com/maryland/bal-timore-city/bs-md-kelly-waverly-20210109-7x3wjvlrwvbgrguekib63sqfuu-story .html

Kelly, Jacques. "Old Burlap Bag Factory Becoming Loft Housing in Baltimore's Washington Hill." *Baltimore Sun,* September 9, 2020. https://www.baltimore-sun.com/maryland/baltimore-city/bs-md-kelly-citysprings-20200919-cj4ppao2xrh kbnee4yozqeqk3e-story.html

Kelly, Jacques. "The Boulevard Looks Forward to a Second Century in Baltimore's Waverly." *Baltimore Sun,* July 25, 2020. https://baltimore.cbslocal.com/2021 /02/10/abandoned-buildings-being-torn-down-to-make-way-for-new-park-in-west -baltimore/

"Ken Cuccinelli Walked into a Bar and Martin O'Malley Lit into Him." *Washington Post*, November 28, 2019. https://washingtonpost.com/local/ken-cuccinelli-walked -into-a-bar-and-martin-omalley-lit-into-him/2019/11/28/d27742lc1191-llea-b0fc -b2cc38411ebb-story.html

Kent Island Heritage Society. "Kent Island History." https://kentislandheritagesociety .org/kent-island-history/

Kilgore, Ed. "African-Americans and Statewide Offices." https://washingtonmonthly .com/2012/03/16/african-americans-and-statewide-offices/

Kirkpatrick, David. "Senator Sarbanes, Maryland Democrat, Will Retire in '06." *New York Times*. March 12, 2005. https://www.nytimes.com/2005/03/12/politics /12sarbanes.html

Kravetz, Daniel. "Who Will Benefit from Port Covington." *Shelter Force*, October 2016. https://shelterforce.org/2016/10/21/who-will-benefit-from-port-covington/

Kromer, Mileah. "Jealous Didn't So Much Lose MD Gubernatorial Race as Hogan Won It." *Baltimore Sun*, November 7, 2018. https://www.baltimoresun.com/opin- ion/op-ed/bs-ed-op-1108-h, ogan-wins-20181106-story.html

Lazarick, Len. "'Change Maryland' Looks for Middle Ground." *Maryland Reporter*, June 13, 2011. https://marylandreporter.com/2011/06/13/change-maryland%E2 %80%99-looks-for-middle-ground/

Leckrone, Bennett. "Talbot Officials Ask Court to Dismiss Lawsuit Seeking Removal of Confederate Monument." *Maryland Matters*, July 2, 2021. https://www .marylandmatters.org/2021/07/02/talbot-officials-ask-court-to-dismiss-lawsuit-to -remove-confederate-monument/

LeDuc, Daniel. "Coy O'Malley Scrutinized—Challenge to Townsend." *Washington Post*. December 25, 2001.

LeDuc, Daniel. "Maryland Democrats Redistrict Morella's District." *Washington Post*. January 15, 2002.

LeDuc, Daniel. "O'Malley Raises Funds, Raises Roof." *Washington Post*. March 25, 2002.

"Legislators Override Ehrlich's Red Line Veto." *Washington Examiner*. https://www .washingtonexaminer.com/legislatiors-override-Ehrlich-s-red-line-veto

Levy, Peter. *Civil War on Race Street: The Civil Rights Movement in Cambridge, Maryland*. Gainesville: University Press of Florida, 2003.

Locke, Brett. "Lawsuit Forces Maryland Democrats to Acknowledge the Obvious: Redistricting Was Motivated by Politics." *Baltimore Sun*. June 1, 2017.

Lublin, David. "Autopsy Part I: Poor Explainers for Why Ben Jealous Lost." *The Seventh State*, November 12, 2018. http://www.theseventhstate.com/?p=11896

Luthans, F., and B. J. Avolio, "Authentic Leadership Development." In *Positive Organizational Scholarship*, edited by K. S. Cameron, J. E. Dutton, and R. E. Quinn. San Francisco: Berrett-Koehler, 2003.

MacGillis, Alec. "Democrats Didn't Lose Governor's Races Because of a GOP Wave. They Lost Because of Bad Candidates." *New Republic,* November 5, 2014. https://newrepublic.com/article/120152/anthony-brown-didnt-lose-maryland -because-republican-wave

Mann, Alex. "Hogan Says Baltimore Has Gotten More COVID Vaccines Than It's 'Entitled to,' Drawing Outrage from City Leaders." *Baltimore Sun*, February 26, 2021. https://www.baltimoresun.com/coronavirus/bs-md-hogan-remarks-20210226 -wdph6hrsarh23jscsgjo2csfi4-story.html

Marbella, Jean and Luke Broadwater. "Former Baltimore Mayor Thomas 'Young Tommy' D'Alesandro III, Brother of Nancy Pelosi, Dies at 90." *Baltimore Sun*, October 20, 2019. https://www.baltimoresun.com/obituaries/bs-md-ob-tommy -dalesandro-20191020-dzzetsbbi5cehdiqupcp5slwca-story.html

Marbella, Jean, Childs Walker and Daniel Oyefusi. "As Preakness Approaches, the Real Winner Could Be Pimlico and the Surrounding Neighborhoods. Here's Why." *Baltimore Sun*, May 6, 2021. https://www.baltimoresun.com/maryland/bs-prem -md-pimlico-redevelopment-preakness-20210506-vpt7v57sjbcbfcwrcbmrx3iqcq -story.html

Maryland Department of Planning. Maryland Citizens Redistricting Commission Website. https://planning.maryland.gov/Redistricting/Pages/default.aspx

Maryland Lynching Memorial Project – Wicomico County https://mdlynchingmemo-rial.wixsite.com/wicomico

"Maryland Representative Jamie Raskin Named Lead Impeachment Manager for Trial Against President Donald Trump." *Baltimore Sun*. https://www.baltimore-sun.com/politics/bs-md-pol-raskin-impeachment-manager-20210113-ftx5yje5lja admm3hkxutt4wbu-story.html

Maryland Stadium Authority. *Baltimore State Center Alternative Land Use Study*. January 2018, 94–100. https://mdstad.com/sites/default/files/State_Center_Site _Final_Report_January_2018.pdf

Maryland State Board of Elections. "Elections." https://elections.maryland.gov/elec-tions/2022/index.html

Maryland Transportation Authority. "William Preston Lane, Jr. Memorial (Bay) Bridge (US50/301)." https://mdta.maryland.gov/Toll_Facilities/WPL.html

Matthews, Abigail. "Abandoned Row Home in West Baltimore Set to Become a Home for the Arts." *Baltimore Sun*, May 18, 2021. https://afro.com/abandoned-row -home-in-west-baltimore-set-to-become-a-home-for-the-arts/

Maxwell, Angie and Todd Shield. *The Long Southern Strategy: How Chasing White Voters in the South Changed American Politics*. New York: Oxford University Press, 2019.

Maza, Cristina. "Black West Baltimore Is Still Waiting for Equity." *Talk Poverty*, January 14, 2020. https://talkpoverty.org/2020/01/14/black-west-baltimore-still -waiting-equity/

McCauley, Mary Carole. "'Everything Was Lit Up': Arch Social Club Seeks Zoning Approval for New Marquee Signaling Rebirth of Pennsylvania Avenue." *Baltimore Sun*, March 2, 2021. https://www.baltimoresun.com/entertainment/arts/bs-fe-arch -social-club-marquee-20210302-vxxn4lhopfh2bm4ltlps65py7a-story.html

McCombs, Maxwell and Donald L. Shaw. "The Agenda-Setting Function of Mass Media." *Public Opinion Quarterly* 36.2 (1972): 176–87.

McGann, Anthony L., Charles Anthony Smith, Michael Latner, and Alex Keena. *Gerrymandering in America: The House of Representatives, the Supreme Court, and the Future of Popular Sovereignty.* New York: Cambridge University Press, 2016.

McKeldin, Theodore R. and John C. Krantz, Jr. *The Art of Eloquence: How to Speak Effectively in Politics.* Baltimore: Williams & Wilkins, 1952.

McLeod, Ethan. "What Happened to Baltimore's Harborplace." *Bloomberg*, January 16, 2020. https://www.bloomberg.com/news/articles/2020-01-16/what-happened-to-baltimore-s-festival-marketplace

Memories of Chesapeake Beach and North Beach. Atglen, PA: Schiffer Publishing, 2007.

Miller, Hallie. "Abandoned Baltimore Fire Station to Get New Life as Museum Honoring Black Firefighters." *Baltimore Sun*, September 16, 2020. https://www.baltimoresun.com/business/real-estate/bs-bz-oliver-fire-fighters-museum-20200916-p6ib7lba6beljkc5c4dat4zo4m-story.html

Miller, Hallie. "Baltimore Penn Station Redevelopment Aims to Enhance Experience for Modern Passengers." *Baltimore Sun*, October 15, 2020. https://www.baltimoresun.com/business/real-estate/bs-bz-baltimore-penn-station-redevelopment-20201015-xghwpr3ul5hrxpdknb7k2jwjbe-story.html

Miller, Hallie. "City Spending Board Approves Sale of West Baltimore's Upton Mansion to Afro Charities." *Baltimore Sun*, May 19, 2021. https://www.baltimoresun.com/politics/bs-md-ci-afro-charities-upton-mansion-20210519-p4gvswaiajg2nnjobpzyxgxmgu-story.html

Miller, Hallie. "Construction on Baltimore's Port Covington Development to Resume After Financing Next Phase." *Baltimore Sun*, January 5, 2021. https://www.baltimoresun.com/business/real-estate/bs-bz-port-covington-moves-forward-financing-20210105-72olijelbzgxxkz5e6qfhuofxi-story.html

Miller, Hallie. "Designs for T. Rowe Price, Other Parcels in Harbor Point Show Mix of Amenities, Green Space." *Baltimore Sun*, December 11, 2020. https://www.baltimoresun.com/business/real-estate/bs-bz-design-plans-harbor-point-update-20201210-lpbsnwfcjrgh5gzk4x4vzekowy-story.html

Miller, Hallie. "Plans for Park Heights Redevelopment Show Mix of Housing Types, Public Park Improvements." *Baltimore Sun*, February 27, 2020. https://www.baltimoresun.com/business/real-estate/bs-bz-apartment-next-to-metro-baltimore-park-heights-20200227-2j6hagku7rbftbosyo4pnv3myq-story.html

Miller, Hallie. "Renaissance Row Apartment Building to Provide 'Affordable' Units in Baltimore's Park Heights. *Baltimore Sun*, September 22, 2020. https://www.baltimoresun.com/business/real-estate/bs-bz-renaissance-row-park-heights-20200922-ingnztxm4zhbjfmzgggmowix6u-story.html

Miller, Hallie. "The Afro Newspaper to Move to Former Upton Mansion, Revitalize Historic West Baltimore Building." *Baltimore Sun*, February 20, 2020. Popkin, Samuel. https://www.baltimoresun.com/business/real-estate/bs-bz-afro-returns-to-west-baltimore-upton-mansion-20200226-cslog5cnvfdypo36z4sfzx63be-story.html

Miller, Hallie, Childs Walker and Daniel Oyefusi. "As Preakness Approaches, the Real Winner Could Be Pimlico and the Surrounding Neighborhood. Here's Why."

Baltimore Sun, May 6, 2021. https://www.baltimoresun.com/maryland/bs-prem
-md-pimlico-redevelopment-preakness-20210506-vpt7v57sjbcbfcwrcbmrx3iqcq
-story.html

Miller, Johnny. "Roads to Nowhere: How Infrastructure Built on American Inequality." *The Guardian*, February 21, 2018. https://www.theguardian.com/cities
/2018/feb/21/roads-nowhere-infrastructure-american-inequality

Minder, Raphael. *The Struggle for Catalonia: Rebel Politics in Spain.* London: C. Hurst and Company, 2017.

Miner, Ryan. "Ben Jealous Still Wants to Be Governor – But Can He Clean Up His 2018 Mess?" *A Miner Detail*, September 8, 2019. https://aminerdetail.com/ben
-jealous-still-wants-to-be-governor-but-can-he-clean-up-his-2018-mess/

Mirabella, Lorraine. "Amtrak and Developers Push Ahead with Multimillion-Dollar Transformation of Baltimore's Penn Station." *Baltimore Sun*, March 18, 2021. https://www.baltimoresun.com/business/bs-bz-penn-station-redevelopment
-20210318-fuen4cjidvh6reaozmsr3sttoi-story.html

Mirabella, Lorraine. "Developer Plans Mixed-Use Project On Westport Waterfront Formerly Owned by Kevin Plank." *Baltimore Sun*, October 6, 2020. https://www
.baltimoresun.com/business/real-estate/bs-bz-westport-development-20201006
-6mrliw4gazfjrfbkx3o65i5f2e-story.html

Moncrief, Gary and Pevereill Squire. *Why States Matter: An Introduction to State Politics,* 3rd edition. Lanham, MD: Rowman & Littlefield, 2021.

Montgomery, Lori. "O'Malley Likens Bush's Proposed Cuts to Sept 11 Attack." *Washington Post.* February 9, 2005. https://www.washingtonpost.com/wp/hyn/
articles/A9117-2005Feb8.2005.html

Mosk, Matthew. "Baltimore Mayor's Profile Is Rising." *Washington Post.* October 15, 2001.

Mumford, M. D., S. J. Zaccaro, M. S. Connelly, and M. A. Marks, "Leadership Skills: Conclusions and Future Directions," *Leadership Quarterly* 11.1 (2000): 155–70.

Mumford, M. D., S. J. Zaccaro, F. D. Harding, T. D. Jacobs, and E. A. Fleishman, "Leadership Skills for a Changing World: Solving Complex Social Problems," *Leadership Quarterly* 11.1 (2000): 11–35.

Nguyen, Tina. "Terrified Aides Say Amy Klobuchar is Just Like Trump." *Vanity Fair.* February 8, 2019.

Nicholson, Jr., Roland. "Baltimore Has Long, Sad History of Housing Bias/Op-Ed." *Baltimore Sun*, February 13, 2019. https://www.baltimoresun.com/opinion/readers
-respond/bs-ed-rr-housing-discrimination-letter-20190213-story.html

Nine and Counting: The Women of the Senate. New York: Harper Collins, 2000.

Northouse, Peter G. *Leadership: Theory and Practice,* 7th edition. Los Angeles: Sage, 2016.

Ocean City History. https://www.beach-net.com/delaware-maryland-beach-towns/
ocean-city-maryland-history.php

Ocean City History. https://www.oceancity.com/history/

Ocean City History. https://www.ococean.com/oc-history

O'Connor, Patrick. "Hoyer, Clyburn: An Impromptu Leadership Fight." *Wall Street Journal.* November 8, 2010.

"Old Railroad to Chesapeake Beach Due to be Junked." *Washington Post.* October 11, 2016.

Olson, Karen. "Old West Baltimore: Segregation, African-American Culture and the Struggle for Equality." In *The Baltimore Book: New Views of Local History,* edited by Elizabeth Free, Linda Shopes and Linda Zeidman, 57–80. Philadelphia: Temple University Press, 1991.

"O'Malley's Budget Cuts Kick Off Long Process." *Ocean City Maryland News.* July 12, 2007.

"O'Malley's March." *Washington Post.* March 17, 2000. http://www.omalleysmarch .com/acclaimwp.htm

O'Mara, Richard. "At Peace in Quiet: For 30 Years, People Have Wondered How Tommy D'Alesandro III, a Born Winner, Could Walk Away from Politics. It Wasn't the '68 Riot, He Insists." *Baltimore Sun,* April 4, 1998. https://www.balti-moresun.com/news/bs-xpm-1998-04-04-1998094106-story.html

Opiolo, Emily and Ben Leonard. "Brandon Scott Sworn in as Baltimore Mayor, Addresses 'Public Health Emergencies' of COVID-19 and Gun Violence." *Baltimore Sun,* December 8, 2020. https://www.baltimoresun.com/politics/bs-md -pol-brandon-scott-inauguration-20201208-e6plg5omprh33lecpchscxf6g4-story .html

Orser, W. Edward. *Blockbusting in Baltimore: The Edmondson Village Story.* Lexington, KY: The University Press of Kentucky, 1994.

Orser, W. Edward. "Flight to the Suburbs: Suburbanization and Racial Change on Baltimore's West Side." In *The Baltimore Book: New Views of Local History,* edited by Elizabeth Free, Linda Shopes and Linda Zeidman, 203–226. Philadelphia: Temple University Press, 1991.

Pearson, Richard. "Clarence 'Du' Burns, 84, Dies." *Washington Post,* January 14, 2003. https://www.washingtonpost.com/archive/local/2003/01/14/clarence-du -burns-84-dies/b90638a5-fd6c-4e34-9b00-77f4b1d098e6/

"Pelosi Names Conferees to FY 2014 Budget Conference." https://web.archive,org/ web/20146704622207/http://www.democraticleader.gov/Peloisi_Statement_on _Conferees_to_FY_2014_Budget_Conference.

Petty, Richard and John Cacioppo. *Communication and Persuasion.* New York: Springer-Verlag, 1986.

Phillips, Christopher. *Freedom's Port: The African American Community of Baltimore, 1790-1860.* Chicago: University of Illinois Press, 1997.

Pietila, Antero. *Not in My Neighborhood: How Bigotry Shaped a Great American City.* Chicago: Ivar R. Dee, 2010.

Pitts, Jonathan M. "Activists Vow to Continue Fight Against 'Talbot Boys' Confederate Monument in County Seat on Maryland Eastern Shore." *Baltimore Sun,* January 21, 2021. https://www.baltimoresun.com/maryland/bs-md-talbot -boys-controversy-20210103-iwqle7gj5nfhlfeu2r64h4ykiy-story.html

Pitts, Jonathan M. "Half a Century After Rioting Ravaged Cambridge, Town Seeks to Embrace History – So As to Transcend It." *Baltimore Sun,* February 12, 2017. https://www.baltimoresun.com/maryland/bs-md-cambridge-riot-1967-20170212 -story.html

Polk, Justin M. "Fort Detrick to Take Over Forest Glen." *Frederick News-Post.* October 7, 2008.

Popkin, Samuel. *The Reasoning Voter.* Chicago: University of Chicago Press, 1991.

Pousson, Eli. "Vacant Houses and Inequality in Baltimore from the Nineteenth Century to Today." In *Baltimore Revisited: Stories of Inequality and Resistance in a U.S. City,* edited by P. Nicole King, Kate Drabinski and Joshua Clark Davis, 52–66. New Brunswick, NJ: Rutgers University Press, 2009.

Racial Wealth Divide Initiative. *Racial Wealth Divide in Baltimore.* Corporation for Enterprise Development, 2017. https://prosperitynow.org/files/resources/Racial _Wealth_Divide_in_Baltimore_RWDI.pdf

Rascovar, Barry. "Rascovar: Why Brown Could Lose Race for Governor." *Maryland Reporter,* October 5, 2015. https://marylandreporter.com/2014/10/05/rascovar -why-brown-could-lose-race-for-maryland-governor/

Rawley, James. "Pelosi Heads Off Democratic Leadership Fight, Backs Hoyer for No. 2 Post." https://www.bloomberg.com/news/2010-11-13/pelosi-holds-off-dem-ocratic-leadership-fight-backs-hoyer-for-no-2-post.html

Rentz, Catherine. "Baltimore Invests $100M to 'Revitalize' 17 Acres of Park Heights; City Presents NHP Foundation as Developer." *Baltimore Sun,* September 18, 2019. https://www.baltimoresun.com/maryland/baltimore-city/bs-md-park-heights -vacants-20190918-a2ryyin3vjfc7bik6q3dttn6qe-story.html

Richman, Talia. "Poll: Majority of Marylanders Surveyed Approve of Hogan's Response to the Coronavirus Pandemic." *Baltimore Sun,* October 13, 2020. https:// www.baltimoresun.com/politics/bs-md-pol-poll-approval-20201013-mbo4gun w2bck7kqglh6ftox6nu-story.html

Rizzo, Mary. "Image and Infrastructure: Making Baltimore a Tourist City." In *Baltimore Revisited: Stories of Inequality and Resistance in a U.S. City,* edited by P. Nicole King, Kate Drabinski and Joshua Clark Davis, 257–270. New Brunswick, NJ: Rutgers University Press, 2009.

Robillard, Kevin. "How Larry Hogan Won in Maryland." *Politico,* November 7, 2014. https://www.politico.com/story/2014/11/larry-hogan-maryland-governor -112681

"Rock and Roll Governor: The Wild Side of Martin O'Malley." https://news/yahoo .com/blogs/power-players-abc-news/rock-n-roll-governor-the-wild-side-of-ma rylands-Martin-P'Malley-110244497.html

Rodericks, Dan. "In Facing Pandemic, Hogan Has Been Sensible, Trump Reckless. Will That Matter in 2024?/Commentary." *Baltimore Sun,* November 6, 2020. https://www.baltimoresun.com/opinion/columnists/dan-rodricks/bs-md-rodricks -1108-20201106-szoqixa4djg3bhj4xsh3qqaeti-story.html

Rodericks, Dan. "In Pigtown, Building Stability and Pride in the Neighborhood Block by Block/Commentary." *Baltimore Sun,* June 24, 2021. https://www.baltimoresun .com/opinion/columnists/dan-rodricks/bs-md-rodricks-0625-20210624-c5vjawk 24zecph52urxzzlqab4-story.html

Rodricks, Dan. "Mikulski's Legacy Starts with 'The Battle of the Road." *Baltimore Sun.* https://www.baltimoresun.com/Maryland/bs-md-rodricks-0303-20150302 -column.html

Rosenwald, Michael S. "Western Maryland Secession Seeks to Sever Ties with the Liberal Free State." *Washington Post.* September 8, 2013.

Rothstein, Richard. "A 'Forgotten History' of How the U.S. Government Segregated America." By Terry Gross. *Fresh Air*, May 3, 2017. https://www.npr.org/2017/05/03/526655831/a-forgotten-history-of-how-the-u-s-government-segregated-america

Rydell, John. "As Scott Delivers His First State of the City Speech, Jack Young Speaks." *Maryland Matters*, March 19, 2021. https://www.marylandmatters.org/2021/03/19/as-scott-delivers-his-first-state-of-the-city-speech-jack-young-speaks/

Sandalow, David. *Madam Speaker Nancy Pelosi: Life, Times, and Rise.* New York: Modern Times, 2008.

Sankofa, John. "Disinvestment in Baltimore's Black Neighborhoods Is Foreboding But Reversible." *Urban Wire*, September 29, 2020, https://www.urban.org/urban-wire/disinvestment-baltimores-black-neighborhoods-foreboding-reversible

Sarcevic, Lejla and Max Bennett. "How Larry Hogan Won In a Blue State." *Capital News Service*, November 6, 2014. https://cnsmaryland.org/2014/11/06/how-republican-larry-hogan-won-in-blue-maryland/

Schaller, Thomas. *Whistling Past Dixie.* New York: Simon and Schuster, 2008.

Schwartzman, Paul and John Wagner. "As Baltimore's Mayor, Critics Say, O'Malley's Policing Tactics Sewed Distrust." *Washington Post.* April 25, 2015. https://washingtonpost.com/local/dc-politics/as-mayor-of-baltimore-omalleys-policing-strategy-sewed-mistrust/2015/24/25/af81178a-ea91-11e4-0767-6276fc9b0ada-story.html

Shaver, Katherine. "Federal Officials Close Civil Rights Complaint about Baltimore Light Rail Project." *Washington Post.* July 13, 2017.

Sheckels, Theodore F. *Maryland Politics and Political Communication, 1950-2005.* Lanham, MD: Lexington Books, 2006.

Sheckels, Theodore F. "Mikulski vs. Chavez for the Senate from Maryland in 1986 and the 'Rules' for Attack Politics." *Communication Quarterly* 42.1 (1994): 311–26.

Sheckels, Theodore F. "The Rhetorical Use of Double-Voiced Discourse and Feminine Style: The U.S. Senate Debate over the Impact of Tailhook '91 on Admiral Frank B. Kelso II's Retirement Rank." *Southern Communication Journal* 63.1 (1997): 56–68.

Sheckels, Theodore F. Nichola D. Gutgold, and Diana B. Carlin. *Gender and the American Presidency: Nine Presidential Women and the Barriers They Faced.* Lanham, MD: Lexington Books, 2012.

Sherman, Natalie. "What Now for State Center Site? Anxious Neighbors Wait for Answers." *Baltimore Sun*, March 31, 2017. https://www.baltimoresun.com/business/bs-bz-state-center-next-20170331-story.html

Sherman, Natalie and Pamela Wood. "99 Workers Moved from Baltimore's State Center." *Baltimore Sun*, January 26, 2017. https://www.baltimoresun.com/maryland/baltimore-city/bs-md-state-center-jobs-20170126-story.html

Shutt, Jennifer. "Governor O'Malley Says He'll Veto Chicken Tax Bill." https://web.archive.org/web/20151117065247/http://archive.delmarvanow.com/article

/20140207/NEWS/30207009/Governor-Martin-O-Malley-says-he-ll-veto-chicken-tax-bill-poultry-S-cent

Smith, C. Fraser. *Here Lies Jim Crow: Civil Rights in Maryland.* Baltimore: Johns Hopkins University Press, 2008.

Smith, C. Fraser. *William Donald Schaefer: A Political Biography.* Baltimore: Johns Hopkins University Press, 1999.

Smith, David. "'The Moral Centre': How Jamie Raskin Dominated the Stage at Trump's Trial." https://www.theguardian.com/us-news/20211feb/13/jamie-raskin-trump-impeachment-trial

Social Network and Archival Cooperative. "McKeldin, Theodore R." https://snac-cooperative.org/ark:/99166/w63v3ctt

Stephens, Taylor. "With Nearly 3 Years Until 2020 Election, Deeply Red Utah Gets Its First Visit from a Presidential Candidate—a Little-Known Democrat." https://www.sltribune/news/politics/2018/01/25/with-nearly-3-years-until-2020-election-deeply-red-utah-gets-its-first-visit-from-a-presidential-candidate-a-little-known-democrat

Stogdill, R. M. *Handbook of Leadership: A Survey of Theory and Research.* New York: Free Press, 1974.

Stogdill, R. M. "Personal Factors Associated with Leadership: A Survey of the Literature," *Journal of Psychology* 25.1 (1948): 35–71.

Streicher, Sean. "Abandoned Buildings Being Torn Down to Make Way for New Park in West Baltimore." *WJZ-TV,* February 10, 2021. https://baltimore.cbslo-cal.com/2021/02/10/abandoned-buildings-being-torn-down-to-make-way-for-new-park-in-west-baltimore/

Studio Gang. "National Aquarium Strategic Plan." https://studiogang.com

Tapscott, Richard. "Congress Votes to Put Reagan's Name on Airport." *Washington Post.* February 5, 1998. https://www.washingtonpost.com/archive/politics/1998/02/05/congress-votes-to-put-reagans-name-on-airport/096c/dd6-7084-48f8-ae2a-71f575afbb0/

The Avalon Project. "Amendments to the Maryland Constitution of 1776." *Yale Law School Lillian Goldman Law Library*, 2008. https://avalon.law.yale.edu/17th_cen-tury/ma03.asp

The Hopkins Diaspora ERG. *The Hopkins Diaspora ERG Celebrates 400 Years of African American History in Maryland.* Johns Hopkins Medicine, 2019 (website). https://www.hopkinsmedicine.org/diversity/_documents/400_Years_of_AfricanAmerican_History_in_Maryland_FINAL.pdf

Theodos, Brett, Eric Hangen, Brady Meixell and Lionel Foster. *Neighborhood Investment Flows in Baltimore With a Case Study on the East Baltimore Development Initiative.* Washington, DC: Urban Institute, 2020.

Thompson, William J. "So What Did He Do." *Washington Post*, August 22, 1999. https://www.washingtonpost.com/archive/opinions/1999/08/22/so-what-did-he-do/762dac88-646c-463b-9ba6-72b2a05fc93a/

Tkacik, Christina. "Retro Baltimore: Central Avenue Car Barn, a Relic of City's Cable Car System, to Get Overhaul." *Baltimore Sun*, January 14, 2021. https://www.baltimoresun.com/features/retro-baltimore/bs-fe-retro-central-ave-car-barn-20210114-srt4hlqp5bcztfbxvl3ub25sla-story.html

Trent, Juddi S., Robert V. Friedenberg, and Robert E. Denton, Jr. *Political Campaign Communication: Principles and Practice,* 8th edition. Lanham, MD: Rowman and Littlefield, 2016.

Turner, Tatyana. "Two Neighborhoods, One Black and One White, Team Up to Bring a Skatepark to West Baltimore." *Baltimore Sun,* June 4, 2021. https://www.baltimoresun.com/maryland/baltimore-city/bs-md-skateboard-park-west-baltimore-20210604-xw2yt6kqlzb65jjyjivdto65cy-story.html

Turque, Bill. "Jamie Raskin: The Most Liberal Congressional Candidate in a Crowded Field." *Washington Post.* April 5, 2016.

United States Census Bureau. https://census.gov

University of Maryland Libraries. "Theodore Roosevelt McKeldin Biography." https://archives.lib.umd.edu/repositories/2/resources/1051#, November 26, 2019. https://www.wbal.com/article/422974/2/gov-hogan-announces-plans-for-redevelopment-of-state-center-complex

Urban Land Institute. *From a Highway to Nowhere to the Road to Revival: Healing a Scar, Reconnecting Our City.* June 26–27, 2018.

Wagner, John. "O'Malley, Archbishop at Odds Over Same-Sex Marriage, Letters Show." *Washington Post,* August 8, 2011. https://www.washingtonpost.com/local/dc-politics/omalley-archbishop-at-odds-over-same-sex-marriage-letters-show/2011/08/08/g/QAL/vR02L_story.html

Wagner, John. "O'Malley Finds Issue Can Cut Both Ways." *Washington Post.* https://www.washingtonpost.com/wp-dyn/content/article/2016/c3/02/AR2006080201812.html

Wagner, John and Jenna Johnson. "Republican Larry Hogan Wins MD Governor's Race in Stunning Upset." *Washington Post,* November 5, 2014. https://www.washingtonpost.com/local/md-politics/republican-larry-hogan-wins-md-governors-race-in-stunning-upset/2014/11/05

Wagner, Rose. "Five Takeaways from Baltimore Mayor Brandon Scott's New Crime Plan." *Baltimore Sun,* July 23, 2021. https://www.baltimoresun.com/politics/bs-prem-md-ci-mayor-scott-crime-plan-takeaways-20210723-z3uquzlzwng4dmltrgbjxiq75e-story.html

Waldman, Tyler. "Gov. Hogan Announces Plans for Redevelopment of State Center Complex." *WBAL-Radio,* November 26, 2019. https://www.wbal.com/article/422974/2/gov-hogan-announces-plans-for-redevelopment-of-state-center-complex

Wang, Sam and Brian Remlinger. "Can Math Stop Partisan Gerrymandering?" *Los Angeles Times,* May 5, 2017. https://www.latimes.com/opinion/op-ed/la-oe-wang-remlinger-gerrymandering-20170505-story-html

Weinger, Mackenzie. "Hoyer: Let Israel Build in East Jerusalem." *Politico,* May 11, 2011. https://www.politico.com/story/2011/08/hoyer-let-insrael-buiild-in-e-jerusalem-061145

Weissert, Will. "Representative Jamie Raskin Links Impeachment with Personal Tragedy." https://apnews.com/articles/donald-trump-capitol-siege-politics-impeachments-trump-impeachment.878fc4csdba85111cecS2f1e8ebd2002772/10/21

Welsh, Nancy H. "Racially Restrictive Covenants in the United States: A Call to Action." *Agora Journal of Urban Planning and Design.* 2018. https://deepblue.lib .umich.edu/bitstream/handle/2027.42/143831/A_12%20Racially%20Restrictive %20Covenants%20in%20the%20US.pdf

Wenger, Luke, Erin Broadwater, and Yvonne Cox. "Mikulski Remembered as a Plain-Speaking Trailblazer for Women in Politics." *Baltimore Sun.* https://www .baltimoresun.com/politics/bs-md-mikulski-career-20150302-story-html

Wheeler, Timothy. "O'Malley Administration Sets Out Path to Fracking in Maryland." *Baltimore Sun.* http://www.baltimoresun.com/feature/green/blog/bs -md-fracking-regulation-20141125-story.html

Wood, Pamela. "In Upcoming Political Memoir, Maryland Gov. Hogan Calls 2015 Baltimore Unrest His 'Baptism of Fire.'" *Baltimore Sun,* July 14, 2020. https:// www.baltimoresun.com/politics/bs-pr-pol-hogan-book-20200714-yepqs2x5xfh dhkghn6zu4zfowa-story.html

Wood, Pamela. "Maryland Gov. Hogan's Coronavirus Precautions: Tests, Masks, Fewer Staff." *Baltimore Sun,* October 20, 2020. https://www.baltimoresun.com /coronavirus/bs-md-trump-hogan-coronavirus-20201002-kvtn6ua5efdg5js4kks 52ib5hi-story.html

Wood, Pamela. "Study Recommends Offices, Retail, Park for State Center in Baltimore, But Not an Arena." *Baltimore Sun,* January 23, 2018. https://www.chi-cagotribune.com/bs-md-state-center-study-20180123-story.html

Wood, Pamela and Justin Fenton. "We've Examined 5 Chapters of Maryland Gov. Larry Hogan's Book. We Have Questions." *Baltimore Sun,* July 16, 2020. https:// www.baltimoresun.com/politics/bs-md-pol-hogan-chapters-20200716-7lfg2s5 3wrb55npxjpli7wndry-story.html

Wood, Pamela, Bryn Stole and Liz Bowie. "Maryland Gov. Hogan Calls on Schools to Bring Students Back to Classrooms by March Under Hybrid Learning Plan." *Baltimore Sun,* January 21, 2021. https://www.baltimoresun.com/coronavirus/ bs-md-hogan-salmon-covid-schools-update-20210121-5r74ewa7nnfg7bq4hjsdrw-cfju-story.html

Zaccaro, S. J. "Organizational Leadership and Social Intelligence." *Multiple Intelligence and Leadership,* edited by R. Riggio, 29–54. Mahwah, NJ: Lawrence Erlbaum, 2002.

Zaccaro, S. J. "Trait-based Perspectives on Leadership." *American Psychologist* 62.1 (2007): 6–16.

Zaccaro, S. J., C. Kemo, and P. Bader. "Leader Traits and Attributes," *The Nature of Leadership,* edited by J. Antonakis, A. T. Cianciolo, and R. J. Sternberg. Thousand Oaks, CA: Sage, 2004.

Zurawik, David. "Five Unconventional Takeaways on Media Campaigns from Hogan's Big Win." *Baltimore Sun,* November 6, 2018. https://www.baltimore-sun.com/opinion/columnists/zurawik/bs-fe-zontv-larry-hogan-media-campaign -20181106-story.html

Zurawik, David. "Maryland Congressman Cummings Redeemed Cohen Hearing with His Passionate, Poetic Closing Remarks." *Capital Gazette* (Annapolis). February 27, 2019.

Index

Afro-American (later, *Afro*), 6, 162, 224
Agnew, Spiro T., 33, 36, 74, 133, 135–40, 144, 147, 149, 271
Allen, Janet, 58
Althusser, Louis, 231–32, 234, 242, 269
Anderson, Carol, 239, 243
Angelos, Peter, 73
Austermuhle, Martin, 63, 105, 114
Avolio, B. J., 120

Babbington, Charles, 129
Bachelor, Tom, 130
Bader, P., 119, 121, 123, 127
Baker, Bobby, 118, 177
Baker, Jeff, 113
Baker, Rushern, 103–4, 106
Ball, Molly, 131
Baltimore, 2nd Lord (Cecilius Calvert), 153, 250
Baltimore and Ohio Railroad, 9, 197
Baltimore Colts, 78, 81
Baltimore-Link, 86
Baltimore Orioles, 11, 73, 98, 265
Baltimore Ravens, 78, 81
Baltimore-Washington International Airport (once, Friendship; now, Thurgood Marshall), 11, 70, 180
Barnes, Robert, 243
Bartlett, Roscoe, 141
Barton, David, 172

Bascomb, Marion, 73–74
Bash, Dana, 27
Bass, R. M., 135, 149
Bealefeld, Fred, 83
Beall, J. Glenn, 10
Beatty, Michael, 217
Becker, Jo, 130
Bell, Lawrence, 81
Beltways, 70, 180–83, 192–93
Bennet, Michael, 24–25
Bennett, Max, 62, 113–14
Bentsen, Lloyd, 17
Biden, Joe, 133–34
Blankenship, Jane, 27
Bogan, Daniel S., 172
Bost, Cheryl, 53
Botton, Alexander, 26
Boutler, Brian, 130
Bouton, Edward, 161–62
Bowie, Liz, 64
Boxer, Barbara, 18–20, 27
Braveboy, Aisha, 100
Brewster, Daniel, 125, 127
Briggs, Jonathan E., 93
Broadwater, Erin, 26, 65
Broadwater, Luke, 92
Broady, Mark, 220
Brown, Anthony, 37, 45–46, 50, 52, 95–106, 108, 110–12, 143, 234
Brown, Gary, 86

Brown, H. Rap, 138, 254
Brown, Thomas, 253
Brown, Travis, 40
Brugger, Robert J., 150, 207
Buchanan, Patrick, 236
Buchanan v Warley (1917), 161
Buckingham, James Silk, 154
Buckley, John, 163
Bullock, John, 170
Burke, Kenneth, 238
Burns, Clarence H. "Du", 79–80
Busch, Michael, 99
Bush, George H. W., 39, 121, 134
Bush, George W., 35, 140
Bzdek, Jeff, 131

Cacioppo, John, 266
Calhoun, James, 69
Cambridge Riots, 138, 177, 254
Campbell, Colin, 65, 94, 229
Caputo, Shelly Moore, 22
Cardin, Ben, 95
Carlin, Diana, 26, 131
Caro, Robert A., 129, 207, 269
Carter, Jimmy, 139
Cassio, Ron, 50, 60, 63, 65, 92
Central Park (New York City), viii
Chafee, Lincoln, 39, 143–44
Chan, Jinlene, 53
Change Maryland, 44–45, 97–98, 106
Charland, Maurice, viii, 221–22, 234,
    243, 269
Charles Center, 70, 212–14
Cheatham, Marvin "Doc", 224
Chesapeake Bay Bridge (William
    Preston Lane, Jr. Memorial Bridge),
    4, 7, 177–80, 184, 188, 248–52,
    255–60
CitiStat, 30–32, 82
Claiborne, William, 250
Clinton, Hillary, 33, 35, 38–40, 123,
    142–44, 267
Clinton, William, 121, 140
Coelho, Tony, 118
Coffin, Isaac, 257

Cohen, Rachel, 106, 114–15
Cohen, Richard M., 150
Cohen, Zeke, 59
Collins, Susan, 22
Columbia, 8–9, 11
Comia, Catalina, 130–31
Connelly, M. S., 119, 129
Coolidge, Calvin, 134, 145
Corrigan, Irene, 162
Corrigan v Buckley (1926), 63
Cox, Erin, 48, 62–63, 99, 107, 113–15
Cox, James, 145
Cox, Jeremy, 246, 260
Cox, Ramsey, 26
Cox, Yvonne, 26
Crenson, Matthew, 56, 75, 78, 80–81,
    91–93, 155–56, 160, 172–74, 227
Cuccinelli, Ken, 35
Cummings, Elijah, 54–55, 120, 122–23,
    128, 234
Cummings, Harry, 160
Curran, Joseph, 31
Curran, Robert, 100

D'Alessandro, Annuciata Lombardi, 72
D'Alessandro, Thomas, Jr., 72, 79, 126,
    212
D'Alessandro, Thomas, III 71–78, 138
Dashiell, Milton, 159–60
Deep Creek Lake, 9
Deer Park, 9
Delaney, John, 134–35, 140–44, 147,
    149
Denton, Robert E., Jr., 150
DeSousa, Mathias, 153
DeVos, Betsy, 49
DiMargo, Carissa, 114
Dixon, Sheila, 82–84
Donovan, Doug, 49, 61, 114–15
Douglass, Frederick, 252, 259
Dresser, Michael, 46, 48–49, 62–63, 65,
    113–15, 207
Drum, Kevin, 243
DuBois, W. E. B., 162
Dugan, John P., 128–29, 131, 134–35, 149

Dukakis, Michael, 39
Duyer, Linda, 261
Dyson, Roy, 247

Eberly, Todd, 49
Edwards, Donna, 234
Ehrlich, Robert, 29, 32–33, 44–45, 50,
  57, 60, 95, 102, 190, 271
Eisenhower, Dwight D., 72, 136, 212
Enten, Harry, 113

Farrell, Greg, 129
Federal Highway Aid Act (1956), 168
Federal Hill, 4
Feinstein, Diane, 18–19, 22
Fenton, Justin, 54, 64, 93
Ferguson, Bill, 57
Finan, Thomas B., 137
Fisher, Mark, 27
Fleischman, E. A., 119, 129
Ford, Gerald R., 134
Fort McHenry, 4, 265
Foucault, Michel, vii, 20, 27
Franchot, Peter, 56–57
Friedenberg, Robert V., 150

Garfield, James, 134, 141
Garrett, John, 9
Gansler, Doug, 98
George, B., 120, 125, 129
GI Bill (1944), 166, 212
Gillibrand, Kirsten, 22
Gill v Whitford (2017), 243
Gingrich, Newt, 121
Glendenning, Parris, 10, 29, 34, 195
Goldstein, Louis, 78
Goldwater, Barry M., 136
Goodman, Phillip H., 72
Gore, Al, 134, 140
Grady, J. Harold, 72
Greater Baltimore Committee, 212–13
Greene, Marjorie Taylor, 126
Grey, Freddie, 48–49, 54–55, 82, 85–86
Grimes, Seth, 111, 115
Gude, Gilbert, 121, 233, 235

Gunts, Ed, 228
Gurry, John, 160
Gutgold, Nichola, 26, 131
Guttierrez, Ana Sol, 100

Hamlin, James, 58
Harbor East, 4, 83–84, 217–18, 225–26
Harding, F. D., 119, 129
Harding, Warren G., 145
Harris, Andy, 247
Harris, Kamala, 22
Hawkins, W. Ashbie, 159–62
Henica, Ellis, 62
Henson, Dan, 221
Hicks, Joshua, 208
Hill, A., 25
Hogan, Larry A., Jr., 4, 8, 33–34,
  43–66, 70, 85, 95–112, 126, 141,
  190–92, 197–99, 242, 266–67, 271
Hogan, Larry A., Sr., 43–44, 102, 106,
  237
Hogan, Yumi, 51
Holden, Charles, 149
Holtje, Melissa, 174
Hoover, Herbert, 145
Hopkins, Daniel, 3
Horseholder, Mike, 129
House, R. J., 135, 149
Hoyer, Steny, 6, 44, 120, 125–28, 235,
  237–38, 268
Hoyt, Homer, 164
Hunt, J. G., 135

Ingraham, Christopher, 243
Inner Harbor (Baltimore), 4, 71, 77,
  181, 214–17, 226
Interstate Highways, Baltimore, 16, 74,
  168–70, 186–87, 190–207, 213–14
Interstate Highways, outside Baltimore,
  183–87, 196, 204, 207
Irsay, Robert, 78

Jackson, Ray, 222
Jackson-Stanley, Victoria, 254
Jacobs, Ben, 40

Jacobs, T. O., 119, 129
Jacobson, Joan, 83–84, 93
Jan, Tracy, 165, 174
Jealous, Ben, 23, 47–49, 95–96, 103–12, 266
Jentleson, Adam, 129
Johnson, Denise, 169
Johnson, Jenna, 62
Johnson, Lyndon B., 118, 134, 136, 139, 269
Jones, Adrienne, 59

Kaltenbach, Chris, 228
Kamenetz, Kevin, 103–4
Kane, Paul, 131
Kassenbaum, Nancy, 22
Keena, Alex, 242
Kelly, Jacques, 174, 223, 229, 230
Kelso, Frank, 18, 20, 22
Kemp, C., 118, 121, 123, 128
Kennedy, John F., 139, 183
Kennedy, Robert F., 138, 267
Kilgore, Ed, 243
King, Garfield, 256
King, Martin Luther, Jr., 74–75, 138, 181
Kirkpatrick, David, 129
Klobuchar, Amy, 22, 24–25, 27
Kopp, Nancy, 56
Kovens, Irv, 76
Kramer, Mileah, 49–51, 60, 63, 66
Krantz, John C., Jr., 72
Kratovil, Frank, 247
Kravetz, Daniel, 228
Kyle, John, 58, 59

Lane, William Preston, Jr., 248
Larson, L. L., 135
Latner, Michael, 242
Lazarick, Len, 44, 62
Lazo, Luz, 208
Leckrone, Bennett, 261
LeDuc, Daniel, 40, 130
Lee, Blair, IV, 46, 100
Leonard, Ben, 94

Levy, Peter B., 150, 207
Lewis, Robbyn, 58
Lierman, Brooke, 59
Locke, Brett, 150
Luthans, F., 120

MacGillis, Alec, 100, 114
maglev train, 90, 202–5, 222
Mahoney, George P., 33, 137
Mahool, J. Berrie, 160
Manchin, Joe, 24
Mandela, Nelson, 120
Mann, Alex, 64
Marbella, Jean, 92, 94, 228
Marenberg, Sandy, 221
Marks, M. A., 119, 129
Marshall, Thurgood, 70
Matthews, Abigail, 230
Matthews, Kathleen, 58
Matthias, Charles M., 16, 32, 121, 124
Maxwell, Angie, 150
McCarthy, Eugene, viii
McCarthy, Joseph, 22
McCartney, Robert, 208
McCaskill, Claire, 22
McCauley, Mary Carole, 229
McComb, Maxwell, 150
McConnell, Mitch, 118
McGann, Anthony J., 242
McGovern, George, 140
McGwire, Mark, 123
McKeldin, Theodore R., 17, 32–33, 37–38, 43, 70–74, 77–78, 212, 214, 248, 271
McKerrow, Raymie, vii
McLeod, Ethan, 216, 228
McMehan, George W. F., 159, 162–63
Meade v Dennistone (1938), 163
Meixell, Brady, 171
Messite, Zach, 149
Metcalf, Andrew, 208
Mfume, Kweisi, 81–82, 122, 234
Mikulski, Barbara, 10, 15–26, 123, 126, 186, 240, 267–69
Miller, Hallie, 228–30

Miller, Johnny, 169, 175
Miller, Thomas V. "Mike", 50
Minder, Raphael, 243
Miner, Ryan, 106, 114–15
Mirabella, Lorraine, 229
Modell, Art, 78
Moncrief, Gary, 1
Mondale, Walter, 134
Montgomery, Lori, 40
Morella, Constance, 120–23, 128–29, 233, 235
Morris A. Mechanic Theatre, 213
Mosby, Marilyn, 54, 61
Moseley-Brain, Carole, 18–19
Mosk, Matthew, 40
Mumford, M. D., 119, 129
Murdoch, Stephanie, 224
Murkowski, Lisa, 22
Murphy, Carl, 162
Murray, Patty, 18, 22
Murtha, John, 126

National Housing Act (1934), 164–65
National Rifle Association, 10, 142
Nguyen, Tina, 27
Nice, Harry M., 146, 201, 271
Nine and Counting, 20, 27
Nixon, Richard M., 43, 133–34, 136–40, 271
Noonan, Peggy, 140
Northouse, Peter, 134–35, 149

Obama, Barack, 54–55, 123, 126
O'Brien, Edwin, 33
O'Connor, Patrick, 130–31
Olson, Karen, 173, 227
O'Malley, Martin J., 10, 17, 29–41, 44–45, 57, 61, 75, 81–82, 84, 87–88, 95, 100–102, 134–35, 142–44, 149, 192, 195, 267
O'Mara, Richard, 75, 92
Opiola, Emily, 94
Orlinsky, Walter, 79
Orser, W. Edmund, 167–68, 173–74
Oyefusi, Daniel, 228

Paterakis, John, 217
Patterson, Roland, 73
Pearson, Richard, 93
Pei, I. M., 215
Pelosi, Nancy D'Alessandro, 16, 75, 118, 120, 123, 126, 138, 212, 268
Pemble, Lisa Gring, 25, 27
Perdue, Frank, 33, 256
Perry, Richard, 266
Philips, Christopher, 156, 173
Pietila, Antero, 170, 173–75
Pimlico, 88, 221
Pitts, Jonathan M., 261
Plank, Kevin, 219–20
Podair, Jerald, 149
Polin, Abe, 181
Polk, Justin M., 207
Popkin, Samuel, 266
Port Covington, 86, 89, 219–21, 222–25
Pousson, Eli, 173, 227
Pressman, Hyman, 137
Preston, James H., 161, 211–12
Pugh, Catherine, 83, 85–87, 89
Purple Line (suburban Washington), 192–93, 197–201

Raskin, Jamie, 120, 124–25, 128
Rawley, James, 131
Rawlings, Howard "Pete", 81, 84
Rawlings-Blake, Stephanie, 54, 61, 84–88
Rayburn, Sam, 117–18, 269
Reagan, Ronald, 121, 130, 136, 140
Red Line (Baltimore), 4, 55–56, 61, 86, 190–92, 200
Reid, Harry, 118
Remlinger, Brian, 243
Rentz, Catherine, 228
Richardson, Gloria, 138, 254
Richman, Talia, 64
Ritchie, Albert, 134–35, 144–49
Rizzo, Mary, 221, 228
Roberts, Samuel, 211
Robillard, Kevin, 45, 62, 97, 113–14
Robinson, Bishop L., 78

Robson, Debrah, 27
Rockefeller, Nelson, 137
Rodricks, Dan, 26, 51–52, 64, 226, 230
Roosevelt, Franklin D., 136, 145–47, 149
Roosevelt, Theodore, 134
Roscover, Barry, 46, 62, 101, 113
Rose, Kwame, 55
Rosenwald, Michael S., 207
Rouse, Jimmy, 216
Rouse, Joseph, 8, 215–16
Russell, George, 73
Russell, Richard, 269
Rutherford, Boyd, 51, 95
Ryan, Paul, 118
Rydell, John, 87, 94

Safire, William, 136
Salmon, Karen, 53
Sandalow, David, 131
Sanders, Bernie, 33, 38–40, 142–44
Sankofa, John, 171, 175
Santorum, Rick, 17
Sarbanes, Paul, 16, 95, 120–22, 240
Sarcevic, Lejla, 62, 113–14
Schaefer, William Donald, 10, 31, 36–38, 73, 75–80, 124, 195, 214, 216, 226
Schaller, Thomas, 130
Schmoke, Kurt, 75, 80–81
Schmucker, Samuel, 161
Schriefer, Russell, 45, 47
Schwartzman, Paul, 40, 93
Scott, Brandon, 3, 76, 83, 88–91, 226–27
Shaver, Katherine, 208
Shaw, Donald L., 130
Sheckels, Theodore F., 26, 131, 150
Shelley v Kramer (1948), 163
Sherman, Natalie, 38, 65
Shield, Todd, 150
Shutt, Jennifer, 40
Sickles, Carlton, viii, 137
Simon, David, 35
Sims, P., 129

Smith, Al, 145, 147
Smith, Anthony, 242
Smith, C. Fraser, 75, 77–78, 93
Smith, Colin, 55
Smith, M. C., 21–22
Squire, Percival, 1
State Center, 56–59
Steele, Michael, 95
Stephens, Taylor, 150
Sterling, Jaymi, 102
Stogdill, R. M., 119, 128–29
Stokes, Carl, 81
Stole, Brian, 64
Streicher, Sean, 230
Swisher, William, 80

Taft, William Howard, 136
Talbot Boys, 252–53, 259
Tawes, J. Millard, 137–38
Theodos, Brett, 171
Thompson, William, 71, 91–92
Thurmond, Strom, 138
Tkacik, Christine, 229
Townsend, Kathleen Kennedy, 29, 33–34
Trent, Juddi S., 150
Tribe, Lawrence, 124
Trone, David, 237
Trudeau, Pierre Elliot, 120
Truman, Harry S., 134
Trump, Donald, 35, 49, 55, 125–26, 135, 147, 237
Tubman, Harriet, 254–55
Turner, Tayana, 230
Turque, Bill, 130, 208
Tydings, Joseph, 137

U.S. Housing Act (1937), 165
Ulman, Ken, 99

VanderRohe, Mies, 213
VanHollen, Chris, 100, 120, 122–25, 128
Vezzella, Laura, 23
Vieth v Jubelirer (2004), 243

Wagner, John, 40, 62, 93
Wagner, Rose, 90–91, 94
Walker, Childs, 228
Walker, Garrett Russell, 163
Wallace, George, 8, 125, 137–38, 184
Wang, Sam, 243
Washington Senators, 11
Watergate, 140
Webb, Jim, 39, 143–44
Weigner, Mackenzie, 130
Weiner, Deborah, 230
Weissert, Will, 130
Wenger, Luke, 26
West, Samuel, 160
Wheeler, Timothy, 40

White's Ferry, 196
Whitlock, George, 161
Whitney, Catherine, 27
Wilkie, Wendell, 147
Williams, Matthew, 256
Wilson, Harry O., Sr., 162
The Wire, 35
Witcover, Jules, 150
Wood, Pamela, 54–55, 57, 64–65, 93
Wynn, Al, 234

Young, Bernard C. "Jack", 87–88

Zaccaro, Stephen, 119, 121, 123, 128
Zurawick, David, 47, 63, 109, 115, 170

About the Authors

Theodore F. Sheckels, PhD (Penn State, 1978), is Charles J. Potts Professor of Social Science and professor of English and Communication Studies at Randolph-Macon College, Ashland, Virginia. He is the author, coauthor, editor, or coeditor of twenty books. Some explore the international English literature written in Canada, South Africa, and Australia; others deal with several aspects of political communication, including election dynamics, presidential rhetoric, and speechwriting. In 2006, he wrote *Maryland Politics and Political Communication, 1950–2005* (Lexington). This 2022 book is, in a sense, a coauthored sequel, bringing the study up to date and broadening its scope beyond political campaigns to important matters of public policy.

Carl Hyden is associate dean for Administration in the School of Global Journalism and Communication at Baltimore's Morgan State University. When still in the classroom, he taught courses that included rhetoric, political communication, propaganda, public relations, and advertising. He has presented conference papers on topics ranging from the Anne Arundel County (Maryland) slots referenda, political advertising, and the rhetorical style of former Maryland governor William Donald Schaefer. Conference papers on local and national 9/11 memorials, the Chicago parks system, the High Line in NYC, Westminster Arcade in Providence, RI, and Maryland's memorials to Thurgood Marshall became chapters in *Public Places: Sites of Political Communication*, a book he coauthored with Theodore Sheckels.

9 781666 928976